RICHARD ALDINGTON: A BIOGRAPHY

Also by Charles Doyle

JAMES K. BAXTER
WILLIAM CARLOS WILLIAMS: THE CRITICAL HERITAGE
(*editor*)
WILLIAM CARLOS WILLIAMS AND THE AMERICAN POEM
WALLACE STEVENS: THE CRITICAL HERITAGE (*editor*)

Richard Aldington:
A Biography

CHARLES DOYLE

Southern Illinois University Press
Carbondale and Edwardsville

© Charles Doyle 1989

All rights reserved. No reproduction, copy or transmission of this publication may be made without written permission.

No paragraph of this publication may be reproduced, copied or transmitted save with written permission or in accordance with the provisions of the Copyright Act 1956 (as amended), or under the terms of any license permitting limited copying issued by the Copyright Licensing Agency, 33–4 Alfred Place, London WC1E 7DP.

Any person who does any unauthorised act in relation to this publication may be liable to criminal prosecution and civil claims for damages.

First published in 1989

Published by
THE MACMILLAN PRESS LTD
Houndmills, Basingstoke, Hampshire RG21 2XS
and London
Companies and representatives
throughout the world

Published in the United States of America and its dependencies by Southern Illinois University Press, P.O. Box 3697, Carbondale, IL 62902-3697

Printed in the People's Republic of China

Library of Congress Cataloging-in-Publication Data
Doyle, Charles, 1928–
Richard Aldington, a biography.
Bibliography: p.
Includes index.
1. Aldington, Richard, 1892–1962–Biography.
2. Authors, English–20th century–Biography.
I. Title.
PR 6001.L4Z59   1989   821'.912   [B]   CIP
ISBN 0–8093–1566–1   88–34922

To Alister Kershaw

To Alister Kershaw

Contents

	List of Illustrations	ix
	Acknowledgements	xi
	Introduction	xiii
1	Chrysalis, 1892–1911	1
2	Pound and H. D., 1912–13	13
3	Egoists, 1914	26
4	Images, Lost and Found, 1915–16	38
5	War, 1916–18	54
6	Aftermaths, 1919–20	68
7	Malthouse Cottage: Working at the Writer's Trade, 1921–25	77
8	Malthouse Cottage: Eliot, 1919–27	90
9	Malthouse Cottage: The Late 1920s, 1926–28	106
10	Port-Cros and After, 1928–29	119
11	A Career as a Novelist, 1929–31	138
12	1931–33	151
13	1933–36	164
14	1937–38	177
15	Farewell to Europe, 1939–40	191
16	1941–42	206
17	1943–46	215
18	1946–50	230
19	1950–54	245
20	The T. E. Lawrence Affair, 1950–55	261
21	1954–57	275

22	Maison Salle, 1957–59	289
23	1959–61	300
24	1962	313
	Notes	326
	Bibliography	355
	Index	370

List of Illustrations

1. Richard Aldington in 1905. (Estate of Margery Lyon Gilbert.)
2. Richard Aldington aged 19, 1911. (Morris Library, Southern Illinois University.)
3. Hilda Doolittle (H.D.) in 1913. (Beinecke Library, Yale University.)
4. A group of fellow-poets visit Wilfred Scawen Blunt, January 1914. (Courtesy of the Rt. Hon. Earl of Lytton, OBE.)
5. A multiple photograph of Dorothy (Arabella) Yorke. (Estate of Professor Alfred Satterthwaite.)
6. Richard Aldington as an army officer, 1918. (Beinecke Library.)
7. D. H. Lawrence's portrait painting of Dorothy Yorke. (Beinecke Library.)
8. Brigit Patmore as a young woman. (Estate of Professor Alfred Satterthwaite.)
9. Osbert Sitwell and Richard Aldington in the gardens at Montegufoni. (Morris Library.)
10. Richard Aldington, by Man Ray, late 1920s. (Beinecke Library.)
11. Richard Aldington, photograph taken for a Harrod's window display in the late 1920s. (Vaughan and Freeman photo. Estate of Margery Lyon Gilbert.)
12. Richard Aldington (photograph by Madam Yevonde). According to Brigit Patmore, this was taken shortly after publication of *Death of a Hero* in 1929.
13. Aldington and Brigit Patmore in the South of France, early 1930s. (From Brigit Patmore's *My Friends When Young*.)
14. Richard and Netta Aldington in the late 1930s. (Courtesy of Catherine Aldington Guillaume.)
15. Richard and Netta Aldington in the early 1940s. (Beinecke Library.)
16. Henry Williamson and Alister Kershaw, 1949. (Courtesy of Alister Kershaw.)
17. Aldington in Montpellier, 1955. (Courtesy of F.-J. Temple.)
18. H.D. in 1956. (Beinecke Library.)
19. Richard Aldington, Lawrence Durrell, Henry Miller and Jacques Temple. (Courtesy of F.-J. Temple.)

20. Aldington with his daughter Catherine in Leningrad, late June 1962. (Courtesy of Catherine Aldington Guillaume.)
21. Aldington and Catherine in the gardens of Petrodvorets, 1962. (Courtesy of Catherine Aldington Guillaume.)
22. Aldington broadcasting in Russia, 1962. (Courtesy of Catherine Aldington Guillaume.)
23. At Valentin Kataev's dacha, at Peredelkino near Moscow. Kataev is on the left, Aldington next to him, Catherine in the centre. (Courtesy of Catherine Aldington Guillaume.)
24. Aldington with a group of his Maison Salle neighbours, 1962. (Courtesy of Catherine Aldington Guillaume.)

Acknowledgements

Special thanks to Alister Kershaw, Literary Executor of the Estate of Richard Aldington, for his assistance and for giving me the opportunity to write this book. Particular thanks for their assistance to Dr Norman T. Gates, most devoted of Aldington scholars, and to Mr David Wilkinson, author of a valuable unpublished study of the context of Aldington's life in Berkshire in the 1920s.

Grateful acknowledgements to: the Morris Library, Southern Illinois University at Carbondale; Mr Donald Gallup, former curator, Mr Louis Silverstein and Miss Marjorie Wynne, Research Librarian of the American Literature Collection, Beinecke Library, Yale University; the McPherson Library, University of Victoria; the Manuscript Division, the British Library; Mrs Ellen Dunlap and the Humanities Research Center, University of Texas; Dr Lola Szladits, Curator, and the Henry W. and Albert A. Berg Collection, New York Public Library; the Houghton Library, Harvard University; the National Library of Australia, Canberra; the Newberry Library, Chicago; the University of Chicago Library, Dergenstein Collection; University of Arkansas Library; Library of the University of California, Los Angeles; University of Illinois Library; University of Iowa Libraries; University of London Library; University of Toronto Library; The All-Union State Library of Foreign Literature, Moscow; The Foreign Commission, Soviet Writers' Union, Moscow; Copyright Agency of the USSR, Moscow; Lockwood Memorial Library, State University of New York at Buffalo; Dartmouth College Library; University of Reading Library; the Huntington Library, San Marino, California; Boston University Library; Cornell University Library; Temple University Library; Princeton University Library; India University Library; New York University Library; Mr Roger Smith and William Heinemann Ltd; Mr Mark Bonham-Carter and William Collins & Sons; Chatto & Windus Ltd; New Directions Publishing Corporation; the Viking Press; Antony Alpers; the late Mrs Netta Aldington; John Arlott; Robin Ancrum; Professor Helen Bacon; the late Dr Miriam Benkovitz; Professor Peter Buitenhuis; Professor Fred D. Crawford; the late W. Denison Deasey; Lawrence Durrell; Mrs T. S. Eliot; Constantine Fitzgibbon; C. J. Fox; Mrs Catherine Aldington Guillaume; Mrs Eunice Gluckman; James Hanley; the late Dr

Selwyn Kittredge; Lady Kathleen Liddell Hart; the late Mrs Margery Lyon Gilbert; Professor Frank McShane; Lawrence Miller; the late Professor Harry T. Moore; Malcolm Muggeridge; Michael Patmore; Dr Lawrence Clark Powell; Benedict Read; the late Professor Alfred W. Satterthwaite; Mrs Perdita Schaffner; the late C. P. Snow (Lord Snow); Philip Snow; the late Vernon Sternberg; M. F-J. Temple; Professor Mikhail Urnov and Mr Eric Warman. Special thanks are due to Sue Mitchell for typing the manuscript.

Introduction

'A writer of great gifts'—thus Richard Aldington, poet, editor, translator, critic, novelist and biographer, was adjudged by C. P. Snow in the late 1930s.[1] 'No one can read him for ten minutes without feeling a glow of power and vitality.' A quarter of a century later, after Aldington's death and not long before his own, T. S. Eliot told a correspondent that 'something more permanent and extensive should be written about Richard Aldington, whose place in the literary world of my time in London is or ought to be secure'[2] Shortly thereafter, in an obituary notice on Aldington, Eliot said: 'We were on the same side for a long time and I was the first to give offence, although unintentionally . . .'[3] Snow, too, had more to say about Aldington, in the middle of a 1966 essay on Stalin: 'There was a break in our friendship because, without doing anything at all or saying a word, I found that I was part of a conspiracy against him. We were, I am glad to say, reconciled before he died'.[4]

At different times Eliot and Snow were good, even close, friends of Aldington. Both are on record as perceiving in him a brilliant but difficult individual. From the mid–1950s until recently Aldington has been almost forgotten in the United States while in Britain a not clearly deserved reputation for making virulent and intemperate *ad hominem* attacks has largely overborne any sense of his considerable literary merits. But there are signs of a revival of interest in Aldington's life and work. In 1975 the New York Public Library published his letters to the scholar Alan Bird, which focus largely on the research done for Aldington's biography of Lawrence of Arabia[5]; in 1981 the Viking Press published his correspondence with Lawrence Durrell.[6] At present a 'Selected letters' is in preparation and a volume of Aldington's correspondence with Pound.

Aldington's earliest literary avocation was as a poet. By the time he was 19 he had experimented successfully with free verse. He deserves an honourable place as an innovator in this medium. Besides being one of the official founders of Imagism in 1912, once the Poundian phase of the Imagist movement got under way Aldington was the most effective English Imagist. Through his work as apologist and editor he was instrumental in sustaining the English end of the movement during its short life and was the prime mover behind the 1930 anthology which was the movement's summing-up.[7] As he saw it, the aim of Imagism was 'to correct certain tendencies, and to foster others',[8] by which he meant banishing Victorian moralisms and 'poetical' flourishes. Significantly, part of his own purpose was to circumvent those kinds of artist 'who, of necessity, write, think and paint only for each other, since there is no one else to understand them'.[9] But perhaps his chief service to Imagism was his early recognition of the greatness of Hilda Doolittle's talent and his encouragement of her.

Along with F. S. Flint and (a little later) T. S. Eliot, Aldington was largely responsible for infusing the influence of contemporary French poetry into English. As literary editor of the *Egoist*, one of his aims was 'a revolt against our intellectual provincialism'.[10] In practice, this revolt became a concentration on French literature, and an awareness of 'international consciousness' acknowledged by Eliot as editorial successor to Aldington at the *Egoist*.[11] Aldington sustained his role as cultural 'good European' and proponent of cross-fertilisation throughout the 1920s in the pages of the *Times Literary Supplement*, the *Criterion* and elsewhere.

All this occurred during a period when Aldington saw himself as recuperating psychologically from experiences in the First World War. 'There are two kinds of men, those who have been to the front and those who haven't', he wrote in his memoir, *Life for Life's Sake*.[12] His first literary response was in poems, *Images of War*,[13] charged by Bernard Bergonzi with expressing 'a purely personal revulsion from the scenes of war',[14] a judgement which might equally well characterise the poetry of Wilfred Owen. But Aldington broke away from the conservatism of his life and writing in the 1920s with a larger statement about the war and an individual contribution in another medium. *Death of a Hero*, which he called a 'jazz novel', claims the musical form Eliot and Pound linked with poetry, and is one of the most powerful works of fiction dealing with the First World War. Since its first publication in 1929 it has been in print almost continuously, most recently in the 1984 Hogarth Press edition.

'I would never have thought that the English would produce a book like it!', Maxim Gorky wrote in 1932.[15] The Russians' immediate response to Aldington's 'bitter realism' quickly expanded into intense interest in his work in general. Confirmation that this engagement continues was provided recently by the participation of a member of the Soviet Writers Union, Professor

Mikhail Urnov of the Moscow Institute of Printing Arts, at the University of Reading's 'Aldington Symposium' in July 1986. Since the appearance of Evgeny Lann's review of *Death of a Hero* in *Novy Mir* in September 1931:

> Richard Aldington has always been accepted in Russia, and still is, as a many-sided figure, a rounded personality. Articles have been written about him as a poet and a novelist, a translator and a critic, a man and a writer . . . articles, studies, reviews and notices about him have appeared in works published in Moscow and Leningrad, in journals and in newspapers published in other cities. . . . His books have reached every part of the country.[16]

A 1930s English critic, A. C. Ward, saw that the novel 'proclaimed that the war had been fatal to a whole generation of youth by inflicting death either morally or spiritually, or both, even when it had spared the fighters' bodies'.[17] For Aldington, the causes of this mass fatality were Victorian materialism, humbug and philistinism, which he attacked here and in his later fiction. As an aesthete, he felt that the arts should be a life-giving alternative to destructive bourgeois social values but, from *Death of a Hero* on, the social snobbery and artificiality of the London literary world were, among his prime targets. Much of the opprobrium which Aldington has suffered derives from the perception that many of his bitter and angry assaults were directed with personal venom against individuals. As to that, his friend Alister Kershaw once observed:

> There's no denying that Richard had an impressive muster of aversions, ranging from left-wing bigots to the Catholic church, but, as Roy Campbell says, his hatreds were jovial and, so to speak, generous; they were never spiteful or vicious. Besides, he rather enjoyed his own tirades and had a lot of fun making his hatreds seem more ferocious than they were.[18]

The question of the quality of Aldington's personal animus comes up with redoubled force in relation to his biographies. In that genre he exhibited great range, from his succinct and still valued study of Voltaire in the 1920s to his sketch of Norman Douglas (which he hoped would provide material for others engaged in full-scale biographies of Douglas) to his rigorously-documented 'biographical enquiry' into the life of Lawrence of

Arabia. What Aldington added to the art of biography, particularly in the 1950s, is an unusual amalgam of substantiated objective fact with a subjective element which often enlivens the 'portrait' he is making. Although he set out to give a full-scale acount of the Duke of Wellington, he soon abandoned the idea of writing definitive or exhaustive biographies in favour of what he termed 'portraits'. *Portrait of a Genius, But* . . . , his study of D. H. Lawrence, is one of the best works on its subject and remains in print. If Aldington's reputation finally foundered because of his enquiry into the life of the 'other Lawrence', the desert soldier, no one has yet demonstrated that its major assertions are, in any important particular, at variance with the truth.

Early in his career, Aldington observed that:

> This question of criticism is of the very essence of our literature. It needs constant discussion. A man of parts who could really work out an original, sincere criticism could determine the literary taste of the next twenty years.[19]

The 'man of parts' turned out to be Eliot, but Aldington also wrote a great deal of effective literary criticism, ranging from numerous book reviews in the *Sunday Referee* and *Vogue*, to the *Times Literary Supplement*, *Poetry*, the *Dial* and the *Criterion*. Some of his best criticism is to be found in the introductions to various anthologies. Perhaps the most useful remark on Aldington's competence in this medium is Selwyn Kittredge's:

> How refreshing it is to be able to cast aside both the ponderous scholarly study and the falsifying popularization and find a critical commentary, such as Aldington's introduction to the *Portable Oscar Wilde*,[20] which is lucid, informed and gracefully written, yet full of balanced critical insights such as only a lifetime of reading for pleasure can unfold.[21]

Aldington had the instincts of a scholar, even if he was strictly and determinedly amateur, and he read deeply and seriously through a lifetime intensely preoccupied with literature, but he also said, in his introduction to *The Religion of Beauty: Selections from the Aesthetes*: 'If we cannot take Art and Literature with a certain lightness, among the many pleasures of life, let us take to grave-digging as a relaxation'.[22]

Largely self-educated, in the Greek and Latin classics and in several languages, he was widely read both in world literatures and general subjects. Kershaw, in a broadcast, has listed tongue-in-cheek the formidable variety of Aldington's interests in the 1940s and later: 'Ethnography, botany, astrology, entomology, anthropology, butterflies, bushmen, beetles; music, sculpture, painting; architecture, history; Purcell, Kant, Hokusai, Piranesi, Newton, Wren'. In other words, he was a person of lively and open intelligence.

It was this intelligence which moved him from his early days to fight off the narrowing influence of a provincial English environment. Although from another social background, this was a matter in which he could instinctively sympathise with D. H. Lawrence. But Aldington was of a different cast of mind. In his 'teens he formed the ideal of the 'good European', that is, the individual steeped in the literature and civilisation of the European past. (Here, of course, he found common ground with Pound and Eliot.) Otherwise, he discovered for himself, as he tells us in his memoir *Life for Life's Sake*, a philosophy which he came to see as Epicurean: 'What I wanted to do was to enjoy life, to enjoy *my* life in *my* way; and that in no wise depended on the three fatal vices, the exercise of power, the possession of property, the esteem of other featherless bipeds'. 'Live your life with gusto', a mentor advises the hero of Aldington's *All Men Are Enemies*.

Art, too, requires 'gusto' most of all. It has been said that Aldington had 'no fund of larger ideas', but he had anticipated this charge and answers it explicitly in the 'Author's Note' to *Artifex: Sketches and Ideas* (1935) where he observes that there are, lingering in the consciousness 'the clouds of ideas or pseudo-ideas which dim the mental landscape of our epoch. They are unsatisfactory material for the artist, who is concerned with life rather than with mental abstractions about life'.

In *Death of a Hero*, and indeed in all his effective fiction, he attributes contemporary social problems (of the early 20th century) to the British caste system and moral values set in the previous epoch. The title essay of *Artifex* advances the proposition that historical explanation should evolve from a tracing backwards, step by step, to the roots. As to 'progress', this results from a series of quantum leaps, most of which have originated in the imagination of one individual:

I think the history of civilization in its essentials might be written in a few hundred biographies, perhaps less. It would be simply an account of the various kinds of impetus given by exceptional individuals to the mass.[23]

Yet Aldington is ambivalent about these individuals, especially in their modern form:

with the aid of these transcendent scientific geniuses we shall either wipe each other out, or we shall make the world a desert in pursuit of imagined gain, or we shall make it an ant-hill of virtuous Socialists. (p. 9)

He deplored the control theologians and scientists have over our lives, although the theologian had lost real influence and had created instead 'the useful little bogeyman of respectability'. In contrast, the scientist's expertise had been put at the service of militarism. Neither theologian nor scientist has power 'where it is most needed—over the military man and the predatory exploiter of the earth and other human beings'. Against these 'modern colossi' stands the 'small, dejected and nervous figure' of 'Artifex, servant of the life impulse, maker of myths, music and images' (p. 11). This figure, puny in our era, attempts to celebrate the 'otherness' and 'wonder' of the world, which is 'to be enjoyed and revered' (p. 18), though the whole idea of an anthropocentric universe is to be questioned.

Artifex, the independent artist, has little to do with fashionable contemporary art:

Certainly there is art now, but it is the art of hyperaesthesia, the art of exasperated neurasthenics. The latest aesthetic giggle, the new *petit frisson*—anything, anything to seem original. The music of atonality, the painting and sculpture of super-realism [that is, surrealism], the literature of the stream of consciousness, the aestheticism of concrete and cocktails—neurasthenia and self-destruction. Intellectual snobbishness is the very essence of its appeal to the gangs and cliques of Paris and London. If it were not inaccessible to common sense they would not want it . . . As to the swinish multitude—abandon them to the venal, the vulgar and the mediocre. (pp. 33–4)

A thinly veiled attack on what later came to be called 'Modernism', this implies Aldington's sense of the nature of his own reader, the adequately educated sensible person who sees the point in conserving and enjoying what is best in the European tradition.

Aldington then compares the peasant and the industrial worker, favouring the former's realism and independence, his capacity for adapting to the rhythms of life, for an approach which is also Aldington's:

> There isn't any paradise, either here or hereafter; there isn't any solution of the 'problem of life', because it isn't a problem. The only thing to do with life is live it, put up with the tough breaks and enjoy the alleviations. To me the arts are among the highest of the alleviations—they are more than that, an indefinite prolonging and intensifying of life here and now. If they do not enrich experience of life both in artist and spectator, I see no point in them. (pp. 40–1)

A summing-up is provided in 'A Splinter of America', Aldington's responses to a first encounter with the West Indies. Once again rejecting theological or scientific overviews of human experience, he says:

> there might be another attitude to life, based on an acceptance of life's mystery and on reverence for its many forms, a more modest conception of man's place in nature, and abhorrence of every kind of greed and destruction. One seems to get glimpses of it in the more ancient civilizations, in the lives of some men, in some poets and even in a few philosophers. (pp. 56–7)

But the world is now too populous and too chaotic for anyone successfully to teach such a philosophy, so that all any individual can do is to follow his own daimon as far as circumstances allow.

Both in his life and writing this is what Aldington attempted, and this accounts for his fascination with such a figure as Charles Waterton, the squire naturalist, an eccentric, which is to say, one who 'is supremely the man who knows what he wants to do, and simply and openly does it. He never thinks of gain or applause, but of the satisfaction of doing, the supreme peace which comes from the object attained—whether it be riding a live alligator on the banks of the Essequibo or standing on one foot on the topmost pinnacle of the Castello de Sant' Angelo in Rome'.[24]

Introducing *The Complete Poems of Richard Aldington* in 1948, he wrote, 'I claim no share whatever in the so-called 'revolution of 1912'. It was a mere accident that what I was writing then chanced to meet with the approval of the verse revolutionaries'.[25] Thus he repudiated his connection with Imagism, the one literary movement associated with his name. Apart from it, during a 50-year literary career he went his independent way, riding more than a few alligators of his own. All this led to his last difficult years in a cottage in the Sancerrois region of France, but an interesting and varied life ends on no dull note and, instead, is wreathed in ironies, most notably a triumphal tour of collectivist Russia. Aldington's last important book was a study of the life and works of Frédéric Mistral, the Provençal poet, the value of whose work derives from the fact that he was deeply rooted in his own community.

1 Chrysalis 1892–1911

When, in his 40s, Richard Aldington first saw the façade of a typical brownstone house in New York City he experienced 'that tenderness we feel at the unexpected revival of childish memories'.[1] He was confronted by a house 'near cousin' to the yellow brick one where he had lived in Dover as a youth. From this English sea-coast dwelling he had emerged, passing the 'sad housemaids' whitening the area steps, on his way to the small private school where as a young child he learnt his first French and Latin. In this town he 'was being manufactured into the sort of human product a not too intelligent provincial society thought I should be'; but fortunately much of his growing up was done in the country, which in retrospect he felt enabled him to develop 'into something on my own'.

Although he grew up in Dover and its vicinity, Aldington was born in Portsmouth, Hampshire, on 8 July 1892. The eldest of four children, he was christened Edward Godfrey (or, as he sometimes insisted, 'Godfree', though this middle name was his mother's maiden name). He chose to be Richard while still a boy, presumably feeling the name had more romantic aura to it than that of the portly future king.

He was proud that his surname could be traced as far back as the early 14th century and his sister Margery described the Aldingtons as 'pre-Norman Conquest Saxon landowners'.[2] But Aldington's father, Albert Edward, practised as a solicitor at Dover and along the South Coast. A man with modest literary aspirations, he was author of at least two books, and his novel *The Queen's Preferment* (1896) met with some success. He is the figure behind the portrayal of George Winterbourne's father in Aldington's *Death of a Hero*, which also reveals something of the quality of Aldington's parents' relationship: 'the pathetic efforts of George Augustus to be an aesthete and WRITE meant something, some inner struggle, some effort to create a life of his own. It was an evasion, of course, a feeble, flapping desire to escape into a dream world; but if you had been George Augustus, living under the sceptre of dear Mamma in the Sheffield of 1891, you too would have yearned to escape'.[3] The need to break out of the confines of a narrow social environment, this was to become a recurring major theme in Aldington's writing.

Of 'Mamma' (Isobel) in *Death of a Hero*, Aldington goes on to say 'she also wanted to escape'. In the person of his mother, Jessie May, she went about it in a more thoroughgoing, if less sensitive, fashion than his father, actively pursuing a writing career and becoming acquainted with professional writers, who thus came early into Aldington's life.

During the first two decades of the century, she published seven books (with a variety of more or less well-established publishers), among them *Love Letters that Caused a Divorce* (1905 or 1906), *Love Letters to a Soldier* (1915) and *Roll of Honour and Other Poems* (1917). These and other books with similar titles later seemed contemptible to Aldington who many times expressed active dislike for his mother, once claiming to his friend Frank Flint that she 'keeps a saloon and writes inconceivable novels'.[4] No matter that the 'saloon' was the commodious and respectable Mermaid Inn at Rye, Sussex! Another friend, John Cournos, heard from Aldington in 1920 that Jessie May had just disgraced herself by testifying as a witness to an adultery and being paid five pounds for it.[5] No such stories survive about his father. Albert Edward appears to have been a gentle, studious, docile man, with a poor head for business, dominated by his wife.

In the dream-like impressionistic early pages of *Life for Life's Sake*, Richard Aldington invokes a ghost or two, but otherwise conveys the feeling of a peaceful, pleasurable, largely rural childhood. His preparatory schooling was at Mr Sweetman's Seminary for Young Gentlemen at St Margaret's Bay, a small fishing village a few miles from Dover. He was immensely happy there. 'I developed a sort of mystic enthusiasm for life. I can remember when I was about ten, leaning from my bedroom window to listen to the thrushes singing on an April evening, with feelings of such intense aesthetic pleasure that one's finest emotions now seem blunt and coarse by comparison.' Always sceptical of received religions, or indeed dogma of any kind, Aldington's 'mystic enthusiasm', especially when he was at the height of his powers, impelled him to live every moment to its fullest intensity.

His sister Margery remembered this period and, in particular, the dominance of their mother, 'strong-willed and emotionally turbulent... [with] a dramatic and highly imaginative mind and a temper she enjoyed displaying... she flourished and thrived on a first class "row" at least once a week, but it shattered the rest of us'.[6] Jessie May's temperament and social ambitions combined with Albert Edward's poor head for business, seem eventually to have brought the family ruinously into debt. Margery's account of their mother is confirmed in many of Aldington's letters, and his feelings about Jessie May are at the back of several savage portrayals of mothers in his fiction, most notably that of Mrs Winterbourne in *Death of a Hero:*

> Although a lady of 'mature charms,' Mrs. Winterbourne loved to fancy herself as a delicious young thing of seventeen, passionately beloved by a sheik-like but nevertheless "clean" (not to say "straight") Englishman. She was a mistress of would-be revolutionary platitudes about marriage and property (rather like the talk of an "enlightened" parson), but, in fact, was as sordid, avaricious, conventional, and spiteful a middle-class woman as you could dread to meet. Like all her class, she toadied to her betters and bullied her inferiors. But, with her conventionality, she was, of course, a hypocrite. In her kittenish moods, which she cultivated with a strange lack of a sense of congruity, she liked to throw out hints about "kicking over the traces." But, as a matter of fact, she never soared much above tippling, financial dishonesty, squabbling, lying, betting, and affairs with bounderish young men, whom only her romantic effrontery could have dared describe as "clean and straight," although there was no doubt whatever about their being English, and indeed sportin' in a more or less bounderish way.[7]

Several late letters from Aldington to his brother Tony throw further light on their mother's temperament, the relationship between the Aldington parents, and the domestic conditions prevailing in his boyhood and young manhood:

Daddy was 56 when he died — heart. [He wrote on 20 December 1958] His refusal to divorce was surely Roman Catholic twaddle?[8] Curious, that though literate, he wrote so badly. Mother's novels, though hideously vulgar and illiterate, have much more vitality. Among the little handicaps you have had to live down is the fact that she caused the windows of (I think) the Kentish Express to be filled with copies of an incredible work coquettishly entitled Love Letters that Caused a Divorce. This work was designed to extinguish Marie Corelli and Elinor Glyn, but unluckily failed to do so.

Unfortunately daddy had (or thought he had) a sense of

humour, but he was always getting into difficulties through misplacing it. . . . Pending the first Alien Act of whatever, the F[oreign] O[ffice] sent officials on the packet-boats to ask the nationality of each person boarding. (Foreigners had of course to justify and show means.) Well, Daddy advanced, the F. O. Bloke says, affable like: "Are you British, sir?" And Daddy replies humourously: "no, Dutch". By the time he had extricated himself, even he did'nt think the joke very funny.

'She had let George down so badly time after time when he was a boy that he was all tight inside'; Aldington might easily have written these comments on George Winterbourne about himself. Ruefully sympathetic as he was towards his father, virulent antipathy lies just under the surface of most of his comments on his mother, whether in letters or in presenting her fictional surrogates in *Death of a Hero*, *Very Heaven* or *Rejected Guest*.

In an interview not long after Aldington's death, Dorothy Yorke (his American companion of the 1920s) made some interesting points about the parents: 'Well, his mother was a good soul . . . And his mother was a very common, stout woman. She had a great deal of intelligence, but she was a very common woman. . . . Edward Albert Aldington was nearly a gentleman. He was a country type. He was a country lawyer and he was of a much greater class than this very common, fat woman that he married — Richard's mother. . . . And I think Richard spent his life trying to get away from the mother in him to attain the father in him'. Thus the contrast between the Aldington parents is made something of a caricature,[9] as in the old comic postcards of Donald McGill, [10] with their large, buxom red-faced and huge-bosomed 'mums' and diminutive, harassed-looking 'dads'.

Another source of early dissatisfaction and insecurity was Aldington's immediate environment. In a late letter to Tony, he says: 'The photo of poor old Dover is indeed shocking. The Victorian houses, with all their drab squalor, still had some remote trace of humanity, but these skyscraping slave-pens, industrial ergastula, give one the creeps. It is the same everywhere, and reflects the age, which will do itself justice'.[11] In his published writings and letters this plaint against dehumanisation of the environment in the interests of industrialism is often repeated. Dover is the locale of his best-known early poem, 'Chidhood',[12] published when he was 21.

The bitterness, the misery, the wretchedness of childhood
Put me out of love with God. . . .

So the poem opens, proceeding for more than a hundred lines to anatomise the dull, hateful town of Dover (renamed 'Dullborough' in *Death of a Hero*). In 'Childhood' Aldington locates a deeply personal metaphor[13]:

> Somebody found my chrysalis
> And shut it in a match-box.
> My shrivelled wings were beaten,
> Shed their colours in dusty scales
> Before the box was opened
> For the moth to fly.

The metaphor reappears, more universalised, in *Rejected Guest*:

> A child, grubbing about in the garden, finds the chrysalis of a tiger moth. An old boot box is begged from the kitchen, a crumpled pile of unnecessary leaves is arranged for the treasure, useless air-holes are punched. Every half-hour or so, the child peeps into the box to see the wonderful change it has been told about. Nothing happens, the box is forgotten, and then one day carelessly opened. The bright-winged creature lying dead. . . .[14]

This image of a stifling environment or nurturing-time is made all the more pertinent by the knowledge that Aldington was a keen amateur lepidoptorist. Collecting butterflies became a lifelong hobby. He had already begun gathering and making specimens, in a boy's way, when he met the Reverend Francis Austin, 'A burly man with thick eyebrows and Henry VIII legs', who encouraged and helped him.[15] Austin was a field-naturalist and avid collector who penned books on such varied topics as medieval seals and flowers in Shakespeare. He was one of several older men with whom Aldington established friendship during adolescence.

Among a list of 'dull' items adumbrated in 'Childhood' is 'the big College' where, as a day-boy from 1904 to 1906, Aldington was apparently himself considered dull. Looking back, he recollected an institution intent on moulding boys to middle-class, Empire-vaunting conformity. His determined resistance of the process may partially explain an undistinguished academic career there. Several times, in letters and memoirs, he records with satisfaction his return years later as an old boy and distinguished author. Walking in the school close with the headmaster, Mr Lee, formerly his housemaster, he was asked: 'And now tell me, my dear Aldington, *where* on earth did you get your scholarly knowledge?' The account of George Winterbourne's schooldays reflects those of the young Aldington:

> He was supposed to be dull-minded as well as obstinate and unmanly.... Maybe he picked up more even of the little they had to teach than they suspected ... he was busy enough inside, building up a life of his own. George went at George Augustus's books with the energy of a fierce physical hunger. He once showed me a list in an old notebook of the books he had read before he was sixteen. Among other things, he had raced through most of the poets from Chaucer onwards. It was not the amount that he read which mattered, but the way in which he read. ... The English poets and the foreign painters were his only real friends. They were his interpreters of the mystery, the defenders of the inner vitality which he was fighting unconsciously to save. Naturally, the School was against him. They set out to produce 'a type of thoroughly manly fellow', a 'type' which unhesitatingly accepted the prejudices, the 'code' put before it. ... The others were good enough fellows, no doubt, but they really had no selves to *be*. They hadn't the flame. ... That's what they couldn't stand — the obstinate, passive refusal to accept their prejudices, to conform to their minor-gentry, kicked-backside-of-the-Empire code.[16]

Some at least of the young Aldington's 'scholarly knowledge' was garnered from his father's library of two thousand books, where he read Scott and the fustian Harrison Ainsworth and, through finding an open copy of Oscar Wilde's *Intentions* on his father's desk, discovered Keats and promptly read through *Endymion*. This was in 1907 and long afterwards he considered it lucky he had stumbled on Keats and Wilde, and not, for example, Matthew Arnold, a sort altogether less appealing to his romantic disposition. The happy encounter led on at once to Aldington's excited scribbling of his first poems, while he was out insect-hunting on the cliffs at sunset. Inverting the field notebook he carried at

Austin's suggestion, he recorded a line of iambic pentameter which had 'presented itself', and felt he had truly begun as a writer. The act of turning the book upside down he later saw as a 'symbolical gesture'; but he was quickly to learn that writing, like field observation, entailed much hard, tedious work.

His interest in Wilde was to reach its high point some 40 years later when he produced a brilliant introductory essay for *The Portable Oscar Wilde* (1946). It would have surprised and amused him to learn that an earlier Wilde apologist, Leonard Cresswell Ingleby, author of some four hundred pages of competent, if unctuous memoir and exegesis, was none other than a boyhood *bête-noire*, his mother's friend, the popular romantic novelist Guy Thorne (and that Ingleby and Thorne were both pseudonyms of one Cyril Arthur Edward Ranger Gull.)

To a great extent, young Aldington was an autodidact but his learning was surprisingly wide-ranging. For example (as he told his Japanese follower Morokimi Megata in 1959) at the time of the Russo-Japanese war he had already come across the writings of Lafcadio Hearn, the Japanese-American scholar. In the 1920s he confided in Herbert Read that he had experienced a wholesale aesthetic awakening when he was around 15. Apart from books, as he tells us in *Life for Life's Sake* this was partly brought about by his seeing beauty in the traditional architecture of country churches and partly through a memorable visit with his father to the Musée Royal in Brussels. He came home from this in a state of high enthusiasm, saturated with sense experiences, and suffused with an indefinable well-being which he never forgot. Shortly after returning, though, he had an apocalyptic and bloody dream, somehow associated with the trip, though perhaps also in anticipation of imminent minor surgery, a hernia operation. Thus even this joyous awakening had its moment of dark counteraction.

The focus of his self-teaching quickly became a desire to write, and especially to write poetry. By 16, he had published one poem in London (in 'an obscure journal', he later told Amy Lowell. It may have been the *New Age*[17]), but now he wrote his first story, promptly read to his mother, and as promptly sent by her to George Bernard Shaw, who responded (Aldington claimed later):

Madam,
    Your son has obviously too much literary talent to earn his living in an honest way.

I enclose a guinea which he is to spend in some thoroughly selfish manner,

Yours faithfully.

A more accessible 'literary hero' appeared in the person of Dudley Grey, a local literatus and a man of 50 when Aldington was in his teens. Grey is portrayed in *Death of a Hero* as Dudley Pollack, who (for unexplained reasons, with a whiff of scandal) had retreated from public life to a small seaside cottage. Despite the difference in their ages, Aldington regarded Grey, who as a young man 'had gone about Venice in a cloak and a gondola, imagining himself another Byron',[18] for some time as his closest friend. Grey now appointed himself Aldington's aesthetic mentor and, under the pretext of playing chess, the two met regularly. Aldington later had to outgrow the Tennysonian droning chant acquired from emulating Grey's style of reading poetry, but some things about Grey he never forgot. Breadth was what this 'second father' had to offer him, for Dudley Grey was 'a good European', who could talk interestingly of London, Paris and Berlin, of the theatre, grand opera, and symphonic and chamber music, or about Homer and Horace, Ronsard and André Chénier. It was at his urging that Aldington made strong efforts to read French, but perhaps the chief gift he imparted was an enthusiasm for Italy. Through him Aldington was prompted to learn Italian, and European history and something of styles and periods in the history of art. Grey also attempted to inculcate a sense of literary patience in the boy and was annoyed when, quite soon, Aldington had a poem accepted for publication (presumably the one in the 'obscure journal'). Grey quoted Horace to the effect that one should shelve one's work for seven years before sending it out to editors, but it was other advice of his which Aldington really heeded. 'You must go to Italy', Grey suggested regularly; but, of course, university should come first.

When he was 17 Aldington's family moved to London, a prospect he initially welcomed. For a few months the family lived at Harrow, which he found mediocre and lifeless. A further move, to Teddington, was an improvement because the place was handy to Pope's Twickenham, to Strawberry Hill and Richmond, and the house was built on part of an orchard owned by R. D. Blackmore. The Aldingtons lived only a couple of hundred yards from Burley Park and Richard liked to walk there under trees planted by Charles II. He greatly enjoyed the park in summer, in the early morning hours when nobody was about, and managed to determine the least popular times at nearby Hampton Court, so he could study in quiet the paintings in the state apartments, the Mantegna cartoons and Raphael tapestries, or enjoy in the very early morning the red and fallow deer and immense, ever-changing seasonal panoply of flowers.

Apparently quite heedless of Dudley Grey's advice, he soon began to submit poems and translations to publications such as the *Evening Standard*, *Westminster Gazette*, and *Pall Mall Gazette*, delighting in the occasional half-guineas these commitments produced. Otherwise, having few friends, he wandered the city alone, trudging the galleries and browsing in the then richly-rewarding Charing Cross Road bookshops ('an Alma Mater for those who know how to use them', he wrote later). The Teddington house itself had mild literary associations. From there he went visiting to Putney Hill where Algernon Charles Swinburne, one of his heroes, had died a year or two earlier. He sent poems to Swinburne's mentor, Theodore Watts Dunton, and was invited to tea at The Pines, Swinburne's last home. Swinburne's writing table and chair, some of his books and a hall filled with Pre-Raphaelite paintings, were there to be gawked at, but afterwards Aldington felt like a tourist or interloper.

London seems to have wrought a change in him. A sentence of *Death of a Hero* is pertinent here. The narrator says of George Winterbourne: 'I imagine that he more or less adjusted himself to ... public-school and home hostility; that, as time passed and he began to make friends, he felt more confidence and happiness'.[19] In 1910 Aldington enrolled at University College, London, where he soon got to know other students. One of these, Vivian Gaster, who was in the same Greek class, met him quite often outside classes. Though Gaster came to dislike Aldington's later iconoclasm, he recalled of 1910, 'I was fascinated with his talk about poetry, and he was (to me) [the] romantic type of Bohemian, wearing a velvet jacket and brownish trousers. I certainly learnt a lot about the poetical outlook and how to understand poetry'.[20] Simplistic as it may be, this suggests that Aldington was young a man who had found his role.

He made two particular friends, Alec Randall and Arthur Chapman. Like him, they aspired to write. Aldington and Chapman shared a bent for poetry, Randall remembered, 'but Richard, with his handsome features, his sparkling merry eyes, his reddish beard and velvet jacket and flowing bow tie was the more romantic'.[21] Chapman, in any case, died young in a boating accident (and was memorialised by Aldington with a poem in the college magazine).

Randall's memoir is both valuable and touching, for it provides a portrait of young Richard Aldington in which many life-long characteristics are revealed, but shows traits for which he was later criticised, or even vilified, as part of a sympathetic picture. To Randall, he was a student-rebel who knew he wanted to be a writer and not (as he said his mother wished) practitioner of a bourgeois profession such as the law. But Randall remembered Aldington's defiance of the established order as being far from angry, and indeed marked by gaiety. He saw in him a pleasant compound of humour, kindliness and well-defined scepticism. This last was directed towards institutions, received opinions and what we might now perceive as ideological 'groupthink'. Aldington had a lifelong distrust of political and religious systems in general, and of state-applied social panaceas in particular. He was strongly committed to individualism and the pursuit of personal fulfillment. Alec Randall saw signs of all these characteristics.

In *Life for Life's Sake* Aldington mentions several teachers encountered at University College, though none had any profound effect on him. Among them were poets, notably the humorous and yet severe A. E. Housman,[22] who attempted to afford his largely-indifferent students access to Virgil and Livy, Cicero and Tacitus. Randall tells us that Aldington scorned Cicero, directing him instead towards the astringencies of Catullus. Somewhat later he introduced him to the mediaeval Latin poets and to Rémy de Gourmont's *Le latin mystique*,[23] a work which was to influence Randall towards conversion to Catholicism. Despite Hugh Kenner's demonstration of Aldington's 'misreading' of a Sappho poem,[24] he does seem to have acquired a remarkable grounding in the Greek and Latin classics. A contemporary, the formidable Rebecca West, comparing the same two men as Professor Kenner, suggested that 'Aldington was extremely well-read . . . I don't think Ezra Pound made that impression on any of us'.[25] Aldington's practice as a poet was to be importantly affected by his grounding in the classics. When still 18 he began to write *vers libre* because he had tired of the effects of rhyme and was interested in poetic experiment. A model was available in Coventry Patmore's 'The Unknown Eros', but he was unfamiliar with it, nor, despite Dudley

Grey's guidance in French poetry, was he aware at first of the French *vers librists*. His practical starting-point was a chorus from Euripides' *Hippolytus*.

Another University College luminary was W. P. Ker, the mediaevalist, known chiefly to Aldington (and presumably to others, as is suggested in *Life for Life's Sake*) for his 'mask-like face'. Rebecca West reported, however, that Ker was impressed by the range of Aldington's reading and his understanding of what he read, and strongly regretted that he later did not follow an academic career.[26] As it turned out, Aldington's university life was short, and he was soon quit of an institution designed to produce 'ten thousand pedants for one poet'. In 1918 he told Winifred Ellerman (Bryher, the novelist) that he had left University College after fighting against the insensitive education system, and that he was 'more or less in disgrace, after insulting the provost'.[27] This explanation contrives to suggest that he was thrown out, but his real reason for leaving was that his father had suffered financial reverses from unlucky speculations. Far from being glad to abandon the 'philistine stronghold', Aldington learned that changed circumstances brought a changed image. Friends and acquaintances who had admired his intellectual gifts now seemed to discover that, after all, he was a rather ordinary young man. Harshly he summed up a valuable lesson gained from trying to solve the 'ancient and fish-like problem' of how to live as you will, and not as you must: 'The bourgeois always rats in money disasters'. Though this, of course, is Aldington the successful middle-aged author looking back to a young Richard hurt by events.

Some of the weight of this depressing problem was still with him a quarter of a century later when he wrote *Very Heaven* (1937). Chris Heylin, the protagonist, learns suddenly that his parents have lost their money and his comfortable student life must cease. The novel opens with Chris wondering how he can confess such disasters to his tutor who coincidentally is asking himself (somewhat indifferently): 'What does one say to an undergraduate whose parents have lost their money?' In 'the Capitalist's pasture' that disappearance of sustaining wealth makes tutor and student inhabitants of different realms. The obvious, acceptable, and respectable route in Aldington's case was towards some mute clerkship in one or other City of London business, but this he did not take. Through friends he met a Mr Beare, 'sports editor of one of the big London dailies'. Beare, planning to take an apartment in

Bloomsbury, offered to share it on condition that for two or three afternoons a week Aldington would act as his assistant, covering sports events the editor could not attend. Besides being given accommodation, Aldington was to be paid the usual copy rates. Though he sometimes claimed disingenuously to have loathed all forms of sport at school and thought it contemptible that adults should waste their time playing children's games, he took the job.

He carried a portfolio of his writings to Fleet Street and succeeded in placing two poems. Reckoning up afterwards, he was delighted that these sales and one week's work as part-time sports reporter had earned him as much as a clerk would earn in a month. All this occurred in the brief period while he was cutting ties with the University of London, a circumstance which found him in a state of some exaltation because he felt that he could survive well enough by relying on his own gifts. Or, as he tells it himself:

> Leaving University College for the last time I walked, as I had so often done before, down Gower Street towards Bloomsbury, Soho, and Charing Cross. In this I detect an accidental symbolism which is rather pleasing — the departure from buttressed respectability towards the freer if frowstier fields of bohemianism.[28]

2 Pound and H.D., 1912–13

His new-found poverty restricted Aldington to a spartan regimen, non-smoking and largely non-alcoholic, with writing as chief preoccupation. Though the way of life appealed, he felt it would be dull if continued too long. He need not have worried, for he was soon involved in the round of literary parties, though he despised their snobbery and fashion-dominated loyalties. At the salon of Mrs Deighton Patmore, known at Brigit,[1] (herself later to play an important part in Aldington's life) he was introduced to Ezra Pound, a tall young American with reddish hair and neatly kept beard. At 26, seven years Aldington's senior, Pound was already a name and for some time to come would be a 'small but persistent volcano in the dim levels of London literary society'(*Life for Life's Sake*, hereafter *LF*, p. 105). Pound proved 'great fun'. Though from the beginning Aldington observed a posturing side to him, he always remembered the Ezra of 1911–13 with affection and gratitude.

Shortly after their first meeting, Pound lectured on Provençal poetry in Lady Glenconner's drawing-room (the milieu in which Yeats had his plays performed). The occasion was chaired by W. P. Ker who, as Aldington remarks, was obliged for once to drop his mask:

> As the lecturer tied himself into a series of inextricable knots, consisting largely of 'I mean to say', 'What I mean is, er'—er', I found myself watching Ker, who by the way was one of the best mediaeval and Provençal scholars in Europe. It was the first time I had ever seen a real expression on his features. His wrinkled and slightly acid face seemed petrified with incredulous astonishment.[2]

But this recollection was 30 years after the event. Much nearer in time to it, Aldington wrote to Amy Lowell in quite a different tone, showing Pound in another light. Of the early months of their friendship, he says:

I showed him my vers libre poems over a beefsteak in Kensington and he said: 'Well, I don't think you need any help from me!' We were great friends, very great friends, and I cannot forget how much his knowledge and sympathy meant to me, after many years of spiritual isolation and almost morbid sensitiveness to general misunderstanding.[3]

Although Aldington had already found his way to *vers libre*[4] and to a wide range of reading, Pound brought him 'news' of Arnaut Daniel and Cavalcanti, Homer and Dante, Villon, Ronsard, Verlaine and the French Symbolists and Pound's 'true Penelope', Flaubert,— a writer who would still be engaging Aldington's attention near the end of his life.

Through Pound Aldington met Hilda Doolittle. His picture of their three-way relationship in *Life for Life's Sake* is good-humoured and mellow. They made pilgrimages together to 'fashionable tea-shops', for which, as Americans, Ezra and Hilda had 'an almost insane relish'. In one such 'bun shop', in 'the Royal Borough of Kensington' around April 1912[5] occurred the now near-legendary meeting which marks the official founding of the 'Imagist movement'. At Pound's instigation, the three agreed on the principles of good writing recorded in 'A Retrospect':

> In the spring or early summer of 1912, 'H.D.', Richard Aldington and myself decided that we were agreed upon the three principles following:
> 1. Direct treatment of the 'thing' whether subjective or objective.
> 2. To use absolutely no word that does not contribute to the presentation.
> 3. As regarding rhythm: to compose in the sequence of the musical phrase, not in the sequence of a metronome.[6]

This familiar passage is quoted here to emphasise the mention of Aldington's name. Numerous books and essays on the history or theory of Imagism have been published,[7] and this is not the place to explore the subject in detail. Shortly after the 'bun shop' meeting Pound called their group 'Les Imagistes', insisting that Hilda should sign some poems 'H.D. Imagiste'. In Pound's *Ripostes*, published in London that October, the name appeared in print for the first time,[8] with an airy note (appended to 'The Complete Poetical Works of T. E. Hulme[9]): 'as for the future, Les Imagistes, descendants of the forgotten school of 1909, have that in their keeping'. Thus Aldington gained a toe-hold in literary history as founder-member of an avant-garde movement.

In May all three members of the new 'mouvemong' (the affectionate phoneticism is Aldington's, mimicking Pound) were in Paris. Aldington was glad they were together. He encountered Paris with a sense of 'vivacious peace', finding that it *looked* 'the most intelligent of cities',[10] though he says in a postcard to Albert Edward: 'It took me two days to get over the vile façade of the Louvre'. Remaining until late June, he wrote a little, but chiefly seems to have savoured Parisian life, exploring Paris with H.D. Later, in her yet to be published biographical novel 'Asphodel', she actually identified Paris with Aldington ('Darrington' in the novel): 'Paris suddenly became (with the coming of Darrington) Paris'.[11] She then stretched the link to the mythological figure of Paris (with Pound, by implication, as Menelaus); but for Aldington himself this trip was free of such overtones; he simply enjoyed the rhythm of the great city. Pound took him to visit his American pianist-composer friend, Walter Morse Rummel, who later set some children's verses written for him by Aldington and H.D.[12] They also saw something of Henry Slonimsky, another Pound contact from Philadelphia and the University of Pennsylvania, whom Aldington had met earlier in 1912 at one of Hulme's Frith Street 'Tuesday evenings'. He was impressed by Slonimsky's skilled arguments against Hulme's explications of the philosophy of Kant and Bergson. He delighted in the spring evenings, sitting under the trees in the Luxembourg Gardens, listening to talk of Heraclitus and Parmenides, and very likely wearing the new black velvet jacket which he had hung out in the rain, to shrink and crease and age into a garment appropriate to his vocation.[13]

Back in London for the second half of 1912, he briefly worked part-time for the Garton Peace Foundation,[14] an organisation which had been founded to forward the ideas of Norman Angell as expressed in *The Great Illusion* (1909), chiefly that 'no war can be *economically* advantageous' and 'our first objective is defence rather than peace'.[15] He came to the job by an odd route, the reading of Whitman's *Drum Taps* (1865) and *Specimen Days* (1883), 'boned up' on for a paper delivered to the London University Literary Society. Quite quickly, he became disillusioned with Angell's ideas for achieving and maintaining peace, but reading Whitman convinced him that war's brutality and widespread suffering made it unthinkable as a course of action. His later dread of the actual conflict may have owed something to this reading. He made use of his experience at the Garton to focus the moment in *Death of a Hero* when George Winterbourne, the protagonist, first learns of the possibility of war:

> 'What nonsense!' said George explosively, 'What absolute nonsense! Haven't you read Norman Angell's *Great Illusion*? He shows quite conclusively that war does nearly as much damage to the victor as to the conquered. And he also says that the structure of modern international commerce and finance is so delicate and widespread that a war couldn't possibly last more than a few weeks without coming to an end automatically, because all the nations would be ruined.'[16]

Meantime, the London poetry front was active. All year had appeared the sixpenny numbers of *Poetry Review*, founded by Harold Monro, whom Aldington had met soon after meeting Pound. Although no poems of his appeared there in 1912 Aldington apparently helped in producing the magazine. The August number is a survey, by another new friend, F. S. Flint, of 'Contemporary French Poetry',[17] which strongly conveys the exploratory vitality of new modes across the Channel. These French intellectual currents were already present when Aldington was experimenting with *vers libre* in 1911, though he came to a more detailed knowledge especially through Flint, of whom he wrote: 'Our friend, F. S. Flint, introduced us to Verlaine, Rimbaud, Laforgue, the Symbolistes and their successors, who were still producing all sorts of new poems . . . .' Two decades later, his recollection is somewhat different. Speaking of Ezra Pound, 'citizen of the world' he says 'Instead of pap, he fed me meat. He gave me Villon, he gave me Verlaine . . . .' and 'we liked F. S. Flint, although the nearest he got to Imagism was reading masses of young French poets and imitating Verlaine'.[18]

In September Pound became foreign editor of *Poetry* and soon forwarded to Chicago some poems of Aldington's. The next month he followed them up with some of his own, but instructed the editor, Harriet Monroe, not to print these until she had used work by H.D. and Aldington. This early flurry of poems included H.D.'s 'Hermes of the Ways', and 'Choricos', which was to become Aldington's best-known Imagist poem. With it Pound sent Aldington's 'To a Greek Marble' and 'Au Vieux Jardin'.[19] This last is perhaps the nearest to an Imagist poem on the Hulme model of 'accurate, precise and definite description'.[20]

> I have sat here happy in the garden,
> Watching the still pool and the reeds
> And the dark clouds
> Which the wind of the upper air
> Tore like the green leafy boughs
> Of the divers-hued trees of late summer;
> But though I greatly delight
> In these and the water-lilies,
> That which sets me nighest to weeping
> Is the rose and white colour of the smooth flagstones,
> And the pale yellow grasses
> Among them.

The November *New Age* included poems by Aldington, and the journal's editor, A. R. Orage,[21] afterwards commissioned him to write a series of 'Letters from Italy'. On 9 November Harriet Monroe wrote to Pound questioning the soundness of Aldington's 'To Atthis (After the Manuscript of Sappho Now in Berlin)', noting that University of Chicago scholars 'wouldn't stand for' something so far from the original.[22] Pound responded that the original text is too mutilated for categorical scholarly judgements. Thinking back on 'To Atthis' a few years later, he considered it one of the few beautiful poems of the period and drew on it in writing his fifth canto, but on this occasion *Poetry* turned it down.[23] The November *Poetry* did contain a group of Aldington's poems along with Pound's report of the state of the art in London. Pound allotted Aldington's poetry a cautious little paragraph to itself, finding in it 'a gleam of hope', presumably for the resuscitation of the 'dead art'; but the 'Notes and Announcements' were more expansive, describing Aldington as 'a young English poet, one of the 'Imagistes', a group of ardent Hellenists who are pursuing interesting experiments in *vers libre*; trying to attain in English certain subtleties of cadence of the kind which Mallarmé and his followers have studied in French. Mr. Aldington has published little as yet, and nothing in America'.[24]

As a consequence, one 'spectral' London day as he was labouring at translating Charles D'Orléans, the mail brought a cheque from *Poetry* for around $40, and a postcard from a friend in Genoa depicting almond trees in blossom on a hillside above the Italian Riviera. 'Why not go?' Aldington asked himself. Armed with the cheque, the commission from Orage, and some assiduously hoarded funds of his own he at last determined to follow Dudley Grey's often-repeated advice. By the time Harold Monro officially opened the Poetry Bookshop in London on 8 January 1913,[25] Aldington was in Italy. John Cournos, a new friend and another protégé of Pound's, had provided a list of hotels and *pensioni*. In Rome Aldington lodged in the Via Sistina, where he remained for eight weeks enjoying the orange trees and cypresses in the garden. For seven months he was a tourist, first in Rome, then Naples, Capri, Florence and Venice, with short excursions to Pompeii, Amalfi, Padua, Vicenza, Verona and Lake Garda. Among the people he met were the writers Violet Hunt and Robert Bontine Cunninghame Graham, the Scots writer-politician, with 'fine hidalgo looks and supple energy',[26] who took him visiting the opulent dwellings of the aristocracy. Alice Meynell, the poet, deplored his taste for Swinburne and solicited interest in Coventry Patmore, a request he 'cheerfully' refused. In a *pensione* at Cava, over a breakfast served with a large bowl of scented honey, he met Stefan Georg, 'and the German poet talked to me of his French friends, Mallarmé and Verlaine and the Symbolistes, and said I must read no more Latin but only Greek, always Greek'.[27] Neither then nor later did Aldington's Hellenism need encouragement.

A notebook labelled 'Anacapri 15/3/13' (English-style dating) gives some indication of his activities. One page contains a calendar, from mid-February to early June, with various places from Florence to Sorrento named at approximately weekly intervals. Elsewhere in the notebook, this is extended to mid-August (the end of his Italian stay) at Vicenza, and some cryptic entries connect a given place with art or literature ('June 12. Theocritus on Capri'). Several pieces date from these months, and show a talent for rhyming, traditional metres, and simple expression; others (which survived into *The Complete Poems*), such as 'Amalfi' and 'In the Via Sistina' are in 'free form' and 'cadences'. Aldington has an interesting comment on all this in the Introduction to his *Collected Poems 1915–1923*:

> I tried my hand at everything from blank verse and rhymed couplets to Spenserian stanzas, ballades, sirventes and villanelles, with fatal facility. At length I grew disgusted with

copying and (influenced by Greek choruses and, strangely enough, Henley) began to write what I called 'rhythms', i.e., unrhymed pieces with no formal metrical scheme where the rhythm was created by a kind of inner chant. Was this merely the result of a surfeit of formal metre? Possibly, though I still think it was a legitimate development *after* considerable practice with the traditional forms. Later, I was told I was writing 'free verse' or 'vers libre', which information I accepted with docility and some surprise. Still later, Mr. Pound (whose early encouragement I record with gratitude) informed me that I was an Imagist. . . .[28]

There is evidence of systematic submissions to editors, but the best poem remained uncollected and apparently unpublished, until discovered some 60 years later by Norman Gates in the files of *Poetry*: 'Pompeii (February 1913)':

> Today the wind is cold in Naples;
> The rattling streets are gusty;
> Beggars moan at every half-sunned corner;
> The Mergellina chokes with driving dust
> And the alleys reek . . . .[29]

In a few rapt pages of *Life for Life's Sake* this is remembered as a time of flowers, savoured, closely observed (there is even a brief passage parallel to 'Pompeii'); yet, from his point of view, he did not see far enough into things. 'On the squalid track to the station [at Paestum] a haggard beggar whined incessantly: '*Cieco, signori, cieco*'—blind, gentlemen, blind—and so we were, but didn't know it.' What Aldington meant by this is summed up by a remembered image: 'Heavy serious Germans bearing rucksacks crunched in their huge hob-nailed boots over the pavement of the Piazza and the ancient floor mosaics of St. Mark's'.[30] Within 18 months of this Italian tour, he and his country would be at war with these Germans, but for the blissful moment it was '*cieco, cieco*'.

In the spring ('The spring of 1913, the happiest of my life') Aldington joined Pound and Yeats at Sirmione, then did some sight-seeing with Pound in Venice. H.D. was there and, for a time, her parents. H.D. and Aldington had several things in common. At this stage both were relative beginners as poets, both were interested in Hellenism, in reading and translating Greek texts. In 'Asphodel' H.D. has recorded appreciation of their work together in the British Museum reading-room. Aldington was at first the more knowledgeable in Greek language and culture, but he modestly acknowledged that she was the more Greek in spirit. From the beginning he greatly admired her poetry

H.D was tall and large-framed, but frail. She had the habit of stooping, in an attempt to minimise her height. Her facial bone-structure was strong, with a definite chin and jaw-line and what Aldington sometimes called her 'too high Flemish forehead'; her nose was perhaps too short for such a face, but her lips were full and sensitive, her expressive, deep-set eyes at once wild and vulnerable. Her brown hair, falling to her shoulders, was often worn in a headband. Aldington, too, was tall, but he was handsomely robust. In 'Asphodel' she has him describe himself as 'a bit florid at times. True British roast beef'. As a pair they must have looked exceptionally attractive.

H.D. had contrived to see something of him in Rome and then to have her family leave her alone with him on Capri. Before rejoining her parents in Venice, she and Aldington went to Naples, and two of her autobiographical notes are very informative. Part of the first reads:

> 1913. Early spring in Capri; mother goes to Sicily. I meet them in Venice, after trip up with R; we stayed longer than they expected. Ezra is there; general feeling of disapproval.

That this feeling concerns herself and Aldington is clear from the other note:

> Jan. 1913, we leave cold Naples . . . we leave for warmth, Amalfi drive, Sorrento, Capri, C.L.D. [her father] leaves, mother joins him in Sicily, I am alone, move from Paradiso to little room in top of house, in garden, R.A. [Aldington] and work on Greek and walks, R. loses watch, rocks, swallows, etc. Roses, figs, goat-cheese, pear-blossom, iris. Monte Solaro, daisies on walls, R.A. talks in half-frightened manner. Naples in little hotel room of Slonimsky's list, given R. in London. Rebellion, stay on in Florence, go Venice, cheap third class . . . .

It was what Pound called their 'unofficial honeymoon in Italy'.[31] One of H.D.'s biographers, Janice Robinson, offers the view that

H.D. was drawn to Aldington partly by the excitements of these shared times in Paris and Venice.[32] He, for his part, wrote:

> Like a gondola of green-scented fruits
> Drifting along the dark canals of Venice,
> You, O exquisite one,
> Have entered into my desolate city.[33]

While he was still in Italy in June 1913, two London feminists, Harriet Shaw Weaver and Dora Marsden, began fortnightly publication of the *New Freewoman*, with Rebecca West[34] as assistant or sub-editor. On his return to London in late summer, Aldington became an active participant in the paper almost at once. This came about after Pound had contrived to establish himself as literary editor. Soon Aldington joined Pound and others in a campaign to change the paper's name so that, from the first number in 1914, it became the *Egoist*.

Pound took over more of the venture for literary purposes than its feminist editors had originally intended. His manner of participation nonplussed West, until she became uncertain who was actually running the paper. She resigned in October and Marsden offered Aldington her job; as she wrote to Harriet Weaver:

Will you please get ready for a shock: though possibly rumour will have made it no shock but ancient history: *This* half of the directors has appointed Mr. Richard Aldington as sub-editor in place of Miss Rebecca West, departed. Mr. Pound was very keen about the appointment: he says it will do the paper a great deal of good in many ways—in particular because of his connections.[35]

Pound's ever-ready editorial advice chafed Aldington, and Marsden quickly noticed how the two men 'spit and scratch at each other'[36] but Weaver was impressed by his eager efforts to increase the paper's circulation. He also attempted to stretch its slender finances by using translations or reprints.[37] Characteristically, he worked hard, but this had its problematic side. Combined with Pound's interventions, it posed a threat to Marsden, who in any case found literary men difficult to work with. Matters were smoothed over, however, and the two men were more than ever vital to the paper under its new name.

Marsden was not alone in her distrust of the Pound-Aldington combination. In the spring of 1913 in Paris Pound had met two American poets, Skipwith Cannell and John Gould Fletcher. Soon afterwards Fletcher sought him out in London; but, distrustful by nature, on 7 September Fletcher wrote warning Amy Lowell not to contribute to *Des Imagistes*, the anthology through which Pound proposed to publicise the Imagist movement. The real editor, Fletcher complains, is Aldington:

> The aim and object—not avowed, but secret—of the whole affair is to boom Aldington—to give him such a send-off in the United States that he and Pound will divide the country between them.
> If Aldington were really any good as a poet, I would not care. But I hate to see a rigged-up game being foisted on the public to boom a silly cub who deserves nothing but a licking.[38]

Fletcher describes H.D. as 'another arriviste' and claims that Aldington is in the business of gathering 'names' to puff his own work, but will take care to choose the weakest poems offered by Fletcher, Lowell and others, so that his own would shine by comparison. According to Aldington, he and H.D. were glad to welcome Fletcher into the Imagist group, though they at first objected to Lowell, discerning in her one published book, *A Dome of Many-Coloured Glass* (1912), 'the fluid, fruity, facile stuff we most wanted to avoid'.[39] The determined and energetic Lowell, after reading about Imagism in *Poetry*, secured an introduction to Pound from Harriet Monroe and headed for London, where Aldington and H.D. met her, liked her, and changed their minds about her participation in the group.

One name Aldington certainly had gathered was Yeats's, though there is no evidence that he exploited it or ever pursued a closer relationship. Since an evening at Woburn Buildings in March 1912 when he had translated the 'stentorian Milanese' of the Futurist Marinetti, he had got on familiar terms with Yeats. This September he turned up at the Holborn apartment to attend one of the Irish poet's soirées, only to find him alone. The two spent a couple of hours talking by the fireside, Yeats reminiscing about his early life in Ireland and London. Impressed by the older poet's unaffectedness, Aldington cherished hearing him read 'September 1913', which be believed Yeats had 'finished that morning'.[40]

Aldington's relationship with H.D., meantime, had flourished and in October 1913 the two were (as Pound put it in a letter to his mother) 'decently married'[41], with Pound and the Doolittle parents as witnesses. As recently as 1912 H.D. had still been disentangling herself from years of emotional involvement with Pound, whom at one stage she had expected, and intended, to marry. Through Aldington's reticence on closely personal matters, in *Life for Life's Sake* nothing is made of his wedding. In H.D.'s so-far unpublished typescript, 'Paint it Today', Pound and Aldington are Raymond and Basil respectively. H.D. wrote: 'After the Raymond fiasco, I couldn't be engaged. I won't be engaged. But I'm going to marry Basil. No, no, no. Just marry him. No one is to come. *No* one'.[42]

H.D. herself, and her biographers,[43] have provided accounts of her closeness to Pound in the years before her marriage. One source, the novel *HERmione*,[44] explores in detail the intensity of the Pound–H.D. relationship and the rivalry for H.D.'s affections between Pound and her Philadelphia girl friend, Frances Gregg. At one moment in *HERmione*, Pound (George Lowndes) calls H.D. (Hermione Girl) 'Narcissa'. Hermione's attitude to George, in contrast, is ambivalent. He has a peculiar power, but he is also 'pig-like'. Yet several fictional recountings confirm H.D.'s shock at discovering the seriousness of Pound's intentions towards his future wife, Dorothy Shakespear.[45] Decisive as they proved to be, it was not the first time Pound had, in effect, deserted her, nor the first time H.D. had found an alternative. As she relates in *End to Torment*:

> Frances Gregg had filled the gap in my Philadelphia life after Ezra was gone, after our 'engagement' was broken. Maybe the loss of Ezra left a vacuum; anyway, Frances filled it like a blue flame. I made my first trip to Europe with her and her mother, summer 1911. Frances wrote, about a year after her return to America, that she was getting married . . . . She said that one of the objects of her marriage to this English University Extension lecturer—or in fact the chief object—was a return to Europe so that she could join me.[46]

According to her unpublished 'Autobiographical Notes' at Yale, H.D. was prevented from following Frances Gregg and her husband, Louis Wilkinson, to Brussels. Pound intervened: 'Says F. has a chance to be happy, but if I go it will complicate things'.[47] Later, when Aldington learned of this relationship with Frances he was sympathetic, being broad-minded about such matters, though in 'Paint it Today' Frances is reported as voicing her hatred for him, declaring, 'I think him under the surface, unclean'.

Though it could not be expected that a relationship as extended and complex as H.D.'s with Pound would simply and suddenly disappear, it is not a necessary inference that Aldington was for her a refuge, second-best, or a 'rebound'. If he was in love with her, so she in some fashion reciprocated. If we choose, as others have done, to accept H.D.'s fiction as evidence, in *Bid Me to Live*[48] she writes of the counterparts of herself and Aldington:

> They had lived then. They had lived that year in Italy, before the war, almost a year of married life in England after. Two years. One married year in England and the time together before that, in Paris, in Rome. In Capri, Verona, Venice.
>
> Words that she did not speak held old cities together; on this fine strand, this silver cord, Venice was a bright glass-bead . . . .

Elsewhere in *Bid Me to Live* hindsight, rather than feeling, holds sway:

> Mrs. Rafe Ashton. That is my name. It was a blithe arrangement. They might have made a signal success of their experiment. They made a signal success of it, but in the tradition not so much of Robert Browning and Elizabeth Barrett as of Punch and Judy. They browsed over their books; they had friends in common. They crawled under the *Mercure de France*, barricaded themselves with yellow-backed French novels . . . .

Admittedly, this makes it sound like a marriage of convenience for both of them and, if we are to take *End to Torment* as proof, H.D. continued then and for long thereafter to have a strong emotional bond to Pound. But a passage in Aldington's *Death of a Hero* may cast his relationship with H.D. in somewhat different light, though he wrote it ten years after they had separated, when his passion for another woman was at its height. He shows the realisation of love between George Winterbourne and Elizabeth (who is more H.D. than not) as genuine on both sides. Walking the evening street, George is thinking of Elizabeth and of a moment of magnetism he has just experienced between them. He begins to sing 'Bid Me to Live' and later cannot sleep, 'for very love of living' and the thought of sharing life with Elizabeth. A romantic, even sentimental, moment, but it is significant that H.D. should pick on Herrick's poem to focus her own novel:

> Bid me to live, and I will live
> Thy Protestant to be
> Or bid me love, and I will give
> A loving heart to thee . . .

Janice Robinson's account of H.D.'s life promotes the somewhat melodramatic notion of Aldington's 'fighting for her', especially with Pound. If correct, this is curiously at odds with the fact that it was the Pound of 1912–13 for whom he often afterwards expressed affection and admiration. Pound has been shown in a bad light in more than one account of these circumstances and those who suggest that H.D.'s attachment to him outweighed her feeling for Aldington, even at the time of their marriage, seem to imply that she, too, should be seen in such a light.

In 1913 into 1914 H.D. and Aldington felt genuine emotional commitment to each other. Her belief in the marriage, and the security and pleasure she drew from it, lasted strongly until they were living in Hampstead in 1915. Aldington's response to her was not sceptical, as William Carlos Williams' was, when she ran, danced and soaked in the New Jersey rain, invoking: 'Come, beautiful rain! Beautiful rain, welcome!'[49] Pound it seems was jealous of Aldington and attacked him as 'The Faun' (H.D. has Frances Gregg also refer to him as a faun) in a poem full of private allusion, where Pound sounds like a limp-handed comedian:

> 'Ha, sir, I have seen you sniffing and snoozling
>   about my flowers.
> And what, pray, do you know about
>   horticulture you capriped?'

3   Egoists, 1914

At this time Aldington made patient efforts to cultivate the friendship of another Imagist, Frank Flint, and to push Flint's cause at the *New Freewoman*. Diffident and defensively class-conscious, Flint was not easy to befriend, but Aldington persisted, keeping review space for him so that he could earn much-needed shillings, making repeated efforts to take him to dine with Hueffer (who had not yet changed his name to Ford Madox Ford) at South Lodge, or to introduce him to John Galsworthy's sister, Mrs Souter. On Aldington's part there was a touch of youthful condescension towards Flint, but while he could be sardonic about him out of his hearing, in Flint's company he was customarily solicitous and painstaking. 'That Blunt affair is to come off on Sunday, 18th, he wrote to him on 8 January 1914. 'We are all to go down to Blunt's place for lunch. I am instructed to see that you turn up. *All* expenses of the committee are paid. I will send you time of trains, &c. later. Perhaps you will travel down with me.' As usual he was concerned about Flint's finances and was certainly aware that he had evaded not one but three invitations from Mrs Souter. Flint, this time, went along.

Secluded at his Sussex estate, Newbuildings, Wilfrid Scawen Blunt, long regarded as a political gadfly, had been banned from Egypt for his part in the attempted promotion of Egyptian nationalism, and jailed for speaking publicly on the subject of Irish Home Rule. For these reasons, perhaps, more than the sonnets on which his poetic reputation chiefly rested, Pound instigated a dinner in his honour. Accounts of it were published by Yeats in *The Times* (20 January), Aldington in the *Egoist* (2 February),[1] Pound in the March *Poetry*, and Flint, in the same month, in the new *Poetry and Drama*.

The delegation presented 'a carved reliquary of Pentelican marble, the work of the sculptor Gaudier Brzeska. It bears a recumbent female figure and an inscription' (Yeats). Pound read a poem in which he confused the Italian revolutionary Mazzini with an Egyptian, Ahmed Arabi. Blunt found Pound's act of homage incomprehensible and did not care for Gaudier's bas-relief, which he considered futuristic and in poor taste. After the poets departed he turned its face to the wall. Perhaps a more successful detail was the roast peacock, suggested by Lady Gregory, served in full plumage and sufficient for most of the poets to have two helpings, though it was eked out by a roast of beef.

A lover of the pleasures of the table and of proper ritual, Aldington enjoyed the occasion, a break in a routine of extremely hard work for the newly-christened *Egoist*, whose 15 January issue contained his adroit parodies of Pound:

> Come my songs,
> Let us observe this person
> Who munches chicken-bones like a Chinese consul
> Mandilibating a delicate succulent Pekinese spaniel[2]

Although in mid-year Aldington's name would be among those attached to the Vorticist Manifesto, he had already, this January, staked out a different, more personal position. He remarked in 'Anti-Hellenism: A Note on Some Modern Art' that:

> ... though I admit as I have admitted before the great value of, say, the sculpture of Mr Epstein and the painting of M. Picasso and the latest poems of Mr Pound ... I find there is still a strange allure about these ordinary uninteresting things which the Greeks loved—health and beauty and youth in the midst of friends .... I do not see why new fashions in artistic creeds should compel us to say that simple and happy and healthy works of art are entirely bad.[3]

From the start his attitude to the modern movement was never unquestioning, but throughout 1914 he contributed to the *Egoist* on subjects central to it: the French philosopher-historian-novelist Rémy de Gourmont (whose work interested him as early as mid-1912), free verse and Imagism.

Guided by Flint, apparently, all three 'founding' Imagists had quickly become interested in French poetry. Aldington's engagement soon broadened and deepened. He first wrote about Gourmont at length in reviewing the reissue of *Le Latin mystique du moyen age*,[4] the Frenchman's anthology of mediaeval Latin poetry. In three successive months Aldington made important contributions to the growing Anglo-French literary *rapprochement*.'Some Recent French Poems' in June 1914[5] showed his interest in Apollinaire and other French experimentalists. July numbers of the *Egoist* and *Poetry* carried his translation of Gourmont's

'Tradition and Other Things', itself a main source of Eliot's 'Tradition and the Individual Talent'.[6] (For Eliot as for Gourmont, tradition is indispensable, but is not a prison. The epigraphs to 'The Perfect Critic', which open Eliot's early book of essays *The Sacred Wood* are from Gourmont's *Letters to the Amazon*, and *The Problem of Style*. From Gourmont he acquired his ideas on 'impersonality'—see the essay 'Philip Massinger' in *The Sacred Wood*—the 'dissociation of sensibility' a term adopted from Gourmont's essay on Lafargue and the meaninglessness of 'absolute originality', and the view that the critic's central aim is to discover the laws behind his personal critical impressions.) In one other respect Gourmont is of special significance to Aldington, when he says: 'My tradition is not only French; it is European'. In August he contibuted a translation, in 'The New Poetry of France',[7] the theories of the *paroxyste* (that is, French futurist) poet Nicholas Beauduin. Introducing the essay, Aldington expressed understanding of its intellectual position, but he was not really in sympathy with theories of literary dynamism or creative violence.

Soon in correspondence, he discovered that Gourmont was in difficulties first through age and ill health and then the onset of the First World War, which curtailed his income. Aldington tried to arrange for translations and writing commissions through Harold Monro, Harriet Monroe and others. He never met Gourmont, a recluse who suffered from *lupus* which badly disfigured his face, but a bond developed between the two and Aldington was more than merely turning a phrase in recalling the French writer as *'mon vieux ami et maître'*.[8] What Aldington and Flint, Pound and Eliot admired in Gourmont's prose is its combination of frankness, fair-mindedness, clarity and graciousness. Such characteristics accorded with the literary aims of the Imagists. Pound once said that Gourmont was 'a symbol of so much that is finest in France'[9] a place which (in contrast to England) was 'the laboratory of ideas' where 'new modes of sanity can be discovered'. After the Frenchman's death early in 1915, Pound wrote: 'De Gourmont carried his lucidity to the point of genius'.[10]

While this French link was being explored much was happening with the Imagist movement. The February number of the American little magazine *Glebe* was Pound's anthology *Des Imagistes*, almost immediately issued as a book, first in New York by Boni and Liveright, then in London by the Poetry Bookshop. Reviews, with the surprising exception of the conservative *Morning Post*, were negative. 'One copy [of the anthology] was angrily returned from the Savoy Hotel by an American', Aldington recalled, 'and an old gentleman came into the shop and made a row'.[11] Pound's biographer, Charles Norman, says: 'Some purchasers charged down Devonshire Street with the book in their hands and demanded their money back'.[12]

None of this can have bothered Pound much, for his interests were shifting elsewhere. With Aldington the situation was rather different. Pound told Glenn Hughes in 1917 that Imagism had begun as a name 'invented to launch H.D. and Richard before either had enough stuff for a volume. Also to establish critical demarcation long since knocked to hell'.[13] That Aldington at least for a time took the 'critical demarcation' seriously may be judged by his *Egoist* review of *Des Imagistes* in June,[14] where he gives his version of the Imagist tenets, though he later several times denied ever having taken them seriously. Pound, meanwhile, had become more closely associated with Wyndham Lewis and the Rebel Arts Centre, which opened in Great Ormond Street in March. Some time about then Aldington visited the Centre with Pound and the two April 1914 numbers of the *Egoist* carried a full-page advertisement for *Blast*, a magazine to be edited by Lewis, promoting a new movement which 'in a backstage transaction whose details are lost to history', Pound named Vorticism.

As Timothy Materer shows in *Vortex: Pound, Eliot and Lewis*,[15] Vorticism in practice had begun at virtually the same moment as the 'official' Imagist movement. Finding common cause with Wyndham Lewis and a means of repudiating the 'Amygism' of Amy Lowell, 'hippopoetess' (these are Pound's terms), Pound in September 1914 declared that, 'Imagisme, in so far as it has been known at all, has been known chiefly as a stylistic movement, as a movement of criticism rather than of creation'.[16] On Pound's formulation, the image now became a VORTEX 'a radiant node or cluster' or 'the point of maximum energy'. The new term, Vorticism, had broader reference and was applied not only to poetry but to other arts, such as painting and sculpture.

Aldington had little to do with all this and at crucial times was out of London. Early in April 1914, he and H.D. took a holiday at Hindhead, Surrey. They were not involved in Pound's wedding, which took place at that time. In early May they were visiting the Aldington parents, at the Mermaid Inn, Rye, where Hueffer came to dinner and amazed Albert Edward with his fund of literary anecdotes. 'My father was swimming in bliss', Aldington recalled, 'although once or twice he looked a little puzzled. And then Ford began telling how he met Byron. I saw my father stiffen'.[17] Ford's embellishments were excused by Aldington as due to devotion to artistic form, though he may have felt indulgent because Ford about then declared him the only true Imagist.[18] Ford later said the same thing about himself, and Pound rated Aldington a Ford imitator.

The Futurist Marinetti was still prominent on the London scene and Lewis and cohorts felt impelled to rout him. On 25 May Aldington wrote asking Harold Monro; 'Are you going to Marinetti's lecture? I am preparing a costoom of violent green orange and blue for the occasion'. Invented by the Aldingtons and Pounds, this garish attire was intended to disrupt Marinetti's disquisition on Futurist clothing (a drably utilitarian single garment fastened by a zipper). Aldington wore his 'costoom' and Marinetti denounced, the 'young Passéists in the audience'.[19] Aldington and Pound co-signed a letter to the *Observer* in mid-June dissociating themselves from the 'Futurist Manifesto', which the newspaper had published the previous Sunday, and which vaunted such tactics as abolition of syntax, punctuation and metre, use of word-distortion (towards a poetry of sounds), and of the graphic or pictorial possibilities of typography. Consistent with this, Aldington was among the signatories of the 'Manifesto' of the 'Great London Vortex', in *Blast*, no. 1, on 20 June. As the tone of the Vorticist Manifesto was akin to that of typical Futurist pronouncements, the suggestion of consistency may be questioned. But Richard Cork points out that Wyndam Lewis, chief composer of the Manifesto, sought: 'an area of synthesis, essentially, that would temper Futurist melodramatics with Cubist sobriety, Italian movement with French monumentality. Despising Futurism for its unconditional love of machinery, and Cubism for avoiding the theme altogether in favour of the old studio repertoire of portraits and still-life, he aimed for a half-way house situated neatly between the two. . . .'[20] Aldington's signature appeared first among the 11 appended to the Manifesto, but when he wrote about the event in the *Egoist* on 15 July, he said, 'Mr Lewis has carefully and wittily compiled a series of manifestos, to which we have all gleefully applied our names'. Cork observes of Aldington: 'To him, *Blast* No. 1 was nothing more nor less than a lively firework which he heartily approved of, in a non-partisan way, as a bracing tonic for English culture'.

A short while after these events, Amy Lowell returned to London accompanied by automobile, chauffeur, and maid. She had met Pound through Harriet Monroe, and others in London through Pound. Now, dissatisfied with her one-poem appearance in *Des Imagistes*, she re-established her ménage at the Berkeley Hotel, opposite Green Park, determined to further the movement with herself in a leading role. She seems to have chosen her moment well as others, too, including Aldington were fed up with Pound's leadership. She now proposed a series of annual anthologies with each poet given equal space and herself overseeing publication in London and Boston and accounting to contributors for royalties.

Aldington soon saw her point of view, but, as is well-known, Pound refused to co-operate.[21] Squabbles between the two Americans over the next several weeks let eventually to what Lowell called a 'schism', but not before two extraordinary dinners which took place on the 15 and 17 of July at the Dieudonné Restaurant in Ryder Street. Lowell, Pound and Aldington were at both. The first, which occurred on the day the *Egoist* carried Aldington's notice of *Blast*, was to celebrate the reverberations of that publication. Gaudier, Pound's sculptor-friend and exemplary Vorticist, was broke and paid for his dinner with a '*Fawn* carving' which he placed on Pound's plate.[22]

But for the Imagists the second dinner was the important one. John Gould Fletcher assumed it was belatedly celebrating publication of *Des Imagistes*. Besides the Aldingtons, the Pounds, Lowell and her companion Ada Russell, the others present were Flint, Cournos, Gaudier, Fletcher, Allen Upward, Hueffer and Violet Hunt. Pound and Lowell sat at opposite ends of the main table, and most of the party seemed aware that she was throwing down a challenge.

Fletcher passed around a copy of *Des Imagistes*, first to Hueffer, who promptly made a speech casting doubt on the qualifications of both Pound and Lowell as Imagists, claiming that he himself had been one long before the movement. 'The only Imagists he saw present at the table were Aldington and H.D. whose imagism seemed to him entirely devoid of foreign admixture. He sat down amidst an embarrassed silence.'[23] Hueffer's was one of many speeches. Upward, prompted by others, championed Pound and mocked Lowell's large girth. Aldington and Gaudier had a set-to, in which Aldington attacked Gaudier's anti-Hellenism and Gaudier rebutted by objecting to Greek idealisation of the human body.

During this exchange, Pound slipped away and came back, flushed and dishevelled, a large round tin bathtub balanced on his head. This, he said, was an appropriate symbol for the new 'nagéiste' school inaugurated by Miss Lowell in her poem 'In a Garden', which concluded with the line: 'Night and the water, and you in your whiteness bathing'. The incident occasioned much hilarity, though participants differ as to its cause, Fletcher, for example, saying that the party laughed at Upward's extravagant championing of Pound. In any event, several of those present were won over to Lowell including Aldington and H.D., perhaps partly because of Pound's overbearing manner, but also because Lowell offered regular financial support.

At Kensington even the Aldington's home life was part of the literary scene. Lewis, for example, upset Aldington shortly after his marriage by coming to their flat and using his razor, notwithstanding that Lewis suffered from a venereal disease. Gaudier came one summer day, giving off 'horrid effluvia' ('Probably the dirtiest human being I have ever known')[24] so they put him on a couch at the far end of the room, only to have Hueffer (who had been to a fashionable luncheon) come in dressed in a top hat and morning clothes. Hueffer soon left and next day upbraided Aldington for allowing 'such a creature' in the same room with H.D. Gaudier, however, established friendships with both Hueffer and the Aldingtons and when he returned to France after the outbreak of war wrote to Richard from the front.

Hueffer lived nearby at this time, as did Pound's mother-in-law Olivia Shakespear. John Cournos had arrived in London that spring and took over Pound's rooms at 10 Church Walk, becoming a regular visitor of the Aldingtons at nearby Holland Place Chambers:

> Hilda was good-looking and charming [he recalled later], a little too tall, perhaps, for a woman according to American standards but not so exceptional in England. . . .
> Here were two poets, man and woman, who were happy together and worked together; at this time, at any rate, their relation seemed to me to be an ideal one.[25]

Soon there were other neighbours, more immediately disturbing. On the day before his marriage, H.D. encountered Pound outside her flat. '"What—what are you doing?" I asked. He said he was looking for a place where he could fence with Yeats. I was rather taken aback when they [Pound and Dorothy] actually moved in. It was so near'.[26] Later in the year H.D. told Lowell that Pound would burst into the Aldingtons' flat unannounced,[27] on the pretext of discussing his current writings. Much of the work in question, both shorter poems and early variations of the *Cantos*, upset H.D. in any case because it referred to private aspects of their relationship. Janice Robinson instances 'Tempora', a poem in which 'Dryad' (a name Pound had given H.D.) cries out to 'Tamuz' (that is, Adonis/Pound) for attention.[28] Pound, as has been said, may have wished to establish a troubador-lover relationship with H.D. at the time, and we may note that 'Tempora' was first published in March 1914 in Harold Monro's *Poetry and Drama*. That Pound's attentions were clearly unwelcome to both Aldington and H.D. need hardly surprise us. 'But,' H.D. remembers, 'we went soon after to Hampstead to a larger flat that a friend had found us'.[29] After that they saw far less of what she calls 'the Kensington group', meaning chiefly the Pounds and Ford.

Perhaps as part of the 'dynamism in the air' John Cournos recollected of that 'hectic summer', July 1914 seems to have been propitious for artists' dinner gatherings. Yet another took place on 30 July, in Lowell's suite at the Berkeley. Guest of honour, seated next to the hostess and that evening won over to be at least a fellow-traveller of the Imagists, was D. H. Lawrence. Meeting Lawrence for the first time, Aldington was impressed by his 'fiery blue eyes and the pleasing malice of his talk',[30] but, seated by the window as he was, Aldington's attention was repeatedly drawn to the Piccadilly traffic below. Lawrence, on entering and before he could be introduced, had said: 'I've just been talking to Eddie Marsh. He says we shall be in the war'. Although war had been rumoured for months, the others wished not to believe it, but in the warm golden light of that tranquil evening Aldington could clearly read a news-stand poster at the corner of the Ritz opposite: 'Germany and Russia at war, Official', and the newsboys were calling a Special Edition reporting the British Army's mobilisation.[31]

Aldington would become a friend of Lawrence's, but never an especially close one, or at least not for any length of time; though he figures significantly in the development of Lawrence's literary reputation. Shortly after this meeting, Aldington encountered, fleetingly, another notable literary personality of the time. Walking with Flint in Piccadilly he met Rupert Brooke clad in a shabby mackintosh, bearing the news that he had been commissioned and was about to join the Naval Division at Antwerp. As for himself, Aldington wrote to Harriet Monroe on 7 August: 'I went the other day to join the Honourable Artillery Company and thanks to my peculiar appearance was temporarily arrested as a spy!' He adds, perhaps intending a joke, 'I went with Hueffer to see Masterman[32] and Ezra and I have put ourselves at the disposal of the government'. This 'arrest' as a 'spy' was nothing more than his being apprehended for accidentally wandering into the Company armoury, but his effort to join the Artillery was prevented because he had undergone a hernia operation in his youth. His direct participation in the war was postponed.

Besides continuing to toil for the *Egoist*, he now worked for a time as 'secretary' to Hueffer (soon to rename himself Ford Madox Ford). With Alec Randall, he became Ford's helper with a volume of propaganda, *Between St, Denis and St. George*. This book, which was designed to overcome pro-German feeling in Britain, explored the significance of French civilisation in world affairs.[33] Aldington explained to Lowell that he was engaged in 'literary research' for the government. Several months after the outbreak of war he was seeing Ford daily. He told Lowell:

> My constantly being with him has dispelled the last of my illusions regarding him. I still think him a good critic—when not blinded by prejudice or *interest*—a good poet in a few of his poems—and a very bad novelist. But he is incurable [sic] vain and self-satisfied. He repeatedly tells me that he is 'the only poet there has been during the last three hundred years' and 'the greatest intellect in England'! And about a fortnight ago he said that he was after all the only real Imagiste! So I shan't be sorry when I am through with this job.[34]

Of course, this judgement was uttered before Ford's finest novels were written, though even after a quarter of a century Aldington appears to have valued him chiefly as a critic. Looking back, one war later, his judgement of Ford's character had not changed much, but was softened by tones of generosity. In retrospect, Ford's *English Review* became 'the best literary journal issued in England in this century'.[35] A complete run of the review was among his effects at Maison Salle in 1962.

Aldington's contributions to the *Egoist* in the first months of the war included, besides his poem 'Childhood', articles on free verse in England, on the Epicurean pages of *Scenes and Portraits* by the Australian writer Frederic Manning,[36] and on 'Parochialism in Art'.[37] His continued link with the French scene is manifest in an obituary essay on Charles Péguy in the mid-October number, where he stresses also the disastrous loss of human talent already being caused by the war.

Not surprisingly, Lowell entered somewhat into the *Egoist* picture. Pound had attempted to interest her in financing the magazine, but she came forward instead with her idea for a series of Imagist anthologies. Once Pound was at loggerheads with her he attempted to run an anti-Lowell article in the *Egoist*, but Aldington intercepted it, telling Harriet Weaver that if it were published he would resign. Clearly he had chosen sides in the contretemps, and now his friendship with Lowell developed by means of a steady trans-Atlantic correspondence, though he avoided complete alienation from Pound. He did, however, advise Lowell how to respond to Pound's diatribes, once giving her a vivid sketch of Pound's response to the prospect of one of her anthologies:

> I have told E. about the bk. I said 'We have practically fixed up the Anth[ology] for 3 years'. His face fell tremendously; he said 'Good', insincerely. I said: 'We are using the title *you* suggested "Some Im[agist] Poems"' [sic]. He nodded. I said: 'We have said in our preface how much indebted we are to you for the word "Im[agist]" & how we regret your absence from this vol. & how we hope to have you in the others'. He sniggered . . .[38]

Squabbling among the Imagists was not abated when Lowell's new book of poems, *Swordblades and Poppy-Seeds* appeared in the United States puffed by advertising which compared her favourably with Yeats, Pound and Ford. Aldington's review has its equivocations. He was able to compare *Swordblades and Poppy-Seeds* to advantage with the poems of 'a member of the school of affected revolutionaries', John Rodker. If he praises Rodker with loud damns, his response to Lowell ranges from 'a sorry performance' for one poem, to the implied spottiness of 'sometimes extremely good'.[39] She would, he thought, prefer such 'sincere' comments to 'log-rolling'.

Throughout this period Lowell continued as something of a financial lifeline for the English Imagists, for Rémy de Gourmont (on Aldington's advocacy) and even for the Aldingtons themselves, though in their case through seeking American jobs for Richard. Weaver also apparently looked on Lowell as a potential 'angel' for the *Egoist*. Pound had written in February asking her if she would like to edit the periodical, saying that the present 'editrix' was ready to quit.[40] Later in the year Aldington accepted some money on behalf of the magazine and Lowell was eager 'to buy her way into' it, but he felt that no English publication should have an American as its sole backer.[41] He responded similarly to her offer of £100 to begin an independent review, though he was (at least in theory) willing to cross the Atlantic and work in an editing capacity on any American publication with which she was associated.[42]

Aldington might well have liked to escape to the United States for there is no doubt that he was disturbed by the war. He wrote to Lowell on 21 September 1914:

> I am sick of 'atrocities'—what d'you suppose our men'll do if they get into Germany? How are we going to keep French and Belgians and Russians and Servians from rape, pillage and [sic] incendarism?

In his very long letter of 7 December 1914, which is otherwise concerned with American publication, in an aside beginning, 'For this war is killing us all, Amy', he makes an uncharacteristic defence of 'democracy against autocracy'. Fletcher, who says he deliberately sought him out at the time, recalled: 'he was no longer the gay, insouciant, jaunty, swaggering Aldington I had known'.[43] Cournos portrays him, as Arnold Masters in the *roman à clef Miranda Masters*, as fearful of the war to the point of neurosis. Aldington, as he told Lowell and others, was willing enough to join the army, but he was already writing on the margins of letters to America, 'I'm sick of war', and Fletcher found what he considered his anti-patriotism bewildering. Yet sometimes Aldington is full of admiration for the war effort. There is an unresolved inner disturbance which we shall encounter again. Perhaps, after all, the First World War was the origin of later private tensions, certainly it aggravated earlier ones. 'Under the stress of inner conflict', he wrote a quarter of a century later, with reference to the war, 'I lost the serenity and harmony which form a large part of real success in life. I thought it was a plain duty to be in the army . . . . On the other hand, I thought war an insanity . . .'.[44] Perhaps because of this very uneasiness of his, H.D. was in the country in October, living in a cottage lent by Ford (quite possibly the one with the 'leaking thatch' and 'creaking latch' mentioned in Part X of Pound's 'Hugh Selwyn Mauberly'). Aldington joined her there at week-ends.

Lewis, busy decorating Ford's study at South Lodge, or painting the drawing-room bright red and converting it into a Vorticist salon,[45] invited the Aldingtons to visit him. Using his own work for Ford as excuse Aldington declined, adding:

> Apropos, if you are publishing a manifesto in the new number of Blast I would be glad if you would exclude my name—that is supposing you thought of including it. I was very happy to sign the first manifesto but I feel that my continuing to associate myself definitely with Blast would be the merest hypocrisy on my part. I appreciate your work immensely, but my conceptions of art are so old-fogeyish that it would be perfectly ridiculous for me to declare publicly as a Blastist or anything of the sort.[46]

That he had reservations about both leading 'Blastists' of his acquaintance, Lewis and Pound, is undoubted. He confided in Amy Lowell:

> The more I think of it, the more I regret having allowed Wyndham Lewis to publish my name in the list [of signatures to the first Blast Manifesto]. I met [Jacob] Epstein the other day and he told me that he had also determined to have nothing to do with Lewis. I said that I thought it had done me harm to print my name in Blast; he said he was sure it had harmed him; I said Lewis was a charlatan, and he said yes, but he was not even a decent charlatan, he was ungenerous. (You won't repeat this, will you?). I think they are all crazed, Lewis, Ezra, Ford: they all certainly have the signs of incipient madness![47]

As 1914 ended the Aldingtons clearly felt more allied to Lowell than to Pound. Not unnaturally, upset by the course of the war, Richard was conscious of the already large casualty lists. Perhaps partly for H.D.'s sake, he had briefly considered crossing to the United States with the idea of working on a literary review there, but he told Lowell, 'I cannot leave England as long as there is a possibility I am wanted in the firing-line' (7 December). While this sounds categorical, it has something of an air of self-dramatisation. Under the prevailing circumstances of international crisis, even Lowell's wealth could not guarantee him a secure American job.

4 Images, Lost and Found, 1915–16

Aldington's efforts to aid Gourmont now began to go awry. Prompted by him, Amy Lowell had arranged publication of a series of the Frenchman's articles in the *New Republic*, but the magazine refused to print two of them. Nor did the signed manuscript of Gourmont's *Nuit Au Luxembourg*, promised to Lowell in response to a gift of $200, arrive. She was good about the manuscript, but Herbert Croly, who had refused the articles for the *New Republic*, was treated to a furious letter from Aldington, who also informed Lowell that 'Any American paper should be satisfied to pay $six [dollars] a time for [Gourmont's] signature'. Later, rejoicing in his 'slanging' of Croly, Aldington declared (not altogether seriously) that he had 'a profound contempt for all things American!'[1] A young man's breezy tactlessness, but Croly had to be placated. Lowell, who had agreed more readily than Harriet Monroe to help Gourmont, now offered Croly apologies, characterising Aldington as 'only twenty-two, exceedingly prejudiced and as far as America is concerned exceedingly ignorant'.[2] Another Philadelphia friend of those times, the translator James Whitall, good-humouredly portrays him as revelling in bad imitations of the American accent. Gourmont's situation was salvaged when his articles were accepted by the *Boston Evening Transcript*.

Whitall's contrasting portraits of H.D. and Aldington in 1914–15 help to deepen our sense of each personality. To Whitall the 'tall, slender, strangely beautiful' H.D. was habitually absent in her own 'mental vision' of ancient Greece, though her sudden returns to the present were marked by 'effortless domination' of the conversation. In contrast:

> Richard may have been a voyager into other worlds, but he never gave evidence of it and always seemed to us to be treading with unmistakable firmness the ground upon which he actually stood. His energy of brain and body was like a fresh, strong wind which invigorated without whipping skirts about or blowing off hats; it was never anything but inspiring to me—I would have quickly wilted in the presence of blustering. For some reason he wore a

black cloak which indicated his temperament no better than a regalia of turquoise and ostrich feathers would have done; a close view and two minutes' conversation flatly contradicted any idea that, from a casual glimpse, one might have formed of a long-haired, languidly-moving Bohemian of trailing speech and tepid enthusiasms. Richard may, in those days, have considered it stupid to bother about regular hair-cutting, but he moved with a grace that was the reverse of languid and his speech was alive with the true accents of the young innovator, passionately opposed to all comfortable mediocrity. He hated publishers, successful authors, critics, Americans and Quakers, but he had friends among them all, consistency being a trait seldom possessed by a dangerously charming person.[3]

When Aldington sought help for the Belgian refugee poet Jean de Bosschère, he again turned to American sources and even became self-conscious about it, telling Harold Monro he was 'absolutely ashamed' of begging from Americans on behalf of indigent artists. But he remained willing to accept financing in aid of publication from that quarter, especially from Lowell. He spoke to her on 1 February of the need for 'a small quarterly to fill the bleeding gap caused by the war'. On this theme he was corresponding with George Wolfe Plank, an American wood-cut artist and friend of H.D.'s, who had produced the *Butterfly* in Philadelphia between 1907 and 1909. Plank and he considered collaborating in a new magazine, with international contributors, prominently including Lowell,[4] but the scheme came to nothing.

The *Egoist*, 1 April, carried Aldington's review of J. K. Huysmans' *A Rebours*, 'Decadence and Dynamism', where he puts forward the view, which was to be an important theme in his novels, that artists were better off under the 'careless corruption' of the *ancien régime* than within the 'growth of commercial democracy—that gigantic conspiracy for supplying manufacturers with slave labour under another name'. He links 'commercial democracy' with the 'socialising of life', but the negative image he had in mind was materialist America.

Almost simultaneously he had a squabble of sorts with another American, Harriet Monroe. Late in March she wrote protesting his *Poetry and Drama* review of her book *You and I*.[5] She resented his belittling of her old-fashioned technique and machine-age subjects, and challenged him to publish the one poem he had praised, 'The Hotel'.[6] She accused him of unthinkingly preferring 'Beauduin & Co', (that is, the French *Paroxystes* or Futurists). When, after deliberate delay, he replied in May he adopted the high tone used with Croly ('Had I written my criticism of you in a personal letter your reply would have been justified, but as it is I can only ignore it'); his letter is endorsed in her handwriting: 'No ans'. In contrast is his treatment of H.D. Writing of 'A Young American Poet' in the *Little Review* this March, he reveals a tenderer side of himself and finds a useful oxymoron for the quality of her work, 'a kind of accurate mystery', which is derived not from meditating on Futurist locomotives and such 'but little corners of gardens, a bit of a stream in some Pennsylvania meadow. . . . obscure sort of broodings with startling and very accurate renderings of detail'.[7] Perhaps naturally enough, he saw the value of her work long before others did.

Life in other respects, however, did not go well for the Aldingtons. On 21 May he wrote to Lowell:

. . . I have been rather distressed, because Hilda was delivered of a little girl still-born about 2 a.m. this morning. She (Hilda) was in a good nursing home and had an obstetrical specialist. I haven't seen the doctor, but the nurse said it was a beautiful child & they can't think why it didn't live. It was very strong, but wouldn't breathe.

Poor Hilda is very distressed, but is recovering physically.

H.D. had learned she was pregnant on the day war was declared. At the beginning of the pregnancy, which she was persuaded to continue by a woman doctor whom she respected (Julia Ashton in *Bid Me to Live* is told: 'Now Mrs. Ashton, you have such a nice body, you will always regret it if you do not have this child'[8]), H.D. spent many weeks away from Aldington, 'the author of her momentary psychic being', at Ford's country cottage. When she was with him in the good years of their marriage, she often found his physical presence overpowering, but otherwise experienced a kind of remoteness. When she 'lived with him, absent, so intensely. He would be almost nearer, once he had gone . . . .'[9] Yet she felt then and afterwards that theirs was a union. Two minds which 'had the urge . . . to dare to communicate', though for her dryad personality his 'true English roast-beef' after the still-birth would become 'over-physical sensuality' (her words). A few days after the desolating event he complained to Lowell about the English! They 'haven't the faintest idea how to heal a fine mind like Hilda's'.[10] Hilda, for her part, was inclined to hold him responsible for the loss of their daughter, which she later blamed on the 'shock and repercussions of war news broken to me in rather brutal fashion'.[11] The news was the sinking of the *Lusitania* on 7 May 1915, which Aldington greeted with odd elation, on the grounds that it might bring the Americans into the war. He was nonetheless upset that sheets from America for the first *Some Imagist Poets* were thought to have been lost in transit. On the evidence of *Bid Me to Live* (she offers no other), Janice Robinson claims that at the time of the still-birth Aldington was in a 'romantic involvement' with Brigit Patmore (Morgan le Fay in the novel). Begun in 1921 *Bid Me to Live* fermented and matured (the metaphor is H.D.'s) over a period of more than 30 years. Deliberately autobiographical, some of it is not so much factual as suggestive, in the following Stein-like vein:

> She had lost the child only a short time before. But she never thought of that. A door had shuttered it in, shuttering her in, something had died that was going to die. Or because something had died, something would die.[12]

As it is, this carries the possible implication that a consequence of the still-birth was the death of the marriage. Throughout, the novel tends to show the husband's obtuseness and the wife's sensitivity. In contrast, H.D.'s biographer Barbara Guest suggests H.D. did not want the child and felt guilty about it, but 'there is little likelihood that the sinking of the *Lusitania* caused this miscarriage'.[13] Peter Firchow, in a straightforwardly objective article, draws attention to a letter written by a close witness, John Cournos, on publication of the novel in 1960. '*Bid Me to Live* is, according to my knowledge of events, rather a white-washing operation (of [H. D. her] self I mean) at the expense of others, and of one person in particular . . . .'[14] Cournos was in frequent touch with H.D. in these war years (something approaching 60 of her letters to him are at the Houghton Library); her contact with him is characterised by a high degree of emotionalism. In fact, she had 'fetched' him and he was in love with her. As to Aldington's insensitivity, so often hinted at in her various fictional treatments of their relationship, she remarked to Cournos towards the end of the war: 'He [Aldington] has a soul, that is why he suffers!' In *Miranda Masters*, Cournos portrayed this 'soul' and portrayed in the eponymous character a version of H.D.

as someone much tougher and more self-serving, though made of finer clay.

Beyond the circumscribed context of the Aldingtons' marriage, Lawrence in *Kangaroo* has given a vivid sketch of the very time and place:

> 1915, autumn, Hampstead Heath, leaves burning in heaps, the blue air, London still almost pre-war London: but by a pond on the Spaniards Road, blue soldiers, wounded soldiers in their bright hospital blue and red, always there: and earth-coloured recruits with pale faces drilling near Parliament Hill. The pre-war world still lingering, and some vivid strangeness, glamour thrown in. At night all the great beams of the searchlights, in great straight bars, feeling across the London sky, feeling the clouds, feeling the body of the dark overhead. And then Zeppelin raids: the awful noise and the excitement.[15]

During one Zeppelin raid, shortly after losing the child, H.D. ran out of their Hampstead flat to peer at what she saw as the leviathan in the sky. Startled by anti-aircraft guns, mistakenly believing that bombs were falling, in her haste she stumbled down the iron fire escape in the dusk, deeply gashing her leg, sustaining what seemed to her to correspond to a psychic wound. Shortly after this, in mid-June, Aldington took her for a three-week stay at a cottage in Albury, Surrey. For the time being, at least on the surface, their relationship held together, though H.D. was to write later:

> Then 1915 and her death, or rather the death of her child. Three weeks in that ghastly nursing-home and then coming back to the same Rafe. Herself different. How could she blithely face what he called love . . . .[16]

Apparently the still-birth meant the 'prospect looming ahead' of continuing married life without sexual relationship, though 'Julia' is careful to record that this state of affairs was imposed by the nursing-home matron.

While the Aldingtons suffered this personal tragedy the activities of the Imagist group continued. Houghton Mifflin brought out *Some Imagist Poets* in mid-April under Lowell's scheme of equal representation for each poet, though Aldington did much of the editing, including restating the Imagist principles in a piece which Read declared 'the locus classicus' of Imagist doctrine:

1. To use the language of common speech, but to employ always the *exact* word, not the nearly-exact, nor the merely decorative word.
2. To create new rhythms—as the expression of new moods—and not to copy old rhythms, which merely echo old moods. We do not insist upon 'free verse' as the only method of writing poetry. We fight for it as a principle of liberty. We believe that the individuality of a poet may more often be expressed in free verse than in conventional forms. In poetry, a new cadence means a new idea.
3. To allow absolute freedom in the choice of subject. It is not good art to write badly about aeroplanes and automobiles; nor is it necessarily bad art to write well about the past. We believe passionately in the artistic value of modern life, but we wish to point out that there is nothing so uninspiring nor so old-fashioned as an aeroplane of the year 1911.
4. To present an image (hence the name 'Imagist'). We are not a school of painters, but we believe that poetry should render particulars exactly and not deal in vague generalities, however magnificent and sonorous. It is for this reason that we oppose the cosmic poet, who seems to us to shirk the real difficulties of his art.
5. To produce poetry that is hard and clear, never blurred or indefinite.
6. Finally, most of us believe that concentration is of the very essence of poetry.

In the preface Pound is thanked without being mentioned by name. At the time Aldington was also editing an Imagist number of the *Egoist* and actively sought poems from Pound (asking, too, about the possibility of obtaining work by William Carlos Williams). Pound did not reply. There is some force, therefore, in Kittredge's claim that while the leadership of the movement passed to Lowell, the 'directing force, although somewhat subterranean, was, however, Richard Aldington'.[17]

In the United States at least, the two publications got in each other's way. Aldington had chosen to round out the *Egoist* presentation with an 'objective' overview by Harold Monro.[18]

Some of Monro's points are useful in considering Aldington's own poetic methods. 'All these poets are primarily impressionists', Monro says. Elsewhere in the issue we find Aldington stating his own sense of Imagism: 'there is an escape from artificiality and sentimentality in poetry, and that is by rendering the moods, the emotions, the impressions of a single, sensitised personality confronted by the phenomena of modern life, and by expressing these moods accurately in concrete, precise, racy language'.[19] In an interesting parallel, the American Imagist William Carlos Williams later described his book, *The Tempers* (1913), as a 'mood book'.

Lowell had arranged for distribution of 150 copies of this *Egoist* through American bookstores, but on 19 May she wrote to Aldington that she, along with Fletcher and Houghton Mifflin's editor, Ferris Greenslet, now thought it a mistake. One reason was that Dora Marsden's work occupied the front quarter of the issue. Another was that Lowell felt Aldington had too docilely incorporated Monro's 'hostile criticism'. But the most compelling reason was the 'far-fetched indecency' of Lawrence's poem 'Eloi, Eloi, Lama Sabachthani'.[20] Lowell felt distribution of the magazine would damage sales of the anthology, already exposed to hard competition from Frost's *North of Boston* and Masters' *Spoon River Anthology*.

Meantime, the nominal 'founder' of the Imagist movement, Pound, took a drubbing from the 'Amygists'. Following Aldington's condescending description of him as 'the producer of occasional brilliancies', in the Mayday *Egoist* (where he also takes sideswipes at *Blast* and Futurism), Lowell and Fletcher, disguised as 'George Lane' reviewed their own anthology in the May *Little Review* and from this camouflaged position declared the book a success despite Pound's 'jejune maledictions', which had done so much to make the Imagist group ridiculous.[21]

Both Imagist publications generated a good deal of reaction. Conrad Aiken, for example, attacked the *Egoist* number in the 22 May *New Republic* though he was soon answered by William Stanley Braithwaite, the journalist-anthologist. An argument developed in print between Flint and Pound as to the movement's origins. Keeping track of reactions in general, Aldington gained the impression that opinion was slowly veering in favour of Imagism, especially in the United States where at first some heavyweight broadsides from commentators such as John Livingstone Lowes, William Ellery Leonard and Padraic Colum seemed potentially damaging. Colum chose Aldington specifically as a target in 'Egoism in Poetry' (*New Republic*, 20 November 1915). Comparing Aldington's 'Daisy' with Byron's 'When We Two Parted', he says that the ostensible subject, a childhood sweetheart who became a city whore, is merely a shell, an occasion for 'the writer's own moment'. Even though such comparisons are necessarily random, this is perceptive enough. The weakness of Aldington's early poems' 'impressionism' is too direct an exposure of self, too obvious an irony. Yet his work displays a management of line and cadence which should not be overlooked. As to egoism, Ford, too, lumping him in with Lowell and Fletcher, called them 'all too preoccupied with themselves to be really called Imagists',[22] though the complexity of the point at issue may be gauged by quoting Ford as saying elsewhere 'that all art must be the expression of an ego'.

An editorial writer in the *New Freewoman* in 1913 had declared Max Stirner's anarchist work *The Ego and His Own* 'the most powerful text that has ever emerged from a single human mind'[24] and the journal's prime concern was to promote Stirnerian egoism; but this kind of egoism is quite contrary to the self-involvement attacked by Colum. It is the reason why the *Egoist* got its name and it betokened a 'hardness' quite in keeping with Poundian Imagism. A month or so before Ford's remark was printed in the *Outlook* Aldington told Lowell his relationship with Ford had deteriorated because he had refused to drop the Imagists and become Ford's 'humble slave and disciple'.[25]

As part of his editorial work, Aldington was then also in charge of production of the Egoist Press's Poets Translation Series, separate pamphlets, actually offprints from the magazine, intended for reissue in book form. His versions of *The Poems of Anyte of Tegea* and *Latin Poems of the Renaissance* were numbers 1 and 4 of the first set. After the war he would contribute two more pamphlets to a second set of six, and all four were combined into his *Medallions in Clay* (1921). But more important from his point of view was year-end publication of his first book of original poems, *Images* (1910–15). By mid-July Lowell had persuaded Edmund R. Brown of the Four Seas Company in Boston to accept the book for publication and Aldington felt Harold Monro would be willing to print a Poetry Bookshop edition from the American sheets. In the event, Brown procrastinated, but by mid-November the English edition was near publication. 'I have been having a deuce of a time with my book', Aldington told Lowell. 'Monro wanted a coloured cover and I asked a "modern" artist to do it—with horrible results. It would ruin the book to use it; it will lose me a friend if I don't! Damn it!'[26] The friend, Nina Hamnett, had taken a pan-like sketch provided by Aldington and given it 'a pot belly, a tail like a horse & a flute up its nose ....', as he complained to Monro on 12 November, emphasising, *don't* print this drawing'.[27]

Images was published in London on 1 December, with a three-coloured line-drawing of trees by John Nash; 27 of the book's 30 poems are in *vers libre* (two others are prose poems, never republished; the third is 'After Two Years', a piece of pastiche mediaevalism which Herbert Read thought 'one of the most perfect lyrics in the English language' and which was set to music by Peter Warlock).[28] The book contains elements of straightforward realistic reportage, but 'Hellenism', so dear to Aldington and H.D. at that time, predominates, interwoven with Swinburnian music and the Pre-Raphaelite traces later noted by Thomas MacGreevy and others.[29] Today, the best-known poem in *Images* is 'Choricos', which certainly made its mark at the time of publication. Norman Gates suggests that 'Choricos' finds its form through line cadences (a Modernist characteristic), but these cadences are caught up in the Swinburnian metronome:

> And we turn from the music of old,
> And the hills that we loved and the meads,
> And we turn from the fiery day
> And the lips that were over-sweet ....[30]

In *A Poet's Life*, Harriet Monroe quotes a wartime letter, written from the trenches:

> A pretty heavy bombardment was going on above and most of us were not without fear. We jerked out an occasional sentence and smoked heavily, and altogether wished we might be some miles back; when some fellow from the west, quite simply—naturally, it seemed then—began Aldington's 'Choricos'. We listened; fell upon it eagerly; were thankful. As he came to the invocation to death he stood up full length, his head at the *abri*, and recited those splendid lines with an aristocracy of accent which gave them sympathy and understanding. I tell you, those lines are immortal; more than that they offered us immortality to share in.[31]

'Choricos' was one of the poems over which Pound remarked, 'Well, I don't think you need any help from me' and (according to Charles Norman) is the particular poem prompted by the chorus from Euripides' *Hippolytus*.[32] An invocation to Death, 'Choricos' is certainly a 'mood poem', and may fairly be said to present (as Pound has it in 'A Few Don'ts') 'an intellectual and emotional complex in an instant of time'.[33] Once a prize exhibit of Imagism, because it is a deftly handled evoking of a state of consciousness, it is a good example of the 'Image' as a non-discursive presentation of psychic experience. But is it a consciously studied piece of technique? One of Aldington's most concise statements of his literary position, the 'Introduction' to his *Complete Poems*, may be cited against it. There, almost as if in rebuttal of a famous Pound dictum, he asserts: 'I do not believe ... that poetry is a matter of technique'.[34] Instead, he believes it a matter of 'reverence' and 'mystery', with the poet as medium for something 'other' than himself.

'Choricos' perhaps remains Aldington's best-known poem. In the late 1940s, summing up the 35 years of his poetic career, he chose to place it first in his *Complete poems*. The opening lines will serve to show its character and quality:

> The ancient songs
> Pass deathward mournfully.
> Cold lips that sing no more, and withered wreaths,
> Regretful eyes, and drooping breasts and wings –
> Symbols of ancient songs,
> Mournfully passing
> Down to the great white surges
> Watched of none
> Save the frail sea-birds
> And the lithe pale girls,
> Daughters of Oceanus.

The most striking thing about the poem, and the reason for its particular effectiveness, is in fact its technique, its musicality, yet it is undoubtedly a mood poem. There is none of the hard particularity of observation for which Owen's war poems are so justly famous. Other war poems of Aldington's to a degree manifest that kind of particularity, but in 'Choricos' he created and sustained an elegiac mood, largely through cadence, but also through classical

Greek reference, stock epithets and images, and the flowing linking device of the conjunction. 'Choricos' is in keeping with early, idealist war poetry typified by Julian Grenfell's 'Into Battle'. Aldington's poem shares some of its trappings with Swinburne and some of its rhythms with the early Yeats. As a vehicle of elegiac expression it is highly successful. Aldington's Hellenic poems in general are not so much concrete specific occasions as notations of a generalised psychological condition, though perhaps Selwyn Kittredge hits it nicely when he says of 'To a Greek Marble' that it 'particularly, achieves a symphonic blending of fragile sense responses'. The free verse line is, throughout, deftly handled to this end:

> There bloom the fragile
> Blue-purple wind-flowers,
> There the wild fragrant narcissus
> Bends by the grey stones.[35]

There are exceptions to this quality of effect, as in the ending of 'Lesbia', with its sudden Catullan shock of realism:

> And through it all [he is speaking of the death of the gods]
> I see your pale Greek face;
> Tenderness
> Makes me as eager as a little child to love you,
> You morsel left half-cold on Caesar's plate.

But even the Italian poems, those gifts of the earnings from *Poetry*, are dominated by Hellenism, as 'In the Via Sistina':

> O daughter of Isis,
> Thou standest beside the wet highway
> Of this decayed Rome,
> A manifest harlot.
> Straight and slim art thou
> As a marble phallus:
> Thy face is the face of Isis
> – Carven
> As she is carven in basalt.
> And my heart stops with awe
> At the presence of gods,

> For there beside thee on the stall of images
> Is the head of Osiris
> Thy lord.

Another of the Italian group, 'Amalfi', offers no 'local colour' or description, but a generalised picture, chiefly of the sea, in almost sacramental tones ('O Thalassa'). In briefly considering the poem, Gates reminds us of some points of Aldington's in the correspondence columns of the *Egoist* on 1 April 1914, to the effect that the poet's task is 'to present the exact emotion, the exact vision, the exact *image*'. These and other remarks show that for him Imagism was fundamentally, though not completely, subjective. 'Amalfi' appears to bear this out:

> We will come down to you from the hills,
> From the scented lemon-groves,
> From the hot sun.
> We will come down,
> O Thalassa,
> And drift upon
> Your pale green waves
> Like petals.

The remaining mode in *Images* is shown by the realistic reportage and air of objective, even pseudo-scientific, recording in 'Cinema Exit' and the 'brutal directness' (the phrase is May Sinclair's) of 'In the Tube'. *Images* as a whole displays a gift for phrasing, a good ear, capacity for observing concrete details. It also reveals some emotional immaturity, shown in 'Cinema Exit' in the misanthropic reference to 'Millions of human vermin' and 'In the Tube', where the 'brasslike eyes' of the other passengers seem to say to the protagonist: 'What right have you to live?'. Another facet of this immaturity is the self-pity interlaced with factual observation in 'Childhood'. Still a very young man when this book was published, Aldington shows deft control of the free verse line, though some confusion at his own centre.

If the Aldingtons left Kensington for Hampstead partly to create distance from Pound, they were quickly to have other literary neighbours. In August Lawrence and Frieda moved to the Vale of Health nearby and Cournos records meeting Lawrence at the Aldingtons' flat, noting in him a sixth sense about other people, especially women. Here was to begin the relationship between Lawrence and H.D. which resulted in her portrayal of Rico in *Bid Me to Live*. Julia (H.D.—She is also Julia, in Lawrence's *Aaron's Rod*) was enraptured by the 'pale face and the archaic Greek beard and the fire blue eyes in the burnt out face'.[36] Rico 'was the only one who seemed remotely to understand what I felt when I was so ill' (from the still-birth). When Aldington pictured him for Lowell he was wearing 'a vast red beard and ... very cantankerous and anti-war. He thinks of coming to California, so you may see him en route'.[37] He also reports on *The Rainbow*, then widely attacked and soon suppressed by the magistrates on the grounds of its 'immorality'. Lawrence's 'California' as it turned out was Florida, where he hoped to found his Utopian Rananim, along with (as Aldington put it later with nice irony) 'such rough-and-ready pioneers as Aldous Huxley and Philip Heseltine'.[38] He might have added to the list a 'rougher and readier' member, H.D. herself. In the event, Lawrence went neither to California nor Florida, but to Cornwall, a circumstance which had indirect effects on Aldington's life.

At the beginning of 1916 he was still thinking of escaping to the United States, where he might edit an 'American Mercure' or even run an American equivalent to the Poetry Bookshop. These ideas are an important vein in his correspondence with Amy Lowell through 1915 and into 1916, but Fletcher recalled that Lowell cooled on the review proposal because she felt Aldington might be hard to handle, and she warmed to it again only in response to 'desperate appeals' from H.D.[39] Fletcher says Lowell 'practically begged' him to write to Aldington, stressing the financial risks and her recent losses on the operetta she had backed, which had played to empty houses in a blizzard.

But other business between Aldington and Lowell went ahead. She saw the Four Seas *Images* through the press, at one point dissuading an impatient Aldington from withdrawing it. He, for his part, was busy with the next Imagist anthology, of which he was again virtual editor. Still seeking a firm sense of the movement's *raison d'être*, on 18 January he wrote:

> We wanted to write hard, clear patterns of words, interpreting moods by 'images', i.e. by pictures, not similes. . . . I think we ought to keep the Anthology for those poems which do in all things express those principles . . . .

About this time he was considering moving to the country,

telling one correspondent that H.D. had been ordered to do so for her health's sake. Pound was suggesting to Harriet Weaver that Aldington's energies be concentrated on the Poets Translation Series, while he and Lewis occupy space in the *Egoist*.[40] 'It is understandable that Richard Aldington sometimes found his position uncomfortable', say the authors of *Dear Miss Weaver*. 'Although it was more than two years since he had taken over, he found Ezra Pound still regarded *The Egoist* as his own domain. Harriet was not sensitive on this score. She never lost sight of the fact that she owed Mr Pound a great deal . . . .'[41]

John Quinn, the American lawyer patron of Yeats, had recently promised Pound a subsidy 'in connection with *The Egoist*,[42] and now Pound's suggestions regarding editorial responsibility ignored the fact that Aldington had charge of the section of the paper he wished to control. At the end of March, when she had seen Pound's proposals, Marsden wrote to Weaver, 'it is a question of E.P. and his friends against R.A. and his friends'.[43] She felt Pound was the more entertaining of the two, but realised that his scheme would reduce her own powers (and even Miss Weaver's) to 'zero'. Yet when these implications of his proposals were put to him, Pound reacted quite strongly: 'I DON'T WANT ALDINGTON FIRED!', he wrote on 4 April. '. . . If he goes off to fight I don't see why his job shouldn't be kept open for him. . . . I thought I distinctly said there would be room for him in the new scheme.' That he continued to respect Aldington's work is suggested by his remark to Harriet Monroe, in March, that 'there were two decent things by R.A. in the *Poetry Journal* some time ago'.[44]

By this time the Aldingtons were at Martinhoe, Devon, from whence Richard assured Frank Flint, 'in spite of the cold and snow we are very happy'. In mid-March they moved to Woodland Cottage in the Exmoor valley, about a mile and a half from the sea, with two other cottages and a large inn as neighbours further along the valley. Through Cournos, they made new friends in the area, John Mills Whitham and Carl and Florence Fallas. Carl Fallas had travelled the world and later would write a novel about Japan, *The Wooden Pillow*. Whitham, strongly puritanical by nature, was a conscientious objector and, according to Cournos (who soon joined the group) both Fallas and Aldington were trying to make up their minds whether to adopt the same attitude.[45]

Cournos began working on a novel, *The Mask*,[46] which he read to the Aldingtons as it progressed. He had a room in their cottage; the Fallases lived half a mile away and Whitham in a village two miles further inland. The conditions encouraged Aldington to work intensively at writing poems. Flint visited at Easter and even considered moving his family down. The whole scene 'recaptured the good fellowship and gaiety which had vanished from London',[47] though H.D. became jealous of Aldington's interest in Florence Fallas,[48] noting in her unpublished journal: 'R goes much to the Fallas Cottage'. The group met three or four times a week for a meal or a long walk, and their effort to forget the war included laying in a stock of Neiersteiner and other German wines. Though Aldington's escapism went much further, and made H.D. suffer intensely:

> But I,
> how I hate you for this,
> how I despise and hate,
> was my beauty so slight a gift
> so soon, so soon forgot?[49]

'She had married him when he was another person, that was the catch, really.' Thus Julia thinks of Rafe Ashton in *Bid Me to Live*.[50] Without providing specific evidence, Barbara Guest says: 'Aldington went about successfully seducing Flo Fallas. H.D. knew of the affair, and others, which were conducted in London. . . . It was Flo's "commonness" and not her attractiveness that bothered her—she feared it would "sully" Aldington's poetry'. Another recent commentator, Fred D. Crawford, notes that: 'the two had both expressed their approval of freedom in relationships, even in marriage . . . but H.D. had difficulty being honest with herself and with Aldington when he sought sexual gratification outside the marriage. When she objected to Aldington's extra-marital entanglements, she tended to focus on peripheral issues rather than on what really bothered her. For example, she frequently confided to John Cournos . . . that her major objection to Aldington's affair with Flo Fallas was that it lowered H.D. to Flo's level'.[51]

Cournos, in *Miranda Masters*, indulging in a little over-writing, portrays Florence Fallas as Ruth, who 'walked with a slow, deliberate gait, strong with the flaunting pride of the female in the presence of the male. She was handsome and buxom, and her skin was pink with the smooth healthy flesh of fruit newly ripened'. In contrast, H.D. is portrayed, stripping for the nude swimming party of the scene, as an alabaster statue, 'a heap of white at her feet, like fallen petals before a white stalk'. Gombarov (Cournos's fictionalised version of himself) from the height of a rock observes the two women and their husbands, 'regarding the women as if in judgment. Each man looked at the other's wife, not his own'.[52]

A coolness, and even a silence, had developed between the Aldingtons and Lowell though Richard was concerned when Lowell's *Six French Poets* was attacked by Middleton Murry in *The Times*. Lowell felt the weakening of the bond, whereas Fletcher's link with Aldington seems to have strengthened. The American had changed his mind about the 'unlicked cub' of 1913; now Aldington is anatomised in the April *Poetry* as the 'precursor and most shining example' of an English 'return to that simplicity and restraint which are the highest qualities of art'.[53]

H.D. experienced similar praise for her version of 'Iphigeneia in Aulis' in the Poets Translation Series. Yeats admired it and on 4 May the *Times Literary Supplement* singled it out as best in the series, saying she possessed 'an interpretive genius which is both provocative and singularly illuminating'. Such bouquets reinforced her growing determination not to return to America even though Aldington was urging her to do so, and because of the war was himself (as she reported to Flint) 'in a rather melencoly [sic] way' waiting to be called up under the new Military Service Act (1916).

Albert Edward, who had a position with the Ministry of Munitions, made an effort to have Aldington inducted into the Officers Training Corps, but there were no vacancies, so he decided to wait until he was called up as a private in the North Devonshire Regiment. Meantime he added to his own volatile state by pondering the number of literary projects he must soon postpone or abandon, but also by inconveniently carrying on his affair with the tall blonde Florence Fallas, in late May and early June sending Flint copies of resulting love poems, plus a cool rationalisation, 'Don't pity H—one learns to appreciate . . . by comparison'. Kittredge remarks that this particular infidelity of Aldington's marked 'the beginning of the dissolution of his marriage,[54] but a year before, just after H.D. had suffered the still-birth, Brigit Patmore frequently was a guest at the Aldingtons' Hampstead apartment and, in Kittredge's words: 'A kind of casual but elusive intimacy developed between Aldington and Brigit, complicated by frequent insinuations on the part of Brigit that she was attracted to H.D.'[55]

5 War, 1916–18

On 24 June 1916 Aldington and Fallas set off for the 11th Devonshire Regiment base at Wareham, Dorsetshire. H.D. was left at Woodland Cottage with Cournos, but in a month moved to Corfe Castle, Dorset, within walking distance of Aldington's camp. From there she wrote to Cournos, who had moved to London, 'you seem to make me feel that there can be love and peace together'. At Woodland Cottage and later, she had flirted with Cournos and he for a time developed an emotional attachment to her ('very nearly fell in love' with her[1]) though according to his novel *Miranda Masters* he at first high-mindedly repulsed her and then, when he succumbed, was told in blunt terms to go and seek out a whore, which he duly did.

Aldington took badly to soldiering and H.D., asking Flint to send him frequent postcards, spoke of his 'foredoomed look'. Aldington told Lowell that as he rolled up his bedding after his first night in barracks he found himself reciting passages from Wilde's 'De Profundis'![2] Lawrence on the other hand wrote to Lowell: 'How Aldington will stand it I don't know. But I can tell that the glamour is getting hold of him: the "now we're all men together" business . . .'[3] Aldington had been in uniform two months. Obviously, from the beginning the experience gave him mixed feelings of elation and depression.

He laced his letters to H.D. or Flint with mockery of army life's inanities. His sardonic eye noted widespread incompetence, the training and facilities seemed everywhere hopelessly inadequate, the men in charge fools. In August he briefly expected to be drafted to Mesopotamia, but after training he and Fallas, who seems to have been unaware of Aldington's affair with his wife, were not sent with their battalion. Each was promoted to lance-corporal and held back for non-commissioned officer training, an outcome Aldington attributed ironically to an officer's noticing his 'remarkable intelligence' in being able to 'take down' and reassemble a rifle. Next he was moved to a base near Salisbury, Wiltshire, and then to Portland, Dorset, where he was utterly depressed. The whole physical and natural scene there weighed on him, from the viaduct-shaped barracks to the huge blocks of Portland stone hewn by long-dead convicts, and the offshore dark grey warships of the Home Fleet.

In contrast, the November 1916 *Little Review* published the first group of Aldington's prose poems which were to comprise *The Love of Myrrhine* and *Konallis* (1917; 1926). An abortive plan by H.D. to sail for America suggests a shift in their relations. The day after she should have sailed, 12 November, he wrote to Flint that while the feeling that he wished her to go had upset her, this particular plan had been her own. Indeed, at one point she had wanted Cournos to go with her. Despite the fact that she wrote a great deal of poetry at Corfe Castle and that her imaginative life prompted her to remain there quietly, she did not stay long. She departed, not for the United States but for London, in effect following Cournos there, thus according to Barbara Guest showing 'her dependency on yet another person to lend her stability'.[4] Later in November, Aldington explained enigmatically to Lowell that H.D. had not crossed to the United States because she 'found so many friends in London and was having such a good time that she decided to stay there until after Christmas'. She had established lodgings at 44 Mecklenburgh Square, which Cyrena Pondrom aptly describes as 'a way-station in the disrupted lives of the entire group of literary figures who had previously gathered in the South of England'.[5]

Aldington was in suspense waiting to be drafted and by early December it had become clear that he was bound for France. A few days before Christmas he and Fallas were among a huge mass of reinforcements. For three weeks they were crowded with 20 others in an eight-man tent, their time spent floundering about in full marching order, desultorily practising with Mills bombs, testing their gas masks, and doing other army routines. Rations had not been supplied for the great increase in numbers, and the temperature soon fell below freezing-point. They were frequently hungry, but presumably the human crush helped alleviate the effects of the harsh weather. As 1917 began Aldington was a non-commissioned officer in the Sixth Leicestershire Regiment, with the British Expeditionary Force on the Western Front.

Meantime his literary work was being taken by such places as the *Dial* and *Seven Arts*, although by mid-year both the Aldingtons' official connection with the *Egoist* had ceased and the masthead carried instead the name of T. S. Eliot. H.D. had sent Aldington's Konallis poems to the Reverend Charles Bubb of Cleveland, Ohio, who ran the small specialist Clerk's Press, and who now planned a fine edition of the prose poems; 'but', Aldington adjured Flint on 13 January, 'see above all things that E.P. doesn't get hold of one. It's an edition I want to keep for my *friends*'. He also asked Flint to see that H.D. was entertained, and even 'if you can devise any sort of "affaire" pour passer le temps, so much the better'. This curious request of a friend, seems to assume that Flint himself was not likely to oblige.

The April *Egoist* carried Aldington's 'Notes from France' where he remarks with light irony, 'I have not done any poems. I am having too good a time', but the best he could devise as a break from the 'coarse and inferior' fare of British Army cooks was a trip to Calais with Fallas. When he went up the line it was to a battalion of pioneers, something between Infantry and unskilled engineers. Days were spent trench-digging, running out wire or road-building, all business Aldington found tiresome, so he was pleased when he was made a runner. His share of 'hairsbreadth 'scapes' are recounted in *Life for Life's Sake* and, more immediately in *Images of War* (1919), then *Death of a Hero* and *Roads to Glory* (1930). The poems record his horror and the desire to protect his artist's sensibility:

> ... every man
> Nerve-tortured, racked to exhaustion,
> Slept, muttering and twitching,
> While the shells crashed overhead.[6]

Or, as in 'On the March':

> I will throw away rifle and leather belt,
> Straps, khaki and heavy nailed boots,
> And run naked across the dewy grass
> Among the firm red berries!
> I will be free
> And sing of beauty and the women of Hellas,
> Of rent seas and the peace of olive gardens,
> Of these rough meadows,
> Of the keen welcome smell of London mud!
> I will be free. . . .
> Party—HALT![7]

In *Life for Life's Sake* he summarises tersely:

It was by chance that I was given just one night off in a period of two months; and that night happened to be one when a shell dropped on a group of our officers and runners, killing or wounding all except Carl [Fallas] and his officer. It was by chance that I lowered my head just as a shell burst beside me in a mine crater, so that instead of hitting my face a splinter merely crashed my tin hat. It was by chance that I shifted my foot a fraction of a second before a bullet neatly took the toe from my boot instead of smashing my ankle. It was by chance that, standing in a trench, I turned my head to speak to the man behind me exactly at the moment a large chunk of shell whizzed so close to my cheek that I felt its harsh and horrid breath. It was by chance that in the last attack of the war my field glasses shifted round over my stomach—when I went to use them I found they had been smashed and bent.[8]

Early in March he told Cournos that his application for a commission was 'going through channels' and he expected shortly to return to England for training. His postscript tells of an interview with a senior field officer: 'The general was fearfully decent. I told him I was a minor poet and he said: "Magnificent, Magnificent, just what we want!"'[9] He asked Cournos to break the news of his possible return tactfully to H.D., of whom Lawrence wrote to Lowell at this time: 'Hilda Aldington is very sad and suppressed, everything is wrong. I *wish* things would get better'.[10] Lawrence says nothing about the cause, but at least part of the explanation is a rebuff from himself.[11]

Aldington was in France until April 1917, but then returned briefly to England. It may have been about this time that he first met Herbert Read, who recalled:

I well remember that first meeting. We had lunch together and strolled up Charing Cross Road, looking at the bookshops and talking about our literary enthusiasms. Aldington looked very handsome in his uniform and I was immediately captivated by the brightness and candour of his features—a boyishness, one might call it, which he retained perhaps all his life, certainly until he left Europe. He was one of the most stimulating friends I have ever had—easy in conversation and very frank, full of strange oaths (mostly in French) his mind darting about rapidly from one aspect of a subject to another. I was to spend many happy hours with him. . . . It was a friendship not free from divergences of opinion—even fundamental differences of outlook.[12]

The enforced military life did not stop Aldington's writing altogether and he contributed reviews to the *Egoist* and the *Dial*. In April results of the *Little Review* 'Vers Libre Contest' were announced, with H.D. and Maxwell Bodenheim joint winners. In her inimitable way, the editor Margaret Anderson noted: 'But it may be interesting to print some of the others. For instance, not a single judge mentioned the following—Aldington's Stream'. One judge, Eunice Tietjens, had admired two other submissions on condition that 'Richard Aldington wrote them'. As he had not, her admiration was withheld on the grounds that they were imitations.[13]

Vers libre was a current subject of controversy in British periodicals, though the argument had started in America between Amy Lowell and John Livingstone Lowes. Eliot quickly joined issue on the matter and in 'The Borderline of Prose' attacked *vers libre*. Among other things, he said: 'Mr Aldington's prose-poems (and I allow them great merit) fail exactly because they seek to evade the technical distinction between two forms' [prose and verse].[14] Debate continued up to a special 'Prose & Verse' issue of Harold Monro's monthly miscellany, *The Chapbook*, in April 1921. Aldington and Eliot met first in 1917 because of management changes at the *Egoist*, brought about partly because Aldington could not then continue with the Egoist Press and H.D. had no interest in journalism. Both Aldingtons were willing to step down in favour of Eliot, though H.D. assumed Aldington would return to his job after the war. He met Eliot to help the latter's takeover at Oakley Place; but their long and complex relations properly began after the war, though Eliot meantime referred again to Aldington's work as a *vers librist* in 'Ezra Pound: His Metric and Poetry' (1917).[15]

On 1 June, when the Clerk's Press published its limited edition (40 copies) of *The Love of Myrrhine and Konallis*, Aldington was in England in a Reserve Battalion awaiting transfer to an Officer Cadet Corps. Besides pressing his 'hearty over-sexed' attentions on H.D. (if we are to go by *Bid Me to Live*, that is) he had an interlude in which to write. On 3 August he sent Bubb the manuscript of *Rêverie: A Little Book of Poems for H.D..*, written in the trenches, probably in the small pocket-book, 'which I carried through gas attacks, two battles, and many months of trench warfare', later presented to Lowell.[16] Bubb had already printed Aldington's translation of *The Garland of Months* by Folgore Da San Gemignano, and was now asked to use the same typeface for *Rêverie*. By the time the Clerk's Press published *Reverie* in August, Aldington had left London for officers' training camp. Seven of the small book's nine poems survived into *The Complete Poems* and, along the way, appeared in either *Images of War* (London, 1919) or *War and Love* (Boston, 1919) or in both. In these and his other war poems one is struck by the combination of vivid reportage and pathos. '*Rêverie*', Alec Waugh wrote nearly half a century later, 'describes how a soldier in a quiet part of the line in France broods over his wife in England. Written in rhythmed verse, it is tender, wistful, nostalgic, uncomplaining. I still think he is one of the best of the English war poets'. Waugh adds that Aldington was at his finest writing of love.[17] He has in mind chiefly the title-poem:

> It is very hot in the chalk trench
> With its rusty iron pickets
> And shell-smashed crumbling traverses,
> Very hot and choking and full of evil smells,—

but the protagonist has located a little shed, and crawls away amid the clamour of the guns 'beating madly upon the still air', to lie there in reverie over his 'unfaltering love'. Poignant as this is, we should of course guard against total identification of protagonist with writer. Life in the trenches does, however, seem to have heightened Aldington's emotional sense of H.D. He wrote her many agonised letters declaring his continued love, but also, as time went on, the inner struggle he was undergoing, his misery in the trenches compounded by his chaotic feelings towards H.D. and another woman, newly come into their lives, Dorothy Yorke.

Just as *Rêverie* was published, H.D. moved to Lichfield to be near Aldington's camp. Expecting to be back in the front line by the end of 1917, to Flint and others he professed terror at the thought of enduring another barrage, like the ones so vividly described in *Roads to Glory* (1930), and in such stories as 'At All Costs':

> 4 a.m. With a terrific crash, which immediately blotted out the roar of the other bombardments, the German artillery on their own front came into action. Hanley half-recoiled. He had been in several big bombardments, and thought he had experienced the

utmost limit of artillery. But this was more tremendous, more hellish, more appalling than anything he had experienced. The trench of the outpost line was one continuous line of red, crashing trench mortars and shells. The communication trench was plastered with five-nines. Shells were falling all along their own line—he heard the sharp cry 'stretcher-bearer' very faintly from somewhere close at hand.

The confusion and horror of a great battle descended on him.[18]

Some paragraphs about George Winterbourne, protagonist of *Death of a Hero*, are to the point:

> Winterbourne walked away from the tent lines, and stood looking over the desolate winter landscape. Half a mile away the tent lines of another huge camp began. Army lorries lumbered along a flat, straight road in the distance. It was beginning to snow from a hard, grey sky. He wondered vaguely how you slept in the line when there was snow. His breath formed little clouds of vapour in the freezing air. He pulled his muffler closer round his neck, and stamped on the ground to warm his icy feet. He felt as if his faculties were slowly running down, as it his whole mental power were concentrated upon mere physical endurance, a dull keeping alive. . . .
>
> He experienced a rapid fall of spirits to a depth of depression he had never before experienced. Hitherto, mere young vitality had buoyed him up, the *élan* of his former life had carried him along through the days. In spite of his rages and his worryings and the complications and boredoms, he had really remained hopeful. He had wanted to go on living, because he had always unconsciously believed that life was good. Now something within him was just beginning to give way, now for the first time the last faint hues of the lovely iris of youth faded, and in horror he faced the grey realities. He was surprised and a little alarmed at his own listlessness and despair. He felt like a sheet of paper dropping in jerks and waverings through grey air into an abyss.[19]

This is memory. At the time, however, Aldington's feelings were much more complex, or at least more mixed, so that Barbara Guest is not entirely unfair when she says it is only necessary to compare *Death of a Hero* with Graves's *Goodbye to All That* 'to realise that Aldington's experiences are not so desperate or tragic as he would have us believe'.[20] At the beginning of 1917, for example, he wrote from 'somewhere in France' to Lowell:

> If I get 'pipped' you'll give an eye to H.D. won't you? She is my chief concern and if it were not for her I should enjoy this experience immensely.[21]

To be fair, it should be stressed that at this moment he had been in France for two weeks.

Of a moment when he was due to return to the front H.D. wrote in *Bid Me to Live*:

> He would be going back to France. To-morrow, to-day. They would brew tea (all this had happened before), they would find eggs in the shelf under the book-case where they kept their shoes. They would smoke, and while a winter-dawn stole over a sleeping city he would say those things that might (God knows) have better been left unsaid. If he had been the ordinary Englishman, he wouldn't have said them; but of course, if he had been the ordinary Englishman, she wouldn't have married him. She had married him when he was another person. That was the catch, really.[22]

On 30 August she wrote to Flint, 'A beautiful lady has my room'. (This was in the Mecklenburgh Square establishment, to which at H.D.'s invitation the Lawrences had also now come, from Cornwall.) At this point Dorothy Yorke and Cecil Gray enter more clearly into Aldington's story. Gray, a 22-year-old Scottish musicologist and composer, had been the Lawrences' friend and neighbour in Cornwall. Like them, he figures in *Bid Me to Live*. He is Vane or Vanio. Rafe asks Julia, in a crucial scene: 'Do you love Vane?' 'I don't think so.' 'Does he love you?' 'I don't think so. We're just two people who belong together like Bella and you'.[23]

Dorothy Yorke, the 'beautiful lady', known as Arabella or Bella in *Bid Me to Live*, was a friend of Cournos, who had obtained the room for her. When the Lawrences arrived, Cournos left with Hugh Walpole and others on the Anglo-Russian Commission to Petrograd, and Arabella moved upstairs to his room. Like H.D. she was a Pennsylvania girl, but closer in age to Aldington. Cournos, who had been violently in love with her, remembered her at 19 as 'tall, slender, graceful; with black copper-tinged hair; with high, and as it were, carven cheekbones'.[24] Of high-coloured complexion, hers was a restrained yet exotic beauty. Qualities like these are in *Death of a Hero* attributed to Elizabeth who, in other respects, is a counterpart to H.D. In another *roman-à-clef* involving the group, Lawrence's *Aaron's Rod*, Arabella, as Josephine Ford, is portrayed as possessing 'dangerous impassivity' or quietness, 'a cameo-like girl with neat black hair done tight and bright in the French mode. She had strangely drawn eyebrows, and her colour was brilliant'.[25] This young woman would quickly figure as importantly as H.D. in Aldington's emotional life.

By now, clearly, H.D. remained emotionally attached to him, but resented his sexual demands. Despite such personal complications, he continued to value her work. On 20 November, writing to Amy Lowell for the first time in nearly a year, he said, 'apart from any personal feelings, H.D.'s poetry is the only modern English poetry that I care for'. Lawrence told Lowell that both Aldingtons were in London. 'Richard has another fortnight or so', he wrote, 'and then heaven knows where he will be sent: let us hope, somewhere in England. They seem pretty happy, under the circumstances. We have had some good hours with them in Mecklenburgh Square—really jolly, notwithstanding everything.'[26] For once perhaps Lawrence was blind to the complexity of interpersonal relationships around him.

Aldington's commission was listed in the December *Army Gazette* and when he commiserated with Flint who had just been called up, he was a Second-Lieutenant with the Third Royal Sussex Regiment based at Newhaven, Sussex. 'Dear boy', he wrote, 'you are sensitive and quickly wounded, proud and a poet—do you need any further composition for misery?' In the line, he said, Flint would feel the bitterness of being separated from those he loved, and sense that his friends had forgotten him. Grasp life, he advised, with extraordinary zest. For himself, he seems to have spent a December leave reading to H.D.—Shelley, Swinburne, Euripides—but with her agreement he spent a great deal of time at Mecklenburgh Square in Arabella's attic. H.D., after all, later wrote: 'But I can not serve God and Mammon, not serve poet and hearty over-sexed ('we have them on the run') young officer on leave'.[27]

The precise comings and goings at 44 Mecklenburgh Square, and who lodged with whom and when, cannot now be made clear, but the Lawrences were there in November and December and when H.D. was in London she lived in the upstairs flat (really one large room, or 'bed-sitter') with Arabella. Since Corfe Castle, a bond had existed between H.D. and Lawrence, as she later re-imagined it:

> Julia existed, parasitically on Rafe and Rico lived on Elsa. But once alive, fed as it were from these firm-fleshed bodies, they were both free, equal too, in intensity, matched, mated.[28]

In the tangle of relationships, Frieda Lawrence was momentarily taken up with Gray, Aldington with Arabella, and H.D. was 'fetched' by Lawrence. Much or little may be made of this last link, but, real or fantasy, it affected the Aldingtons' marriage. Perhaps the distance Lawrence kept affirmed the 'spirituality' of the link in contrast with the 'firm-fleshed' grossness of Aldington's infidelities.

In the thick of it all H.D. was writing, copiously, and Aldington, too, was able to write. H.D. apparently destroyed a good deal of what she produced and he admired her artist's relentlessness and her spiritual growth and originality, while at the same time his own work shows depression (a whole run of poems has titles like 'Doubt', 'Apathy', 'Defeat'). There is irony then in the fact that Harriet Monroe's review of *Rêverie* that spring recounts yet another incident in which a soldier in the line was moved by the invocation to 'Choricos'.[29]

When the review appeared, Aldington was once more in the trenches. 'I believe he was glad to go', Lawrence told Cecil Gray on 18 April.[30] 'It is harder to bear the pressure of the vacuum over here than the stress of congestion over there.' Lawrence should have been well aware of the instabilities of Aldington's life on the home front. John Cournos, on the other hand, was not, and Aldington was now forced to write and explain his involvement with Arabella—'we fell in love with each other, that is all'.[31] Cournos was bitterly hurt, because he felt that H.D. had connived at shifting Arabella's affections from him to Aldington, but had this been the simple truth Aldington's next year or so might have been less agonising. 'The truth is', he wrote to H.D. on 20 May, 'I love you and I desire—l'autre.' While in this instance he could with some justice claim to have been precipitated into the dilemma, it would not be the last time in his life he was to experience such a condition.

In reaction to this and to an apparent rebuff of her fantasies of cerebral empathy with Lawrence, H.D. soon departed with Gray for Pendeen, Cornwall. 'Do be happy with Cecil', Aldington wrote magnanimously, but adding the touch of melodrama: 'I shall get over this some day'. Combined with the sheer nastiness of trench life, this crisis undermined him so that, he claimed, he twice attempted to be killed in action. Yet he envied Carl Fallas, who had just suffered a 'blighty' (a war wound sufficiently serious to have one sent home from France, but not fatal or permanently disabling). It was at this time that H.D. wrote of Aldington to Cournos: 'O he is a queer, tortured soul, He has a soul, that is why he suffers'.[32] Torn as he was between her and Arabella, he continued to write H.D. passionate letters. Characteristically reticent, he kept news of the state of his marriage from friends, though he told Randall of his 'Gargantuan disgust' for the war, and confessed that he had nothing to live for. He felt isolated even in denouncing war in his poems and spoke accurately of 'the indignation, the pity, the anguish underneath' his own work.[33]

Aldington now felt that, out of solicitude for H.D., Brigit Patmore had dropped him. Brigit had been part of their relationship from the beginning. They had first met at her house. Their link with her was ambivalent, in the sense that she was sexually attracted to each of them. (Kittredge reports her as exclaiming, 'I think it would be lovely to have a woman-lover' and—to H.D./Julia—'Oh, darling, it's really women I love'.[34]) When H.D. had professed shock at Aldington's carnal attitude towards Arabella, Brigit in fact dismissed it as an instance of predictable male cynicism. In *Bid Me to Live* Brigit (as Morgan le Fay) is included as one of the responsive objects of Aldington's carnality. Yet early in August 1918, when news came that H.D. might be pregnant by Gray (despite their proposed platonic relationship) and that Gray's call-up was imminent, Aldington advised H.D. to seek help from Brigit, whom, oddly, he calls 'the only trustworthy woman friend you have'.[35] Though Arabella objected 'rather fiercely', he took a very British line regarding the child's parentage. 'I will accept the child as mine if you wish', he wrote to H.D. on 3 August. Gray, assigned to the Army Pay Corps, apparently was anxious to avoid responsibility for the pregnancy, and H.D. considered an abortion. Aldington begged her not to go through with it. Considering his state of nervous near-exhaustion and debility, this was generous indeed, especially as the complex of circumstances had given rise to so much personal and emotional confusion. At another point, he was more dubious about her having the child, as he felt it would confirm her relationship with Gray. News of H.D.'s pregnancy pushed

Aldington towards a resolution, kept for some time, to see neither H.D. nor Arabella again, though his offer held regarding the child.

Having spent much of an August leave in London, disconsolate, he must have been relieved this time to return to France. In September he was behind the lines, taking a signalling course, perhaps to assume duty as Battalian Signals Officer. Despite occasional sorties by German planes, he seems to have become happier or perhaps oscillated towards the gung-ho attitude H.D. scoffs at in her novel. On one occasion he informed Flint that, 'There is something great about the expeditionary force—Whitman would call it "abrupt, huge, hairy, testicular".' It was to Flint, too, that he wrote of his last assignment up the line, when he found an 'old' corpse, 'a dead boche' in a derelict house.[36] Several similar incidents are recorded in poems such as 'Trench Idyll', 'Soliloquy I' and 'Soliloquy II'. Interestingly, each is seen as an affront to an ideal of beauty:

> But—the way they wobble!—
> God! that makes one sick
> Dead men should be so still, austere,
> And beautiful,
> Not wobbling carrion roped upon a cart . . .
> Well, thank God for rum.[37]

In November the war ended and with it the weeks and months of fear and depression. Now to be faced was the 'sinister degradation' of English life which had taken place in the latter part of the war and which Aldington was later to find anatomised once and for all in the 'Nightmare' chapter of Lawrence's *Kangaroo*.

'I was in London in November', Lawrence wrote to Lowell, '—saw Richard, who was on leave. He is very fit, looking forward to peace and freedom. Hilda also is in town—not so very well. She is going to have another child, it appears. I hope she will be all right. Perhaps she can get more settled, for her nerves are very shaken: and perhaps the child will soothe her and steady her.'[38] In more mischievous mood, Lawrence wrote to Arabella's mother in mid-December: 'Poor Hilda. Feeling sorry for her, one almost melts. But I *don't* trust her—other people's lives, indeed!'[39] Evidently, their special relationship, in which she was one of the select band chosen for Rananim, and in which their blue flames might burn together, was at an end. 'Kick over your tiresome house of life' Rico had told Julia, that is, Lawrence had told H.D.) in *Bid Me to Live*. There is the famous paragraph in the novel where she seeks physical confirmation of the 'track between them, written in the air':

> She got up; as if at a certain signal, she moved toward him; she edged the small chair toward his chair. She sat at his elbow, a child waiting for instruction. Now was the moment to answer his amazing proposal of last night, his 'for all eternity'. She put out her hand, then had touched his sleeve. He shivered, he seemed to move back move away, like a hurt animal, there was something untamed, even the slight touch of her hand on his sleeve seemed to have annoyed him. Yet, last night, sitting there, with Elsa [Frieda Lawrence] sitting opposite, he had blazed at her; those words had cut blood and lava-trail on this air. Last night, with the coffee-cups beside them on the little table, he had said 'It is written in blood and fire for all eternity'. Yet only a touch on his arm made him shiver away, hurt, like a hurt jaguar.[40]

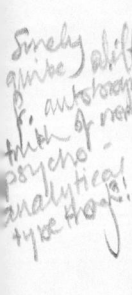

Louis Martz, in his Introduction to H.D.'s *Collected Poems 1912–1944* says that: '*Bid Me to Live* constitutes a special case, for it was written under advice from Freud himself that she should write history'.[41] This is to say that the book may be regarded as having somewhat more autobiographical authority than usual. But when Freud gave his advice in the 1930s, H.D. had already been writing fictional accounts of her marriage for perhaps 15 years. And it is not too much to claim that her versions of any events in her life have a tendency to be self-serving. Most opinions of the Lawrence-H.D. relationship, given that the letters quoted in *Bid Me to Live* were at some point destroyed, and given that a full explanation of the relationship can never be available, tend to conclude that it was in essence cerebral. By November 1918, in any event, Lawrence had placed the Aldingtons, in his mind, firmly together. Aldington's leave began the day after the armistice was signed. On the way home he had passed through Cambrai, which had been fired and looted by the retreating Germans. At Boulogne on 15 November, he observed the signs of privation in the pinched and yellow faces of French prisoners of war returning home. On this short leave the Aldingtons' marriage effectively came to an end, which compounds the ironies of Pound's remark to Joyce that Aldington represented the competition of the returning troops. The war, Pound thought, had done Aldington good. 'Must say the effect on Aldington is excellent', he observes nonchalantly. 'He went to the fields of glory full of doctrinaire bosh contracted from a returned English hun [Ford?], but he has come back purged, and with a surface of modesty.'[42] When Aldington arrived in London, H.D. had left.

6 Aftermaths, 1919–20

In the early weeks of 1919 Aldington, in Belgium, was teaching unwilling 'tommies' arithmetic and English grammar. H.D., suffering pneumonia, was being nursed by her new friend Bryher, in the country outside London. 'Bryher' was the pen-name, and later adopted name, of Winifred Ellerman, a novelist, daughter of a shipping magnate. She admired Imagist poetry and especially the writing of H.D., whose whereabouts and sexual identity she discovered through May Sinclair. On meeting H.D. in July 1918 she quickly asked her to go on a holiday to the Scilly Islands, and was soon in love with her. From this time onwards, H.D. was to discover in Bryher a curious mixture of hard-headed scepticism and weakness. In the first phase of their relationship, she and Bryher would be rescuing each other. H.D. decided almost at once to throw in her lot with Bryher. This must have been evident to Aldington, and may well explain his subsequent behaviour concerning the daughter, Frances Perdita, born to H.D. on 31 March 1919.

Momentarily revitalised by the war's end, Aldington was full of writing plans. He mentioned a novel to Lowell, which suggests the possibility he had scribbled notes towards what eventually became *Death of a Hero*, as he says in the letter to Halcott Glover which prefaces it: 'I began this book almost immediately after the Armistice, in a little Belgian cottage—my billet. I remember the landscape was buried deep in snow, and that we had very little fuel. Then came demobilisation, and the effort of readjustment cost my manuscript its life. I threw it aside, and never picked it up again'. By the time he had finally returned to England his positive mood was gone. 1919 may well have been, as Norman Gates says, 'Aldington's *annus mirabilis* for publication of poetry', but it was otherwise an extremely difficult year, prelude to a period of intense inner conflicts. 'The year 1919' he wrote 22 years later and taking refuge from another war, 'was certainly an *annus mirabilis*, if you take the "mirabilis" ironically'.[1] With real or affected hardness, H.D. later told Conrad Aiken, Aldington 'had or pretended to have a sort of lapse of memory and dissociation, they called shell-shock. One could not, could one, unequipped, be expected to deal with that'.[2]

Aldington experienced the war's last phase and the immediate post-war as a period of insomnia, and unaccountable depressions, when 'it seemed to me that my mind had deteriorated, because of the difficulty I found in concentrating on mental work'.[3]

Disillusionment was rapid on homecoming to London, which he found dirty and shabby, with everything in short supply except military uniforms and debts. People seemed hostile to the demobilised troops and motivated largely by self-interest. Luckily the threads of a literary life were there for him. Herbert Read wrote for contributions to the new *Art and Letters*. Aldington met Holbrook Jackson and formed a link with the journal *To-Day*, and became a contributor to Henri Davray's *Anglo-French Review*. During the year four Aldington poetry titles were published: *Images of War* (Beaumont), expanded edition (Allen & Unwin); *Images of Desire* (Elkin Mathews); *Images* (Egoist Press), and *War and Love* (Four Seas Company, Boston.)

His short association with the Clerk's Press ended. Apart from private reprints of Aldington's titles in the first Poets Translation Series, Bubb, during the war, had issued *Rêverie* and *Myrrhine and Konallis*. But other advertised titles never appeared, and there are hints of a hiatus between the two men in their letters.[4] Aldington told Lawrence Clark Powell some 30 years later that Bubb had 'got mad at me about something which he thought disrespectful to Jesus'.[5]

Quite soon Aldington was pursuing an alternative. In the latter part of December 1918 he began mentioning to contacts the possibility that Bryher might subsidise a translation series. This link with Bryher was to affect him seriously, both immediately and in the long term. Almost at once after she had contacted him by letter while he was at the front in mid-1918, he had suggested she get in touch with H.D., an act far-reaching in its consequences. Quite soon, the Aldingtons had dined with Sir John Ellerman, Bryher's father. Though Aldington lampooned him in *A Fool i' the Forest* and wrote of him acidly in *Life for Life's Sake*, he was through Ellerman's influence commissioned to write for the *Sphere* and the *Times Literary Supplement*. The latter became his steady source of income for most of the 1920s.

Eliot suggested Aldington apply for the assistant editorship of the *Athenaeum*, under Middleton Murry, but he was more interested in the job Murry was vacating, French literature critic for the *Times Literary Supplement*. He soon felt London had lost the flavour of pre-1916. The West End streets, raucous and tense, seemed indecent and debauched, an insult to the war dead. He felt cut off from those who had not suffered front-line life. A new-found friend such as Read, who had comparable war experience, could not help to alleviate Aldington's sense of being isolated somewhere between the Hugh Walpole middlebrows and Modernists like Joyce and Pound.

Aldington, lodged at the Author's Club in Whitehall, slowly worked his way back into social life. The spring appearance of his poem 'Reverie' in the *English Review* helped cement a new friendship, with Alec Waugh, another returned subaltern. They met at one of Harold Monro's Poetry Bookshop bachelor parties. Waugh came to think Aldington's prose ill-tempered, but always retained an admiration for his poetry. 'His talk did not scintillate', Waugh remembered, 'but it was sound, varied, entertaining. . . . Parties went better for his presence. He enjoyed good company and good wine. I have never heard him speak spitefully of another writer.'[6]

Early in March Aldington dined at Bellotti's restaurant with Pound, who spoke of his growing disillusionment with the English and intention to move to Paris, 'where he could be among intelligent people'. Aldington felt little sympathy with this mood, which brought out his Englishness. But he was restless and this, combined with his need to earn, drove him into what was to become a lifelong bad habit, overwork. Soon he was writing for a range of periodicals, including the *Pall Mall Gazette*, *Athenaeum*, *Spectator*, *English Review*, the short-lived *Coterie* and, before long, the *Criterion*. Late in March, he told Lowell: 'I am not at all well; my nerves have got in such a state that I have a sort of "sympathetic" neuralgia in my neck and arms; I sleep badly; I have a "trench throat" and cough; I have ague directly I get cold. This sounds a devil of a grouse, but it's true, only for Heaven's sake don't mention it to Hilda'.[7] Like Antony Clarendon, hero of his *All Men are Enemies*,[8] Aldington may well have felt suicidal.

If he did not wish H.D. to know, one reason may be discerned in her remark to Aiken that, 'one could not . . . be expected to deal with that', that is, the condition of his health. He complained to Lowell several times about his state of nervous debility and physical exhaustion, headpains attributable to deferred shell-shock, an eruption of boils, and so on. Another better reason was that, having recovered from her pneumonia, H.D. had given birth to a daughter,

Frances Perdita, and was in the aftermath, 'terribly ill and thin'. She spent three weeks in a West London nursing home, which she found detestable despite Bryher's devoted attentions. From Ealing, still weak, she moved to central London, the Hotel Du Littoral in Moor Street, the last accommodation she was to share, very briefly, with Aldington, presumably to settle matters over the child's official parentage. Later, she made harsh accusations against his conduct during these weeks. When he wrote on 26 April his tone suggests that something unpleasant, but by no means unspeakable, had happened between them. She was still unwell. Nonetheless, he said 'I shall see a lawyer and hand the matter over', but also, 'And I *do* sincerely want you to be happy somehow in your own way'. Regrettably, he offers no specifics, but this is not quite the tone of someone who had uttered grim threats, as H.D. later claimed, though she makes no mention of them in her 'Autobiographical notes' which do say, however, that 'Richard comes to lunch at Bullingham Mansions [Kensington]' where she lived after the Littoral, after a spell in Pound's flat at Holland Place and after her holiday with Bryher in the Scilly Isles.

When Aldington began work for the *Times Literary Supplement* in May the editor, Bruce Richmond, seemed at first to treat him with polite insolence, but quite soon Richmond's attitude 'improved'. The two men established cordial working relations which lasted throughout the 1920s. Aldington liked to think his professionalism prompted Richmond's apparent change of heart.

Once Aldington had the job he thought of his friends. Within a month or two (though he misdates it in his memoirs as 1922)[9] he had introduced Eliot to Richmond, after a 'most complicated piece of diplomacy'. He recalled with some relish that Eliot almost flubbed the opportunity by 'wearing, if you please, a derby hat and an Uncle Sam beard he had cultivated in Switzerland'.[10] Over a steak and a pint of bitter in the pub, however, Eliot retrieved the situation by the quality of his conversation. Aldington also agreed to share the French literature reviews with Flint, Flint to review poetry and Aldington prose. Thus each continued involvement in the intense interchanges between French and English writing. Aldington attempted unsuccessfully to have Lawrence accepted as contributor to the *Anglo-French Review,* only to complain shortly to Lowell that Lawrence was engaged in purveying 'dreadful stuff' in the *English Review.* The 'stuff' in question became part of Lawrence's *Studies in Classic American Literature.*

The long-anticipated American-published volume *War and Love* appeared in spring 1919, and was reviewed in the *Dial* in late May. Calling Aldington an 'honest war reporter' and recorder of 'ecstasy and exquisite suffering', the reviewer remarked that the 'war has produced no more genuine poetry'.[11] Aldington saw these war poems as a contrast to the work of Brooke and Noyes, written by a common soldier for common soldiers, though he believed them too hastily composed. The *Poetry* reviewer preferred the love poems and felt the writer was too sensitive to record successfully the inarticulate feelings of ordinary men.[12] Another reviewer, declaring the book 'the finest poetry of its kind published since the war',[13] sees in it the maturity of Aldington's 'genius'. The war poems have not the raw force of Rosenberg's best work, but their value is in accuracy of observation presented with a characteristically understated intensity. The book's other dimension is a display of the fine lyricism with which Aldington could evoke heterosexual love.

When Harriet Monroe wrote in September asking him to become *Poetry's* London correspondent, he temporised to avoid offending Pound (who still had the job). At the same time he reacted angrily to negative comments on *War and Love* in the *Little Review* by Pound's friend William Carlos Williams.[14] Williams grumbled about the war poems' lack of objectivity, a complaint of which Aldington wrote angrily to Harriet Monroe: 'Did he—a doctor—imagine that artistic calm, detached vision, were possible to men who were reduced by inadequate diet, sleeping in wet clothes out-of-doors, months of physical torment and mental stagnation in a desert of mud, broken walls, hell?'[15]

Although he enjoyed some aspects of the literary scene and deepened some relationships, such as that with May Sinclair (in whose novel *Mary Olivier* he is the workaholic Richard Nicholson, with whom Mary Olivier 'the woman who translated Euripides', falls in love) he now made a surprising move. Before Lawrence left for Italy in mid-November, Aldington had agreed to take over his tenancy of Chapel Farm Cottage at Newbury, Berkshire. He moved there in December, yet at this very moment accepted from *Poetry* the assignment of contributing a 'London Letter' three or four times a year at three dollars a page.

At Chapel Farm he began settling into the task of earning an income. Writing for *The Times* proved no sinecure, because of his then relatively limited knowledge of general French literature. Most of the 1920s was for him a life of unremitting labour, wide reading, and writing about 200 000 words a year. During these years he published, apart from journalism, a large number of books. Soon after beginning work for *The Times* he became a regular reviewer for the *Nation* and then assistant editor, sometimes acting editor, of the *Criterion*. At Chapel Farm and later Malthouse Cottage, Aldington accumulated a library of some 6 000 books including, after 1921, much of his father's library. Perhaps setting the seal on his new life, in late January 1920 he wrote to H.D. wishing her *bon voyage* on her first trip to Greece, locus of the Hellenism which meant so much to each of them. Although at first he continued to further H.D.'s literary interests in England and the United States, the two were not in direct communication again until 1929, although (as Arabella suspected) they remained interested in one another's lives throughout the decade.

Aldington quietly and quickly immersed himself in the writer's daily life, with poetry and translation as central preoccupations. He seemed anxious to work towards broader connections between English and American writing, telling both Lowell and Harriet Monroe that the *TLS* would be taking more frequent notice of the American literary scene. His contributions to *Poetry* increased, and thus contact with Monroe. He alerted her to the post-war emergence of Dadaism from its Zurich cafe, deploring that the *Dial* was about to take it seriously. 'Some sort of squelch seems necessary', he declared, as he set out to attack the 'imbecility' of Gertrude Stein and her associates.[16] The eventual result is his article 'The Disciples of Gertrude Stein',[17] in which he perceives Stein as following Poe and Whitman in influencing the French, linking up with a French capacity for verbal play which of itself dates back to the *fabliaux*. With typical irony, he speaks of Blaise Cendrar's work, for example, as 'frequently tainted with intelligibility', but his real target is Dadaism, for which ultimate responsibility is attributed to Stein. Whatever the merits of his argument, the piece is chiefly interesting as one more indication of Aldington's literary conservatism. Yet it was not an insular conservatism, like that of many English writers, who ignored or condescended to the Americans, and in another *Poetry* article he gave open-minded welcome to the emerging American idiom.[18]

Early in May an unsigned *TLS* article attacked American poetry, though without mentioning the new generation of Pound or Eliot or H.D.[19] Aldington nonetheless sent copies to Lowell and Monroe, urging the latter to respond. The *TLS* subsequently embarrassed him by refusing to print her letter. At this stage, despite doubts about the poetry of both Pound and Eliot, Aldington seemed to find fellow-feeling with the expatriate Americans. Several times during the year he expressed his liking for and admiration of Eliot to Lowell and others, though he already had clear reservations about Eliot's poetry. In June he was particularly positive:

> His manners are charming and ironical, his conversation really witty, his point of view always finished and sometimes profound; he is a really polished American and I know of no greater praise to give a man. His influence as a critic is much greater than as a poet, though there he is exceedingly admired and attacked, but his critical articles give him great prestige.[20]

Such admiration did not prevent him, a week or two later, from citing to Harold Monro Eliot's lines 'Polyphiloprogenitive, the sapient sutlers of the lord' as an instance of fundamental literary insincerity.[21]

This whole question of sincerity engaged him and indicates another crucial difference from Pound, and Pound's often-quoted: 'I believe in technique as the test of a man's sincerity'. Only recently Aldington had translated from Edouard Dujardin's *De Stéphane Mallarmé au prophète Ezéchiel* the passage: 'An artist's first problem is sincerity. To be sincere does not mean to tell others the truth; it means, at least in art, to tell oneself the truth'. Dujardin was probably close to Pound in his ideas about technique, but the passage provoked Aldington into seeing the question of truth to one's material more literally than did Pound. Relevant here are 'Personal Notes on Poetry', recently retrieved from a holograph notebook[22] and dating from this period. One complete entry, Section 8, reads: 'Sincerity in poetry is a valuable thing: it means knowing exactly what you feel and saying it as well as possible'. *Vers libre* seemed to offer brevity, precision and clarity, but the central quality of poetry is passion or emotion ('A poem deeply felt ... makes its own cadence'). Where Pound or Eliot perceive the poem as a fusion of intellect and emotion, Aldington's view is more personal, nearer D. H. Lawrence's. Concluding the notes he speaks, typically, of poetry as, after all, 'a sort of religion in which men put down their guesses about the universe and the meaning of things'. For him as a humanist aesthete, poetry was the highest manifestation of human consciousness.

Pound and Eliot, Flint and Harold Monro, these were Aldington's literary friendships of the time. Towards Flint, as always, he was a model of solicitude. In April Flint's wife, Violet, died of pneumonia, in childbirth, though the child survived. Aldington wrote to Flint several times, full of sympathy, with suggestions about care of his daughter, Ianthe. He got the *TLS* to advance Flint £20, and wrote a poem, 'The Walk',[23] which speaks tenderly of Flint's grief and recalls Flint's companionship when Aldington had undergone similar suffering in 1915. In May Flint heard from H.D.: 'I feel so utterly understanding as I went through it all almost exactly as she did. ... It was coming back to life that was anguish to me'.[24] Aldington often urged Flint to overcome his hypersensitivity, to be less modest. While warning against the vanity of such as Pound and Ford he suggested the advantages of a 'tempered ... assumption of superiority' such as that adopted by Eliot or Aldous Huxley. He identified with Flint in the hazardous business of holding one's own in the literary world and urged Pound to champion Flint's new book of poems, *Otherworld*, reviewing it himself for *Poetry* in October.[25] There he pictures Flint as an idealist who suffers from his material disadvantages and plebeian origins, and portrays Flint's as 'a healthy mind struggling against bitterness and discouragement', whose work is characterised by intense sincerity.

Towards Pound Aldington's feelings were considerably more ambivalent. He frequently praised his American friend, but also congratulated himself that his work was accepted in places becoming closed to Pound. In June, for example, he had articles in *To-Day* and the *English Review*, poems in *Art & Letters*, the *Nation* and *Coterie*. In under six months he had earned £200 by his pen, a competence, as he called it—noting that he had one for the first time. Pound at the same time found his literary fortunes in England at their lowest. Aldington vacillated in feeling about Pound, often exasperated with him, yet calling him to Dujardin, '*le plus intelligent des poètes et le plus charmant de mes amis*'[26]

Aldington wrote often at this time to Harold Monro, treating him as a confidante. Monro sent his poems to Aldington for comment, Aldington sent his for the *Chapbook*. Despite the amount of publication he was doing, twice at this period he asked Monro to print the poems under an 'inoffensive pseudonym',[27] claiming that he had a 'neurasthenic horror' of seeing his name in print. This is a glimpse of the darker side of Aldington's life, an effect of the war, compounded by a growing sense of solitariness. Later, he claimed

..Monro that merely to 'keep on' was 'a triumph of optimism'.[28] A sense of being in retreat seemed to govern him and he confessed to feelings of supineness and futility. To disturb his listlessness there were complications over his tenancy of Chapel Farm Cottage, misunderstandings which arose because Lawrence's friends the Radfords absent-mindedly forgot to pass on rents he paid them, so that he had to hire a lawyer to prevent eviction. This cottage, though it had a garden and the nearby meadows and coppices were full of wild flowers in spring, was secluded and silent, fit scene for a 'misanthropic cell' located in a nondescript hamlet in charmless and featureless country. As appropriate tenant, he confessed to Monro that he felt in his own poetry 'a certain dullness, only to be expected from a man who has been spiritually stunned'.

This stunning of the spirit did not prevent him, on 20 August, from offering Monro a self-described 'simple' line of philosophy:

> We have no evidence of 'God', no evidence of any superior intelligence directing the universe. The only intelligence we know is the collective intelligence of men (I mean the best of men). Why then should men not create 'God'? Why shouldn't the knowledge and intellect of men—immensely developed—enable them to become 'God', i.e. the directing intelligence? We can shoot a mass of metal 50 miles with accuracy . . . .

From September 1920 onwards he sought a new cottage, but at first could find nothing and asked if Monro could put him up in a room over the Poetry Bookshop should he need to return to town. He broached with Monro the idea of a chapbook on the prose poem, with himself, Eliot and Frederic Manning as contributors. He knew Eliot was against the form, but respected his reasons. He also promoted Eliot's new book of criticism, *The Sacred Wood*, published on 4 November, mentioning it enthusiastically to Flint and others. In December he moved into Malthouse Cottage, near Reading. His interest in the prose poem continued strong and, despite the fact that the English edition of *Images of War* was 'a dreadful fizzle' and had sold only 91 copies, he planned a major collection of his own poems in this new and exotic genre.

7 Malthouse Cottage: Working at the Writer's Trade, 1921-25

With the exception of several literary friendships, to which we shall return, Aldington's life for most of the 1920s contained few of those high moments which can tempt and delight a biographer. His retreat to the cottage at Padworth, roughly halfway between Reading and Newbury in Berkshire, was undoubtedly caused in the first instance by war-weariness and London-weariness, and possibly, as he himself hinted at one time or another, shell-shock and poison gas. In any case, he was in a bad state of nerves and perhaps still engaged in wrenching his soul from H.D.

He settled into Malthouse Cottage with Arabella who, like all his women partners after H.D., stayed in the background. So, this Bella of *Bid Me to Live*, this sexual 'star-performer' filched from John Cournos, this young Pennsylvania woman whom H.D. claimed had had 'a lot of lovers', who had even 'been slashed about by abortionists', she with a certain Oriental look, 'tight-pulled dark eyes' and 'insect black updarting eyebrows', with her 'toneless one-tone voice', who 'was so very quiet', a 'beetle with a hard shell ... metallic', somehow merged for most of the 1920s into the cramped setting of Malthouse Cottage. 'Elegant but poor', so Lawrence described her in a letter to Cynthia Asquith in November 1917.[1] Dorothy-Arabella's presence in Lawrence's *Aaron's Rod*, in the guise of Josephine Ford, seems to confirm H.D.'s picture, in some respects: 'Her movements were very quiet and well-bred; but perhaps too quiet, they had the dangerous impassivity of the Bohemian, Parisian or American rather than English'.[2] Installed on the straight, still banks of the Kennet, this Arabella made friends with some of Aldington's friends, and she was quiet, but she seems to have been no danger to anyone.

Aldington laboured long and hard to make a modest income, his routine broken only by work in the garden, a visit from a friend such as Harold Monro or Eliot, or an occasional trip up to town. One such trip in this spring of 1921 had a melancholy occasion. Unexpectedly, Albert Edward collapsed and died at the Authors'

Club in Whitehall. There was an inquest, which Aldington had to attend, and the funeral, which he arranged. There was momentary financial anxiety, when he felt the burden of responsibility especially for his sisters. But apart from interrupting his work, his father's passing caused only a ripple. One of the last communications between them was a note from Albert Edward thanking Aldington for Knopf's edition of *Medallions in Clay*, his collected translations, published in New York that winter. Aldington's attitude to his father was somewhat mixed—affection, some gratitude (partially for the library of English classics, most of which he inherited) together with a degree of contempt for his father's capacities and energies as a lawyer and administrator, and his feebleness as a man.

Aldington's income at this time derived almost entirely from literary journalism, supplemented by selling boxes of review books to Cyril Beaumont in Charing Cross Road. As Beaumont good-humouredly remembers: 'I came to know Richard Aldington primarily from his selling books to me, rather than I to him'. Beaumont pictures 'an alert brisk figure, sometimes wearing a clipped moustache, sometimes a small beard in the French style. He was always very frank and to the point. Sometimes he dressed simply, sometimes he sported a romantic sombrero and cloak'.[3]

The beautiful spring turned into a hot summer and in July Aldington took a walking tour. On 20 July he wrote from Tewkesbury asking Beaumont for money for his latest batch of books and, this sum in hand, he walked Radnor forest and the Welsh Mountains. He returned to Malthouse to a series of gloomy letters from Manning, so in late August he travelled to Bourne, Lincolnshire, for a few days to help organise Manning in his labour on the biography of Sir William White (1923).

During the same period Aldington was consoling Eliot, who was overworked and had marital difficulties, Flint, who was in a state of depression and withdrawal, and Harold Monro who had problems with alchohol and lack of confidence in himself as a writer. No wonder that Aldington told Lowell his own work was delayed because of 'having to rush off from time to time to save people from nervous breakdowns'.[4] For the present it seems, his own war-damaged health did not impede him. He relished his bookish, bucolic life and, after Monro had spent a November weekend with him, declared, 'I don't want to be "modern" or successful or anything but cheerful and contented'. Thus he seemed to be, whatever the local legend around Padworth (largely induced by Monro's bouts of intemperance) that he 'regularly indulged in "filthy orgies" . . . with deboshed Londoners'.[5]

Apart from reviewing, and producing a thin stream of poems, Aldington worked hard at translations. In 1922 Beaumont published his version of Goldoni's *The Good-Humoured Ladies* and late that summer he completed work on Cyrano de Bergerac's *Voyages to the Sun and Moon*, which appeared the following year in Routledge's Broadway Translation Series, and thus became the ninth separate title he had translated, from five languages.

After finishing the *Cyrano*, Aldington, with Arabella and his friend Halcott Glover, headed for Italy, with an overnight stop in Paris. When they arrived in Florence there were few tourists and the heat of summer was over. An exhibition of *cinquecento* painting at the Pitti Palace introduced him to the work of the Caracci, Guido Reni and Caravaggio. Thronged with girls in thin summer dresses, hair braided with flowers in the traditional Florentine style, the streets seemed 'a carnival of Venus'. In contrast, Rome was Bacchic, the heatwave and drought of the previous year having produced a superb vintage. In quest of improving his Italian, he found considerable intellectual life in the local papers. Otherwise, he was absorbed in reading Dryden's plays, the work of a 'wonderful craftsman'. He was to return to the 17th-century poet in Jamaica more than 20 years later, finding an affinity in Dryden's measured, sceptical rationalism. This Italian trip prompted memories of before the war and in gratitude (because its fees had enabled him to make his first trip to Italy) Aldington sent *Poetry* a batch of work. Touched by his letter, Harriet Monroe took none of the poems.

'I had a wholly delightful time in Rome and Florence', Aldington told Harold Monro on 19 October. 'Among other valuable sensations was that of sitting in a warm golden sunset on the Palatine watching the light fade on the old bronze gate of the little temple of Romulus—you know the one—which has been there untouched since 300 A.D. I had one of those complex feelings one can hardly express—involving a real sense of *duration*, almost a revelation of time as an *absolute*, and a kind of religious resignation (you won't misunderstand the 'religious'?), an acceptance of being a mere transitory link in a mysterious progress. . . . ' He felt this trip helped restore his war-shattered equilibrium, but he sent Flint in November a poem full of images of smashed statues, profaned sanctuaries, bestial faces:

> Basalt and marble are broken
> Desecrated the once holy earth ...

The lines could fit well enough into Eliot's allusive and elliptical vision of the waste land. In complete contrast are the 'Four Songs' in the December 1922 *To-Day*. Beautifully timed, in full rhyme and traditional measure, these are pastiche of 16th- and 17th-century modes, but, quite rightly, Aldington retained three in his *Complete Poems*[6] and never published the piece sent to Flint.

During 1923 four titles appeared under Aldington's name. Two, *Voyages to the Moon and Sun* and *French Comedies of the XVIIIth Century* are in Routledge's Broadway Translation Series. The other two are poetry, *The Berkshire Kennet* and *Exile and Other Poems*. *The Berkshire Kennet* is a one-man rearguard action against modernism, nicely-turned octosyllabic couplets in pastoral mode, mimicking late 18th-century models, even to the sentiments expressed. To an extent the poem is symptomatic of the fact that Aldington was uncertain of his position in relation to the new poetic; but when the American reviewer and anthologist Louis Untermeyer declared that the work of Marianne Moore and Eliot was not poetry Aldington disagreed, citing Horace, Boileau and Pope to prove that poetry may incorporate criticism, declaring that 'any fool can be emotional'. 'But to write like Miss Moore "it is at least necessary to read and think"'.[7] He approved of what he saw as the reaction against Romanticism, but *The Berkshire Kennet* reverts to the stock responses of an earlier period, and is in *The Complete Poems* in a section headed 'Metrical Exercises'.

The opening section of *Exile and Other Poems* clearly demonstrates that Aldington has abandoned the central principles of Imagism. Fundamentally discursive, the poems are in free form, but with a pervasive iambic underlay. The limitations of this section may be reduced to a single fault: poems pointed in the wrong direction, back towards the poet. Observation of others amounts here not to insight but self-exposure. Only occasionally, as in 'Bones', is resonance derived from some measure of wit and detachment:

> Now when this coloured curious web
> Which hides my awkward bones from sight
> Unrolls, and when the thing that's I—

Malthouse Cottage: The Writer's Trade

> A pinch of lighted dust that flashes—
> Has somehow suddenly gone out,
> What quaint adventures may there be
> For my unneeded skeleton?[8]

The book's second section, 'Words for Music', which includes 'Songs for Puritans', 'Songs for Sensualists' and 'Metrical Exercises' is beautifully accomplished but largely pastiche:

> If all my senses still conspire,
>   Ere their meridian be past,
> To set the blossoms of desire,
>   The worm shall not exult at last;
> Her children and my words I trust
> Shall speak her grace when we are dust.

Yet if we return a moment to the suggestion of self-exposure, we find that the opening lines of the book's title poem ask: 'How shall we utter/This horror, this rage, this despair?' More personally, in 'Eumenides', the poet says:

> I have lived with, fed upon death
> As happier generations feed on life;
> My very mind seems gangrened.

Later he asks:

> Have I not striven and striven for health?
> Lived calmly (as it seemed) these many months . . .

'What is it I agonise for? My own murdered self. . . . It is myself that is the Eumenides'. In another poem, 'Meditation', he rejects the 'lie' of immortality or the 'legend' of a possible future life, but partially counter to this is 'A Gate By The Way'. Standing in a field, the speaker addresses a bookish, unnamed friend:

> We are nearer the gods than those who run and fly.
> The shadows we pursue may not be shadows . . .

This poem circles around the word 'peace', which Aldington sought at this period and sometimes claimed to have achieved. But the general feeling of the 'Exile' section of poems is one of moroseness. The book in some sense marks a crucial moment in his literary life. Imagism had given his career impetus, but his poetry of the immediate post-war years is a falling off. *Exile and Other Poems* is a dim book to be represented by at the very moment when Eliot had published 'The Waste Land' and Americans such as Pound, Williams and Marianne Moore were establishing the canon of modernist poetry.

Aldington's turning to imitation of pre-Romantic models in fixed forms bothered Frank Flint, but in the January 1923 *Fortnightly Review* Aldington paid tribute to Flint, endorsing his dictum that the important attributes of a poet are sincerity, personality and style. To put effect before meaning he finds a symptom of decadence, and singles out the work of Apollinaire as example. If only because it forces the poet to attend to his meaning, *vers libre* may be a positive development. For two reasons the article is worth attention. First, Aldington's vaunting 'sincerity' again separates him from Pound, Eliot and their emphases on technique and effect. Second, he comes out positively if not wholeheartedly for *vers libre*, though he had ceased to make it central to his own practice.[9]

He continually boosted Flint, trying to help him overcome a characteristic hypersensitiveness, joshing him for his recurring doubts about their friendship. Acting the older brother, Aldington repeatedly attempted to get Flint to steel himself against criticism, not to take himself or his friends too seriously. Flint had made a real contribution to contemporary poetry in his handling of *vers libre*, and it was a pity, Aldington felt, that personal inhibitions prevented him from full and free involvement in the writing scene, with the consequent opportunities for recognition.

A great deal of Aldington's writing in the early and mid/1920s continued to be translation. His work in 1923–24 included *Les Liaisons Dangereuses*, a version still current today and, most curiously, *Sturly*, a book on oceanography by Pierre Custot. *Mercure de France* called this version *'un véritable tour de force'*, a judgement Aldington concurred in, as he claimed to have completed the translation in three weeks after reviewing the French edition for the *Times Literary Supplement*, and after T. E. Lawrence (a figure to loom large in his future) failed to bring it off. Aldington solved the problem of technical vocabulary with great resource by taking from the London Library parallel scientific texts in English and French on Mediterranean sea-life '(ichthyology, algae, and what-not)'. His translation had the curious result that Custot, a director of the aquarium at Monte Carlo, who may have believed Aldington to be a scientist, suggested that he come and live with him!

More important from a personal standpoint was *Literary Studies and Reviews*, Aldington's first collection of literary criticism, direct fruit of the influence of Dudley Grey, the 'good European' mentor of his teens. Two-thirds of these studies are on French writers and are collected from the *Times Literary Supplement*, but perhaps his non-French topics are most worth our notice. Aldington himself was proud of his championing of modern writers, including Proust, Joyce, Lawrence and Eliot, although as we have seen Joyce was not especially delighted with his attentions.

Placed between the Proust and Joyce essay, 'The Poetry of T. S. Eliot' merits separate comment, if only because it goes against the grain of both precept and practice in Aldington's own poetry. Some questions he raises here he will approach again many years later in a very different mood. But despite reservations he wishes to show that Eliot is no mere imitator of Laforgue and the French but is their intellectual peer, and that his capturing of the tones of Donne and Chapman is deliberate strategy. Denying obscurity in Eliot's poetry (the comments were written before the publication of 'The Waste Land') he notes instead density of thought and 'a healthy reaction against the merely pretty and agreeable'.[10]

Besides displaying Aldington's self-acquired scholarly grounding, these essays are remarkable for a gracefulness exemplified in the cadences of the concluding piece, 'Theocritus on Capri', and for independence of judgement, of which 'Landor's Hellenics' may serve as evidence. Aldington came to value the economies and the aesthetic sense of the 'tender old Englishman', and Landor's range of culture and incisive critical judgement, but most of all he admired the same mixture Yeats had found suggestive in his lucubrations on the anti-self, the antithesis between Landor's intellectual life and his 'English emotionalism':

> He lived in a series of emotional explosions; of wrath, pride, generosity, tenderness, indignation. How natural that he should turn for discipline to the pure serenity of Attic Greek; and knowing him as we do, how natural that Walter Savage Landor, fuming with rage over some trifle, should invest his indignation (at some local squire) with the Jovian dignity of Pericles or the

cynic indifference of Diogenes. The English Landor is always visible through the Greek Landor, even in the 'Hellenics'; the matter, the form, almost the very speech is Greek, but the voice is English.[11]

A new feature, 'Books of the Quarter', was introduced into the *Criterion* with the 1 July 1924 number and Eliot embarrassed Flint by asking him to review *Literary Studies*. Flint, as in so many other circumstances, appealed to Aldington and was invited to visit Malthouse and help stem his friend's workaholism. Aldington felt Flint's task in writing the review might be complicated by the feeling that he should himself have compiled such a book, but Flint overcame all anxieties and provided a useful and graceful discussion, centred on the point that the book's ultimate purpose is 'the illumination of the epicurean philosophy in literature'.[12]

Flint saw Aldington's epicureanism as a reaction to his war experience, but it was also natural to his temperament, just as was an affinity with Voltaire's incisive rationalism. For Routledge's Aldington was working on a study of Voltaire, which he found congenial although, for a 60 000-word book, he claimed that he had to consult nine volumes (4500 pages) of 'official' life, eight million words of the writings and 10 000 letters, plus secondary sources. His *Voltaire* was praised for its objectivity and for his empathy with the subject, whom he praised for possessing 'a European mind'.[13] 'Mr Aldington presents [Voltaire] as a living force in his own century', wrote Kingsley Martin.[14] Alyse Gregory in the *Dial*[15] wrote of Aldington's being 'saturated ... with his subject', of his 'determined veracity', 'impartiality held up on the wings of enthusiasm', 'sober insight', 'clear and incisive thought' and 'critical sense, combined with historical perspective, personal intensity and literary craft'. The anonymous *New Statesman* reviewer says that Aldington is 'sane, unheated, well informed and above all really curious ... vivid and intelligent ... has written a book which ... should remain the standard English short biography for many years'.[16] As all this suggests, the book is a highly successful exercise in accomplished compression and balanced perspective. Its favourable reception was, as we shall see, in sad contrast to that given Aldington's biographies of the 1950s.

He discussed the book with Herbert Read. The two friends regularly participated in fortnightly luncheons in town, along with Eliot and others, but Read now noted with regret that Aldington had retired into being 'a country old Tory'. Certainly he was working intensely on the Voltaire. He told Read he had also just completed a 1400–line poem, which, he thought, 'will amuse you and a few other honnêtes gens'.[17] He sent a copy, but did not put in an appearance.

When, in November, his friend George Gribble travelled from Rome to England, Aldington saw to it that he made the right social links, so the Gribbles were entertained to lunch by Edith Sitwell and to dinner by Eliot. They spent a few days at Padworth in December and George Gribble's notes show that Aldington's bucolic isolation was by no means grim: 5 December, 'warm reception, very jovial'; Aldington took him walking in the countryside which he found much to his taste, as he did their talks late into the night; 7 December—'Another "binge" with Aldingtons'. Two weeks later, just before leaving for the Mermaid Inn, Rye, Aldington wrote to thank Read for his comments on the long poem, *A Fool i' the Forest*. Read apparently found it loose and lacking in intensity, eliciting from Aldington the view that 'intensity' is a dangerous ideal, a way to possible sterility and eventual silence. *A Fool i' the Forest* 'may be loose, as you say. But I have grown to dislike extremely all expression which is elliptic and alembique; I abandon it, I give it to the devil. I hate Rimbaud, I dislike Valéry, I have a contempt for Mallarmé. Clarity and verve are what I want, variety and fertility—Balzac, not Flaubert. I want to destroy self-consciousness in my writing.'[18]

Balzac, not Flaubert, which, in an odd way, is to say 'Yeats, not Pound'. At this moment Aldington felt that Pound and Flint, and now Eliot and Read, had been led astray by this quest for intensity. Only Sacheverell Sitwell had escaped! Put that way, his view is unfairly made to seem ridiculous, but he had a point—as he saw it, reason was giving way to feeling. On the other hand, eschewing the self-consciousness of a calculated style, he allowed an opposite defect in much of his writing—lack of distancing, too strong a direct presence of his own personality, of (in Yeats's phrase) 'the bundle of accidents that sits down to breakfast'.

The *Times Literary Supplement* for 22 January 1925 carries a review of *A Fool i' the Forest* characterising the poem as 'suggestive allegory . . . at once ribald and poignant'. Aldington's 'looseness' is seen as giving 'entirely free play to its author's faculties', so that 'Mr Aldington's apparent formlessness, his ironic frivolity, is an index of poetic sincerity'. The book is 'a spiritual and psychological autobiography' centred on three characters who are both individual and symbolic, three and yet one. These are 'I', Mezzetin and the Conjuror, and the theme is the struggle of 'I' to attain harmony with the world around him. Mezzetin symbolizes 'the imaginative faculties—art, youth, satire, irresponsible gaiety, liberty'; the Conjurer 'symbolizes the intellectual faculties—age, science, righteous cant, solemnity, authority—which is why I make him so malicious'.[19] (A careful reader will find in the Conjuror, too, some hint of Eliot.) The four-beat unrhymed narrative line is interspersed with many snatches of song, and combines with swift kaleidoscopic shifts of mood and pace—in a montage technique which has since become familiar in the works of Brecht, Behan and others. Scenes shift from Venice to Athens, to the trenches, to London; time shifts between past and present, between memory and consciousness. As Glenn Hughes puts it in what is still the best generally available account of the poem, 'Aldington the man is dragged from place to place by Aldington the poet and Aldington the scholar'.[20] In these travels, the 'I's' soul is fought for by the other two. Mezzetin, the artist, is killed in the trenches by the Conjuror. Once back in London 'I' disposes of the Conjuror, and then is free of both, to realise 'himself'—to become a typical petty bourgeois, white-collar worker and family man.

Some reviewers, though not the *TLS*, saw *A Fool i' the Forest* as deriving from *The Waste Land*. For example, a passage beginning 'O Pall Athena / America loves you ... '[21] was said to imitate the famous Eliot passage 'O O O O that Shakespeherian rag', but Aldington had already demonstrated his own gift for parody and deliberate pastiche, and other poets besides Eliot and Aldington (Vachel Lindsay, for example) were employing the jazz rhythms novel in the 1920s. The reviewers' linking his work with *The Waste Land* must have galled Aldington for, as he several times assured Read, he was attempting to evade the 'costiveness' of Eliot's kind of poetry and 'write for all men of good will'.[22] Later he said his model was a narrative poem by another friend, *The Dark Night* by May Sinclair, and that *A Fool i' the Forest* repeats and unifies themes in his own earlier book, *Exile and Other Poems*. Within the poem there is a correspondence between Mezzetin and the Conjuror and Shakespeare's Jaques and Touchstone, in *As You Like It*, from which Aldington's title comes.[23]

Work on this poem and the Voltaire study taxed his health. After posting the Voltaire typescript to Routledge's, he and Arabella celebrated by going for a long country walk, but he collapsed with heart palpitations, had to be taken home by car and carried to bed. He explained the episode as 'influenza, of the kind which attacks the heart'.[24] The collapse may have been in part a reaction to his tapping of the subconsciousness which fed *A Fool i' the Forest*. A London specialist diagnosed 'rapid nervous exhaustion' and prescribed rest and change, a regimen later converted into a three-week walking tour during part of which Aldington walked 20 miles a day in the most mountainous area of Wales.

At the beginning of March 1925 he received from Boston a copy of Lowell's book on Keats. He wrote at once, thanking her flatteringly for it. The exchange revived a link which had become tenuous. Pound, too, after a longish interval, renewed contact with him, and displayed 'the same old prejudices and phobias, the same old pretences and affectations'. 'I don't know if he has retained any reputation in America, but here he is almost forgotten', Aldington told Lowell, 'and as the rest of us go up, he goes down'.[25] News reached him at Shrewsbury that Lowell was seriously ill, and he sent a commiserating postcard. It was their last communication, as she died a week later.

From May onwards American reviews of *A Fool i' the Forest* began to come in. Typically they perceived Aldington as working in Eliot's shadow; the *New York Times*, for example, commending the book, says that Aldington's 'phantasmagoria unmistakeably suffers when placed in comparison with "The Waste Land"', while he is 'an able secondary figure' lacking Eliot's 'concentrated poetic force or ... beautifully condensed ironic power'.[26] Paul Rosenfeld, then at the height of his influence in New York, saw this secondary role of Aldington's differently, perceiving him as an intermediary between the experimentalists and the traditionalists.[27] If Aldington found reviewers' condescensions irksome, he responded by uttering some of his own. In a long article-cum-letter dated 19 May 1925 he wrote to *This Quarter* about Pound in terms of mixed compliment and deprecation, terms which suggest that in England at least Pound and his work were passé.[28] Although Aldington does not deal with the specifics of Pound's work, the letter is worth reading in full as it contains some sharp insights which, in effect, predict Pound's future and at the same time reveal much about Aldington:

> To appreciate the work and personality of Pound needs a certain amount of intelligence and discrimination. He invites misapprehension, from his extreme sensitiveness (wrongly sup-

posed to be conceit) and from a wilful disregard of certain obvious conventionalities. He takes immense pains with his poetry and writes prose with preposterous carelessness. He has none of the arts of persuasion and invariably begins his prose blandishments by insulting his readers and wounding their self-conceit—unpardonable error! Somebody said of Villiers that he had genius but no talent which is almost true of Pound. At any rate, he has the poorest literary strategy I ever met with; some may think that a trait entirely to his honour. But the result is that both his personality and work are misunderstood (especially in England, where it is hopeless to try to get people to take him seriously) and a man of great parts has been more or less driven into the wilderness.

Pound's character is a strange mixture of sweetness and tartness, generosity and unfairness, enlightenment and prejudice, profundity and flippancy. His impatience of restraint and the necessary donkey-work of literature does him grave injustice. His critical flair is remarkable, certainly the most remarkable I have ever met; no man has more unerringly picked out the unrecognised genius of his age and few have worked more generously towards getting that genius recognised. He has wide knowledge, with strange gaps of ignorance, especially when he leaves the one subject he really knows—i.e. poetry. Possibly his credulity in matters of occultism and economics, for example, is due to a complete lack of the philosophical training so conspicuous in T. S. Eliot. Pound's polemics resemble the noisy discharge of a blunderbuss, which harms the firer more than the quarry; . . . Personally, I shall always be grateful to Pound (and I hope always ready to acknowledge it) for the charm and stimulus of his personality and talk in the years 1911–12. Since then we have gone different ways and for me at least much of the old magic has gone; but Pound's kindness to me was great and generous in many ways.

Late in June, Monro stayed at Padworth. Both men were in a relaxed mood. Aldington, obviously seeing him as an ally, wrote after Monro's return to London to celebrate country life, fit subject for poetry rather than the ponderings of 'Bertie Russell and Eddington and Einstein and Rivers and the Waste Land and all their desolating train'.[29] Whatever he may have supposed about Pound's reputation declining, by now the rise of Eliot's stock was inescapable.

Yet when Pound was planning the enlarged 1926 edition of *Personae* he consulted Aldington, who responded that he was 'very much flattered' that his opinion should be valued, and followed this with a long paragraph eulogising most of Pound's earlier poetry. In this letter of 5 October 1925, he took the opportunity to complain about Eliot:

> I don't know what he is doing with his quarterlies and to tell you the truth I have not even looked at the last two books he sent for review. When one is a professional whore of letters it is not much fun to whore far under the skeduled [sic] price and be treated as if it were a favour! However, I think he means well.

8 Malthouse Cottage: Eliot, 1919–27

By 1925, then, Aldington was prepared to use hard words about Eliot. Yet in the early 1920s the two men were friends and intellectual allies. To explore their relationship, we must briefly move back a little in time. Before their friendship, in 1917 Eliot had praised Aldington's prose poems in what was otherwise an all-out attack on *vers libre*.[1] In the same year Eliot briefly echoed this praise in his well-known essay, 'Ezra Pound, His Metric and Poetry'.[2] For his part, Aldington within months of demobilisation in 1919 several times felt the impulse to convey to Eliot an admiration of his critical essays. He did write in July and praised Eliot as 'the only modern writer of prose criticism in English'; but there was another side: 'I feel compelled to add that I dislike your poetry very much; it is over intellectual and afraid of those essential emotions which make poetry'.[3]

Because of his grounding in contemporary French writing, Aldington was aware of Eliot's French models and did not fully concur in the impression of Eliot's originality as a poet which grew up during the 1920s. His common ground with Eliot, as with Pound, was a wide-ranging interest in European literature and a perception that contemporary writing needed to be rooted in the great literatures of the past, a project which could be aided by a new criticism and sensitive translation.

As mentioned briefly above, it was through Aldington that Eliot came to write for the *Times Literary Supplement*. In *Life for Life's Sake*, Aldington dates this 'about 1922', but the evidence fixes it in 1919. In a letter written from 15 Noon Street[4] and dated simply 'Tues. 23rd', he tells Eliot that Bruce Richmond, editor of the *Times Literary Supplement* 'has a great admiration for your critical prose and, I think, would be willing to publish a leading article by you . . . he would offer you that chance of writing a leader on the new edition of Ben Jonson. Would you undertake it, and if so could you be at the Times office (Queen Victoria Street entrance) at 11:30 a.m. on Monday next so that I could introduce you?'[5] Eliot's article on Jonson appeared in the *Times Literary Supplement* on 13 November 1919.

As to Eliot's poetry, it is easy to demonstrate that Aldington's immediate unease about it was not merely a generalised negative reaction to the unfamiliar. On 11 June 1920 he wrote from Hermitage:

> I know it is exceedingly brilliant and thoughtful; I see it as miles above most contemporary stuff; I recognize an irony which is 'vraiment supérieur'. But, I do feel sometimes, that you, like Ezra, have sacrificed something to this exquisite surface. And you do mix metaphors! What does a 'gesture' which 'rises' 'in steam' really mean? It doesn't hit my senses. Again in 'Rhapsody on a Winter [sic] Night'—what is a 'lunar synthesis'? how do 'whispering lunar incantations' 'dissolve' 'the floors'? Why *'fatalistic* drum'?? And then the 'dead geranium'—'drum' rhyme![6]

With Imagism had arisen questions about the nature of verse forms. In England, the controversy narrowed down to the status of prose-poetry, and 'the prose-poetry controversy was the most visible effect of Imagism'.[7] After first declaring that *'Vers libre* does not exist', in 1917[8] Eliot went on to select the prose-poem as a target, on the grounds that 'poetry is written in verse and prose is written in prose'.[9] He singles out Aldington, 'a poet who has done interesting work in what is unfairly called *vers libre*' as making prose-poems which are an unsatisfactory hybrid of the two media.

Through Harold Monro, Aldington pursued a plan to issue a *Chapbook* on 'poetry in prose', at first intended as a fourfold exchange, Eliot and Manning *contra*, himself and Aldous Huxley in favour. In the event, Huxley did not participate. Eliot's piece establishes the context, claiming the distinction between prose and verse as technical, demonstrating by example that mere intensity cannot be the criterion for the prose-poem, showing that some sustained prose masterpieces have greater intensity than some briefer classic poems. What Eliot sees are two categories of writing classified according to technical characteristics, and he feels that any merging of the two simply leads to confusion. (At this time in the United States, William Carlos Williams, who came to see himself as Eliot's arch-rival, was deliberately experimenting with such *con*fusion). Manning, with much reference to Aristotle, objects to the received attitude that in some sense prose is more nearly 'raw material' than poetry. The thrust of Aldington's response is that 'human ideas, sentiments, perceptions, emotions, feelings, are not arranged in two separate categories labelled "prose" and "poetry", but are interfused and interdependent'.[10] Neither side of the argument is particularly incisive or conclusive. Interesting as it is in showing the contrasting views of Aldington and Eliot, the chapbook is, as Monro felt, dull.

Eliot spent an occasional weekend at Malthouse Cottage in the early 1920s. Aldington liked hiking in the Kennet valley region, rejoicing in the unexpected encounters with history. Both Lawrence and Eliot joined such excursions, Eliot once accompanying Aldington on a 15-mile trek to Sherbourne St John. Eliot seemed knowledgeable about wild birds, but was responsive most to the place's history. Lawrence, as might be expected, showed his gift for an intensely vivid awareness of nature.

In March 1921 *Poetry* carried Aldington's review of *The Sacred Wood*, which praises Eliot in terms echoed by other critics, singling out 'Tradition and the Individual Talent'. He is particularly impressed by Eliot's sense of a continuing, and continuously modified, order. Lowell reacted with reservations about Eliot, but Aldington declared him the most attractive critic produced by America. 'He has that charm and vigour of the early Ezra, plus a soundness, a coolness, and urbanity, Ezra could never have.'[11] In a letter to Eliot several months earlier, Aldington spoke of 'a book which I believe spans a new period of vitality in English culture, *The Sacred Wood* is probably as important to this generation as Arnold's *Essays in Criticism* [were] to his . . .'[12]

Aldington was also asked to review *The Sacred Wood* for *To-Day*. Typically, he attempted to get assignments from the journal for both Manning and Eliot. 'I am supporting Eliot for all I am worth', he told Holbrook Jackson, and in his review he praises Eliot's 'exquisite mind, originality and disinterestedness'.[13] Eliot came to Malthouse Cottage in September, after the conclusion of a long-awaited visit from his mother, his brother Henry and sister Charlotte. In a bad state of nerves, he did not share Aldington's high opinion of *The Sacred Wood*, which was receiving mixed reviews, and which Eliot thought 'a very imperfect production'.[14] He confided in Aldington plans for launching the *Criterion* and asked him to correspond often as 'it is a great pleasure to me'.[15] By late September he was feeling so ill that Vivien Eliot arranged for him to see a specialist, who told him he must go away for three months' rest quite alone, must follow a strict regimen and must in no way exert his mind. Generously, his employers at the bank had agreed to pay his salary, so he had reasons to refuse writing assignments. 'I really feel very shaky', he told Aldington, 'and seem to have gone down rapidly since my family left.'[16]

A week or so later he wrote that he would be leaving for Margate the next day, would remain there a month and then travel abroad to Lady Rothermere's cottage at La Tourbie, Provence. Hoping Vivien could join him at some stage, he asked if Aldington could look after their small cat, 'a very good mouser'.[17] On the advice of Ottoline Morrell and Julian Huxley he changed plans and travelled instead to Lausanne, offering Aldington six weeks use of his London flat in his absence.

Meanwhile, Aldington had asked Jackson to send copies of his review of *The Sacred Wood* to various people, including Amy Lowell, Bruce Richmond and Scofield Thayer of the *Dial*. He hinted mysteriously that he had 'a plot' to get Eliot more time for writing.[18] But soon he was obliged to reveal news of Eliot's breakdown and consequent inability to contribute to *To-Day*. 'I know you will sympathize with this misfortune', he told Jackson, 'and understand how I feel about so dear a friend'.[19] Two days later, on 7 October, he informed Jackson that a specialist had diagnosed Eliot as suffering from 'an effusion of lymph at the base of the brain', a malady, Aldington noted, which had been fatal to the renowned 18th-century classical scholar, Richard Porson.

Eliot kept in touch with him by postcard. Aldington, as he told Lowell, continued to admire Eliot's exact learning combined with originality of mind. Eliot is 'the one dear friend I have made since my return' (from the war).[20] He felt that he could get enough commissions from editors to rescue Eliot from his labours at Lloyd's Bank. In an undated letter, Eliot wrote to thank Aldington for a cheque, which he says he will keep to use in an emergency. Eliot is effusive about their friendship. Giving his Cliftonville address, he notes: 'I have not betrayed it to anyone but yourself and the bank, so do not expose it to any person'. Urging him to write, Eliot signs himself, 'ton bien dévoué.[21]

An exchange of views with Aldington is the origin of one of Eliot's most celebrated essays, 'Ulysses, Order and Myth'.[22] Aldington's 'The Influence of Mr James Joyce' appeared in the *English Review* in April 1921. According to Margaret Anderson, Pound thought it hilarious.[23] Joyce considered any mention of his

...ok an advantage,[24] but when seeking reviewers in 1922, he told Harriet Shaw Weaver, 'I don't think Mr Aldington ought to be asked to write a second article'.[25]

In fairness to Aldington, it must be noted that he wrote to Eliot on 14 September 1920:

> The Joyce article is mighty far from perfect. I wrote it on an impulse, with no preliminary thought, without rereading or consulting a line of Joyce; it took exactly and hour and a half to put down and I have not altered it at all. It was written first for the *Dial* as an expression of my annoyance with a lot of American imitations of Joyce. Therefore it is plain to me that the article is fallible at many points. But it does express my thesis which is:
> 1. James Joyce is a great writer but
> 2. his 'Philosophy' is too ascetic and gloomy (for my taste)
> 3. his prose is by no means flawless
> 4. the influence of his 'philosophy' will be deplorable because we shall get shoals of Rodkers and worse
> 5. the influence of his prose will be deplorable, because incoherence will pose as genius
> 6. a classic style—sobriety, precision, concision—is and must be the most beautiful thing in literature and all deviations from it are retrogression.

Certainly, 'The Influence of Mr James Joyce' reads somewhat strangely today, in the light of Joyce's settled fame. *Dubliners* is seen as a mere offshoot of French Naturalism; *Portrait of the Artist* (which Aldington nonetheless greatly admired) is 'sordid'; what he had seen of *Ulysses* is 'a tremendous libel on humanity', harsh and sneering. At the very time Joyce was explaining to Valery Larbaud the Odyssean scheme of *Ulysses*, Aldington wrote that 'Mr Joyce, with his great undisciplined talent is more dangerous than a ship-load of Dadaistes'. Several years earlier he had observed to H.D. that Joyce, like 'all of us', lacked a guiding principle, and damagingly believed in nothing except himself.[26] Such comments may seem funny from the viewpoint of 'Mr Pound, champion of *Ulysses*', but they lead on to questions which manifest Aldington's ultimate conservatism: 'Joyce's influence, which I dare to prophesy will be considerable, cannot be a wholly good one. He is disgusting with a reason; others will be disgusting without reason. He is obscure and justifies his obscurity; but how many others will write mere confusion and think it sublime? How many dire absurdities will be brought forth with *Ulysses* as midwife?'

As Kittredge has pointed out, Aldington urged Eliot to respond to the article, perhaps even at the same time as its English publication,[27] and admitted that his own piece had been hurriedly written. Eliot's reply, outlining the 'mythical method' of Joyce's prose, did not appear for a couple of years. In the May 1921 number of *Poetry*, Aldington reinforced the statement of his general views, in 'The Poet and Modern Life'. He deplores the drift to materialism in our age of 'mental anarchy', and the current English poets' having 'thrown violently aside the reflective, the intellectual aspects of their art to create something which is essentially only vital'.[28]

His involvement with Eliot continued throughout 1922. On 7 January the *Outlook* carried 'The Poetry of T. S. Eliot', where he discusses Eliot's literary antecedents, French and English metaphysical poets, and defends him against charges of obscurity, insisting that Eliot's poetic theory and practice are unified.[29] Some of these points he makes in a letter to Sturge Moore a few days later,[30] where he suggests the older man should meet Eliot and contrasts Eliot's 'reasonable and charming' demeanour with Pound's 'hysteria' and the 'infernally emotional' Middleton Murry. He does suggest that Eliot's problem is over-control for fear of his emotions.

In February Aldington and Pound became concerned that Eliot was on the verge of another collapse. By mid-March Pound, in Paris, had developed a plan, which Natalie Barney dubbed 'Bel Esprit', to seek 30 donors among working artists and patrons, each to pledge ten pounds a year, 'for life or for as long as Eliot needs it'. Pound made clear that he and Aldington were the initial donors of ten pounds, and each had made the required pledge. Already in Pound's mind the scheme had broadened so that after Eliot it might be applied to others, and he sent Kate Buss a copy of the circular printed at Quinn's request for 'Bel Esprit' by John Rodker, in which Pound, Aldington, and Sinclair are mentioned by name and described as 'the initial life members of Bel Esprit'.

In an undated letter, Pound suggests that arrangements for fund-raising should be two-pronged, with himself responsible for the Americans, Aldington for the English. In correspondence with Pound following the First World War Aldington is for some years business like and to the point, discussion being confined mostly to literary matters. Pound appears to grow more proprietorial, more than once addresses Aldington as 'Dear Infant' and eventually declares: 'You and H.D. both stopped progress about the time you ceased to desire perfection', presumably under the tutelage of Uncle Ez. 'You began to back up each other's egoism and consider me as a gaga old adlepate [sic], and to cease to desire castigation.'[31] Clinching the charge, he notes: 'neither Yeats nor Tummus [Eliot] have ever been so high of stomach'.

Undoubtedly, the Bel Esprit scheme was Pound's, and he quickly succeeded in raising subscriptions. Already by 5 April 1922 Wyndham Lewis had applied to him for support, but Pound fended him off. In May he suggested that Aldington and Sinclair should be trustees for the scheme on Eliot's behalf. Eliot, invited to Padworth, could not come, but sent an effusive message of friendship: 'You do not know how valuable your encouragement has always been to me'.[32] Aldington many years later told Lawrence Durrell that when he got into the Bel Esprit with Pound he thought the scheme was being initiated with Eliot's knowledge and consent, only to discover otherwise.[33]

Eliot quickly became uneasy about Bel Esprit. On 30 June he wrote to Aldington that he appreciated the motives behind it and was not 'above' such a scheme, but that it was proving tiresome and embarrassing. Pound's proposed implementation was 'rather bordering on the precarious and slightly undignified charity'. Nonetheless the scheme was continued, with Pound generating publicity and with its proponents at some cross-purposes. Aldington attempted to persuade Lowell to overcome a dislike and distrust of Eliot and to contribute and even become the organiser of the American arm, but she discovered Pound had made the same suggestion to Harriet Monroe.

The English arm of the scheme, centred in an account at Aldington's branch of Lloyd's Bank, 67 Kingsway, went ahead with Aldington, Lady Ottoline Morrell and Virginia Woolf as signatories. It continued throughout the year with Virginia Woolf playing an ever more central role. On 19 October she wrote to Aldington to say that Eliot would not leave the bank without an absolute guarantee of £500 a year, with a deposited capital sum or securities to back it. By making such a suggestion, Eliot may have been looking for a way out of the situation altogether. Morrell and Woolf both felt his conditions could not be met and proposed a fund merely to augment Eliot's income. Eliot was reaping insults, too, from the scheme. One donor sent sixpence, another four penny postage stamps, and on 16 November the *Liverpool Daily Post* carried some libellous comments.

At the end of the year, on 19 December, Woolf proposed Eliot be sent a cheque, but, she said, he would only accept it if there were not strings attached and would refuse any funds from writers in circumstances like his own. Eventually, the scheme bogged down, but Eliot wrote to Aldington that he appreciated the work he had done towards the fund and would continue to value his friendship.

Efforts to float the Bel Esprit scheme on Eliot's behalf continued into early 1925, at which time Eliot was offered, and refused, editorship of the *Nation*. He left the bank in September that year, with the support of Lady Rothermere, to write and edit the *Criterion*. In the meantime, collaboration with Virginia Woolf afforded Aldington a social opening he did not take. In mid-November 1924 she wrote, 'I hope you'll come one day to see us, not on business, which is dreary enough'. Apparently he did come, but 'on business', for her diary for 21 December 1924 records:

> We have also seen Aldington, who calls like a tradesman for orders; a bluff, powerful, rather greasy-eyed, nice downright man, who will make his way in the world, which I don't much like people to do. All young men do it. No young women; or in women it is trounced; in men forgiven.[34]

Perhaps he was impressed by Woolf's fame, or intimidated by her manner. Perhaps she was simply insensitive to a certain delicacy on his part. A parallel may be seen in his handling of Eliot. Recollecting it, Arabella told Selwyn Kittredge: 'they got along very easily indeed, although Aldington was always a little formal with him. Eliot is the sort of person one *is* a bit formal with'.[35]

In the thick of his Bel Esprit efforts Aldington continued uneasy about Eliot's influence as a poet. Yet his article 'The Poet and His Age'[36] in the September 1922 *Chapbook* is much influenced by Eliot's 'Tradition and the Individual Talent', though Aldington uses the occasion to suggest that the new poetic 'lacks ordonnance', and that its products do not give pleasure, as poetry ought to do.

Eliot asked him to organise the foreign section of the *Criterion*, which began publication in October 1922. Read felt that Aldington (and Wyndham Lewis) held off participation at first, but by April 1923 when Aldington wrote to congratulate Read on his Eliot-influenced essay, 'The Nature of Metaphysical Poetry'[37] he himself had been drawn in, supplying what amount to jottings on current French periodicals. He appears actually to have edited the July number of the *Criterion*, as Eliot was again in difficulty, due largely to his wife's health, but also to the strain of working at Lloyd's. This number contains in the notes separate statements on 'The Function of a Literary Review', one by Eliot, the other by Aldington. Shortly before the number appeared Aldington told Harold Monro that he was urging Eliot to use little poetry, to present virtually a journal of criticism. There was, he said, a 'huge wad' of Pound's poetry to hand, of which he could make nothing. The 'huge wad' proved to be the Malatesta Cantos. He censored them because Pound characterised Pope Pius II as a 'swelling s.o.b.', which, offensive to Roman Catholics, might also have run afoul of British libel laws. 'I cut it out; whereupon Ezra promptly transferred the epithet to me by mail'.[38]

After initial coyness Aldington quickly became deeply involved in the *Criterion*. When the first instalment of 'Foreign Reviews' appeared in April 1923 he provided the French section; Eliot had earlier told him that he respected his French translations more than anyone's. As a possible explanation of Aldington's delayed involvement, in the summer of 1922 there had been some misunderstanding between the two, perhaps over the name of the journal, which, Aldington pointed out, was that of a London theatre, but which Eliot retained possibly because it had been suggested by Vivien. Now, in a pre-Whitsun letter to Flint, Aldington notes: 'I fear I have offended T. S. Eliot with one of my untimely (yet timeless) jests. He went to the country for a short holiday, so I wrote and asked him if he was cultivating his waste land. Ominous silence!' Eliot may have read more into this remark than was intended, interpreting it as a slur on very private aspects of his life, either with Vivien or his sex life in general.[39]

Aldington, in any event, saw the July 1923 number of the *Criterion* through the press. An article in it was a direct cause of tension between Eliot and himself. This was his 'Et in Arcadia Ego', on pastoral in the Italian Renaissance. Eliot found it too mild, apparently said so and was surprised at Aldington's strong reaction. When he suggested he should take it elsewhere Eliot demurred, but the incident caused some cooling of friendship and the task of French reviewer quite soon went to Frank Flint.

After Aldington and Arabella took a holiday in Beenham, Devonshire, in July, a time he used to try some verse experimentation, in writing unrhymed odes, they returned to find that he had to assume more responsibility for the *Criterion*. Because of Vivien's ill-health Eliot had been forced to relinquish most of the routine work towards editing the October number. Both editors contibuted 'Notes' and, Aldington provided comments on French periodicals, but he felt others associated with the project were treating him as the hack who would undertake all routine chores. What seemed a graceful way out occurred when, early in November, he and Arabella left for Rome. On New Year's Day he wrote from Hal Glover's apartment there declaring to Harold Monro his happiness at having severed himself from the *Criterion*—'to hell with coteries and to hell with snobbery!'

This severance lasted about 18 months, but in the middle of it Aldington's *Literary Essays and Reviews* brought him back to the subject of Eliot, in 'The Poetry of T. S. Eliot', in generally positive terms. By April 1925 there was some measure of reconciliation with the *Criterion* 'coterie', as is evident from the inclusion in the April number of 'François Villon', a long essay in which Aldington obviously relishes the paradoxical mixture of brutality and tenderness, ribaldry and grace, characteristic of the French poet. In the same number, in a review stitched together almost entirely from summary and quotations, Humbert Wolfe treats Aldington's *A Fool i' the Forest* as a 'slice of life', ending in 'undiluted, broken bitterness', a farouche conclusion to a piece which plunders the poem somehow without managing to do it justice.[40] A month later, his 'Ever aff.' friend Eliot was writing to him asking for a softening down of his review of Cocteau's *Poésie 1916–1923*, which would appear in the *Criterion* in July, and Aldington and Herbert Read were exchanging letters bolstering each other through the hazards and stresses of the literary life. 'Eliot has funked his responsibilities to us since 1921', he complained in a letter of 19 June 1925, '. . . in the first flush of enthusiasm for the *Waste Land*, he could have had us all organized . . . Do you blame me for going into the wilderness once more?' What he expected Eliot to do is not clear, and he appears to overlook the existence of the *Criterion* as evidence of Eliot's 'responsibilities'.

As he had done for Eliot and Flint earlier, Aldington now approached Bruce Richmond to enlist Read for the *TLS*. His friendship with Read had begun in 1917 and at this point continued smoothly. A strong bond was that each had served as a military officer on the Western front. Through the 1920s, Aldington was the more established literary figure, though the two were close in age, and he praised and encouraged Read both as critic and poet. Read was also a friend of Eliot's, but now Aldington did not hesitate to tell him: 'I think Eliot ought to have introduced you to Richmond long ago. One thing in Pound's favour—he was never afraid to shove forward a new man. T.S.E. hasn't the energy (or the disinterestedness?) to do it. He is much too afraid of compromising his reputation'.[41] Read was to replace John Middleton Murry on the *Times Literary Supplement*. Aldington's pertinacious coaching helped Read make a good impression on Richmond, and he was hired.[42] (A year later, on 4 August 1926, Aldington declared himself 'proud' of having assisted in getting some of Read's essays published in the *Times Literary Supplement*).

In July 1925 Read took a long week-end in Padworth. Aldington's increasingly negative feelings about Eliot, of which Read was aware, had not yet publicly surfaced, and Eliot told Read at the end of July that he wished he, too, could have come to Padworth, and that he eagerly anticipated some three-way conversations among them that autumn. On 31 July he wrote to Aldington that he looked forward 'hungrily' to seeing him. Eliot asked him to do a small book on Gourmont, one Epicurean writer on another. He enquired when he would be in London, but Aldington seemed intent on staying away. Clearly in his own mind he had no wish to become an Eliot disciple, a contingency against which he warned Read.

The *Criterion* was taken over by Faber and Gwyer and Eliot, who had become a director of the firm, began to develop plans for a series of monographs on foreign men of letters. For this series Aldington was asked to write on Gourmont and Read on Bergson, though Read soon found himself in a predicament involving his two friends.

Aldington's *Voltaire* was published this year by Routledge in their 'Republic of Letters Series', planned in 1923 and under the general editorship of W. K. Rose. Aldington, recruited to help Rose with the series, had asked both Eliot and Read to contribute, though both had declined.[43] Eliot's new proposal cut across Routledge's existing scheme and, often seeking Aldington's advice, Routledge's proposed combining the two. Aldington became upset because Eliot was backed by people who had earlier shown no interest. Aldington's claim to Read that he had warmly supported Eliot both publicly and privately is just, when one considers his published comments on Eliot's work up to this time, his support of him personally in the pre-Lausanne period, his introduction of Eliot to Bruce Richmond and, not least, his efforts towards the Eliot Fellowship Fund or the Bel Esprit. So his statement to Read on 2 October 1925: 'But I have lost faith in him and I feel suspicious—I mean I do most vehemently suspect him of condescension to us all . . . ', is a sad moment. He was certainly prickly, but on the other hand condescension was an admitted weakness of Eliot's. He had shown Eliot considerable generosity and, for the time being, continued to do so.

Late in November, when negotiations between Routledges and Fabers were still going on, he had heard that Alec Randall was to leave England for diplomatic service in Rome. Randall was a tried translator and Aldington told him, 'Routledge are appointing me editor of a series of 18th century translations and joint editor of the Republic of Letters'. He gave the same information to Professor Glenn Hughes, when Hughes spoke of the possibility of Aldington's obtaining a post at the University of Washington.[44] The Routledge appointment, he told Hughes, would establish him as 'the accepted English authority on French literature', an area in which he had worked enormously hard for six years. As if to reinforce the claim, he delivered to the publishers in November his version of *The Fifteen Joys of Marriage, Ascribed to Antoine De La Sale* with his customarily substantial background introduction. This was the fifth volume he had completed for the series since 1923, a three-year period in which he had published no less than 12 separate titles.

To Read, he expressed irritation that Eliot expected him at a moment's notice to drop other work to review for the *Criterion* and, in any case, offered him low rates. In negotiations over the two series he was obliged to mask his real feelings. In fact, he was in a genuine dilemma. A joint editorship between Eliot and Rose meant he would be cut out as a possible co-editor, whereas Eliot's refusing such a proposal would mean that the Routledge series remained limited in scope, with a single editor, which would rob Aldington of the opportunity to supply a number of monographs. Partly in his own interest, therefore, he persuaded Stallybrass of Routledge's to co-operate with Faber and Gwyer. Once Eliot's editorship was an accomplished fact, Aldington was distraught enough to write two confidential letters to Read, on 9 and 13 December, expressing the urge to withdraw from working for Routledge's in either the Republic of Letters Series or the Broadway Translations for which he had only recently been asked to translate 18th-century French novels. Obviously he was hurt, especially as the change occurred at the very moment he was about to assume joint editorship with Rose. 'This affair', he confided in Read on 13 December, 'is the biggest setback I have had since the war and loses me the fruit of years of work.' Cock-a-hoop over the whole matter and unaware of the agonising Aldington had been forced to, Eliot wrote that the new situation 'will require a bottle of fizz'. And what must have struck Aldington with savage irony, 'Whatever happens, you have my sincere and respectful gratitude'.

Read saw how much Aldington had lost, through 'blind force of circumstances', but believed these carried the benefit of affording a very strong link with Eliot. Perhaps remembering Aldington's complaint that Eliot had not provided a lead when it might have been expected, Read, while complimenting him on his skill and initiative in linking Eliot's 'brains' to a big commercial undertaking, concluded: 'I personally think the essential thing is to recognize Eliot's leadership'.[45]

Aldington, in the event, continued to work for Routledge, commissioned to obtain manuscripts for both the Broadway Translations and the Republic of Letters Series. Read, ready to write his study of Diderot, was greatly relieved at the Routledge-Faber settlement and hoped it meant a clearing of the air between Eliot and Aldington, so that the three could have friendly foregatherings. Given the circumstances, Aldington seems to have dealt magnanimously with Eliot and was indeed having greater difficulties with Flint, who asked for a better contract, because Jack Squire had remarked that 'Flint is a Harley Street specialist in French translation'.[46] Read, to whom Aldington passed on this remark, was his main confidante of the time, the two feeling close because of similar war experience. Aldington was moved and impressed by Read's war book *In Retreat* while Read found *Voltaire* 'masterly', especially its compression of Voltaire's work and ideas. In April Read and his wife stayed at Malthouse Cottage. Eliot again said he wished he could join them, but hoped in any case that he, Read and Aldington could get together for a week-end later in the year.

So matters went between Aldington and Eliot. A promising relationship, at moments even close, but with potential for misunderstandings, with Eliot growing in worldly assurance and Aldington retreating into his shell, though there is some evidence in the mid-1920s that he continued excursions up to London and may even have had a studio there, and that he renewed links with Brigit Patmore, a potential contributor to the Broadway Translation Series. Then the August 1927 *Criterion* carried an item which caused another difference between Aldington and Eliot, John Cournos's contribution on 'Russian periodicals',[47] though, in fact, Cournos had contributed the item, which appeared over his initials on several previous occasions. Cournos had offended Aldington by his *roman-à-clef*, *Miranda Masters*, which dealt with the Aldington marriage and was critical of H.D. Although then and later Cournos saw the marriage and its breakdown more from his point of view than H.D.'s, Aldington nonetheless took the attitude that he and Cournos could not appear in the same publication. As Eliot told Read, confronted with a choice between the two, he would have preferred to keep Aldington; but editorial impartiality came first. Eliot felt that if Aldington's view of life had been more normal, Cournos's participation would not have mattered to him:

> ... I have urged him [Aldington] to come to London for six months. His position is not in the least unique, and anyway nobody is in the least interested except his private friends who know that Richard would like to have children and can[']t. I hope when you get the opportunity you will induce him to this step. He would find that all the people whom he wanted to see would receive him and Dorothy. My own social circle has been considerably restricted in the last year or two, but I would guarantee him the Woolfs and Morrells, and the Fabers (who are highly respectable) if he liked.
> I feel in general that this respectability obsession has spoilt his work: has ruined his verse, and has made him run to these tedious adacemic [sic] scholarly essays and editing. But (except for the children part of it) it is all a delusion; and, apart from that (and I really don[']t know how much that counts with him) there are plenty of people suffering from much more *real* torments than his own.[48]

Read, the recipient of all these confidences, tended to agree and came to believe that Aldington was powerfully jealous of Eliot's literary reputation, but for the time being his own relations with Aldington remained unaffected.

Despite the sour tone of his letters to Read,[49] culminating in the remark on 30 August that Aldington 'is full of false pride', Eliot continued to feel that it would be good for Aldington to emerge from his Malthouse retreat. In October Eliot passed on a suggestion from J. B. Trend, *Criterion* music critic, that Aldington might like to give a course of lectures on English literature (to be given in French or Spanish) at the University of Madrid.[50] He reiterated that it was a common complaint among their friends that Aldington did not come to London more often. The two did actually meet in late October 1927 at a London party which both found silly. Meantime, Eliot was the subject, as Aldington told Read on 7 October, of 'the most difficult review I have ever had to write'. The *Nation* had set him the 'nasty problem' of reviewing the Tudor Translation Series edition of Seneca's *Tenne Tragedies*. He considered the plays 'appalling bilge' and wondered why the editor, Whibley, thought an expensive edition worth while. Privately he was greatly disappointed with Eliot's introduction and felt it had been 'uneasily executed', but 'Mr Eliot on Seneca', which appeared on 29 October, is a careful consideration of Eliot's scholarship and critical method.[51] Unaware that in private Eliot had, with some redundancy, alluded to Aldington's 'tedious academic scholarly essays', he by chance took some measure of revenge in speaking of the 'laboriousness' of Eliot's writing about Seneca, and of the 'scholastic' nature of the project. More sweetly, he says of Eliot, 'He is one of the few literary critics who take the trouble to find out what the scholars have to say on their subjects'. He manages to judge Eliot's piece on Seneca 'a disappointment', his theme 'arid', and yet to sound respectful of Eliot. His review damns the whole enterprise, but with considerable tact.

Aldington concludes a letter to Eliot the next day, 'God bless you, dear Tom, I would do anything for you'. Eliot himself thought well enough of 'Seneca in Elizabethan Translation' to include it in his *Selected Essays*.[52] In writing to Read, the question of 'disloyalty' to Aldington crossed Eliot's mind. This, and his confident assumption that he knew Aldington's problems to be partially based on the inability to father a child, suggest a considerable closeness between the two men. Such a degree of intimacy accounts for Aldington's effusiveness, but the volatility of his actions in general suggests that he was suffering through a period of temperamental instability.

When Eliot wrote in mid-November, Aldington was still part of the *Criterion* set. The September number carried his favourable review of Helen Waddell's *The Wandering Scholars*. The number which had sported the offending Cournos carried William King's review of Aldington's *Candide*, credited as a 'thoroughly competent' piece of work, with a 'quite excellent' introduction. Eliot now urged Aldington to come to London again soon and, possibly taking up a conversation they had had at the October party, said he wanted them to discuss theories of 'impersonality' in writing. Eliot's views on the topic are extremely well known, and they obviously differed from Aldington's whose personality is present to a fault in so much of his work.

Just before Christmas he wrote to Eliot on the question of Faber and Gwyer's publishing the British edition of his translations of Gourmont. 'Now my dear old friend', he wrote on 17 December, 'we know each other well enough for you to tell me quite bluntly that you don't want the books. All I ask is a quick decision.' These books, *Letters to the Amazon* and *Remy de Gourmont: Selections from all this Work* were published in London by Chatto and Windus in 1931 and 1932 respectively.

9 Malthouse Cottage: The Late 1920s, 1926–28

Shortly after Read's stay in April 1926, Aldington received a telegram from *The Times* asking his help during the General Strike, which began on 3 May. Stuffing underwear and a book into his army pack, he hitch-hiked to London where he assisted in loading bundles of newspapers into private cars for circulation, and in wrapping individual copies. When each night's work finished he walked along the Embankment to breakfast at the Authors Club in Whitehall. Immediately after the events he wrote to the American art patron, Crosby Gaige, unequivocally expressing support for the employers, admiring the comportment of the police, the army and the volunteer workers, and also Stanley Baldwin's 'great leadership'.[1] The remarks about Baldwin may well have been tongue-in-cheek and the whole statement pitched to what he imagined Gaige wanted to hear. A different perspective is given in *Life for Life's Sake*: 'I suppose I ought really to have been on the other side, for I had no particular liking for Mr. Baldwin and his friends or what they represented. On the other hand, a dictatorship of wooden-headed trade union leaders seemed no great happiness. . .'[2] As to the latter, Aldington wrote to Read on 9 June: 'The T[rades] U[nion] C[ongress]'s little attempt to emulate Moscow hit me. Which is why I turned out with every intention of hitting them if necessary'. How was he hit? He explained to Read that 'a general strike cuts off all sources of income for a one man business'.

The equivocation implied here is expressed in his romantic novel *All Men Are Enemies* (1933) in the long section of Part III, which deals with the hero Anthony Clarendon's involvement in the strike. Clarendon, in the whole context of the novel, is torn between bourgeois respectability and the romantic demands of an individual love relationship. Through contact with friends, he is provided opportunities to consider political questions, such as the validity of socialist utopianism or Marxism/Communism. Fundamentally, however, Clarendon is a bourgeois individualist. Yet, as he is about to leave for London to work against the strike, he thinks 'Another bloody war, and on the wrong side'.[3] When he hears that the Navy is to be used to bring supplies from the Continent, he considers this unfair, because the Navy 'belongs to the unions as much as it does them' (that is, the government).[4] As he leaves the London train: 'he noticed enthusiastic passengers shaking hands with the driver and stoker—a couple of hoary old blacklegs . . .'[5] When Clarendon encounters an old friend among a group of militant strikers, he helps him escape the police. Such an incident is typical of Aldington, and carries the symbolic force of vaunting individual relationship over group concerns. Again, when Clarendon's wife rings him up at the end of the strike, to exult, 'the Trade Unions are smashed!' Clarendon replies, 'Are they? I sincerely hope not'.[6] Part of Aldington's complexity, always, was a tendency to see both sides of a question, another part was to distrust any covenants beyond the personal and individual, so he was frequently in the state of mind which says 'a plague on both your houses'. In the present instance, he provides Clarendon with a rationalisation which may well have been his own, that he 'turned out to help maintain essential services in a crisis, not to fight the employers' battle for them'.[7] Looking back from a cool perspective of 15 years, Aldington could indulge in a touch of ironic humour:

> I suppose my real motive was dislike of inactivity in a crisis, and as I couldn't get on with my own job the best thing to do was to take on somebody else's. Actually I had a variety of jobs, which included standing by, consuming sandwiches and beer at 2 a.m., loading large bundles of *The Times* onto private cars for distribution, protecting the said cars from possible attack on their departure, and wrapping up individual copies to be mailed to subscribers. I sent Mr. Lloyd George his copy, and Mr. Leon Trotsky his, and then a crowd of diplomats, ending up with British Consuls exiled in Manchurian towns I had never heard of. By the time that job was finished it was generally about 6 a.m., and I had a nice morning walk along the Embankment to my club, where I invariably quarrelled at breakfast with a philoprogenitive parson who believed in the duty of man to beget as many legitimate children as nature permitted. Obviously another Labourite.[8]

Meantime, a further volume of his essays, *French Studies and Reviews*[9] appeared to few but respectful notices. It manifests his sense, shared with Eliot and Pound, that the bearers of culture are a handful of 'honnêtes gens' (see his piece on St Evremond, and elsewhere). In contrast to his strike-breaking activities, he was translating mediaeval French and Italian poets for *Fifty Romance Lyric Poems* (published by Crosby Gaige in 1928.) Arabella worked at Hugo's Italian course while he pored over books on Tuscany and Umbria, for a trip to Italy. Working hard, 'living with almost fiendish parsimony' to afford the trip, he was glad to report to Glenn Hughes that *Voltaire* had sold nearly 2000 copies in England and about half that in the United States. But the constant toil of writing undermined him and by early August his ebullience had disappeared and he told Read he was 'damned ill', by which he meant that overwork had fatigued him to the verge of collapse.

They had been invited to stay with the Lawrences at Villa Mirenda, Scandicci, near Florence, but to Aldington's surprise he saw the Lawrences well before that projected visit. He received a note from Lawrence, who was in London, and invited Frieda and he to Padworth. A parcel of his recent books preceded him and Aldington read them and felt he had underestimated Lawrence, who, he now found, had a great deal to say to him though the visit began, 'inauspiciously'. This was because Lawrence found Malthouse Cottage 'sinister'. 'I can't imagine why', Aldington said 'as it was sunny and full of books, with bright curtains and a smiling head of Voltaire over the piano; and the garden was brilliant with late summer flowers.' He felt the true cause was the spartan fare he was able to provide, which Lawrence took as a failure of hospitality. Yet Lawrence was not unfamiliar with frugal living, but this may simply be a case of Aldington's defensiveness. Earlier in the year the two men had exchanged invitations, though when Lawrence wrote in April he did not know when he would be in England. 'Sounds nice, your little cottage .... Don't talk nonsense to me about primitive conditions, do you imagine I've suddenly turned up my nose at the brass tacks of life?'[10] Whatever the case, Lawrence was mollified by provision of a bottle of whisky for his bedtime hot toddy. This sojourn at Padworth was part of his last visit to what he called the 'hopeless attraction' of his native land, sun-starved and with over a million unemployed. He was ill and 'horribly depressed', facts which, with the benefit of hindsight, might have seemed the explanation for his responses.

The visit as a whole went off very well. Aldington arranged to have books sent from the London Library, so that Lawrence could read towards writing on the Etruscans.[11] In the afternoons the two couples wandered in the summer fields and in the evenings they sang French and German songs together. Something had gone wrong with England, they agreed, so that they felt like aliens in their own home. Lawrence advised Aldington to get out and stay out. Aldington admired Lawrence's conversational gifts, his great prowess in mimicry and vivid evocations of the Tuscan pinewoods, olive groves and vineyards. The visit awakened in Aldington a resolve to write strongly from his own feelings, without abandoning ambition to become deeply versed in European culture. It also fed in him a growing desire to be quit of England.

Lawrence's whole stance towards life, as focused in the conversations of this visit, helped to concentrate Aldington's 'vague rebellious tendencies', to make him see (of his journalistic essays and reviews) that 'all this literary stuff was trivial drudgery'. Lawrence was poor but free he thought, 'whereas I had one leg chained to a library and the other to the London literary press':

> The upshot of this was that I wrote a pamphlet about Lawrence and some of his books, in which I abandoned the hocus-pocus of 'objective' criticism and the dessicated style it imposes, and wrote entirely from my own feelings.

When, the following year, he published *D. H. Lawrence: An Indiscretion* he thought it 'my first real bit of prose'.[12] The 'pamphlet' (or, as it became, chapbook) places Lawrence as one of the great English heretics, but, as its subject was quick to see, 'It's more about you, my dear Richard, than about me'.[13] It was, indeed, Aldington's declaration of independence, but as he was swamped with writing commissions he did not perceive at once how he could liberate himself.

Lawrence left England for the last time in late September, to return to Florence and the Villa Scandicci. Aldington and Arabella arrived soon afterwards. Lawrence was comparatively fresh and relaxed, between books. As Aldington records in *Portrait of a Genius, But....*,[14] he made notes of one afternoon of the visit, warm and golden, the chestnuts falling and the peasant children fetching the two men bunches of grapes as they sat in the deck chairs beside the villa. Lawrence rewarded the children with chocolate or sugar, brought from indoors, excusing his extravagance on the grounds that they needed sugar for their health's sake. This portrait is in contrast to that of Comrade-Editor Bobbe (that is, ...ence) in *Death of a Hero*:

> Mr. Bobbe was a sandy-haired, narrow-chested little man with spiteful blue eyes and a malevolent class-hatred. He exercised his malevolence with comparative impunity by trading upon his working-class origin and his indigestion, of which he had been dying for twenty years. Nobody of decent breeding could hit Mr. Bobbe as he deserved, because his looks were a perpetual reminder of his disease, and his behaviour and habits gave continual evidence of his origin. He was the Thersites of the day, or rather that would have been the only excuse for him. Intellectually he was Rousseau's sedulous and somewhat lousy ape. His conversation rasped. His vanity and class-consciousness made him yearn for affairs with upper-class women, although he was obviously a homosexual type. Admirable energy, a swift and sometimes remarkable intuition into character, a good memory and excellent faculty of imitation, a sharp tongue and brutal frankness, gave him power. He was a little snipe, but a dangerous one. Although biased and sometimes absurd, his weekly political articles were by far the best of the day. He might have been a real influence in the rapidly growing Socialist Party if he could have controlled his excessive malevolence, curbed his hankering for aristocratic alcoves, and dismissed his fatuous theories of the Unconscious, which were a singular mixture of misapprehended theosophy and ill-digested Freud.[15]

Back in England, Aldington told Read he had found Lawrence cantankerous, self-centred, and 'hideously narrow-minded', but added, 'he is someone'.[16] These two portrayals say as much about the split in Aldington as they do about Lawrence, but this split turns to a positive value in the weighing-up of Lawrence which he made to write *Portrait of a Genius, But* . . . .

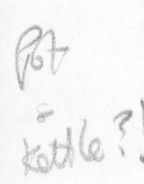

Once back at Malthouse Cottage, he had to produce more 'wolf-scarers' (that is, articles and reviews), though in November he received a very welcome $100 from Crosby Gaige in payment for editions of his works (Gaige collected privately-printed books by favourite known authors). He arranged to meet Gaige in London in December (though he first had to travel north to lecture on Gourmont to the Newcastle Literary Society), where Gaige arranged for him to edit *Fifty Romance Lyric Poems* which was designed by the great typographer Bruce Rogers and became Aldington's favourite object among his own books.

Late in 1926 he went to Rye to help his mother sort out finances. Before leaving for Rye he attended one of the Frith Street gatherings, met Eliot and argued epistomology, Eliot declaring that it does not matter whether there is any objective reality or not, Aldington claiming that to the artist it matters a great deal. Writing to Read about it later, he contrasted Mallarmé and the Symbolistes with the implicit acceptance of objective reality in Balzac. His own position was not in doubt.[17]

At the end of January 1927 he delivered his Gourmont lecture to the 'Heretics' at Cambridge. He was also taking some interest in the *Criterion* and Pound's new Paris periodical, the *Exile*, supplying 'Natal Verses' for its first number.[18] Meantime he had received a copy of the protest against Samuel Roth's American pirating of *Ulysses* and on 10 March wrote suggesting that Joyce might be able to take action through Margaret Anderson, as the *Little Review* presumably had copyright over those portions of *Ulysses* published in its pages. Joyce was evasive about his offer to have a version of *Ulysses* published by Routledge in London. Thanking Aldington for signing the protest, he said that an action had been started against Roth on 23 March. He also asked for the return of a *dossier* on the English Players which he had sent him years earlier. As Joyce complained several months later to Harriet Weaver, Aldington, who had lost it, made no reply.

The typescript of *Fifty Romance Lyric Poems* was despatched to New York at the end of March. By the time Joyce wrote, Aldington and Arabella were in Paris, where they hoped to remain for several months. They settled into a small, grubby apartment near the Luxembourg. After two weeks complete break, Aldington re-established his pattern of morning work, enjoyed the café life, was ecstatic about the elegance and magnificence of Versailles and delighted in seeing the plays of Molière, Marivaux, Beaumarchais and others at the Odéon, where a good seat in the 'second gallery' cost the equivalent of 15 American cents. Such self-indulgences were made possible by a cheque for $250 from Pascal Covici, who had recently published the trade edition of *The Love of Myrrhine and Konallis*.

From Paris on 5 May Aldington wrote somewhat querulously to Gaige that he had heard nothing about *Fifty Romance Lyric Poems*. Nor had he heard from George Doran, of Doubleday, Doran and

Co., whom Gaige had seen as potential publishers for him. A letter from Gaige arrived next day and, at the same moment, Doran arrived on the 'S. S. Berengaria'. When writer and publisher met, it quickly became evident that Doran knew nothing of Aldington's work or reputation and he offered poor terms. Aldington was offended, though Doran claimed that on Gaige's recommendation he was prepared to undertake a 'Collected Edition'. But the two men must simply have clashed in personality and, with some show of acerbity, Doran withdrew. Aldington's effort to establish himself with a major American publisher had turned out to be 'a frost'. His querulousness with Gaige, and presumably Doran, was due in part to his tendency to lapse into habits of overwork, which in turn led to depression. A letter from Lawrence cannot have helped much either. Thanking him for a copy of *D. H. Lawrence; An Indiscretion*, Lawrence says:

> No need to be in any trepidation on my account—you hand me out plenty of bouquets, as you say: I shall save up the ribbons. But *caro*, you are so funny. Why do you write on the one hand as if you were my grandmother—about sixty years older than me, and forced rather to apologize for the *enfant terrible* in the family? Why will you be so old and responsible? *Sei un giovanotto piu crudo, sai!*—And on the other hand, why do you write as if you were on hot bricks? Is the game worth the candle, or isn't it? Make up your mind. I mean the whole game of life and literature—not merely my worthy self. You don't believe it's worth it, anyhow. Well then, don't worry any more, be good and commercial. But don't, don't feel yourself one of the pillars of society. My dear chap, *where* did you get all this conscience of yours? You haven't got it really. *Et iteratum est ab omnibus: ubi est ille Ricardus?* I never knew a man who seemed more to be living from a character not his own, than you. What *is* it that you are afraid of?—ultimately?—is it death? or pain? or just fear of the negative infinite of all things? What ails thee, lad?'[19]

Apart from this passage, Lawrence is friendly and informative, but such penetration into his peculiar *angst* and obviously divided personality must have been hard for Aldington to bear at that moment, a time when, as we have seen, he was also at loggerheads with Eliot.

Why on this occasion did Lawrence flourish his stiletto? After all, in the course of what is ultimately a eulogy, Aldington values him as 'a great character. And a great Englishman'. He attributes to Lawrence: 'A remarkable intuitive insight into character, a subtle sense of complicated human relations, an exquisite sense of beauty, a sense of the mystery of things, a power of using countries and landscapes and animals to interpret the human mind and its moods and tragedies ... ', but also a lingering provincialism and a condescension towards women (and yet a 'rather fanciful intuition' into them). He contrasts Lawrence to the kind of writer 'who lives and thinks and writes in invisible inverted commas'. Far beyond 'remarkable intuitive insight', Lawrence's uncanny plumbing of the depths of people's psyches has often been noted. Perhaps behind his letter, especially the remark concerning conscience ('You haven't got it, really') Lawrence had encountered evidence of Aldington's sexual restlessness. In such matters, in his own way he was at least as likely as Eliot to take offence and make judgements. But ultimately the most penetrating thrust is what amounts to an accusation of 'false consciousness', what amounts to throwing Aldington's 'invisible inverted commas' back in his face. Both men were individualists in a world where individualism is more and more under siege from every direction. The question is, and Lawrence appears to have seen it, what does Aldington's individualism amount to?

Aldington felt the Lawrence chapbook was too frank for British publishers, and now his work turned towards less controversial matter. Glenn Hughes had commissioned for his University of Washington series a similar chapbook on Gourmont and Aldington obtained from the French publisher exclusive rights to issue a two-volume anthology of Gourmont's works translated into English, to be published in New York by Covici. Aldington soon found himself entangled in another bout of heavy work, producing a thousand words a day, with Arabella typing.

Spending much of the year in Paris, he continued translation work and in 1927 Routledge published four of his titles including two selections of Voltaire's letters, Voltaire's *Candide*, and the letters of Madame de Sévigné. With winter's coming, he began to spend more time in London than he had for nearly a decade. He was irritated by the widespread assumption that this betokened his recovery of his senses and nerve. Perhaps influenced by the suggestions of several friends, but also because of deep changes in his personal life which had yet to be revealed, his ties with

Malthouse Cottage were loosening. He might have settled in London, among familiars, but quite soon opted to return to Paris. He wished to rent Gourmont's old apartment in the Rue des Saints Pères, an idea perhaps prompted by Eliot's opinion that his Gourmont chapbook was the best thing in English on its subject and might well be a Hogarth Press item.[20] Aldington, in any case, was working on his larger Gourmont project.

His idea of renting Gourmont's apartment 'permanently' as a Paris base suggests that his financial situation had greatly improved and consequently he intended to live a somewhat different life, especially as he was beginning to find regular *TLS* reviewing irksome. Once he and Arabella crossed to Paris in late March 1928, he quickly felt released to turn back to poetry, and applied his customary working intensity to it. His 'idling in Paris' this spring included writing up to four hours a day, although his later claim that he was working on *A Dream in the Luxembourg* is problematical, because of the subject-matter, a somewhat sentimental treatment of a love affair. He was certainly, as he told Henry Slonimsky, translating Julien Benda's *La Trahison des Clercs*, and had begun work on Gourmont's letters to Natalie Barney (*Lettres à l'Amazone*).

Throughout this period he was in touch with Pound, who had just received the 1927 *Dial* Award, accompanied by Eliot's favourable review of the enlarged edition of *Personae*. Aldington's review, less fulsome, had appeared in the *TLS* of 5 January. Although he praised Pound's craftmanship, the 'reworking' of Propertius and the imitation of Waller's 'Go Lovely Rose', Pound felt his admiration too qualified; but Aldington responded that at least his review would help revive British interest in Pound's work. Through him, Pound's rendering of *Ta Hio or the Great Learning* appeared in Hughes's University of Washington chapbook series in 1928. Pound nonetheless felt tetchy enough to ask of the Gourmont chapbook, 'Why the hell in talking about Remy can't you pick out his POSITIVE value?' Pound, 'yr prore ole farver', allowed that Aldington's *Voltaire* was 'better than might have been expected'. 'Do try', urges Pound, in his undated letter in response to the *Personae* review, 'to practice the mental activity labled [sic] by the late Remy "dissociation" ',[21] by which he appears to mean 'objectivity'.

Where Eliot had urged him out of Padworth, Pound had trumpeted, 'GET OFF THE GOD DAMN'D ISLAND for at least six months', thus adding his voice to those urging, 'Away then: it is time to go'. Pound, like others, seems to have felt that Aldington's bucolic life led to damaging introversion, but Aldington was not completely self-involved. He continued to concern himself about Frank Flint, for example. More than once Pound saw fit to remind him that Flint had more money and security than either of them and that, in any case, in Pound's opinion, Flint's work was relatively dull, indistinguishable from what could be done by 30 or 40 other writers, that he was unknown in the USA, that he fell between scholarly snobbism and the 'modern moderns', and so on.

Pound reacted to the Covici *Rémy de Gourmont* more magnanimously than to the chapbook. On 5 August he sent a postcard: 'Gourmont, best job you have done. Congrats. E.' A week later: 'I don't see how you cd. have got more into 2 vols. or made it more generally representative'.

Gourmont is presented in the chapbook as one whose writing is partly defensive, who had experienced the boredom of over-introspection, and who had difficulty in choosing which of his several literary gifts to develop. To locate Gourmont's relation to a writer such as Flaubert, Aldington hit upon the term 'journeyman', which irritated Pound, who might have used it for, say, Flint. Obviously, if Aldington meant Gourmont was no more than a workaday craftsman he would not have remained so long devoted to his ideas. While admitting that Gourmont left no single masterpiece, in his Introduction to *Rémy de Gourmont* he presents a different picture, of Gourmont's 'greatness' and 'complexity', his superb intellectual curiosity. Borrowing Eliot's phrase, he agrees that Gourmont is 'the critical conscience of a generation', though he finally judges the Frenchman's work 'a series of brilliant parts which only just cohere'.

In mid-1928 Aldington and Arabella returned to England, remaining in London for the first week of July, when he met Wyndham Lewis, attempting to arrange for him a meeting with Bruce Richmond with a view to obtaining *TLS* assignments. Lewis, in fact, had no wish to undertake full-time reviewing, but suggested to Aldington some unspecified collaboration between them. The two men exchanged books, *A Fool i' the Forest* for *The Childermass*. On Aldington's recommendation, Lewis obtained a copy of Eugene Jolas's *transition*, but found it 'full of offensive material, it is indeed a reservoir of foul doctrine'. Lewis, like Pound, was bursting with vehement certainties, whereas Aldington (as the recommendation of Jolas's magazine shows) is torn between his innate conservatism and a desire to keep up with current trends.

Glenn and Babette Hughes were expected in Europe on a Guggenheim Fellowship. Meantime Aldington and Pound wrote to each other at length, prompted by Hughes's projected book on the Imagists, and on 7 August Aldington suggested that the founding Imagists could perhaps 'agree on an official version of the origins of Imagism'. In a long and lively reply[22] Pound provides his own account of the evolvement of Imagism. 'At least nobody ever made a "movement" out of less matter', he notes, 'i.e. five poems by you, five by H.D. and one by Bill Williams'.

Under cover of his habitual sending and receiving of book parcels, Aldington was helping to distribute in England copies of Lawrence's *Lady Chatterley's Lover*. Though he later expressed reservations, he had written to tell Lawrence that he got 'a great kick out of it'.[23] Frieda responded that such praise had come at the right moment, part of a small chorus, while people generally seemed horrified by the book. Lawrence, wretchedly ill, felt he was losing friends over it.

Unexpected events now prevented Aldington from carrying on this subversion and from being at Malthouse Cottage to greet the Hugheses on their arrival from the United States. For some months Alec Randall had been seriously ill with typhoid in Italy. Now he was convalescing at a hotel in Vallombrosa. Feeling she should return to England and fetch their children and anxious about leaving her husband alone, Amy Randall telegraphed Aldington, who set out immediately. 'It was a characteristic generous response', Randall remembered, 'and I know I am not . . . the only friend of his who has received such kindness. He was the ideal companion for a convalescent, so thoughtful and adaptable, so gay and cheerful'.[24] Aldington was translating the *Decameron* and they made a pastime of discussing the work's vocabulary.

Meanwhile the Hugheses had been left to their own devices in England, with Malthouse Cottage and the housekeeper Mrs Stacey, with introductions to Eliot, Flint and Brigit Patmore at their disposal. On 31 August Aldington wrote to them outlining plans for the next several months. He would be in Italy for September and then travel north. 'Paulhan, editor of the *Nouvelle Revue Française*, had offered to lend us his house on Port-Cros (an island off the south coast of France, near Hyères) for the autumn months. We shall probably go straight there from Rome, and we want you to come and join us, picnic and bathe etc. Mrs Patmore will be with us, and probably the Lawrences .... Try to meet us on the island in October.'[25]

He had been growing restless, with both his personal and literary lives. Dorothy Yorke claimed that in the late 1920s he became promiscuous, frequently fell in love, began to drink heavily, and underwent a personality change.[26] ('It seems to me that after several years of strenuous work I was entitled to take a little ease at mine inn.')[27] Aldington, in his 1928 chapter of *Life for Life's Sake* says, on the other hand, 'it seemed to me that I had completely recovered from the effects of temporary heroism at the front and that retirement was no longer indicated as the proper treatment'.[28] In recollection, after a dozen years, he saw himself as having abandoned England in an exuberant frame of mind. He is reported, however, to have staged an exit scene in sombre mood.

In one version, the performance was set in the Comercio Restaurant, Soho, though Richard Church gives two different and confusing eyewitness accounts of it, neither of which firmly establishes a date.[29] The occasion was one of the Frith Street dinners which Aldington had largely been avoiding. Besides Church, the group included Eliot, Read, Flint and J. B. Trend. Aldington came in after the others had concluded the modest meal of cheap Chianti and oxtail. In Church's eyes he was a Byronic figure, towering and defiant. The company's general reaction to his appearance was embarrassment and curiosity. Some, Church thought in retrospect, were aware of events leading up to this moment. Church noticed that Read's expression became opaque, Eliot's quizzical. Aldington said: '"I'm on my way to Paris" . . . "I've done with this country." He waited for protests, but none came. We were all silent, and I saw Eliot slowly nod his head, several times, by way of reluctant understanding'. Flint, relaxed with wine, made several good-natured efforts to persuade Aldington to join the group sociability. Instead, he departed 'magisterially', though 'chased by some fury or demon in his character'.[30]

Much later, talking to Kittredge in 1965, John Cournos provided a similar account but with different details. He places the incident at a pub near the Victoria and Albert Museum, a haunt of the *Criterion* contributors. Cournos recollected that Aldington came in suddenly and declared: 'I have sold my library; I am leaving England forever'. 'A few days later . . . he sent Eliot a card on which was written a single four-letter word'.[31] Behind this last action may have been

Eliot's response of distaste on reading Aldington's *A Dream of the Luxembourg*, which Eliot found vulgarly intimate and indelicately personal.

Wherever the exit scene occurred, if it took place prior to Aldington's leaving for Paris in 1928 then obviously he had made up his mind long before the journey to Port-Cros to change his mode of life. The trip to Rome in Randall's aid was either a pretext or was too unpremeditated to be preceded by such a scene, unless the scene itself came from a sudden strong impulse. Wherever and whenever it happened, the real farewell was to Eliot and Eliot's influence. Church's perception of Eliot's 'reluctant understanding' was intuitively right.

10 Port-Cros and After, 1928–29

Lawrence told the Huxleys that Frieda and he might start for Port-Cros around 1 October. Aldington on his way there first drove south to Naples to meet Brigit Patmore. From early 1926 on, he was in touch with her. At that time, her marriage to Deighton Patmore collapsed and she may have been in financial difficulties. Aldington obtained a commission for her to translate a volume in Routledge's series of translations of 18th-century French novels, for which she was to receive £65. He claimed later that he 'did not see her until 1928',[1] but when he set out for Port-Cros in the autumn of that year he was at least half in love with her.

From Naples he sent Pound an ardent enigmatic postcard: 'Dear, dear Ezra, I was happy indeed to see you and you . . . gave me back life'.[2] From Rome in September he had written Pound twice, and the two met to discuss Hughes's projected book on the Imagists. Pound became confidante for the convolutions of Aldington's emotional life. One of these was involvement with Nancy Cunard, whom Aldington met 'after a party at Ezra Pound's apartment'.[3] Cunard's Hours Press quickly printed a pamphlet of his 'Christmas' poem *Hark the Herald*. He asked Gaige's permission for Nancy to publish a limited edition of 'The Eaten Heart', from a manuscript Gaige had in hand. Focused in the troubadour lore Pound had used in Canto IV, *The Eaten Heart* proposes that human isolation may be overcome by intense passion, which should be lived out, even to death. Thematically, this anticipates Aldington's romantic novel, *All Men are Enemies* (that is, of lovers). To a point, it 'anticipates' his own life.

Fearful that Port-Cros might prove a 'fraud', he was in the event delighted with it, as he recollects in *Life for Life's Sake*. Covered with pines and 'marvellous aromatic plants', the island had a semi-tropical feel—eucalyptus trees, palms and pampas grass. There were no roads, only rough paths, and Paulhan's *vigie* (a small, moated hilltop fort with inward-facing windows) was an hour's walk from any human contact. Communication with the mainland was by donkey and motor-boat.

Lawrence waited at Le Lavandou, near Hyères, for Frieda to

arrive, which she did on 12 October, bringing 'a raging Italian cold', caught in dalliance en route and promptly passed on to Lawrence. The Lawrences still had not taken the boat to Port-Cros when Aldington bragged to Randall on 13 October: 'Here we jape and jest and giggle and talk bawdy and commit adultery from dawn to dusk and dusk to midnight'.[4] Meanwhile, the Lawrences awaited a calm sea to enable them to cross to the island. Once he had made the crossing, Lawrence at first thought Port-Cros 'fun', and found Aldington, Arabella and Brigit all 'nice', but, Aldington recollected, 'it sounds ungracious to say so but we had a better and more harmonious time before [the Lawrences] arrived'.[5]

Aware of Lawrence's illness, he heard him cough at night, but noticed that he gradually improved. Lawrence's indisposition put a crimp in their bathing parties, however, as someone had to remain with him each day. Worse still, he received by mail reviews of *Lady Chatterley's Lover*, which Aldington thought an 'enormous wodge' of vulgarity, spite, filth and hatred. He admired Lawrence's tranquil way of continuing to write but Lawrence's concentration was proof against more than merely bad reviews. Brigit Patmore describes how she rushed into his bedroom, to find him sitting in bed wearing the homburg hat he used to protect his head from draughts. Excitedly, she told him there were not one but *three* rainbows in the valley. With a weary smile, he soothed her like a child and went on with his work.

Aldington, too, worked, translating Boccaccio and writing poems, but also on a much larger project. Several times in the past he had attempted to begin a war novel. Now, thanks largely to funds provided by Covici and Gaige, he had leisure, and he was overcoming earlier self-doubts. He knew how he wished to proceed, to combine the method of Greek tragedy with techniques of satire. 'The plot was to be revealed in the first pages', he wrote later, 'so that if anybody read on it would not be for the trivial purpose of finding out what happened, but because they were interested in what I had to say and the way I said it.'[6] He had in mind a novel of ideas, which he had attempted to work on in 1919 and again in 1925 and 1927 though his habit of humming old war songs while writing suggests that the feeling of his material was equally important. Held up, unsure how to open the first paragraph, he finally got it; then the book's whole first phase (Prologue and Part I) came irresistibly, with a mysterious sense of someone's dictating it:

The moment I had that sentence down, the whole book began to flow with irresistible force; and I had nothing to do but write it down each morning until I felt tired. I wrote the prologue and part one in ten days, and then stopped dead. The mysterious sense of somebody dictating vanished, and I was prudent enough not to force the pace.[7]

Lawrence disliked it, declared it would ruin Aldington's reputation, and that 'he'd go mad if he went on with it'.[8] On the other hand, the women at Port-Cros were in favour, Frieda especially (Aldington says in *Life for Life's Sake*). And, presumably, Brigit Patmore, who praises the novel in her memoirs, but says nothing of how she felt about its author when it was being written in those island-bound days.

What, in any case, was she doing at Port-Cros? As Aldington told Hughes, she was part of the social-intellectual life of London before 1914 and an intimate of the small group of Imagists. Until the mid-1920s she was a close friend of H.D.'s A couple of years before Port-Cros, Aldington obtained for her a commission to translate the Memoirs of Marmontel. When they met at a studio party in 1926, Brigit noticed Aldington had become 'more handsome with the years. He was tall, broad shouldered and so healthy that he looked exultant and his blue eyes were full of light'.[9] After that meeting they kept in touch. In some sense, they were in touch earlier as is revealed by two 1924 letters from H.D. to Brigit. On 18 February, she wrote from Territet:

Now about Richard. Don't let yourself get worried or involved. It is only a matter of separation. I never drempt of divourse [sic]. It would be impossible, I believe. It is simply a legal procedure, I had supposed. Mutual consent. If R. is against it, that is the end. It could more or less, I imagine be forced on him, but I am not, have never been out, to be unpleasant. He can have his A.[rabella] and all the rest of it. What I can never get over is the fact that even now SHOULD I care for any one or want a little freedom, HE can come down on me. Perhaps just a PHOBIA. I don't know. If he were really a 'gentleman' I would not think twice about it. But we know in certain ways, he is totally unreliable. I think, still think, he is a little cracked. Anyhow that seems most charitable. His note to you savoured of Ford. What hypocracy [sic] and humbug. He would I suppose, try that on me. 'I always wanted to be your friend' and so on.

More ebulliently, she wrote on 29 November 1924: 'What a joke your seeing R[ichard]. Yes, it would have been funny if you had spoken. I am still rampantly curious to know what he is up to'.

In *My Friends When Young* Brigit Patmore gives the impression her love affair with Aldington began after Port-Cros. Without naming names he confided in Pound that he had a new love affair, though he contrived to give the impression its object was Nancy Cunard. According to Miriam Benkovitz,[10] at Port-Cros he slept wearing neck beads which had been worn by Nancy. There are signs in his letters of this period that he was in some fashion emotionally involved with Cunard, but there is no doubt at all that the Port-Cros episode ended with his establishing a serious bond with Brigit Patmore. In conversation with Selwyn Kittredge in September 1965, John Cournos claimed that 'when Bridget [sic] arrived at Port-Cros, Arabella invited her to join Richard and herself in bed. This arrangement continued throughout most of their stay . . . . in addition to this *ménage à trois*, Arabella was having an affair with a Sicilian servant at the *vigie*'.[11]

Lawrence, becoming aware of the shifting sexual loyalties at the *vigie*, did not like it. Although quite ill, he suggested he, Frieda and Brigit should leave. Irritated by stormy weather and torrential rain, he wrote to his friends the Brewsters that he did not care for islands, especially small ones. After first planning to remain at Port-Cros into December, he now hoped to be on the mainland by mid-November. In contrast, an elated Aldington would happily have abandoned his plan to leave at Christmas, and would have remained all winter. He later claimed Lawrence openly sided with Arabella 'in a series of demented scenes from some southern Wuthering Heights'.[12] Writing from Port-Cros to congratulate Aldous Huxley on *Point Counter Point*, Lawrence shows his feelings about the situation at length, but without revealing the specific context:

> . . . *caro*, however are we going to live through the days? Preparing till another murder, suicide, and rape? But it becomes of a phantasmal boredom and produces ultimately inertia, inertia, inertia and final atrophy of the feelings. Till, I suppose, comes a final super-war, and murder, suicide, rape sweeps away

the vast bulk of mankind. It is as you say—intellectual appreciation does not amount to so much, it's what you thrill to. And if murder, suicide, rape is what you thrill to, and nothing else, then it's your destiny—you can't change it *mentally*. You live by what you thrill to, and there's the end of it. Still for all that it's a *perverse* courage which makes the man accept the slow suicide of inertia and sterility: the perverseness of a perverse child.—It's amazing how men are like that. Richard Aldington is exactly the same inside, murder, suicide, rape—with a desire to *be* raped very strong—same thing really—just like you—only he doesn't face it, and gilds his perverseness. It makes me feel ill, I've had more hemorrhage here and been in bed this week. *Sporca miseria.* If I don't find some solid spot to climb out of, in this bog, I'm done. I can't stand murder, suicide, rape—especially rape: and especially being raped. Why do men only thrill to a woman who'll rape them?[13]

By 18 November Lawrence was at Bandol. Aldington accompanied him and the two parted for the last time in the salon of the Hotel Sélect opposite Toulon station. On leaving, Lawrence exhorted cryptically, 'Possess your soul in patience'.[14] A month later Aldington wrote to Brigit: 'I shall never forgive Lorenzo certain things, never, never. I cannot forgive anyone who is rude to you. Also he tried to humiliate each one of us in the eyes of the other'. In January, Lawrence, not wanting Brigit Patmore to distribute copies of *Lady Chatterley's Lover*, told his friend Koteliansky, 'I don't know if she's very stable'.[15]

What exactly happened in the second half of November is not clear, but it appears Aldington, Arabella and Brigit each headed for Paris separately. In late November Aldington told Hughes he intended to give up Malthouse Cottage because 'We are going to be so much on the continent'; he adds that Arabella 'will be down before long to tell you all about it'.[16] Early in December he wrote to Gaige and Hughes that he and Arabella had separated. To the Hugheses he qualifies it, 'at least for a time'.

December occasioned a passionate outpouring of letters to Brigit, who had returned to London and family responsibilities. Evidently Aldington was sexually aroused to a greater degree than ever before. At his new quarters, in the Paris Hotel Sélect, Nancy Cunard had thoughtfully paid a week's rent in advance. Arabella, meantime, wrote apologetically, feeling 'she has been lacking in "dignity" (Lorenzo!)'. But this was to no avail and, obviously 'madly' in love with Brigit, Aldington with seeming frankness told her of his Paris routine, which included an 'understanding' friendship with Nancy Cunard, who took him to her friend Henry Crowder's 'most amusing nigger cabaret'.

Such interludes and dalliances did not prevent Aldington from working at his Boccaccio translation and resuming the novel, of which he had written 30 000 words at Port-Cros. (To Brigit he confessed, 'I'm a bit surprised that it's so bad'.) Meeting *TLS* assignments still, he produced short pieces on Diderot and Gérard de Nerval.

Brigit had difficulties to deal with. Besides two sons and a sick husband, she had on hand the tail-end of a moribund love affair, with a lover both tenacious and threatening. Obsessed with her now, Aldington hoped they could be together permanently, but he was practical enough to see that it was best for the present to plan times when she could come to him. Expecting her on 30 December, he booked a room at the Sélect and a table for an evening at Crowder's cabaret, the Plantation.

Largely through Cunard, his Paris connections developed quickly. How closely he became involved with her is not clear, partly because he used her for a time as smokescreen for his affair with Brigit, rejoicing that he had persuaded Pound, for example, that Nancy was 'the one'. Cunard used to claim that when they first met, in Rome, Aldington attempted to 'pounce' on her sexually.[17] Several of his letters to Brigit play evasively with the suggestion that he was involved with 'someone' else; but Nancy, in any case, had Crowder plus a strong emotional grip on her devotee, Louis Aragon. Eventually, Aldington revealed to Nancy his relationship with Brigit. Characteristically she was strongly supportive.

Aldington met many expatriate Americans in Paris, including Hemingway, at Sylvia Beach's bookstore. Aragon, bringing from Nancy proofs of *Hark the Herald*, introduced him to William Bird of Three Mountains Press. Bird later took him to the Café du Dôme, where they met Bryher's husband, Robert McAlmon. McAlmon told him both Bryher and H.D. wanted divorces, and that Bryher hated him. Because of his passion for Brigit, the idea of divorce meant more to Aldington than it might have earlier, but he decided to do nothing until he and Brigit had talked it over. She, after all, was in a far worse marital tangle than he. As to McAlmon, at each meeting Aldington was repelled by the American's coarseness and pose of brutality. But McAlmon was a link with H.D., whose situation in Switzerland he portrayed as miserable, while Bryher held over her the image of a hulking and dangerous Aldington. Ironically, Brigit in England had to contend with a threatening lover whom she found it nearly impossible to shake off. Aldington confided this and the full intensity of his feeling for Brigit in a long letter to Pound on 27 December. 'D [that is, Arabella] threatened and tried suicide at Port-Cros,' he says, with seeming callousness, 'but I held out'. Of the love affair with Brigit, 'it has only been intense for almost three months now, but it has overwhelmed us both'. In more down-to-earth vein, he ends: 'O I forgot, have found our train times and tickets for Rapallo ... Will stop at Aix and Genoa on the way'.

His approval of Pound contrasted with his continuing disgust with a Pecksniffian Eliot. Pound's review of *Rémy de Gourmont*, in the January *Dial* praised the 'lucidity' of Aldington's work. Pound located for Aldington and Brigit a small hotel at the east corner of the bay in Rapallo. The Yeatses, who arrived late in 1928, had a flat on the other side of the bay. Sometimes Aldington and Brigit had morning coffee with the Pounds at the hotel and sometimes the four went to an afternoon tea-dance at a small local hall. Pound astonished them by dancing peculiar steps to his own rhythm, though Mrs Yeats assured them he could dance quite well in the accepted way if he wished. Brigit delighted in what Aldington called the Yeatses' 'Irish humbug'. From his window he would watch Yeats on the beach, once noting a look of 'amazement' on his face on picking up a dried bone and peering at it. Shortly afterwards the Yeatses invited them to tea and Yeats chanted a new poem with the refrain, 'Sang a bone upon the shore'. Aldington observed that whatever Yeats's poems said, Yeats on the beach, except for once watching a dog-fight, was oblivious even to the enticing glances of young ladies.

Both Aldington and Brigit later gave accounts of when they invited the Yeatses to dine. Yeats arrived wearing socks to keep his hands warm and during dinner, according to Aldington, attempted to swallow a lock of his own hair with the spaghetti. Suddenly he asked: 'How do you account for Ezra?' He explained that he thought Pound one of the finest contemporary poets, but often found his behaviour tactless, even outrageous. Further, Yeats objected to the number of slim volumes Ezra plied him with, by young 'shell-shocked Walt Whitmans'. Brigit, who observed the moment with a nice sense of irony, appropriately caps Yeats's comments: 'George [Mrs. Yeats] had acquired the habit of bending her head over her plate and, with her eyes fixed on some ice pudding, she said in a low voice, "Willy talking poppy-cock?"'[18] Aldington thought Yeats in general was having 'a bad fit of Spenglerism'.

Aldington worked at poems and his novel. Gaige was finding him outlets in the United States, but Pound also took a hand. He sent off some Aldington poems to the *Dial* and *Poetry*, causing embarrassment by duplicating Gaige's efforts. 'Aldington seems to have awakened from his slumber', Pound told Harriet Monroe, perhaps feeling he had regained a disciple.

Returning to Paris, Aldington met Covici's partner Donald Friede, who took to London with him the completed portion of *Death of a Hero* and within days cabled approval and encouragement. It was the impetus Aldington's daimon needed and he resumed work at furious speed. For two months the pages 'galloped off the typewriter'. He worked all day for 51 days, finishing the last pages in an uninterrupted eight-hour sitting. On 11 May 1929 with the help of the young American poet Walter Lowenfels, he bundled up the manuscript and sent it to London.

Through Friede's enthusiasm for *Death of a Hero* Aldington made one of the warmest friendships of his life. Friede asked him to offer the book first to Chatto & Windus. Chatto's editor Charles Prentice read it, liked it and, through meetings in Paris, Venice and London, Prentice and Aldington became firm friends. Of the three men portrayed later in Aldington's memoir *Pinorman*, Prentice receives the most benevolent treatment by far, much as Aldington delighted in the idiosyncrasies of Pino Orioli: 'We have given up praising people for being good or virtuous men, but if I were asked to name a really "good" man I have known I should at once say "Charles". He became for me a kind of human touchstone'.[19] He never abated in friendship for Prentice even when their business interests diverged, and warmed to him despite recognising from the outset that among writers Prentice's greatest admiration was for Norman Douglas. What Aldington and Prentice shared was that both were epicureans, believers in the 'good life', and both were devoted to Greek studies (Prentice had taken honours in classics at Oxford).

Aldington's personal relationships took another turn in March, when he resumed correspondence with H.D. after a decade's silence. Arabella had suspected throughout the Malthouse Cottage years that he was still emotionally attached to H.D. and in letters to

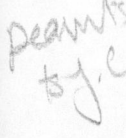

Cournos in the early 1920s H.D. shows awareness of this. She intimated that she, too, felt an emotional bond, but feared that continuing intimacy with Aldington would endanger her psychologically. In the early years of their separation, the two found ways of keeping track of each other's lives.[20] In 1924 H.D. told Brigit, then a close friend, that Aldington had threatened legal action against her for registering her daughter in his name. Now she told Aldington that for years she had feared reprisals, that he would harm her. To this, he professed complete surprise. Partly through Pound's agency (though he insisted that Pound, who tended to 'stage manage', not be present) he and H.D. met in Paris in April. She even went ballroom dancing with him.

As Aldington completed *Death of a Hero* Brigit was obliged to return to London. He wrote or telegraphed daily, even several times a day. The novel done, he experienced depression and utter weariness. His first reaction was to go teetotal and to avoid Cunard-Crowder company, but two days after despatching the typescript he dined at the Soufflot with Janet Flanner and met Djuna Barnes at the Deux Magots. He was also seeing something of two Irishmen, Thomas MacGreevy and Samuel Beckett. He had been introduced to MacGreevy, who became a close friend, at Joyce's apartment. Through Louis Aragon he met Picasso, whom Friede asked him at once to contract, if possible, to illustrate a book. Aldington was also photographed by Man Ray.[21] On 14 May he heard that Chattos had accepted *Death of a Hero* and would advance £100, so he decided to buy a car.

His antipathy towards England was reinforced when he saw performed R. C. Sherriff's war play *Journey's End*, and by a list of deletions requested for *Death of a Hero*, including words such as 'orgasm', 'hymen', and such like, and passages on free love and contraception. He at once asked the editor, Charles Prentice, to procure unexpurgated foreign language editions and vowed prophetically: 'And I'll give the book to Soviet Russia'.[22] He instructed Prentice to indicate each letter of each deleted word by an asterisk.

He had begun to read Gérard de Nerval's writings with a view to translating *Aurélia*. Prompted by Walter Lowenfels, he was working on a new Imagist anthology; he had written some poems, and finished *Love and the Luxembourg* (in England, *A Dream of the Luxembourg*), 'a sort of dime novel, and a break away from the "incomprehensible" school of modern poetry'.[23] He and H.D. were again 'friends and brothers', and she was enthusiastic about the anthology. A sour but predictable note disrupted the current harmony, as he relayed to H.D.—the discarded Arabella was making a nuisance of herself by writing to Brigit and even by telephoning him.[24]

After a short holiday at La Rochelle in early July Aldington went south to Fabregas, near Toulon, moving up to Paris again for the October publication of *Death of a Hero*. In late September he received two large envelopes full of American reviews. These were either violently for or against the book, and in several American cities it was a bestseller. English sales at first went slowly. Circulation libraries such as Boots, Mudie's and Smith's held off purchasing. Nonetheless, by October 5, Chattos had sold 4000 copies (of a first run of 5000) and by the year's end sales were close to 10 000.

In June 1929 he wrote to ask H. G. Wells if he would read a typescript of the novel, as Donald Friede thought it useful to gather some pre-publication comments from notable literary people. Wells obliged, although he did not reply until 29 September, within a few days of publication. 'I was deeply moved by it', he said. 'I don't think the state of mind in London among intellectual people has ever been done so well or nearly as well. At first there is a slight flavour of Samuel Butler, but as soon as your are fairly started it is all your own. It keeps on giving the effect of being absolutely real and true.'[25] Arnold Bennett reviewed it favourably and Wyndham Lewis thought well enough of it to send a telegram of congratulations. By late September Swedish and German rights had been sold and more than 170 reviews had appeared, including Lewis's laudatory one in the *Daily Express*. Shortly, a French edition was arranged. Aldington, with an income of $60 a day was living in an undreamed of state of wealth!

When *Death of a Hero* was reissued in the mid-1930s, it was touted by George Orwell as 'much the best of the English war books',[26] but Aldington at the outset thought it a hastily written book. To Gorham Munson in 1936 he mentioned earlier abortive attempts at a war book, and said that he had in mind models other than strict realism and, among English novelists, preferred Sterne to anyone:

> So far as the form of the Hero went I determined it should be organic, not pre-conceived, i.e. the shape had to grow out of the

matter and emotions. But I gave myself a couple of guides. I kept a rough concept of the Euripidean tragedy in mind, which is why I give the whole plot of the story in the Prologue—the intention there being to avoid false surprise . . . . The other guide was a rough concept of a symphony . . . . [Beethoven's 'Eroica']

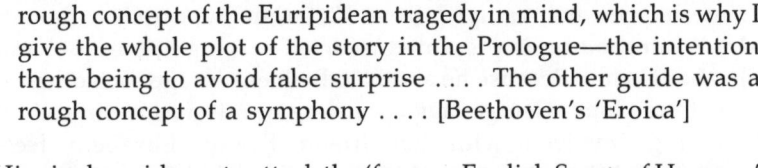

His aim he said was to attack the 'famous English Sense of Humour' which is 'the bolting hole of cowardice, mediocrity and stupidity. I thought something sharper and more ferocious would be salutary'.

'Now, after seven years, there isn't a word I want to alter', he assured Munson, but commenting on Friede's reaction that *Death of a Hero* is 'great in the fullest meaning of the word', he told H.D., 'I'm sure it's not that'. Declaring 'It's not really very good', he asked H.D. not to judge it too harshly, and claimed that by writing this novel he might learn to write a better one.[27] In dedicating the novel to his friend, the playwright Halcott Glover, Aldington noted:

> The technique of this book, if it can be said to have one, is that which I evolved for myself in writing a longish modern poem (which you liked) called 'A Fool i' the Forest.' Some people said that was 'jazz poetry'; so I suppose this is a jazz novel. You will see how appropriate that is to the theme.[28]

The book is really (as he put it) 'a threnody, a memorial' with an implied idealism, a belief in fundamental human integrity and the possibility of comradeship in adversity. This truth, this sincerity, was his primary concern rather than the form or 'way of saying'.

The 'Hero' (the title is ironic) is George Winterbourne—and much is implied in the name—whose life is loosely patterned after Aldington's. Son of a weak-natured father and a promiscuous and insensitive mother, George from the start is victim of his environment and circumstances. He suffers years of the barbaric heartiness of English public school life only to have his prospects destroyed when his solicitor father loses most of the family resources through unwise speculation.

In time-honoured fashion, George's response to his ineffectual father and indifferent mother is to strike out on his own, and head for London with the plan of becoming an artist. He has some success as an art critic and so has entry to the salon-life of London artists, intellectuals and hangers-on. He meets Elizabeth, a follower of the ideas of Havelock Ellis and with Winterbourne's assistance a feminist proponent of 'free love'. In a sense, she is a mother Winterbourne half-escaped from Victorian hypocrisies, though Mrs Winterbourne is presented as a self-serving 'grotesque' and Elizabeth is not. Because he and Elizabeth encourage each other in sexual 'freedom', George lays up a store of misery for himself by becoming involved with her friend Fanny. Elizabeth feels emancipated enough to take a lover of her own, but George's liaison does not please her. Especially when she imagines, or pretends to believe that she is pregnant, she resorts strategically to the older generation's humbug about the sanctity of marriage, recovering her liberated sentiments the moment any threat has passed. Elizabeth and Fanny struggle for George's favour, but he is, ironically, half reprieved by the war. Called up into the army, he is temporarily rescued from the dilemma posed by the two advanced young women.

George's background, his parents' hypocrisy, his half-aware attempts at freeing himself only to land in the morass represented by Upjohn (Ezra Pound) and company, and his efforts to respond to the supposed doctrines of Havelock Ellis and Freud—these matters occupy two-thirds of the novel. From the narrator's standpoint, Winterbourne represents the ordinary man, cannon fodder who must pay with his life for Victorian humbug and Edwardian hypocrisy. After despatching George in the Prologue and demonstrating that he is 'unwept, unhonoured and unsung' especially by his women, the narrator, (in Part I *Vivace*), deals with George's family history and school career. Aldington employs a conventional narrative line, which is disrupted by sudden outbursts of narrator (sometimes indistinguishable from author) intervention, asides, disquisitions and commentary, all of which do not really allow the reader to become immersed in the characters as such. Dickens' influence as Aldington indicated to Munson is evident in the use of caricature and exaggeration, but Sterne's method of digression is also part of the fabric. Kittredge speaks for many critics in judging the book's 'lack of stylistic and rhythmic unity'.[29] Sometimes this point is allied to a judgement about Aldington's state of mind when he wrote it, as when W. C. Frierson labels it 'a bitter novel, savage, wrongheaded and ruthless'[30] and Bernard Bergonzi 'a massive ejaculation of pent-up venom'.[31] Kittredge brings the two concerns, form and attitude, together: 'Aldington simply poured into it the accumulated bitterness, anger and anguish that had been gathering within him since the end of the war, without seriously attempting to give the book more than the superficial trappings of novelistic form'.[32] But this is to undervalue Aldington's claim that this is a 'jazz novel' (the implied formal analogy is with *The Waste Land*). Surely, too, the 'accumulated bitterness' is successfully attributed to the putative narrator, who is committed to a view which condemns the war as a desolation of human waste promoted by the inhumanly smug, obtuse, hypocritical and self-serving attitudes of the monied and aristocratic classes. Take a relatively mild passage, commentary on the romanticising of the marriage ceremony after the wedding of George's father:

> How could they rise to such bilge? But they did, they did, they did. And they believed in it. If only they'd had their tongues in their cheeks there might have been some hope. But they hadn't. They believed in the sickish, sweetish, canting bilge, they believed in it. Believed in it with all the superhuman force of ignorance.[33]

That the narrator should have held such a view is credible and this holds true with even more vituperative passsages. But there are two problems. Through his narrator, Aldington launches a wide-ranging attack on cant and sentimentality, plus an iconoclastic barrage against Victorian views of social institutions. His weakness is that he is too direct, he uses sarcasm where he should use irony. His targets seem to be indiscriminately chosen and he undermines not only manners and attitudes but also the individuals manifesting them.

George Winterbourne, despite his background and antecedents, is of artistic temperament. He hates the regimentation and sports fetishism of school and loves nature and solitude. In all this he is at odds with his human environment. As a boy, he resists efforts to inculcate 'manliness' into him, and prefers to wander alone, dreamily, in the countryside. As portrayed, his friends who introduce him to literature, natural history and the pastime of hiking, are derived from boyhood contacts of Aldington's such as Dudley Grey and Malcolm Hilbery. George's ambition is to be a painter, but he is thwarted when his father's financial ineptitude lands the family in poverty. The intention of this part of the narrative is to portray the hazards endured by the individual of aesthetic temperament who lives in an environment of bourgeois social and economic values and becomes dependent on inherited wealth.

In London George meets, among others, Messrs Upjohn, Shobbe, Tubbe and Bobbe, lampoon versions of Pound, Ford, Eliot and D. H. Lawrence. In Upjohn are portrayed Pound's habits and mannerisms, his hectoring and his hesitations, his entrepreneurship of the arts. The Middle Westerner, Waldo Tubbe, is the first in a series of Aldington's fictional portrayals attacking T. S. Eliot. Though middle-American by birth and upbringing, Tubbe 'was an exceedingly ardent and patriotic British Tory, standing for Royalism in Art, Authority in Politics, and Classicism in Religion'.[33] all of which are based on Eliot's well-known revelations in *For Lancelot Andrewes* (1928). Tubbe is an 'unshakable Anglo-Catholic' who hinted at his aristocratic English ancestry, had his possessions marked with a coat-of-arms and knew only 'the best people'. Tubbe, Shobbe, Upjohn and Bobbe each is described as 'a very great man'.

Just as Aldington appears to have taken his notion of the nation's blood-guiltiness for the war from Lawrence's ideas, so he may have derived these satirical portrayals of figures in the pretentious London literary milieu from Lawrence's gallery of portraits in *Aaron's Rod*. Certainly, his picture of Comrade Bobbe is adequate revenge.

Unlike the Winterbourne parents, the two women closest to George are not 'grotesques'. Elizabeth and Fanny are rivals for George's love. To a degree, these two have real life counterparts in H.D. and Arabella, though Aldington has crossed over their physical attributes so that Elizabeth physically somewhat resembles Arabella but temperamentally is closer to H.D., and (with some over-simplification) the reverse may be said of Fanny. Aldington claimed, perhaps disingenuously, to H.D. that his 'heroines' were drawn from Valentine Dobrée and Nancy Cunard, with their permission.[35] Part II (*andante cantabile*) of *Death of a Hero* anatomises London intellectual life and examines the nature of George's relationships with Elizabeth and Fanny in the years immediately before the war, but with deliberate analogy:

> How curious are cities, with their intricate trench systems and perpetual warfare, concealed but as deadly as the open warfare of armies! . . . The warfare goes on behind the house-fronts—wives with husbands, children with parents, employers with em-

ployed, tradesmen with tradesmen, banker with lawyer, and the triumphal doctor rooting out life's casualties. Desperate warfare—for what? Money as the symbol of power; power as the symbol or affirmation of existence. Throbbing warfare of cities! As fierce and implacable and concealed as the desperate warfare of plants and hidden carnage of animals.[36]

Thus the life of a great city is seen as part of the scheme of 'survival of the fittest', with its concomitant division of human beings into victors and victims. In England the model for this survival is the class system, sustained throughout the Victorian years by cant, or humbug, which control especially the economic and sexual lives of the people.

Sexual morality, what Aldington regards as religiosity and its attendant hypocrisy, and cant-ridden, comfort-loving bourgeois materialism—these are his targets and they dominate Part II as elsewhere. But Elizabeth and Fanny are not mere cardboard cut-outs serving to illustrate a thesis. They are brought to life as characters (though the Cambridge man, Reggie Burnside, remains a stereotype). Aldington's aim seems not to have been 'well-rounded' internal verisimilitude, but satirical projection. His targets are perhaps too broad (the whole quality of English life, the life of the London intelligentsia and its self-serving over-estimation of the importance of art), but on its own terms the writing is lively and effective, good use being made of a technique of allusion not unlike that of Pound or Eliot, but employed to relate the scene chiefly to current ideas (as in references to Havelock Ellis, Norman Haire, Frank Crane, Bertrand Russell). The technique of setting up a network of relationships—between George and Elizabeth, George and Fanny, George and a casually encountered stranger who remarks on the possibility of war: 'Oh, liven things up a bit. We're getting stale, too much peace. Need a bit of blood-letting'[37]—is not unlike Brecht's method of 'alienation', distancing the audience for pedagogical purposes. Perhaps Aldington is attempting it (unconsciously) in the wrong medium, but it was his object, after all, to teach us a lesson.

Death of a Hero has as Epilogue an elegaic poem, but the long section which precedes it, Part II (*adagio*) is the book's most effective unit and might almost stand on its own, or at least with a much briefer lead-in to sketch the protagonist's earlier life. It shows Winterbourne's existence in military camps, in the trenches, at the front—one filled with demeaning experiences: dirt, filthy and infected drinking water, lice, boils, and diarrhoea, but worst of all the blunting of the senses and fogging of the mind.

One other dimension of that experience may be the most trying of all, loneliness. In the grim setting of trench warfare Winterbourne meets few of his own kind among either officers or other ranks. He is reluctant to become an officer because his sensibility is not so thoroughly invaded while he remains among the more or less mindless four-lettering routine of the other ranks. The bleakness, tedium and banality of the life have him reflecting that 'The road to glory was undoubtedly devious in our fair island story'.[38] Less encroached on as a private soldier, his loneliness does not afford the benefit of solitude. He is swept along with the great drafts of men being gathered in to be fed, after interminable waiting, waiting, waiting, into the front line, and the narrative of these events makes the body-punishing and mind-numbing boredom graphic in accurately perceived concrete detail. As to the cause:

> But what were they really against? Who were their real enemies? He saw the answer with a flood of bitterness and clarity. Their enemies—the enemies of German and English alike—were the fools who had sent them to kill each other instead of help each other. Their enemies were the sneaks and the unscrupulous; the false ideals, the unintelligent ideas imposed on them, the humbug, the hypocrisy, the stupidity.[39]

Yet Aldington's account is by no means completely one-sided. In the portrayal of Lieutenant Evans, for whom Winterbourne becomes runner, he depicts 'the usual English public-school boy, amazingly ignorant, amazingly inhibited, and yet "decent" and good-humoured'.[40] Evans has all the prejudices of his class and training, including a strong belief in the status quo, snobbery, philistinism, xenophobia, and yet he is far superior, in Winterbourne's mind, to the people 'at home' who had only the sketchiest sense of trench warfare and sustained all the old pre-war illusions. This at least is what Winterbourne discovers when at last he returns to England to take courses for a commission. The blindness and callousness he encounters exacerbate the effects of the grim and inhuman battlefield.

With the horrors of battle and dreariness of the trenches Winterbourne carries the added tension of his double involvement with Elizabeth and Fanny, and the knowledge that his front-line experiences are, in fact, alienating him internally from both of them. But it cannot be helped, he is one of the generation born specifically to fight this war, fated to it, and so at last he comes into the great battle which is to be the war's, the book's, and Winterbourne's finale. Here, too, the quality of the writing is sustained, as it is throughout Part III, an economical portrayal of chaos and 'timeless confusion'.

The war has only a matter of days to run its course, the Germans are already virtually defeated and an armistice is at hand. George, now supposedly a leader amid the infernal chaos, cannot know this as he leads his men in the vanguard of the fighting close to the retreating German army. Like the Germans, he is all but used up. He endures weeks and months of further trench warfare as a responsible officer, with a respite which confirms his separateness from, and boredom with, even those closest to him on the 'home front'. In the book's final scene, amidst a German machine-gun attack, many of his men are casualties or fatalities. One of his runners is mortally wounded and lies groaning, pleading to be killed, to be released from agony:

> Something seemed to break in Winterbourne's head. He felt he was going mad, and sprang to his feet. The line of bullets smashed across his chest like a savage steel whip. The universe exploded darkly into oblivion.[41]

To friends, Aldington was modest about *Death of a Hero*, though he hoped it would help make his literary reputation on a scale which had hitherto eluded him. He quickly became interested in sales and it may be said that this novel made him a fully professional writer. A serious career as a fiction writer lay before him. But what of the book in other respects? It has been either ignored or attacked (for example, in Bernard Bergonzi's *Heroes' Twilight*, or Jon Silkin's *Out of Battle*. Silkin says: 'resentment . . . gets the better of his aesthetics'),[42] but some recent writers have shown it favour. Robert Wohl, in *The Generation of 1914*, for instance, sees it, with Graves's *Goodbye to All That* and Remarque's *All Quiet on the Western Front*, as one of the most important of the great number of First World War novels published in the late 1920s. Wohl observes that 'anyone trying to understand the attitudes of English survivors of the war would be well advised to read it'.[43]

Another recent writer, Andrew Rutherford, in *The Literature of War*,[44] indicates an aspect of the book which has been almost unnoticed, that is, Aldington's feeling for the soldiers' preservation of their essential humanity, despite the overwhelming horror of their experiences. Rutherford also praises 'Aldington's brilliant evocation of front-line experience'.

If it loses formal coherence because too many social targets are attacked at once and lambasted virulently and stridently, the book remains important. First, because the targets needed to be attacked and *Death of a Hero* is a forceful salvo. But more than this, the long account of life in the wartime army, in the trenches and in the front line, is unquestionably truly observed and incisively recorded. It is an essential document in the imaginative reconstruction of the First World War. With all its flaws of distancing (and in this period of a broader conception of the possibilities of the novel, these might well be re-examined) *Death of a Hero* contains in its *adagio* section an integral work worthy of comparison with, say, *The Red Badge of Courage* as a classic of war.

When he forwarded a typescript of the novel to Herbert Read in July 1929, Aldington said, 'I have purged my bosom of perilous stuff',[45] but this proved not to be so. Rather, he had found his immediate central theme, that the First World War had an inescapable effect on the generation which lived through it and especially on the men who fought it. Aldington confided that he did not expect a fair press in England, but in retrospect Read felt that *All Quiet on the Western Front* had prepared the way and 'Aldington sailed to fame and freedom on this new wave of "war books"'.[46] Almost immediately, the tone of his letters to Read changed, possibly because Read's response to *Death of a Hero* was not wholehearted, but Read felt that with the success of *Death of a Hero*, Aldington 'was never to be quite the same friend so far as I was concerned—not that his affection ever diminished, or that he grew distant or conceited, but I have experienced in other cases the desolation that popularity brings to friendship'. Of course, this was a watershed in Aldington's life in matters far beyond the success of his novel; he committed himself to living on the Continent, and abandoned Arabella for Brigit. As to the success of *Death of a Hero* in England, sales figures picked up remarkably by the end of 1929 and MacGreevy brought news that the book was talked of everywhere. As to friendship, what of Mr Tubbe? Fred D. Crawford has suggested that there are echoes of *The Waste Land*, but shows only a small number of shared allusions.[47] The musical 'form' and desolate urban setting are common to both works, and we may see in Elizabeth and Fanny some parallel, say, to the Thames daughters, but the links are not that simply explained. Aldington's characteristic personal and *ad hominem* 'voice' is one explicitly rejected by Eliot, but shared with Pound in much of his correspondence and criticism and even the *Cantos*. Wyndham Lewis has something of the same flavour. In Aldington's case, it may be obtrusive, but it may be his work's determining characteristic and therefore its strength.

11 A Career as a Novelist, 1929–31

Fortified financially and psychologically by the burgeoning success of his first novel, Aldington and Brigit headed south in November 1929 for Italy. Pursued by rain, they stopped only briefly in Florence and Rome. After renewing acquaintance with Lawrence's friend, the publisher Pino Orioli, in Florence and meeting Alec Randall and other friends in Rome, with a copy of Norman Douglas's *Siren Land* in hand Aldington made for Naples and remained for some time at Amalfi before going on to Palermo and Agrigentum.

Before leaving Paris he had completed work on the Imagist anthology, occasion of rapprochement with Cournos, the offence of *Miranda Masters* set aside. From Amalfi he told Cournos he had received 'a letter from your Russian friend' with news that the Moscow State Publishing House would have *Death of a Hero* translated.[1] Although this proposal bore no fruit for several years, it was to prove momentous.

Armed with introductions, from his French translator Henri Davray,[2] to the governors of Tunisia, Algeria and Morocco, Aldington and Brigit spent the first two months of 1930 in North Africa. The trip afforded him material for a brief section of *All Men Are Enemies* where Waterton, friend of the protagonist Tony Clarendon, suggests visiting the Tunis oases. In Clarendon's 'tourist kind' of experience:

> It was disconcerting to discover that many of the natives in Tunis wore florid socks and fancy Boston garters in full view under their short trousers; and it was also a blow to discover that the call to prayer was a long blast from a factory siren on the top of a minaret. Moreover, nobody in Tunis seemed to pay any attention to it.

Thus even conservative Islam joined step with the march of progress.[3] But the sardonic Aldington is matched by the lyrical:

> Tony was shy of speaking to Waterton about other experiences which had touched him more deeply. Going inland by the little

night train from Kairouan, he had awakened from the uneasy sleep of *couchettes* about two hours before dawn. In spite of the hot-water pipes the carriage felt chilly. Tony looked out of the window, and immediately forgot all about being cold. The dome of the sky was clear and vast, filled with white moonlight which shone over a great sea of lion-coloured sand. There was a tinge of yellow in the white of the moonlight, a tinge of white in the yellow of the sand. Here and there were tiny patches of dark scrub, which looked very like floating seaweed in the uncertain light. The train moved slowly and, it seemed, gently, not unlike a ship, so that the sensation was of sailing over this ocean of tawny sand under a bell of yellowish crystal.[4]

Meantime his literary life went on of its own momentum. He recruited for his squad of English antagonists with 'What is Wrong with English Poetry' (*Everyman* 16 January 1930) where he contrasts its insipid good taste with American vitality. Harold Monro reviewed his *Collected Poems* in the April *Criterion*,[5] noting Aldington's stoic-epicurean view of life, the conversational quality of his *vers libre*, his manifest rejection of Eliot's doctrine of impersonality and the difference between his view of 'sincerity' and Pound's. Monro detects an air of finality, as if the book were summing-up a poet's career. As it proved, though he was only 37 the main impetus of Aldington's life as a poet was already in the past.

From 1929 onwards his attention was centred on full-length fiction, but perhaps because he was based in Paris where a number of small private presses were initiated by Americans in the 1920s, he became interested in these. His first involvement was through Nancy Cunard's printing *Hark the Herald* and then the Hours Press edition of *The Eaten Heart*. Through awareness of small press work he helped the career of James Hanley, the novelist, writing introductions to private editions of Hanley's *The German Prisoner* and *The Last Voyage*.[6]

In 1929 Aldington discussed with Edward Titus, financier of *This Quarter*, the setting up of a poetry prize. With new wealth and new assurance he decided with Cunard to become a patron and award a prize for a poem on a given subject:

Nancy Cunard, Hours Press, in collaboration with Richard Aldington, offers 10 pounds for the best poem up to 100 lines, in

English or American on TIME (for or against). Entries up to June 15, 1930.

The idea was to discover new talent and in the process publicise Hours Press. There were pervasive rumours that Lowenfels was the predetermined winner. He was indeed on the short list with Samuel Beckett and an unnamed Englishman; but the winning poem, Beckett's *Whoroscope*, arrived late on the last day, saving the competition because the remaining hundred or so entries ranged from doggerel to sham metaphysics. Nancy chose Beckett, with Lowenfels as runner-up, saying later that Beckett's name meant nothing to either Aldington or herself. But, as we have seen, Beckett had already been introduced to Aldington by MacGreevy. Deirdre Bair, Beckett's biographer, relates that early in 1930 Beckett 'frequented the cheaper cafes near the rue d'Ulm with MacGreevy and Aldington; or the Café Mahieu on the boulevard St. Michel when Aldington wanted him to meet "a lady worth impressing"'.[7] Between them, Cunard and Aldington may be credited with discovering Beckett, who made a gesture of reciprocation in the 1950s, when Aldington was experiencing tough times, and later wrote in a typically cryptic memorial that he retained few memories for long, but 'among the ghostly few' is Aldington's 'great kindness' to him in Paris in the late 1920s and early 1930s. Aldington helped Beckett further by putting him in touch with Chatto & Windus who published his small book on Proust in their Phoenix Series. Not without reason, then, Beckett wrote in 1965: 'I think of him with affection and gratitude'.[8]

Unfortunately for Aldington, deciding the winner of the other prize, the Aldington Poetry Prize first publicised in *This Quarter* in 1929, for 'the ablest young American poet' was much more difficult and remained undecided throughout 1930. Like Pound, who wrote to him of his disciples Louis Zukofsky and Basil Bunting, Aldington felt free to champion *les jeunes*, in his case the Irishmen, MacGreevy and Beckett, and the somewhat troublesome Lowenfels, who pestered him about poetry prizes.

In March 1930 Brigit again returned to London. That month the *Yale Review* carried Aldington's poem to her, 'Inscriptions',[9] 'Through you I have inherited a world –/Myself'; but he seemed intent on giving it all to her, plying her with telegrams of avowal and graphic love letters. A typical effusion reads:

My body longs and yearns for yours. I want my mouth on yours and to feel your soft breath and all your lovely woman's flesh against mine. I dream of holding your little breasts, so tender and feminine in my hands; and oh how I want to feel that quiver of your body and the leap of you when you so eagerly and lovingly draw into you the life which leaps out from me to you.[10]

Eventually he crossed to London himself, for two weeks quartering at Garland's Hotel and negotiating publisher's contracts through his new agent Ralph Pinker. *A Dream in the Luxembourg* (American title *Love and the Luxembourg*) was published and the reviews, a mixed lot, began to come in. Back in Paris in mid-May, where he dined with Pound ('very sweet and charming') and Olga Rudge, Aldington received in proof a review by James Reeves. He responded that he believed the ordinary reader is interested in narrative and 'Simple but deep emotion', hence the 'magazine story' framework of *A Dream in the Luxembourg*. Reeves was entertained to one of Aldington's clearest statements of his case against Eliot (not unlike that of William Carlos Williams, a contributor to *Pagany*).

> The revolt against Eliot in *Pagany* and the *American Caravan*, seems to me utterly ineffective, because it is made entirely with weapons furnished by Eliot himself. . . . It is insane to question Eliot's genius as a poet or his extreme skill as a critic. What can be attacked, and should be, is his expressed and implied attitude to life; and the over-intellectual, non-specialised type of poetry he has created as a refuge from life.[11]

A Dream in the Luxembourg seemed no effective answer, however. Reviewers dismissed the poem as too personal.[12] Aldington saw such negative responses as 'Establishment' revenge for the success of *Death of a Hero*.

His two-part essay on Wyndham Lewis appeared in the *Sunday Referee* in June, an extended review of *The Apes of God*,[13] perceived as 'the greatest piece of writing since *Ulysses*', its latter part 'a new *Candide*', though ammunition wasted on miniscule targets, 'a set of Bloomsbury and Chelsea parish pumpers'. Lewis's novel caused quite a to-do in literary London, with writers choosing sides, and neither Lewis nor Aldington became more popular. W. K. Rose, editor of Lewis's letters, cites specifically Montague Slater's *Daily Telegraph* notice, 'Satire in the Novel'. Tying together *The Apes of God* and *Death of a Hero*, Slater says these will make the reader ask, angrily, 'Who made you a judge over us?'. With sweeping condemnation, he dismisses Joyce, Lewis and Aldington as perpetrators of the 'inept' novel of satire. Lewis counter-attacked with *Satire and Fiction*,[14] which includes part of Aldington's *Referee* essay.

By the time Slater's attack appeared in London, Aldington had taken up summer quarters at the Villa le Bouquet, Aiguebelle near Le Lavandou, Var. Read sent him *Ambush*, a small book of war pieces which he liked only moderately, perhaps because he was proofreading his own book of war short stories, *Roads to Glory*, while working on his next novel, *The Colonel's Daughter*. To Read, who scorned Lewis's *The Apes of God*, he declared that Lewis with passion would have been the paramount artist of their times, but instead was unjustly neglected. Aldington was seeing something of Michael Arlen (once one of Lawrence's unlikely canditates for Rananim) whom he liked for his modesty, wit and good-temper, and Aldous Huxley, who visited one day in a Bugatti motor-car, apparently 'the spoils' of *Point Counterpoint*.[15]

In August *Everyman* published Louise Morgan's interview with Aldington, 'Writing a Best-Seller in Seven Weeks',[16] which claims that the first draft of *Death of a Hero* was typed partially 'on a Spanish typewriter that belonged to D. H. Lawrence, where the exclamation and question marks were upside down' and partially at Rapallo on a typewriter owned by Pound. More interestingly, Morgan provides a physical description of Aldington— exceptionally broad shoulders, bronzed skin and hair, which 'gleam with vitality. His clear blue eyes shine with the excitement of living. He gives the impression of exuberant health and well-being, of a man who spends the greater part of his time in the open air. One is struck with his irrepressible good humour as well—his smile is always just below the surface, and his habitual expression is one of repressed amusement and mischief.' Obviously his current successes, with Brigit and with the novel, were manifest in his physical presence.

The English edition of *Roads to Glory* was published in October when he and Brigit were in Italy, heading for Venice via Milan, Verona and Vincenza. Read's response was mixed; he felt that some of the writing lacked restraint. A new friend, Sidney Schiff (the novelist Stephen Hudson)[17] suggested war is too brutal a theme for art. Aldington reacted eloquently:

War is the translation into violent action of the hatred and loathing which surges between people under the social and family masks—that is one of the themes of *Death of a Hero*, which perhaps someone will someday perceive. So long as all this hate exists in the world there will be War. But to say that War is not a theme for art seems too absurd. It is self indulgence to shrink from it because it is painful.[18]

Just as *Death of a Hero* is crucially divided between the hero's pre-war and wartime life, so the 13 stories in *Roads to Glory* are centred on two concerns, trench existence and the post-war return to civilian life. The title carries a charge of irony like *Death of a Hero*, but straightforwardness here replaces the earlier book's sarcasm, in story titles such as: 'At All Costs', 'Deserter', 'Of Unsound Mind', 'Killed in Action','Booby Trap' and, reminiscing, 'Meditation of a German Grave' and 'Farewell to Memories'. Trench warfare is vividly evoked, as are a variety of human responses, desertion, courage, fear, callousness: contrasts are made between front line soldiers and base officers and indifferent or uncomprehending civilians; the cant and deceit are scourged which led to the war and cashed in on men's loyalty. Throughout there is great empathy with the soldier victims of the system, but the book does not lapse into one-sided propaganda. In one story, 'A Bundle of Letters', for example, Lieutenant Walter Bracegirdle is depicted exploiting the system to his own selfish advantage, in contrast to the loyalty and understanding of senior officers.

Part of Aldington's purpose still was to purge himself of the 'perilous stuff' of indignation and rancorous horror. Many reviewers found the stories overstated or exaggerated,[19] but it is difficult today to sustain such a judgement. In style, they are bald and direct, at times one-dimensional, but not sensationalist. The view of society conveyed is scathing, but by no means unfair. If the book is sometimes shrill, it is fittingly shrill. 'Who are you to judge us?' asked the reviewer Mr Slater. It would appear that any soldier with extended front line experience in the First World War had every right to judge those who put him there. A *Times* critique said (Aldington told Lewis) that the stories are 'rather narratives than the finished products of fiction'. If this means that the author has worried less about creating a fictional illusion than about presenting 'facts', there is some justice in the criticism.

Throughout 1930 the agent Ralph Pinker worked to improve Aldington's publishing position. The American *Collected Poems* sold much better than the British, so an attempt was made to issue a cheap edition in Chatto's Phoenix Series. This failed, but Aldington made a very favourable contract with Covici Friede. They at last brought out the *Decameron* and Chattos a smaller scale translation, Euripides' *Alcestis*. Aldington's hard work to fulfil contracts may be gauged from 18 days in Venice that October. He produced three *Sunday Referee* articles, a long short story for Cunard ('Last Straws'), another story, and 7 000 words of *The Colonel's Daughter*.

Five hundred copies of *Last Straws* were printed by the Hours Press at the end of 1930 and, to everyone's gratification, the run (largest up to that time for the press) virtually sold out before publication. The story was of a piece with *Roads to Glory*, the portrayal of a group of disenchanted war veterans. Wyn Henderson, temporary manager of Hours Press, delightedly forwarded Aldington a royalty cheque only to have him react angrily because it had not been sent by Nancy. This pomposity gave Cunard ammunition in the 1950s to rebut his 'misrepresentative picture' of Norman Douglas in *Pinorman*. She recalled a divided Aldington, 'the gay, friendly, good-natured side of him, plus his charming enthusiasm—all apparent and delightful with people he liked—and the angry, denunciatory bitter mood and the criticism of so much which had begun to appear in some of his work'. Of the anger of the three protagonists in *Last Straws* in recollecting their war experiences, she says: 'Who doesn't know that mood? It ran with fluency down Aldington's pen, an excellent implement for spleen'. But the occasion for those feelings was long in the future.

Norman Douglas now enters the picture. Shortly after despatching *The Colonel's Daughter* to London, Aldington abandoned a plan to holiday in Corfu, headed once more for Florence, renewed contact with Orioli and, through him, met Douglas. From reading Douglas he had formed a sense of a witty and high-spirited man, with a sane view of life, a wide range of interests and a fund of recondite knowledge. Aldington spent much of 1931 in Florence and became friendly with Douglas though his feeling for Orioli proved ultimately deeper and sunnier.

His two accounts of his first meeting with Douglas, in *Life for Life's Sake* and *Pinorman*,[20] are similar in surface observation, portraying Douglas as physically striking, widely-read, with slightly comic pretensions to gastronomy. Yet there is a distinct difference. By the 1950s Aldington's attitude to Douglas, as to much else, had become mordantly acerbic; but it would be rash to assume that one portrayal is more or less true than the other.

Orioli found for Aldington a large room overlooking the Arno in the Gran Bretagna Hotel, its ceiling painted with a mythological scene centred by a Venus with a huge cut-glass chandelier descending from her navel. The ante-room to the bathroom served as a study. From these quarters, Aldington ventured out to lunch with Douglas almost daily for some months. Douglas's deep knowledge of southern Italy appealed greatly to him, and also a certain flavour of hard-shelled wit masking a sensitive intelligence. (He recalled, for example, Douglas's personal version of his family's motto, 'Tender and true'—'Hard as nails, my dear'.) The two talked at ease on many topics, and in *Life for Life's Sake* Aldington provides affectionate summary of the range of their first conversation. The topics included Southern Italy (and Douglas's book *Old Calabria*), the birds of the Greek Anthology, early German epic poetry, the deforestation of the Mediterranean and a translation of Athaneus, which many years later became a contentious issue.

Shortly before Aldington and Brigit arrived in Florence, Frieda Lawrence had come and Orioli was attempting to advise her how best to deal with publication of Lawrence's works, including the letters. Soon drawn in, Aldington sent an appeal to A. S. Frere, Heinemann's managing director, holidaying at Cannes. Frere came to Florence and agreed that Heinemanns should resume as Lawrence's publishers, allowing Orioli certain priorities for his Lungarno Series of limited editions. Accounts of these negotiations are given in Orioli's *Adventures of a Bookseller*[21] and in *Pinorman*. Aldington claims Orioli's version is a travesty, essentially written by Douglas, magnifying Douglas's part in the business and minimising Aldington's. Douglas's biographer, Mark Holloway, despite his generally poor opinion of Aldington, says: 'He was almost certainly right'.[22]

When Douglas returned to Florence in late 1930 Aldington had just written a *Sunday Referee* column on *Paneros*,[23] which, as its title might suggest, outlines Douglas's philosophy of love. Holloway calls the *Referee* piece 'an appreciation', but in *Pinorman Paneros* becomes one of Douglas's pieces of book-making 'a pedestrian compilation of learned trifles', 'like an appendix or very long footnote to Burton's *Anatomy* tricked out in the sententious style of Sir Thomas Browne'.[24] That this judgement is not unjust may be gauged from Holloway's comment on *Paneros*: 'Paradoxically, and typically, this short treatise written in seventeenth-century prose style, though whimsical in conception, contains little whimsy' (p.

384). But in 1931 these and other obnubilations (to use a favourite Latinism of Aldington's) were over the horizon and he gave a set of proofs of *The Colonel's Daughter* to Douglas, another going to the indigent but companionable MacGreevy.[25]

Aldington needed Douglas as a social diversion, for by early February Brigit had once again returned to England and was in receipt of his fervent and frequent letters. A new acquaintance, the American poet and translator Leonard Bacon, helped him purchase a second-hand Ford car. At once he invested in driving lessons and a month later when he took the test he had already driven 1000 kilometers, including chauffeuring MacGreevy on a weekend trip around San Gimigniano, Arezzo, Siena and in the Appennines.

Meantime he had shown his long story 'Stepping Heavenward' to Orioli and Prentice. Orioli offered £300 outright to print it as a small book in his Lungarno Series. Prentice's agreement was needed, as arrangements had been made to include it in Chatto's Dolphin Series. Both editions were published, Orioli's in a surprisingly large run of 800, on 'Pescia hand-made paper' with eight additional copies for the Canterbury Literary Society.

Stepping Heavenward (1931) is a biting lampoon of Eliot, now transformed into Jeremy Pratt Sybba (later Cibber), son of a doting, overreaching mother and crass, mercantile father, born in Colonsville (St Louis, Missouri), but of an old New England family. In forwarding his career in England Cibber is sketched as an ambitious and social-climbing historian, though he adopts the surname of one of England's least distinguished Poets Laureate. The link with one side of Eliot's achievement is clear:

> Cibber's positive contributions are little short of meagre. Where he excelled was in pointing out the errors of others. Thus, while a man may spend eight or ten years in the composition of a book, Cibber could pick out all its faults in as many days, while the writing of one of his brilliant 'exposure' essays would not occupy him more than six months. Thus, he acquired the reputation of always knowing more than the most learned, of possessing more abilities than the most talented.[26]

Cibber's cause in England is forwarded by a fellow-American, Lucas Cholmp (Pound). When Cholmp meets Cibber at Victoria station, Cibber, with bowler hat and beard, looks exactly like the Eliot who had once all but deterred Bruce Richmond from taking him on as a *TLS* reviewer. Both Pound's and Eliot's mannerisms are satirised in *Stepping Heavenward*, though Pound never seems to have resented the unflattering portrayal. Eliot did. In the course of his guarded, and some might say pusillanimous, memorial comment on Aldington published in 1965, he says 'he wrote a cruel and unkind lampoon of me and my wife who died some years later'.[27] Vivien is introduced into Aldington's story thus:

> It was at any rate a period of intense intellectual activity, for in that short time Cibber wrote the first page and a half of his (unfinished) essay, 'A Plea for Royalism in Western Europe', an exceedingly able paraphrase of Maurras. Considering the storm and stress of his mind, this is little short of miraculous. On the one hand, he had financial worries, the growing hostility of his father and agonising doubts about his vocation in scholarship; on the other hand he had the acute personal problem of Miss Adele Paleologue.[28]

Eliot might have taken offence at allusions here and elsewhere to his ultra-conservatism in religion, politics and social attitudes, or he might have picked up and resented the hint about plagiarism (a line Aldington was to follow and amplify in later statements), but the portrayal of Vivien Eliot as 'Miss Adele Paleologue', whom Cibber marries, must have stung him:

> Adele became more and more unhappy. It is always *rather* unpleasant to live with a genius, but quite awful when he is a Cibber. Few persons now take the view that marriage is or should be a merry bacchanal, accompanied by flutes and the capering of panisks to the tune of 'Hymen Hymenaee!' But Cibber considered it as an inviolable legal contract, implying none but social obligations. So long as Mrs Cibber had the honour to be inscribed in the correct register, got her oats and fig-leaves, and received social consideration by reflection, what the devil else could she want? So, many a time poor Adele gazed into the mirror, clutching her hair distractedly, and whispering: 'I'm going mad, I'm going mad, I'm going mad.' Cibber invariably stood up when she came into the room, and their quarrels were conducted on coldly intellectual lines.[29]

In November 1931 Prentice informed Aldington that Geoffrey

Faber had written to Chatto's protesting the publication of *Stepping Heavenward*, suggesting that it be withdrawn because it would offend Eliot and Vivien. Faber claimed Eliot was unaware of the little book's existence (Faber himself, it turned out, was unaware of the Lungarno edition), but pleaded Vivien's neurasthenia. 'His letter also contained what looked like the threat of a libel action, and I asked whether he wished me to send on the letter to you. But no! And I was asked to say nothing about it to you at all'.[30] Now, however, with the proposed inclusion of 'Stepping Heavenward' in *Soft Answers*, Prentice felt obliged to raise the issue. Chatto's suggested that Faber apprise Eliot of this, but he refused to mention it, and neither Aldington nor Prentice appears to have had qualms about republishing the story, presumably because it had appeared twice already and no action had been taken. Aldington felt Eliot knew of it, and that the attempt to squelch it was underhand. He told Schiff he would probably feel obliged to cancel publication if Eliot sent him a straightforward request, that is, not one that was 'too Christian-slimy'. Whether he knew about it or not, Eliot was not forthcoming.

By 1940, when he was writing *Life for Life's Sake*, Aldington's view of Eliot had mellowed and even showed traces of his magnanimity of the early 1920s, but throughout the 1930s his animus towards Eliot grew, or rather his feelings of antipathy for everything Eliot seemed to represent. Indeed, not long before Aldington wrote his memoirs, in 1939, when for a time he considered applying for academic posts, he developed some lectures for university audiences. One of these is on Eliot, whose poetry he attacks as overrated and pretentious.[31] He excoriates Eliot and Pound as poets of the library, claims that Eliot works through 'arbitrary juxtaposing of the grandiose and the trivial',[32] that he is anti-emotional and detached from the realities of life, and that he displays both intellectual snobbery and, in effect, dishonesty by over-allusiveness and the 'annoying trick'[33] of extensive unacknowledged quotation which amounts to plagiarism. He is particularly scornful of Eliot's strategy of 'escape from emotion' and declares that 'Eliot himself is extremely deficient in the capacity for feeling emotions unless they are those of disgust, despair and suicidal impulse, which in real life has resulted in the hara-kiri of Anglicanism'.[34] As to sexual love, Aldington sees *The Waste Land* as filled with 'anti-sexual perversion'[35] and as manifesting Eliot's central motivation, the death-wish. This sense of Eliot's deathliness carried forward through the whole decade after Aldington wrote *Stepping Heavenward*. In reviewing Aldous Huxley's *Do What You Will* in the *Sunday Referee* for 15 December 1929, he contrasts what he sees as Huxley's life-affirmation with the *weltanschauung* expressed through Eliot's 'The Hollow Men':

> I am sick of death and death-worshipping in all its forms, from senile gentility to the cold butchery of intellectual suicide. Let me give an example. A greatly admired poem by the most admired poet of the day may be summarised in the following excerpted words:
>
> Hollow-dried-meaningless-dry-broken-dry-paralysed-death's-hollow-I-dare-not-deaths's-broken-fading-death's-final-twilight-dead-cactus-stone-dead-fading-death's-broken-dying-broken-last-sightless-death.
>
> The poet's genius is not in question, but I hate this exhibitionism of a perpetual suicidal mania which never, never, comes to the point. ... It is the War despair which involved so many of us and from which the healthy-minded have been struggling to escape, not yearning to wallow in.[36]

Aldington in retrospect saw the 1920s as a period in which he slowly recovered from psychological damage inflicted by the war. He judged his own sexual adventuring as symptomatic of that recovery, which was also marked by an epicure's delight in good food and wine. In contrast, what he perceived as Eliot's religiosity, anti-sexualism and pose of rigid propriety, seemed to him life-denying. He was particularly embittered by the fact that someone with Eliot's attitudes to life should have been so hugely successful in commanding public interest and reputation.

The £300 from Orioli for *Stepping Heavenward* meant that Aldington could plan a motor trip with Brigit. His intention was to stop en route for a day or two each week and work at *Sunday Referee* reviews. He had recently received a bundle of books, including a volume of *Scrutiny*, which he grumbled was full of attacks on Lawrence, Huxley and Lewis with, in contrast, plaudits of Eliot. With MacGreevy along, he and Brigit set off for Rome, motoring there in five days, visiting out of the way places. MacGreevy, afterwards Director of the Irish National Museum in Dublin but then poor and unknown, remembered details of frescoes and paintings seen, and told Miriam Benkovitz, 'It was all a wonderful chance for me. And Richard at the height of his success as a writer seemed glad to be able to provide it for me'.[37]

12 1931–33

By May Aldington was back in France, settled at the Villa Koeclin, Le Canadel, on the Côte des Maures, from whence he forwarded to Sidney Schiff details of villas the Schiffs might rent the following winter. During 1931 he wrote frequently to Schiff, who made efforts to obtain him a better contract from the *Sunday Referee* than the £400 a year retainer already agreed on. Always in need of financial reassurance, despite his largesse to MacGreevy and others, Aldington was the more grateful to Schiff because of what he saw as an intensive campaign by English reviewers against his new novel, *The Colonel's Daughter*, mostly written in a burst of intensive work in the summer of 1930. Prentice was highly enthusiastic throughout its production at Chattos and proposed a huge run until dissuaded by Aldington, who feared enormous numbers of unsold copies. The reviews were once more mixed, larded with accusations which were to become sadly familiar—of Aldington's rawness, sneering, venom, lack of taste and lack of humility; sometimes (as in the *TLS* of 30 April 1931) such charges occurred in otherwise favourable notices.

Sales of the novel were slowed because Smiths and Boots circulating libraries withdrew the book. Aldington at this time was still attempting to interest American publishers in his work and wrote some interesting notes to be sent to Nelson Doubleday about the intentions of *The Colonel's Daughter* and circumstances surrounding its publication: 'It is the mockery at the Colonels, the Smales, Mrs Eastcourts ... which has roused the burghers of Carlisle, London and Cambridge ... ' The note goes on to say that Messrs Smith refused the book on the grounds that it is 'sexually improper':

> Two weeks after publication the directors of Boots (the second biggest book-distributing firm after Smiths) held a Board meeting and decided to withdraw the book. With delicious candour they informed subscribers that the book was 'withdrawn', which ambiguity at least suggested that the publishers had withdrawn it. This *suggestio falsi* was spiritedly countered by Chattos, who put up large posters advertising the book in the most populous parts of London. . . .

Meanwhile the reviewers did their duty. ... I am bad tempered, venomous, vulgar, utterly without taste, coarse, cruel, insufferably affected; I have not one atom of humour, not one grain of pity and humanity; my characters have scarcely any relation with human life; I am cheap, I sneer, I cannot write, my book is intolerable, indecent.... And yet 'In spite of it all' (says one ingenuous reviewer) 'I could not help being interested and read the book to the end'....[1]

Aldington then cites 'the Secretary (a well-known lawyer) of the Freedom Association of Great Britain' as saying that the real reasons for attacks on the book are that it targets 'shams and evils of all kinds' and that 'some people ... hide their dislike of this uncomfortable iconoclast by declaring that the book is sexually improper—which, in fact, it is not'.

Aldington himself provided a convenient and innocuous-sounding plot summary of *The Colonel's Daughter* for Herbert Read on 27 November 1930:

The period is about 15 months anywhere between 1921 and '26, before the General Strike, and of course the whole of the action takes place in England—in an abstract English village, just outside the Home Counties area. The theme is roughly a twin one, combining the life of a village with the life of a girl (virtuous) of our generation or a little younger—a girl whose possible husbands we helped to bury. There is a good deal which is meant to be humourous as well as satirical (you may not find it so!) and I have even ventured on a certain amount of pathos (not bathos). ... There is no 'experimental writing', but I've used the Prologue device differently from that in the Hero, i.e. in the Colonel's Daughter it is used to indicate the general background of world affairs and of English economics—of course, in a symbolic way. I do believe you'll like my local 'magnate'!

The heroine, Georgina Smithers, the plain, kindly child of ostensibly puritanical parents, is willing enough to accept the social conditions which in fact imprison her. In a conventionally structured novel Aldington's purpose is to portray Georgina as an average middle-class girl of her time (as Winterbourne in *Death of a Hero* is an average young man of his). Her life is circumscribed, first, by her very ordinariness of intelligence and looks (though she has a good figure), by the financial poverty which strikes her family, on her father's death, and by hypocritical moral values imposed by her parents. Georgina is the victim of sexual double standards, the expectation that because she is a woman she will remain virginal until marriage (whereas her father has secret sexual liaisons). She is also victim of the social fact that the First World War has decimated the eligible male population. She therefore becomes an easy sexual target for intellectual idler Reggie Purfleet. When she meets a potential suitor in Geoffrey Hunter-Payne, she proves not to be bright enough or attractive enough to charm him.

When Aldington attributed 'a certain amount of pathos' to the story, he was exact. Because of his tone of sustained sarcasm towards everything, his heroine can never rise above the pathetic to the tragic; thus the narrative tone is the book's limitation. Yet within this tone there is a serious concern about the numbers of women limited to spinsterhood (at a time when marriage was the normal expectation) because of a war fought for the profit of a small group of super-capitalists, of whom the killjoy 'magnate' Sir Horace Stimms is prime example.

In its incidentals, such as details of village life, or in the portrayal of some of the minor characters, *The Colonel's Daughter* has a substance which is elusive in the whole. Aldington, not entirely at ease as a novelist, comes nowhere near bringing the full expanse of his mental life to bear on this book. He wrote to Schiff comparing the public attack on *The Colonel's Daughter* with Aristophanes' 'slanging' of the Athenians in *The Wasps* for their not having understood *The Clouds*: 'You who found a poet to battle with the ills of this land and to purify your ways of living, him last year you abandoned, when he had sowed new thoughts which you have prevented from springing up, because you have failed to understand them. Yours is the shame . . . ' 'Do read Aeschylus and Aristophanes', he concludes—'they said it all and so well. Justice is not in Moscow, nor in Detroit, nor in Rome, but in the hopes and longings of mankind'.[2] Admiration for the great classic writers is everywhere apparent in Aldington's letters, but perhaps *The Colonel's Daughter* could have been finer if some sense of true classic gravity had permeated it.

Anxiety about sales of the book began to dissipate and by late June over 7000 of Chatto's edition had gone, but at this moment another niggling anxiety surfaced, the unsettled question of the

Aldington Poetry Prize. *This Quarter* proposed the 1931 award for E. E. Cummings, but Aldington protested Cummings did not need it: 'It is almost like giving it to Eliot'. He proposed Lowenfels. The matter was settled by dividing the prize, but the magazine editorial made reference to Aldington's 'iron fist within a velvet glove'.[3] Coincidentally, Lowenfels embarrassed Aldington, who had promoted his work for its 'imaginative treatment of entirely intellectual material', by writing to *This Quarter* forswearing poetry for ten years 'because of a vacuity of heart'.[4]

In the autumn Aldington took a short trip to England, gladly leaving again almost at once, having persuaded Prentice to take an Italian holiday the following year. Far better than the sojourn on his native heath was the journey away from it, down the Rhine Valley, through the Black Forest, along the French and Italian Rivieras to Florence to settle for a period in an apartment in the Piazza Santa Croce, a most 'seignieurial residence' where he worked on Lawrence, completing the introduction to *Apocalypse*,[5] which he found difficult to write because of lack of sympathy for Lawrence's mystical side. To Henry Slonimsky, Aldington wrote: 'There is some mystical experience, which he fails to communicate, but which stirs me deeply, because it is outside Christianity and its tortured metaphysics and (to me) utterly unhealthy psychology. . . . I prefer to look for the gods on the hills and by the sea. . . . '[6]

At this moment a new dimension was added to his literary career, with a review of *Death of a Hero* in the September 1931 *Novy Mir*, Moscow. As early as 1915 his work was mentioned in an article on 'English Futurists' in the St Petersburg journal *Strelets*, but little subsequent attention had been paid him until this piece entitled 'English literature—a novel about Aunt Sallies and the arrows of the spirit'.[7] The reviewer, Evgeny Lann, collaborated in translating *Death of a Hero* (State Fiction Publications, 1932), which impressed Maxim Gorky. In a letter of 29 March 1932, Gorky asked if his fellow novelist Konstantin Fedin had read it, and remarked, 'Such an extremely harsh, angry and "desperate" book; I would never have thought the English would produce a book like it!' In an article published in both *Pravda* and *Izvestia* on 27 April 1932 (and in the *New Statesman*) Gorky spoke of the novel as 'full of sinister despair', a further extension into pessimism from the writings of Thomas Hardy (an interesting point, as Aldington's hero shares surnames with the Giles Winterbourne of Hardy's *The Woodlander*). Along with *All Quiet on the Western Front* and *A Farewell to Arms* it seemed part of a response to the threat of another world war.

From August onwards Aldington suffered intermittent throat infection and neuralgia. In mid-December he became quite ill. Alarmed by a large swelling on the side of his throat, Brigit called in Dr Torregiani, Italy's best throat specialist. For several weeks Aldington suffered constant neuralgia from an abscess which could not be lanced. Orioli and Douglas were 'angelic' in their attentiveness, Orioli providing plenty of books to read. Aldington tried to work at *Referee* assignments, but Brigit was forced to cable the editor, Hayter Preston, that he was momentarily out of action. Early in February he still could not work or even wear a collar, but by mid-month he was again labouring at Lawrence, editing the *Last Poems*, and told Reeves he had found a manuscript of 67 poems half of which were among the best Lawrence had done. The find included fragments of a long poem on death, in which he saw extraordinary grandeur and dignity.[8]

Now Prentice turned up from London for a planned motor trip south. Douglas and Orioli were invited along, but Douglas felt it too early in the year for such a trip and Aldington himself, still convalescent, quailed at the prospect of setting out in late February in windy, cold and snowy weather. A chilly *tramontana* pursued 'Romolina' (the car) and her party all the way from Florence to Rome; there was snow around Naples and they drove through Salerno, Sicily, in a blizzard, after which they had to be dug out of the snow at Campo Tenese. Apart from the weather conditions, Aldington was an erratic driver, though he resented Pino Orioli's implying as much in his memoir *Moving Along*.[9] Yet despite misadventures he remembered the trip as the most amusing and adventurous he ever made. Prentice could identify and expatiate on the ancient sites they visited. Largely because of his distinctive flavour of personality, Orioli was an endless source of amusement, an Italian *improvisatore* full of verve and raunchy laughter, with a sort of comic dignity. On this trip he was the self-appointed expert on the lavatory facilities, which he classified euphemistically according to Italian art schools, such as 'Quattrocento, scuola di Botticelli', or 'Trecento, Taddeo Gaddi'. Soon he returned from an investigation in some out-of-the-way town with a look of baffled consternation: 'My gawd, zhis vun is *Etrusco!*'[10]

In 1932 Chatto's published two more Aldington titles, *Soft Answers* and the translation of Gérard de Nerval's *Aurélia*, plus the English edition of *Rémy de Gourmont: Selections from All His Works*. The Nerval was well-reviewed, and *Soft Answers* sold better than expected. By the end of April few copies remained of the 2500 first run. Such sales were needed. Aldington earned over a thousand pounds in 1931 (including his *Sunday Referee* retainer and 648 pounds for *The Colonel's Daughter*, but nonetheless ended the year with nearly £200 debit at Chattos. Such a state of affairs was typical for much of his writing life and contributed to the habit of overwork which undermined his health. He was always consious of the need to earn, and even in his best years spent much of his writing energy in working off publishers' advances.

In May he was already sending parts of his new novel to Prentice, who preferred to receive his authors' books that way and thus gain a vicarious sense of being in the writer's workshop. Much of the work on *All Men Are Enemies* was done at Anacapri that summer. Despite a minor motor accident soon after arrival and his depression at the destruction of much of the local natural flower life over a 20-year period, Aldington was able to work there and each successive instalment of the new novel found Prentice more enthusiastic. He offered detailed advice throughout on modifications and amplifications, but rejoiced in the book's scale and declared that if it wasn't authentic writing he did not know what was. Aldington enjoyed that period of work because the process was comparatively uninterrupted by other tasks. That summer he wrote 70 000 words, getting up at seven, working until noon, walking out along the sea coast, lunching, resting and reading through the hot afternoons, and walking again before dinner.

At summer's end he headed north into France, and after stops at Le Lavandou and Bormes stayed for a time at Brantôme. At Bormes he read proof copy of Heinemann's edition of Lawrence's letters with Huxley's introduction. 'When the book came out I found that either Huxley or Frere had cut out one or two cracks at my expense—I can't imagine why. It is surely an important point in Lawrence's nature that he didn't like anybody all the time, not even himself and Frieda.'[11] He was apparently not unsympathetic to Lawrence's inveterate habit of spearing friend and foe alike.

Aldington liked Brantôme despite the fact that from there Brigit was obliged to return to London, for family reasons. Continuing to work at the novel, he suffered stomach troubles and was forced to diet, taking leisure in the heatwave weather by walking or sitting in a little café opposite the abbey. Several times he wrote, in the spate of postcards he sent to London, that the novel moved him to tears, that its world was more real to him than the flesh and blood one he inhabited. His usually ardent letters to Brigit were replaced by bulletins, the one on the morning of 19 September saying that he was working on the final chapter. In mid-afternoon he sent a cable to say he was finished. Next day, suffering severe toothache and neuralgia, he nearly collapsed in the post office. Thus his stay in this village of old stone houses with carved balconies by the Dronne river was intensely emotional, but writing about it later in his memoirs that is all set aside and he conveys a sense of the place's sunniness and his own appreciation of the Abbé de Brantôme, anecdotalist of *dames galantes*.[12]

Aldington crossed the channel with Wyndham Lewis, who had a London exhibition. Lewis offered to draw him but Aldington was obliged to spend a week in a nursing home at Porchester Square and this prevented it. He was still unwell when he returned to France, starting recovery, he felt, only on enjoying an authentic Anjou wine at Saumur. He had not again seen Lewis or seen his show, but wrote a note from Brantôme on 20 October expressing admiration for his genius, though it was apparently the painting he had faith in, for he had written of Lewis's satirical fiction a year or so earlier: 'It is butchery, not artistry. And it is fundamentally inhuman'.[13] Yet Lewis's 'gift of vituperation' (Aldington's phrase), although it has individual flavour, is not unlike similar traits in Pound and Aldington. In all three, rancour against institutions and individuals tends to take a personal edge, which a reader may sense as lack of aesthetic distance.

Both Lewis and Aldington aimed to concentrate the reader's attention on their view of their targets. Like Lewis, Aldington seems to have been influenced by Gourmont's 'art of the *visuel*',[14] that is, detached observation of people's external behaviour, but each injected a personal animus into his portrayals.

By early November Aldington and Brigit were in Portugal, planning to remain for the winter, partly because of the favourable exchange rate. At Coimbra he started daily Portuguese lessons from a university man, possibly the English philologist John Opie who was on the point of retirement after 20 years at the University of Coimbra. Aldington also made contact with a group of poets centred on the journal *Presença*, and arranged to send them English books on his return home. When the rains came at Coimbra he decided to move to Lisbon and from there south. At Setubal he found one of the finest stretches of Riviera scenery in Europe, and rejoiced in the daily supply of fresh seafood.

This trip was unexpectedly curtailed by Chattos' proposal to make 28 cuts in *All Men Are Enemies* (over 4000 words in all) because the typescript was too sexually explicit. Aldington was confronted with the choice between acquiescing or losing his income. He thought momentarily of resuming review work for the *Sunday Referee*, but Aldous Huxley had replaced him. Bowdlerisation would make his novel useless, he felt, but the alternative, he was told was prosecution. In the event, only about a quarter of the proposed cuts were made and he backed down from his insistence on employing the same asterisk device he had used in *Death of a Hero*. He told Schiff that the editor's (he meant Harold Raymond) attitudes in discussing the text had revolted him. For his part, he felt his novel was delicate in its language and passionate in its plea for tenderness between men and women, 'a poem of touch'.[15]

While he was dealing with this crisis, Read called on him to help with another. Read, for the moment, felt conflict between pursuing a career and living by his writing, and apparently contemplated a deliberate study of American best-sellers to discover a 'formula', but Aldington told him 'the only way to make books people will want to have is for Herbert Read to write what Herbert Read passionately wants to write',[16] He explained how he had given up his own secure source of income with the *Referee*, but advised caution, for Read shortly had a six-month leave due in which he could write exactly as he wished and see what he made of it.

At the same time Aldington attempted to forward the literary career of a new Friend, Erik (later Eric) Warman, who had contacted him a year or so earlier to express admiration for *The Colonel's Daughter*. Aldington was advising Warman about two separate book projects, including an attempt at a novel. Warman now proposed to write an appraisal of current literature with Aldington's work featuring as centrepiece. Aldington thought Heinemanns might like this project and went so far as to interest Ralph Pinker in Warman, though for the moment nothing came of these ideas.

Towards the end of January 1933 Aldington lectured at Oxford on literature and censorship, with particular reference to D. H. Lawrence. He had in the back of his mind the possibility of lecturing in the United States, but began negotiating a return to book reviewing, being recommended to the *Evening Standard* by Michael Arlen as replacement for J. B. Priestley. Arlen saw Beaverbrook personally and Aldington was commissioned to supply four articles.

On 2 March *All Men Are Enemies* was published and on a Café Royal menu card dated that day he wrote a pastiche which Norman Gates believes to be 'a graceful tribute to Brigit Patmore':

> Alas! how soon this love is grown
> To such a spreading height in me
> As with it all must shadowed be?

All Men Are Enemies combines a concern about the after-effects of the First World War with a further championing of the individual's right to live his own life. Antony Clarendon, the hero, is characterised in the 'Author's Note' as 'an example of the modern romantic idealistic temperament'. One limitation of the character is that he has no particular calling in life, though he comes to believe that the true focus of an authentic existence is a full heterosexual relationship. As in *Death of a Hero*, the story's outcome is revealed at the start, this time through the mouths of the Olympian gods, who inform the reader that Clarendon's idealism will be continually thwarted by a combination of circumstance and human wrongdoing.

Clarendon's pre-1914 rural English childhood and adolescence at Vine House are portrayed as a contented pastoral, the hero in tune with the natural and social world around him. Part of the portrait is his development of sexual awareness. From all this a full life seems to him to depend on the development of the senses and contact with the forces of instinct, but with the addition of consciousness of culture and a habit of reading. Some critics have perceived a derivative link with D. H. Lawrence, but Lawrence's 'dark gods' of the unconscious have little to do with the world as Aldington sees it, presided over by the Greek nature-gods (in this he is closer to Pound). Vine House and its surrounding country are Clarendon's education in nature, and in a progression of women, starting with his childhood nurse Annie (later fantasised as 'a white fleeting body'), followed in adolescence by his cousin Evelyn, who foreshadows the eventual heroine, Katha.

Clarendon (like George Winterbourne) is average in attainments, mediocre in scholastic performance, with a commendable (if weak) ambition to be an architect. In boyhood he establishes relationships with several older men, chiefly Henry Scrope of New Court (modelled on Wilfrid Scawen Blunt), who formulates his basic philosophy for him:

Don't be duped by general ideas and high-sounding abstractions. Travel, see the world, get to know what men are, work at something that interests you, fall in love, make a fool of yourself if you must, but do it all with gusto. That's the main thing—to live your life with gusto. There may be other lives hereafter, but you'll deserve them, if they come, all the more for having lived this one to the full.[17]

Epicureanism comes naturally to Clarendon, but he has the material world to cope with, 'a world chiefly devoted to getting money'. He is confronted by it in several guises as is suggested by the 'Author's Note', recording the second of the hero's 'instinctive beliefs': 'that living implies much more than acquiescence in a set of formal beliefs, more than getting and spending money. Just as he abandons the secular religions of Nationalism, Socialism and Communism, so he abandons a false marriage and a false career'.

The false career has, at Scrope's instigation, started Clarendon on his travels, to Italy; travel leads to the furthering of the romantic, free-spirited aspects of his life. The-isms, on the other hand, are presented through friendships, with Stephen Crang (Marxist) and Robin Fletcher (socialist), while nationalism is shown in practice through incidents demonstrating after-effects of the First World War (one example, the suspicion by French customs that Clarendon has a visa to enter Austria in 1919). Fletcher, an activist, lives with a certain gusto and wants to found a colony of socialist idealists, but his limitation is that he is programmed by his faith, presented in a great deal too much doctrinal dialogue. Clarendon's reply in one conversation (with another character, Waterton) will serve to show both what he thinks of Communism and one of the shortcomings of the novel. To 'are you a Communist?', Clarendon replies:

No. I think that Communism in practice is poisonous bunk. I don't believe in the class war. I hate it, as I hate all war and killing. The alleged dictatorship of the proletariat is such a swindle that only the proletariat would swallow it. In practice it's the dictatorship of a junta of unscrupulous quasi-scientific fanatics, who'll turn human society into a desert of ennui. But Communism is only Capitalism upside down. Any real revolt must go far, far deeper, and . . . But what's the good of all this? I'm concerned with my own individual life, and at least I'll say this for Capitalism, it doesn't wholly prevent my having one.[18]

Throughout there are rather many conversations about one or other -ism, and by and large they do nothing to develop plot or character. Rather, they afford Aldington an opportunity to express his views.

Clarendon meets Katha on a Greek island a few months before the outbreak of the First World War. They fall in love and plan to marry, though first to make an enlightened try at living together once he has come into a small income. War intervenes, they are cut off from each other and lose contact. Part II, a time shift to 1919, presents a new Clarendon, night-sweating and war-haunted, who crosses frontiers in search of Katha, but fails to find her. Another time shift, Part III, brings us to 1926, Clarendon's marriage to Margaret and his realisation that it, and the business world it is centred in, have prevented him from living with gusto, though it is also true that the war and the loss of Katha have been inner deaths for him, leading him to feel that life itself is worthless, that is, to the furthest reach possible from the experience of full living. Leaving Aeaea after the soul-destroying failure of his search for Katha he feels 'as if he were a dead soul ferried over the waters of death'.[19] Now, in fleeing Margaret and the world of money-death, he heads again for the Paris of his first travels and begins to rediscover the quick of that early experience, although in a maturer configuration, but it is what happens on his return to England that finally shakes him loose from the middle-class death-in-life.

All along, Clarendon's efforts to live his own life, the life of an individual, cost him friendships. Back in England in 1926 he becomes involved in the General Strike. At first he refuses to collaborate in strike-breaking, but personal loyalty, this time to Margaret's brother Julian, eventually draws him in. Involved in a fracas between temporary newspaper workers and strikers, he is struck from behind by someone who turns out to be his old friend Robin Fletcher. He helps Fletcher escape, pleading with him to drop political violence, but the response is a vehement, 'And to hell with *you*'.[20] Clarendon is upset with himself at having taken sides, and this could have been the moment when he abandons England.

Instead, he stays on and has another disillusioning meeting with a figure from his past, this time Evelyn, who has become a shallow social product typical of her caste. But soon after this he discovers by chance that Katha returns to Aeaea for a short stay at the same time every year, and so eventually they are reunited, after he has raced against time to catch her before she leaves. The last hundred or so pages of the book celebrate this reunion, not as spontaneous as their first meeting but full of tenderness, and the story ends on a tremulous note when the two vow to each other to protect their precarious happiness from the world at large.

All Men Are Enemies is too long, much longer than is necessary. There is too much talk. Another problem is that there is no serious choice between Margaret and Katha. Margaret represents an unacceptable ideology (bourgeois materialism) and so is portrayed as unattractive—possessive, domineering and narrow-minded— from the outset. That our romantic idealist should marry her at all is not altogether credible. Though it verges at times on the mawkish, the love relationship is quite well handled (apart from wordiness) though its implied values (the world well lost, and so on) seem shallow.

Evocations of the English countryside and the life of the senses are two of the book's strengths. Clarendon's early sexual encounter with Evelyn is economically handled, because they need say little to each other. The feeling for the love affair of Antony and Katha is genuine enough though their talk is stilted and somewhat stereotyped. A deeper strain in the book is its adumbration of the decline of personal values after the war and of how difficult it has become to live an individual life. Aldington knows how to rhapsodise feelings and how to explore nuances of behaviour which are the outcome of social conditions.

Aldington reacted strongly to a review which appeared in the *TLS* on 2 March. Giving an account of the book, the reviewer says: 'This summary may convey an empression of crudity, but it is not unfair; crudity there is, at least of ideas. The workmanship, on the other hand, is so good that it disguises this. Yet to one reader at least [Aldington's] men are infinitely more satisfactory than his women. . . . The scenes of action, such as the strike and the hunt for Katha in Vienna, show Mr Aldington at his best, and that is very good'.[21] A week or so after this, Louise Morgan in *Everyman* provided a portrait of the artist as epicurean bon vivant, the poor boy who has made good by his own efforts: 'He makes excellent company, for his good humour is as inexhaustible as his memory, and his tact and sympathy are unfailing'.[22] This picture of positive buoyancy is a sample of one kind of portrait, a kind which is regularly interspersed among depictions of Aldington's misanthropic pessimism.

Despite Chattos' excisions, the novel was nonetheless banned in

Australia, a circumstance which amused him but which aided in undermining his health and spirits, both lowered by overwork. Opposition to *All Men Are Enemies* may have contributed to its appearing on the best-seller lists and Pinker shortly negotiated an agreement with Twentieth-Century Fox Films who took out an option on the book for £2500, sufficient income to allow Aldington freedom to concentrate on fiction for three years. Pinker also negotiated a comprehensive Italian agreement and sold Danish and Norwegian rights. In a period of widespread retrenchment, Aldington's career was flourishing and expanding.

13   1933–36

After the publication of *All Men Are Enemies* Aldington and Brigit spent most of 1933 in France, chiefly at the Villa Devos, Pramousquier, near Le Lavandou. Despite an infection caused by dust under the eyelid, he enjoyed the life, getting up at six in the morning to listen to the nightingales in a huge ilex tree. A rather neglected garden, with irises, geraniums, roses, marigolds, mimosa and mesembrianthums, delighted both of them. After his daily stint of writing, he soothed himself weeding the unkempt flowerbeds. As the house was protected from the wind they rejoiced in its long, seaward verandah with its cool floor of large black and white squares. They relaxed in the knowledge that the small inflow of tourists was still months away.

Once again Aldington felt free to stop *Referee* reviewing, recommending Herbert Read as his replacement. He had begun notes towards his next novel *Women Must Work*, but spent part of the summer collaborating with Derek Patmore in writing a dramatic version of one of his own short stories, 'Now She Lies There'. *The Life of a Lady* was published but never produced and remains, as Patmore rightly says, a 'literary curiosity'. The play is based on an 'outstandingly vicious' lampoon of Nancy Cunard, portrayed as Constance, 'the temporary wife of a series of *faux grands hommes*', who comes to a bad end as the diseased mistress of an Arab living in North Africa.

When the visitors came, Charles Prentice was among them and Alexander Frere, of Heinemanns, who was remarried at Villa Devos in June. Another visitor was Professor Gustave Cohen, discoverer of the Liègeois 15th-century work *The Mystery of the Nativity*, which Aldington had translated into English several years earlier. Cohen, a severely wounded war veteran, became a firm friend.

When the playscript was completed, Aldington broke a four-year silence to seek Gaige's interest as a potential theatrical producer. Pinker sent Gaige the script, for which Derek Patmore had been the source of practical stage experience and had helped in planning scenes. There is no evidence that Gaige replied, and Aldington's playwrighting career ended almost as quickly as it had begun.

The autumn of 1933 he spent motoring in Spain, but by early December he was back in London, settled in at Carlton Court, Pall

Mall Place, another London address he suggested was 'mostly inhabited by whores', but which was inexpensive and convenient. Once again he met Wyndham Lewis, who was acting somewhat strangely, receiving mail at a Pall Mall box number, and even leading importunate visitors to it, as his actual 'address'. Despite this, Aldington provided Lewis with introductions to Paris friends. When Lewis returned to London at the end of January 1934 he suggested that he make a drawing of Aldington, which would require two one-hour sittings. After a delay due to recurrence of 'trench fever', Aldington did sit, though the project was never completed, because late in February Lewis was taken into a Baker Street nursing home due to the aftereffects of venereal disease. Aldington had advanced £10 for the drawing and now, learning that Lewis was in straitened circumstances, followed this with another £10. Lewis intended to travel to southwest France and Spain to recuperate and Aldington sent information on eating and lodging places in the Pyrenees and on the Biscay Coast. When, late in April, Aldington sent a cheque for £25, Lewis judged his mood well when he replied that the money would be 'bloody useful and more than useful during the next few weeks, in obtaining for me convalescent *extras*—better and brighter invalid Port!—cream with my asparagus, and *really* new-laid eggs, in addition to settling a debt or two which otherwise would be demanded once a week with menaces'.[1]

Aldington, as usual, was putting in long days at his writing table and had his novel *Women Must Work* three-quarters finished. His Secker edition of Lawrence's *Selected Poems* came out at this time, following *Last Poems* (1933), where he had observed that all Lawrence's writing 'forms one immense autobiography'. *The Poems of Richard Aldington* (an update of *Collected Poems*, 1929) appeared this year. Of it, the noted American critic, R.P. Blackmur wrote: 'Experience catches Aldington by the throat or beats him in the face, and he answers back as vigorously as he can' and 'His poems make powerful personal documents of a life, but they do not often do the necessary work to make them powerful poetry'.[2] *Vers libre* may for Aldington he believes, have been a trap, a slack medium which lent itself to 'what Henry James called "the terrible fluidity" of self-revelation'.

Apart from a section of 'New Poems' the book is substantially the 1929 volume. Blackmur's charge of 'terrible fluidity' seems not entirely fair when levelled against the new poems. Admittedly, they are direct comments on immediate experience and neither allusively recondite nor transformed by metaphor, but they are measured:

> So for a little time I stand among the pines
> Above the clean dry water-course
> Where all sounds are hushed.
> There I am at peace, there I am at one with all things.
> But up here I am not at peace,
> Never truly and wholly at one with all things.[3]

Another reviewer, John Wheelwright, suggests, perhaps more justly, that this group of poems shows a return to 'mastery of the direct and elegant record of sensation and opinion'.[4]

Shortly after his helping Lewis, Aldington heard from Norman Douglas that both Orioli and Reggie Turner were in financial difficulties because of the collapse of an Italian bank. Pino, Douglas said, was also suffering from 'inflammation of the parotid gland'. Aldington sought out the nature of this ailment from a medical encyclopaedia and at once sent a cheque for £100, being quickly repaid by Orioli's comic English: 'I only wished you had been here when I open your letter and I should have jumped to your neck and kissed you'.[5] Orioli's zest and spontaneity were among Aldington's treasures.

Having completed *Women Must Work* in April 1934, he spent some months in Portugal, Spain, and then Switzerland. Warman sent him an account of the film of *All Men Are Enemies*. Aldington noted savagely that while the book had been 'mutilated' and even banned, 'this bloody offensive film' was cleared for 'U' (general) circulation. In Spain and Portugal he attempted unsuccessfully to link up with Lewis on his recuperative excursion. Soon he himself needed convalescence. On the road between Feldkirch and Bludenz in Austria, he was involved in one of his car accidents. An oncoming car skidded, hit him side-on and smashed in his car's front end. Brigit's forehead was badly cut by the rear-view mirror. Aldington was more seriously injured, with a broken knee-cap, which meant spending at least six weeks in the Feldkirch Spital. 'Owing to the obsolescent treatment of my friend Dr. Gutessen-Guttrinken, so dubbed because of a breezy bedside manner I emerged from the Spital with my fracture imperfectly healed and a leg stiff as a poker.'[6] He was first removed to Adetzenburgerhof just outside Feldkirch, and then to Fontanella, a tiny hamlet 6000 feet up with a view across a deep Alpine valley. By the beginning of July he was able to move around on crutches and towards the end of the month, on sticks. In early August he was back at the typewriter, at work on his novel *Very Heaven*. By then, Austrian police had absolved him of responsibility in the accident. The other driver, besides incurring costs for car repairs, surgery, hospital charges, lawyers and compensation, also received a three-month gaol sentence.

While at Feldkirch, Aldington heard Chancellor Dollfuss speak and was struck by the audience's listlessness. A few weeks later, at Fontanella, he heard Dollfuss had been assassinated and wondered momentarily whether he and Brigit should flee the country, At Feldkirch and in the Alps he was unable to work steadily, but gave sporadic attention to a long poem and to planning a collection of essays. Meantime *Women Must Work* was published. Subscription was a disappointing 4000; he felt the reviews 'mouldy' and the book itself a pot-boiler.

Etta Morison (whose name echoes Brigit's original name, Ethel Elizabeth Morrison Scott), a contrast with Georgie Smithers, is in some ways a surrogate for Aldington. More ambitious than Georgie, Etta has more initiative. She is attractive, but poor, and she grows up in dreary Dortborough (Dover). The novel covers the first quarter of the century, up to the General Strike. Its theme is the possibility of true individualism, how difficult it is in a conformist and materialist society, and how doubly difficult for a woman.

Apart from the brief prologue, the novel concerns Etta's life from the age of 19—her efforts to escape Dortborough, her experience of poverty in London, contact with the suffragettes, an office job in which the boss inevitably attempts to take advantage of her poverty to seduce her, and her rescue from a degrading situation by Ada Lawson, a rich suffragette. Through Mrs Lawson, Etta experiences a fuller and more comfortable life in Knightsbridge and is grateful, but she begins to realise that a woman in her circumstances must fight for what she wants: 'Without perceiving it, she had become a little ruthless, more than a little calculating and wary. She thought her eagerness to please Ada Lawson came from gratitude and devotion; and so it did, but there was a grain of calculation—Etta wanted so much not to be sent away, and what better means of avoiding it than by making herself indispensable?[7] But this was a natural reaction in a world where her education had been skimped and her liberty circumscribed because she was female.

The thrust of *Women Must Work* is the conflict in individual experience between the need for self-preservation and desire for self-fulfilment. Etta Morison's twin disadvantages are poverty and femaleness. The first leads her away from Ralph, the man she loves, initially into becoming the mistress of Francis and eventually, as a successful business-woman, into buying a husband and also Dymcott, the property of her former benefactor. In the book's final scene, Etta has her child, husband and newly-acquired estate, but when her husband, Maurice, suggests they dance on the lawn, she responds: 'We can't dance here. There are too many dead leaves'.[8] This Ibsenesque symbol indicates that, a success in the world of Mammon, she has betrayed the authentic life of love and spontaneity.

Woman Must Work, like other Aldington novels, gained critical approval in Russia. He does not provide a warm or especially deep potrait of Etta, but outlines in clear, dispassionate writing the plight of woman due to her implicitly inferior status in British society, a theme he had addressed in a different way the *The Colonel's Daughter*. Etta fights circumstance and, superficially, solves the problem by finding her way into the customarily male position of material power and dominance. Ironically, her success is the instrument of her failure, because she has denied love and so at the end has not the dancing spirit.

In some respects, notably objectivity of presentation, *Women Must Work* is Aldington's most satisfactory novel. Its limitation is that its ultimate purpose never becomes fully clear. As a critique of the position of women, it is not detailed or penetrating enough; as a sortie against the moneyed bourgeoisie, it is not pressed home. Nor, because the protagonist Etta does not live it out, is Aldington's epicurean philosophy a cohering element in the novel. Yet the book commands respect because its author has overcome the tinges of sentimentality in the presentation of erotic love which flaw *All Men Are Enemies* and the underlying hysteria of the society-baiting in *Death of A Hero*.

From Austria, Aldington had started out northeast for Alsace and Lorraine, but he changed direction and headed for the Pyrenees and Spain. From Spain he at first planned to return to the Riviera for the winter of 1934–35, but set out instead for London. On the way from the coast, visiting Halcott Glover in Sussex he reinjured his damaged knee by slipping on a footpath. This meant another operation, another spell on crutches and canes and some time wearing an orthopaedic steel brace (which Brigit called a 'moveable splint'). During recovery in November and December 1934 he completed *Life Quest,* a poetic celebration of 'the singular prerogative of consciousness'.

'There is no argument, but a loose string of moods and meditations, variations on the theme of the 'Life Quest'', says the 'Author's Note',[9] to this poem-sequence, in 20 loosely-related parts. Its title and some background come from 'Sir G. Elliot Smith's *Human History* (1934)'. Replete with historical and cultural allusions the poem is yet a denial of history, and even society, a plea for individuality. This existence is the only one we experience, *Life Quest* asserts, in the tones of Wallace Stevens:

> We shall not see, we shall never see
> Gold islands of the blest in sweeter air . . .

The 'ankh unlocks no door', but we make gods in a vain effort to enlarge our human horizons. Our latest attempts are to seek gods in science. We should distrust 'Heroes and Saviours' and the 'mortal soul' to live for the 'immortal' body, and especially for human (that is, heterosexual) love. We should be 'Avid for much living' and the endlessness of death is worth the 'moment of pure life'. *Life Quest* celebrates what Aldington, echoing Lawrence, calls, 'the magnificent here and now of life in the flesh',[10] but this celebration is discursive and its phrasing and allusiveness have not altogether escaped Eliot's cadences ('Under the Guadarrama in the spring/I heard the nightingales in the ragged park').

At this time Aldington strongly felt that he was finished with Europe, just as earlier he had finished with England and earlier still Lawrence had gone through both processes. He was bothered by a sense of the stress of ancient quarrels, which impeded the free life he envisaged, the wish to pursue his writer's calling and otherwise to live pleasantly. In the autumn at Bordeaux he had experienced the same feeling about France, and his thoughts began to turn to the American continent, his first idea (perhaps linked back to his childhood experience of reading Henry Walter Bates) being to explore the Amazon. One possible cause of the direction of his thought was correspondence about Read's South American novel *The Green Child,* published by Heinemann in 1935.

Aldington thought of trying the West Indies and his first idea was to head for Tortola in the Virgin Islands which was remote and had only one small guest house, but he eventually decided on Tobago as a place where he could stay indefinitely and revisit occasionally, and which had the double advantage of being outside the tourist and the hurricane zones. There he could continue writing fiction and tackle the D. H. Lawrence survey he had discussed with Martin Secker. He told Secker that another writer he found a tempting subject was Norman Douglas. He believed he could be 'wholehearted' about Douglas, on the literary side if not otherwise, though he would be happy to gun down Douglas's 'alleged philosophy', an apparent reference to Douglas's open sexual pursuit of Italian peasant boys. The Douglas idea bore no immediate fruit, but the topic was to be crucial in Aldington's future.

Besides completing his book on essays *Artifex* in Tobago, he also finished compiling *The Spirit of Place*, which he later described as 'an anthology of the most beautiful prose passages from Lawrence's books'.[11] Two sketches from *Artifex* preserve Aldington's impressions of his Caribbean voyage, in what he variously describes as a 'banana boat' and a 'cruise ship'. The commercial materialism of Scarborough township, Tobago, where he landed, and the way of life implied by it thoroughly depressed him. His quarters at Terry Hill, Mt St George, eight miles from town were on 40 acres of derelict plantation 800 feet above sea level, with a Caribbean view, but accessible only by track. At the conclusion of one sketch, 'A Splinter of America', he expresses relief at having escaped Europe, but he intimated to Lewis and others at the time that he rather regretted it.

Aldington was a reacter, and a sceptical one, with a vein of general misanthropy, but also an epicurean. From Tobago he said: 'It seems to me there might be . . . a more modest conception of man's place in nature, and an abhorrence of every kind of greed and destruction'.[12] Thus much was suggested to him by this new environment, and among the advantages of life at Mt St George were absence of machine noises, availability of cheap milk and vegetables and an exotic list of fruits (all varieties of citrus, pawpaw, shaddock, bananas, sapodillas, plantain). He intended to remain until the beginning of the rainy season in June. Living was cheap; for five pounds a month he and Brigit rented a bungalow with large living space, two bedrooms, two galleries (one enclosed, and one along the seafront), loggia, kitchen, bath and shower. A further £3.15sh. employed a laundry woman, a yard boy and an indoor boy who cooked well and liked to call himself 'de butler'. Apart from 'de butler', who received a little bread and sugar, these three had to find their own food. Aldington and Brigit were pleased, too, with the dry season climate, a cool trade wind and 70–80°F temperatures, with unexpectedly little mosquito trouble, because of the height above sea level. If one had company, the place was ideal between December and June, the only problem being the local humans, who (he informed Lewis) were yahoos. But, although he worked well enough, Aldington soon found Caribbean life enervating and his June departure for New York was a flight from lethargy:

> ... I soon fell into the easy rhythm of life in the tropics, varied only by excursions about the very beautiful island and bathing picnics, where I swam in a sea as clear and warm as the Mediterranean. But the most valuable part of that three or four months' experience was the living so close to nature, in an exuberant phase which was new to me.
> 'Isn't it very quiet up here?' a chance tourist visitor asked.
> 'Beautifully quite!' I said enthusiastically; and then, seeing the astonishment on her face, realised that for some people 'quiet' is synonymous not with happiness but with dullness.
> My two books were finished in a long spurt of concentration, and then I idled away some days or weeks, with no mental effort beyond reading a few modern books in English. I didn't want to write anything ; I felt as if I should never want to write again . . . And then suddenly I became aware of a danger lurking in this seductive life of the tropics. It was delightful, rapturous even, to live so natural a rhythm; but it was nature in the mood of the Lotus-Eaters.[13]

He was in New York to make publishing and literary connections. He met such people as Burton Rascoe, and Irita Van Doren, book editor for the *New York Herald Tribune*, but this was a kind of milieu he disliked. 'Curiously enough', Derek Patmore recalls, 'Richard hated being lionized and really enjoyed small gatherings of friends'.[14] Meanwhile, in Moscow appeared the second Russian edition of *Death of a Hero*. In the foreword, Ivan Anisimov[15] praises Aldington's 'bitter realism', portrayal of 'the bankruptcy of capitalism' and closeness to the 'completely new field of conceptions, values and relations' available in the Communist world.[16] A Russian translation of *The Colonel's Daughter*, which also appeared in 1935, was accorded respect although it was noted that the book was not on the same heroic scale as *Death of a Hero*. Given their particular tenor, Anisimov's comments occur at an interesting moment—when Aldington, with his particular ideal of 'the good European', had grown altogether weary of Europe:

> It was particularly easy for a man like Aldington, who has translated Euripides and Anacreon with great delicacy of understanding, who has made a profound study of Voltaire and the Latin poets of the Renaissance, and who has a profound feeling for historical tradition, to come to the conclusion that contemporary 'civilization' was barbarism. . . . And Aldington writes about 'the decline of the West' directly without reserve, mercilessly.

At about this time, Ford Madox Ford's disciple Douglas Goldring, in his autobiography *Odd Man Out* characterised *Death of a Hero* as a 'bitter masterpiece'. Goldring also offers a list of 'men and women I have met whom I have particularly appreciated'. Among the 20 names are included Ford, Lawrence, Douglas and Aldington. Attempting to define the 'quality which singles out those individuals', Goldring writes:

> It is an indefinable something which the 'Socialites', with their 'getting on' preoccupations, completely miss. How greatly one values, in this standardized world, infatuated by the Bitch Goddess, 'the character!' How one admires 'the eccentric': the man whose values are his own and not the herd's![17]

While Aldington's work was making its mark on one version of the 'new world' (Anisimov uses the phrase), he was engrossed in his first contact with the other. Between brief summer and autumn sojourns in New York City he spent the summer at Brockway Manor, Old Lyme, a farmhouse on the Connecticut River with 200 acres attached. While he was there, the Overbrook Press, Stamford, Connecticut, published a handsome limited edition of *A Dream in the Luxembourg*. Before leaving New York on the *SS Berengaria* on 11 October Aldington made what seemed to be a major publishing contact. He and Brigit spent a week at Oyster Bay, Long Island, with Nelson Doubleday, the publisher. He had met Doubleday in the summer of 1933, in the company of Somerset Maugham's secretary,

1. Richard Aldington in 1905. (Estate of Margery Lyon Gilbert)

2. Richard Aldington aged 19, 1911. (Morris Library, Southern Illinois University)

3. Hilda Doolittle (H.D.) in 1913. (Beinecke Library, Yale University)

4. A group of fellow-poets visit Wilfred Scawen Blunt, January 1914. (Courtesy of the Rt. Hon. Earl of Lytton, OBE)

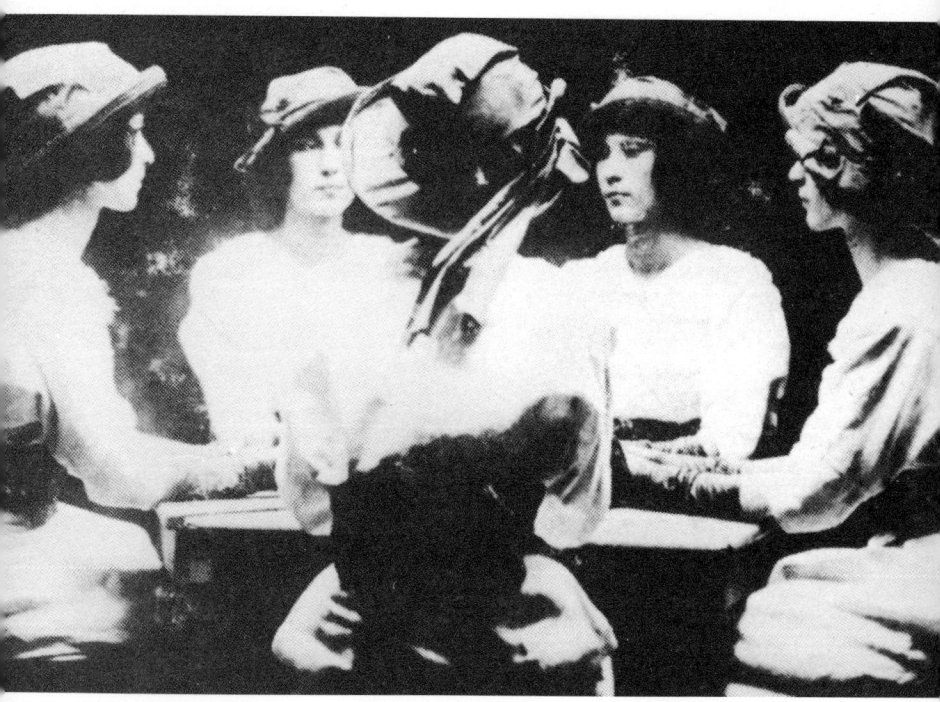

5. A multiple photograph of Dorothy (Arabella) Yorke. (Estate of Professor Alfred Satterthwaite)

6. Richard Aldington as an army officer, 1918. (Beinecke Library)

7. D.H. Lawrence's portrait of Dorothy Yorke. (Beinecke Library)

8. Brigit Patmore as a young woman. (Estate of Professor Alfred Satterthwaite)

9. Osbert Sitwell and Richard Aldington in the gardens at Montegufoni. (Morris Library)

10. Richard Aldington, by Man Ray, late 1920s. (Beinecke Library)

11. Richard Aldington, photograph taken for a Harrod's window display in the late 1920s. (Vaughan and Freeman photo. Estate of Margery Lyon Gilbert)

12. Richard Aldington (photograph by Madam Yevonde). According to Brigit Patmore, this was taken shortly after publication of *Death of a Hero* in 1929.

13. Aldington and Brigit Patmore in the South of France, early 1930s. (From Brigit Patmore's *My Friends When Young*)

14. Richard and Netta Aldington in the late 1930s. (Courtesy of Catherine Aldington Guillaume)

15. Richard and Netta Aldington in the early 1940s. (Beinecke Library)

16. Henry Williamson and Alister Kershaw, 1949. (Courtesy of Alister Kershaw)

17. Aldington in Montpellier, 1955. (Courtesy of F.-J. Temple)

18. H.D. in 1956. (Beinecke Library)

19. Richard Aldington, Lawrence Durrell, Henry Miller and Jacques Temple. (Courtesy of F.J. Temple)

20. Aldington with his daughter Catherine in Leningrad, late June 1962. (Courtesy of Catherine Aldington Guillaume)

21. Aldington and Catherine in the gardens of Petrodvorets, 1962. (Courtesy of Catherine Aldington Guillaume)

22. Aldington broadcasting in Russia, 1962. (Courtesy of Catherine Aldington Guillaume)

23. At Valentin Kataev's dacha, at Peredelkino, near Moscow. Kataev is on the left, Aldington next to him, Catherine in the centre. (Courtesy of Catherine Aldington Guillaume)

24. Aldington with a group of his Maison Salle neighbours, 1962. (Courtesy of Catherine Aldington Guillaume)

Alan Searle. But Searle's presence had prevented Aldington's working to establish a business connection with Doubleday. At this point, the possibility was still open.

For the winter of 1935–36 Aldington was back in London, this time at the Cavendish Hotel, Jermyn Street. During this period he saw Alec Waugh occasionally. The two had first met at the Poetry Bookshop in 1919 and Waugh had praised Aldington's poetry in *To-Day*. Several times in Berkshire days, Aldington had gone to see Waugh play cricket, but they lost touch in the mid-1920s. Waugh renewed the link in an unexpected way, by reading a column in the *Daily Express* in which 'Beachcomber'[18] quoted Aldington's long poem *The Eaten Heart* and scoffed: 'This is what they call poetry nowadays'. Waugh concluded that it was what he, at any rate, called poetry. He bought and read *The Eaten Heart*, then *A Dream in the Luxembourg*, wrote to Aldington and for several years they met from time to time in London or at Waugh's home in Silchester.

Waugh later realised that, while he met Aldington at Douglas Goldring's and elsewhere, he never met him on his own ground. 'I have missed the clue to him', he recalled, 'But it is my belief that he was one of those men who cannot be bothered to organise a social life, who socially live from hand to mouth, making the most of what happens to be around'.[19] Others noted in Aldington an aura of solitariness. He needed company and from time to time made good friends, but it was not characteristic of him to establish a fixed network of social relationships, perhaps because of his semi-nomadic existence.

That winter he heard from Read for the first time in more than a year, a lapse which caused him to grumble to Lewis about Read's ingratitude for help in placing *The Green Child* with Heinemanns. Despite the justness of Waugh's perception about his social life, Aldington could be touchy if a friend slighted their relationship, so now he mentioned to Read that the silence had offended him and suggested a meeting. Whether this meeting occurred is not known, but there follows a ten-year gap in their correspondence (though Read was surprised later to realise this and felt that some letters at least must have been lost.)

Through March 1936 Aldington remained at the Cavendish working on his novel *Very Heaven*. But early in April he and Brigit left England, travelling with the Glovers. Hal Glover, still an unsuccessful playwright, was in poor circumstances and suffering from tuberculosis. His friends took turns looking after him, though

Aldington found the task not very congenial as Glover had discarded his early Fabianism to become 'pro-Musso and pro-Hitler and admire Catholicism!', a state of mind which Aldington characterised to Leonard Bacon as 'gagaism'. In mid-April they landed at Lisbon, en route to Spain. Once there, they saw signs of the coming civil war—two fascisti under arrest at Cordoba, village children giving the Communist salute, and Aldington felt an air of unreality about the political situation. 'Spanish communism must be a queer thing', he wrote to Eric Warman, 'since 90% of the people are bigoted Catholics. Also, the Spaniards are the most intensely individualist people in the world'.[20] A month later they were still travelling, but moving eastward and, possibly gifted by hindsight, Aldington claimed he had felt uneasy during the whole Spanish visit and so had curtailed it.

His apparent detachment about Spain, which contrasts with the involvement of so many intellectuals of the time, may be explained by a passage in *Life for Life's Sake*, where he examines his reactions in the mid-1930s to loss of contact with friends in Germany:

> Though I hadn't many friends in Germany, there were a few I should have liked to read my poem; but their unbroken silence was an only too sinister hint of their fate. It was obvious long before this that the peace had failed to be a peace; now the indications were that Europe was slipping back into barbarism. Unconsciously in boyhood, later on consciously, I had given a lot of energy to the task of trying to fit myself to be a good European—an ideal which is very much older than Nietzsche and without his absurd arrogance. And on that winter evening I perceived with dismay that there might very soon be no Europe in which one might try to be good. The whole conception was being as ruthlessly destroyed as the early Christians destroyed the cosmopolitan Graeco-Roman culture. Violent minorities were betraying and murdering all that had dignified their countries. Reluctantly and ruefully I had to admit that there was no longer anywhere in Europe I wanted to live in; and that there was no place for me among intellectual fanatics who were busy labelling themselves leftists and rightists, and who constantly summoned one to stand and deliver on one silly side or the other.[21]

From Geneva in June he wrote a 'fan letter' to H. G. Wells. Wells had responded positively, if briefly, on publication of *Death of a Hero*, but had irritated Aldington by failing to defend the book against jingoistic and Mrs Grundyish reviewers. Brigit, having met Wells many years earlier through Violet Hunt, had a long-standing friendship with him. When in the early 1930s she visited him several times at the Villa Lou Pidou at Grasse, Aldington did not go. In *My Friends When Young* she muses, 'I find it significant that H. G. Wells had not invited Richard too'. Certainly Wells was in no position to be prudish about Brigit's liaison with Aldington, but Derek Patmore makes a point regarding writing:

> Although he was fond of her [Brigit], he did not seem to take much interest in Richard or his books. In fact, Richard, with his savage attack on English life and his inherent bitterness, was not the type of author who would attract H.G.[22]

Early in July, Aldington and the Glovers were at the Alpenhotel, Fernpass in Tirol, five-hours into Austria from the Swiss frontier. Because the political situation was volatile, Aldington wanted to stop at one of his earlier haunts, Vorarlberg, near the Swiss border, but the Glovers did not like the place. As they travelled Aldington worked steadily at *Very Heaven*. His aim was to complete the novel by September, and despite the conditions of travelling he seems to have been able to work steadily when the opportunity was there. From Austria he told Warman he had received a note from a young German critic who was writing a book on him and stated that the 'official' German view of Richard Aldington portrayed him as rootless, cynical and irresponsibly wealthy, a picture which suggested to its subject that German critics were not unlike those in the 'dear homeland'. Interestingly, writing of *Very Heaven* in the *New York Herald Tribune* the following March, William Soskin employed a German phrase to sum up what he saw as Aldington's focal position, the view that there is 'something rotten ... in the *verdammte kapitalistische Ordnung*'.[23] Had it ever appeared, the young German critic's book might have made an interesting contrast with current Russian views of Aldington and his work.

With typical generosity, Aldington was helping Warman, offering loans and advice on how to pursue magazine-writing assignments, even paying half his London Library subscription. He advised Warman to try Allen Lane, the publisher who had started the spectacularly successful pioneering paperback venture of Penguin Books. Aldington's *Death of a Hero* had appeared in May in the now-familiar orange, white and black covers, within three weeks selling 23,000 copies, a spectacular-sounding figure but even at 15 per cent royalty the author would have netted well under £100.

Very Heaven was completed in the first week of September while he was still in Austria. By early October he and Brigit had returned to London. He decided to continue at the Cavendish Hotel, partly to save Brigit household chores, but undoubtedly to give himself more freedom of action. He had begun courting Brigit's daughter-in-law, the young and attractive Netta Patmore. So, for the third time, he was finishing a long-term relationship with a woman. Characteristically, he was too reticent to confide in friends, rather tending to disguise the real situation and delay revealing the new circumstances for as long as possible. Nor do Brigit's otherwise chatty memoirs, *My Friends When Young*, reveal anything.

Brigit saw H. G. Wells a number of times over the next few months. Writing to him on 27 November, she apologised for annoying him with repeated notes and visits, offering the excuse that she was in considerable pain. This is a veiled allusion to her relationship with Aldington, though in a note a few days later she conveys his greetings to Wells, perhaps as a way of signalling that Aldington was still with her. Then in a letter dated only 'Friday', probably written in December, from the Cavendish she refuses Wells's invitation to a luncheon the following week, saying: 'My son has got to get away in order to avoid a nervous breakdown and I must go with him'. She and her son Michael, Netta's husband, took a vacation in Nice.

When he sailed alone on the *SS Normandie* for new York on 22 December, Aldington had a new romance on his mind, although at this stage a future with Netta was still no more than a possibility. He had a week or two earlier set up his writing affairs very satisfactorily, by signing a six-year contract with Heinemanns to cover all his work from 1 December 1936. His friend Charles Prentice had preceded him in leaving Chattos.

14 1937–38

On 2 January 1937 Aldington wrote from Bonnie Hall Plantation, Yemasee, South Carolina, explaining to Henry Slonimsky that he had decided to come over for Christmas in response to an invitation from the Doubledays, but that Brigit remained in London 'with the boys'. Aldington's seriousness about his new love relationship may be gauged from the fact that 'On board MS Lafayette, approaching England' on 15 January, he wrote to warn H.D. that she would shortly receive evidence of his adultery with Netta, who, by chance, she had met with Aldington in a London tea shop. H.D. had moved to London in 1934 after completion of the famous series of analyses which resulted in her book *Tribute to Freud*.[1]

Overtly, the love affair had been inaugurated the previous October, but now Aldington admitted, 'It's been going on for over a year, with each of us trying to be "honourable" and suppress our feelings...' The relationship had begun to form just a few months after Netta's marriage to Michael Patmore. Once it became known, Netta twice nearly ran off with Aldington before he left for the United States in the *SS Normandie*. His departure caused a flurry of cables between them, with Netta finally capitulating and agreeing that they should 'run away together', so that he set out to return to England on 7 January. 'With me', he told H.D., 'she can live the adventurer's life for which she was born and' (with conscious irony, he invokes another and more distant Patmore) 'not be just one more domestic angel-in-the-house...' He carefully informed H.D. that he was giving Brigit part of his income. As if taking a line from *All Men Are Enemies* he concludes: 'Lovers are selfish. They have to be. The world is against them. Don't be against us'.[2]

When she heard Aldington and Netta were headed for Italy, H.D. wrote to Bryher: 'It was Richard's fourth honeymoon in the heel and toe of Italy and environs, very Byron?' Later, when the divorce proceedings were being forwarded H.D. was very sensitive, remembering her own circumstances, to the fact that Netta was pregnant; but this did not prevent 'some backbiting on her part'. Frere, Aldington's editor, also approached H.D. on his behalf, for she wrote to Frances Gregg on 10 February: 'I feel he looks upon R. as a sort of Byron de nos jours and treats me like a noble woman, which is always so trying'.[3]

By mid-February this latter-day Byron and mistress were at the Pensione Balesti, Florence, in a room with painted ceilings and an enormous bed. Aldington was back in Norman Douglas territory. During this stay, Douglas offended Aldington's anti-homosexualism on being taken with Pino on a drive to Lucca, by having the 'insolence' to bring along uninvited 'a depraved-looking slum child whose behaviour during the day left absolutely no doubt as to the nature of their relationship'.[4]

From Florence, Netta's introduction to Italy took them as far as Capri, where in an almost empty hotel she became ill (presumably reaction to several months of strain). Once she recovered they headed north for France, but did not arrive without further misadventures. The car blew a gasket, so Aldington was put to the expense of sending it by train from Spezia to Nice. It took a long time to arrive and further delays in its retrieval were caused by customs problems, but by April they were settled at Le Canadel. Their new home, the Villa Koeclin, was a cottage on a low cliff, surrounded by an acre or so of thick coppice, but with a fine view of islands. A summer cottage, it had no heat and the roof leaked, but the only bad winter months were January and February and it was possible to swim in the sea nearby until as late in the season as December.

While they were still in Italy *Very Heaven* was published in London, with a good pre-publication subscription. By early May, British sales had reached 9000 and the novel was already being translated for an Italian edition. From a sales point of view, Aldington's career as a novelist continued along the successful course maintained throughout the 1930s, but there is a significant change in the focus of his work. The hero of *Very Heaven*, Chris Heylin, is of the post-First World War generation and thematically the novel is concerned with the 'generation gap' between him and those who have suffered through the war. The novel's title comes from famous lines in Book II of *The Prelude* where Wordsworth celebrates the French Revolution, a time at which 'to be young was very heaven'. Chris Heylin lives in what is potentially such a time, when the whole society is suffering the consequences of economic breakdown, a failure of capitalism; but Aldington's use of Wordsworth is ironic, there is no revolution and Chris Heylin is not forceful enough to be a revolutionary, though years later Aldington told his friend Alister Kershaw that he saw *Very Heaven* 'as a study of a young man inevitably heading towards communism'.[5] In an essay-length note on the novel he makes clear that Heylin is not 'a genuine philosopher or writer or artist' though he considers himself something of an intellectual and has a critical turn of mind. He is a man of action thwarted by his parents' loss of wealth. 'With the money, his caste and caste-training would have been an asset; without money, it's a liability. . . . The professions are closed to him because he hasn't the proper training—a mere university education is no good. The kind of job he could hold down normally in business is closed to him because his father has lost "influence". . . . Most manual labour is closed to him by Trade Union rules. . . . All that is open is the underpaid white-collar job.'[6]

Heylin makes a virtue of criticising the Victorian humbug still clinging to his seniors and his caste, but his candour aggravates the misfortunes of others and thematically serves no real purpose. In the concluding paragraph of his notes Aldington says: 'This novel differs from many others of its kind in that it offers no short cut, political, economic, or otherwise, to universal human felicity'. Unlike his protagonist, the author does not believe in that possibility, but holds that we have left the young a muddled, puzzling world and should be sympathetic towards their efforts to cope with it. In any event, 'there seems to be nothing to do with life except to live it as heartily as possible'. The implied critique of *laisser faire* capitalism is answered only with what is all too easily seen as a *laisser faire* philosophy about life in general. As writing, the book is a highly competent piece of professionalism, but it does not go into depth regarding the causes of Heylin's predicament and it is too pat a conclusion that he should resolve a bitter awakening to daunting practical and material realities by acquiring an 'almost ecstatic confidence in positive goodness of life'.[7] Like all of Aldington's novels up to this point, *Very Heaven* is loosely related to his autobiography. Perhaps it is unreasonable to feel that he should have gone 'into depth' seeking the causes of Chris Heylin's predicament. The negative effects of capitalism are always perceived in his work as a prime cause of individuals' problems; but state socialism is never seen as a bearable solution. The epicurean approach to life, sometimes coupled with a humanist view of human goodness, is the prevailing view in Aldington's work. That he was often savage in his attitude towards human nature is one manifestation of his own divided being—goodwill on one side, distrust on the other.

When he wrote *Very Heaven*, his sense of the immediate political future of Europe was split, between the probability of another war and participation in the widespread feeling that it could not happen. in 'Letter to a Young Man' in *Artifex* he poses again the question of individual fate: 'You didn't make the world, you cannot influence the governments and the armament makers, you are not responsible. Quite true. But then, are you absolutely willing to resign your fate into other people's hands, without the slightest effort to assert your own convictions?'[8] Aldington's answer on this occasion, when the League of Nations still had some credibility, was to urge his 'young man' (born in 1914) to work for world government. But there is no evidence that he ever did such work himself.

Yet, in the context of its time his fiction had a social effect, as may be illustrated by two contemporary responses to *Death of a Hero*. Late in July Ralph Bates[9] wrote from a camp in the Encantadas in Spain to say that his own writing had been greatly influenced by Aldington's, and that after the 1914 War he had found, read and imitated poems in *Images of War* and *Images of Desire*. His response to *Death of a Hero*, read recently in Spain, was: 'I wish I could hate like that'. The same day Bates wrote, the *Liverpool Daily Post* poked editorial fun at Bootle City Council, which decided by a large majority that *Death of a Hero* was a vile and vulgar book and must be removed from the library. To Aldington this event seemed another symptom of British national hypocrisy. At that very time two people who would figure in his future (one as a close friend) were invoking his name. He was among the many writers who had written to Henry Miller in appreciation of *Tropic of Cancer* (1934). Now, in an attempt to sell the book, Miller and Lawrence Durrell made a brochure of excerpts from all their letters, including Aldington's and even an 'absolutely imbecile' one from Pound.[10]

That summer was one of seemingly endless sunshine on the Mediterranean coast. Aldington already had another book, *The Crystal World*, a long poem and an account of his affair with Netta, in the press in London and had made a good start on his novel, *Seven Against Reeves*, a 'comedy-farce' over which he reported, 'Netta laughs herself into tears'. That was the lighter side of life, a new shoot. But all summer divorce proceedings, from both sides, hung over them. On the Patmore side, Aldington faced the prospect of fighting damages claims for £2500, a large sum even for one whose literary career was prospering. He made unsuccessful efforts to settle out of court for a much smaller sum (£250) and waxed sardonic over the degree to which people with 'aristocratic pretentions' appeared to love money and be willing to create public scandal to obtain it. Yet the basic outcome can never have been in doubt and in granting a decree nisi, with costs and £1500 in agreed damages, the President of the Court, Sir Boyd Merriman, noted that the sum seemed in no way too large. The money was to be paid into court withing 14 days of the hearing on 23 November 1937.

Over the same period H.D. was going through divorce proceedings, and the matter in this instance was less clear-cut. In June she furnished the London high Court with a 'Statement of Facts', that Aldington after experiencing conditions on the Western front became very oversexed; that she discovered his relationship with Dorothy Yorke, and herself became 'unfaithful' only after this discovery; and that he had threatened her with divorce and legal consequences for registering her daughter's birth under his name. She also testified that a psychiatrist in 1919 had advised against continuing to live with him because his behaviour was affected by the shock of war experience. A full year was to pass before the decree was made absolute in this proceeding. A somewhat different light is cast on it in an undated letter H.D. wrote Ezra Pound from Territet, in which she repeats the charge that Aldington had threatened her (this was the 'octypus' she felt she had to live with over the years, but which Aldington was amazed to hear about) though, she says, she loved him very much: 'I seem to remember always the indignity of being unsheltered and then the treachery of the betrayal. It doesn't make any difference to my LOVE and I will always love Richard' and 'I mean I wanted A. and R. to be "happy", as R. was too forceful for me and to exigant [sic] and I knew all the time he did not get enough of the sort of thing he wanted. I don't blame myself because I was not strong enough . . . and I don't blame R. But you see I want R. to know that THIS time, I want to make up for anything he thought disloyal in me. I did the only possible thing but I heard it "whispered" that H.D. was "hanging on because I was 'winged' ", I had no place in the air and no place on earth. Now maybe I have a place in the air and a place on earth . . . and I want to make things as right as I can for R. or anyone he happens to love or wants to marry'.[11]

Why was H.D.'s divorce testimony so harrowing if its sole purpose was to oblige Aldington and to ensure that his child would be of legitimate birth? She wished to make him writhe a little, but did not want to inflict pain. 'What happened was that H.D. began simultaneously to suffer from and to enjoy the fancy drama of the foresaken wife who now controlled the fate of the negligent husband.'[12] H.D. upset herself more than she did Aldington. She was thrown back into the stresses experienced during the war and, on Bryher's advice, she went to a psychoanalyst.

Amid these concerns, Aldington's literary life continued. A pleasanter occupation that summer was his re-reading Balzac and Anatole France and taking particular interest in the work and career of Flaubert, reading the novels and looking out for their reception from reviewers when they were published. He saw similarities in one respect between himself and Flaubert, whose masterpieces *Madame Bovary* and *L'Education Sentimentale* were dismissed as gutter productions, and who was attacked as a pornographer, without literary style, imagination or vitality. Aldington saw irony in the fact that Flaubert was prosecuted for obscenity in 1856 whereas when a statue was erected in the Luxembourg in his honour in 1921 the Minister of Education characterised him as 'the greatest moralist of nineteenth-century France!!!' He always enjoyed such instances of hypocrisy, which banished at least for the moment his sense that humans were naturally good, and brought out his other side, the savagely ironic.

Wary of all human systems, he was no less sardonic about Communism than he was about capitalism and Christianity, yet the Russian interest in his work, which had begun with *Death of a Hero*, was to continue. Nine of his poems, translated by Mikhail Zenkevich, were included in *An Anthology of New English Poetry* published by the Leningrad branch of Golitizdat.[13] Also in 1937 there were two separate Russian translations of *All Men Are Enemies* despite the fact that passages in it directly criticise practical Communism. Mikhail Urnov tells us that initial reception of the book was mixed and it was regarded as a decline from *Death of a Hero*, but it withstood criticism and became widely popular. 'The rhapsodical account of how feelings are awakened and how they mature, the hero's spiritual searching, the dramatic love story, the writer's sincere, painful confessions, his exposure of social injustice, the robbery of wartime and the predatoriness of the post-war period—all this attracted the Soviet reader, as it still does', Urnov wrote in 1965.[14] Such remarks are heavily shaded with irony when we realise that, many times, Aldington expressed distaste for Communism and Fascism because they failed to take into account the individual human element. In the mid-1930s when his Russian reputation was burgeoning he had observed to Warman, in a long letter about the Soviets' possibilities of success: 'To have a real democracy you must have real democrats. And it takes a long time to make a great body of them. In fact, though it sounds a paradox, democracy is the ideal of aristocrats'.[15] He goes on to suggest that democracy rests on the desire to give more to the community than one takes from it. The 'wage-slave' is compelled to take, and when he gets the opportunity, reacts by becoming an exploiter.

Perhaps to protect himself from the tensions and unpleasantness of divorce proceedings, he wrote hard all summer and into the autumn. Just before Netta's divorce came to court in November he completed work on *Seven Against Reeves*. By late October 1937 he could boast to Warman he had written 85 000 words in 85 days. It was about this time that they learned that Netta was pregnant, the baby due in June. On Christmas Eve Aldington wrote to Orioli that they intended the accouchement should take place at Lausanne.

The first number of *International Literature* for 1938 contained the Russian version of *Very Heaven*, which was widely reviewed,[16] as Mikhail Urnov notes. Urnov himself gave a conference paper on Aldington that year at the Moscow Institute of History, Philosophy and Literature, a circumstance he recollected as indicating widespread interest in Aldington's writings and appreciation of his 'progressive civic outlook'. Urnov agrees with the view of another scholar, Dilyara Zhantieva, that in the late 1930s Aldington was close to being the Russians' favourite contemporary English writer. A welcome by-product, which surprised him and helped offset the divorce settlement, was receipt of 2383 roubles in royalties.

Another Soviet writer, V. M. Moldavsky, was to note many years later that Aldington had a special feeling for gardens and garden flowers.[17] At Malthouse Cottage, gardening had been a solace and an avocation. Now the garden made him happy at the prospect of a further year at the villa Koeclin, which had about an acre of pine, arbutus, giant heath, mimosa, cork-trees, cistus and cornomilla, breaking down to the sea in rocks of mica-sandstone and quartz, to about 50 yards of sea frontage (the satisfying catalogue was given to Sidney Schiff). Beyond the natural garden were splendid views of islands, including Port-Cros, of such mixed memories.

As Aldington rather expected, reviewers did not much care for *Seven Against Reeves*, which Heinemann published early in 1938 to a subscription of 6000, higher than any of his earlier books. Although some reviewers suggested that it was a pot-boiler, on the whole they were kinder to the novel than he anticipated. He thought this was because it seemed to be a defence of the bourgeoisie in the person of a successful recently-retired businessman, John Mason Reeves. Reeves quickly becomes bored and in the way, and subject to his wife's proclivity for social-climbing. Mrs Reeves draws him into the world of her social aspirations (something he had no time for while busy making money) and the life proves to be very expensive, partly because it engages them in the activities of 'arty' types, such as the young composer whose opera the Faddiman-Fishes persuade them to subsidise. After a number of like encounters and a variety of farcical and fatuous conversations, the Reeveses go to Venice and encounter Philboy and Paiderini (Douglas and Orioli). Here pressure is put on Reeves to subsidise a new literary review and, to avoid it, he is forced to flee to Cannes. Eventually, extracting a promise from his wife to quit social-climbing, Reeves happily returns to work to pay off the bills incurred by their various misadventures and to avail himself of some 'decent companionship'.[18]

Aldington was amused that a book clearly labelled a 'comedy-farce' should be discovered by one reviewer after another to verge on farce, though the American reviewers failed to locate the comedy. The *Daily Mail* had made moves to purchase serialisation rights, but finally settled for a single extract. *Lloyds List* declared that Reeves is 'the kind of solid capable fellow with whom any decent man in the city would be glad to take a chop'. Frere decided to issue a showcard to this effect to all the City bookshops, as Aldington told Warman, with the remark that 'Ours is as ignominious as any other trade'.[19]

At the end of March, his old friend George Gribble, the playwright, arrived in the Var. The Glovers had been there most of the winter, though Hal Glover's tuberculosis made him restless. During April Gribble and Aldington saw a good deal of each other, often lunching together. One of Gribble's typically terse diary entries, for 3 April, reads: 'with Glover to Le Canadel to lunch with R.A. and his new wife, expecting a baby, R.A. physically changed genial as usual. . . .' Shortly after the Gribbles left, the Aldingtons headed off for Lausanne in driving rain. They rented a house for three months, but Aldington despised Switzerland, which he saw as a bourgeois utopia where everything which is not obligatory is forbidden. In any event, they did not stay and by early June had crossed the channel to London. There on 9 June he visited H. D. at

Lowndes Square and, despite the harsh 'facts' she provided for the divorce case, they met on friendly terms.

There next followed a scene so typical of the actors and so enjoyable, in retrospect, to those who had followed their careers. A heavier, older, tousled, repentant Aldington showed up at H. D.'s charming flat. He stayed long enough to drink eleven cups of tea. The two were alone together for the first time in years. He proceeded to throw himself on her mercy. He had no money to pay the court damages, charges, or lawyers. [Long before, in a letter of 20 March 1929, he had written H. D. that he should be the 'guilty' party, and: 'Of course, I would share the expenses'.] The baby was expected any day. Would she waive charges or, more accurately, would she pay off the lawyers for both sides herself? A special plea had been placed that the divorce decree be made active immediately, so that when the baby arrived it would be legitimate. All was now in jeopardy.[20]

Later in June he wrote to thank H.D. for applying for the divorce decree absolute, which came through on June 22 when Netta was more than eight months pregnant, and enabled Aldington and Netta to marry on 25 June. Almost immediately Netta had to go into a nursing home. The Aldingtons' daughter, Catherine, was born on July 6 (two days before his 46th birthday) and by the end of the month the family had moved out of London, to Bramshott Cottage, Liphook, Hampshire. Aldington was working on a new novel, *Rejected Guest*. The divorce proceedings pitched H.D. back into the past and at the end of the month she wrote to Pound that Cournos had blamed her 'vituperatively' for throwing Aldington and Arabella together.

Heinemann were planning a uniform edition of Aldington's work and by this time six titles had been prepared, *Voltaire, Soft Answers* and four novels—*Death of a Hero, The Colonel's Daughter, All Men Are Enemies* and *Very Heaven*. C.P. Snow wrote a booklet to accompany the edition, similar in format to the Lawrence piece Aldington had done for Heinemann's several years earlier.[21] In what Aldington labelled a 'panegyric', Snow speaks of the intensity of his work: 'no one can read him for ten minutes without feeling a glow of power and vitality: a gusto both of the senses and of the mind. . . . ' Praising Aldington's passionate directness, Snow also defends him against charges of bitterness, and in considerable part the essay reads like an apology for Aldington's personality, and in particular his hypersensitivity. In Snow's eyes, the 'bitterness' becomes 'romantic idealism'. A defensive quality in Aldington gives way in the presence of genuine talent. Besides all this, he is 'a very learned man' and, interestingly for someone of Snow's especial bent as a realistic novelist, his poems seem his 'most perfect achievement'.

Partial support for this view of the poetry may be found in a book of that time, Herbert Palmer's *Post-Victorian Poetry*.[22] Noting, rather curiously, that Aldington's poetry is 'often bitter or sensual', Palmer praises his warmth of feeling and his imagination, and suggests that his reputation as a poet has swung back and forth continually between unreasonable depreciation and over-estimation. Almost as if in illustration, Aldington's *The Crystal World* (1937), his last long poem and regarded by Snow as his finest work, was subjected to a highly critical review by Kirker Quinn in the June 1938 *Poetry*. Early in this review Quinn suggests negative criticism has overlooked the fact that Aldington, as a poet, has valued 'the spurt and flare of imagination' more than formal control; Quinn notes that his themes have been reckoned limited and his treatment plodding: 'But at least he has searched them deeply, sometimes in unforgettable language; furthermore, his approach to them and his tone have been remarkably varied'.[23] From this promising preamble, Quinn goes on to castigate the 'utter commonplaceness' of the lyric sections of *The Crystal World*, their 'cloying lushness' and quagmire of clichés, lack of concentration and self-criticism. Norman Gates concurs in this unfavourable evaluation,[24] but another recent critic, Richard E. Smith, agrees with Snow's praise for 'some of the best love-poetry in English'.[25]

Quinn's judgement is certainly too harsh. The opening lyric sets the tone and establishes a convention, which may be linked to the Oriental poetry of pathos:

> Nile-lotus among women, dear flower of girls,
> Exquisite as a slender dark hibiscus,
> Take my head on your breasts, beloved,
> Touch my cheek with your delicate hands
> And—break, O my heart, break with longing.

With slight variations and despite occasional risky bathos ('Go catch a falling star, go climb a tree') this tone is well-sustained throughout 21 of the 22 parts. Far from being 'intensely personal', as Quinn suggests, these lyrics are highly conventional, though intended to convey deep personal feeling. Presumably Aldington felt that such expressions had been made thousands of times before, yet by accomplished use of the conventions one can arrive at a true expressionist offering of one's feelings. This is what Section 22 discusses, on behalf of

> the artist
> Who is always seeking exact equivalences
> For the experiences of the sensibility,
> But in the common terms of common men—
> She is flowers, the sea, a young queen,
> Primitive symbols.
> The emotions are intense, not subtle,
> In no way intellectualised.

In this section the writer shows he has meditated deeply on the experience of human love, its ecstasies and pain. He wonders 'What is poetry?' in connection with love, and with life. The poem's unfashionably discursive mode is handled very well. First, it makes a positive of one of Aldington's weaknesses as a poet, the tendency to explain; second, the use of convention in Sections 1 to 21 largely controls a propensity for mawkishness, sometimes a weakness of his more personal writing. In Section 22 the discussion of poetics is very level-headed in stating a counterview to allusively intellectual poetry. Given acceptance of a stylised treatment of love, *The Crystal World* is Aldington's most coherent, fully realised work in the medium and fittingly concludes *The Complete Poems*.

While he was continuing his writing career and working through a rough passage in his private affairs, war threatened in Europe. Despite his 'Letter to a Young Man' in *Artifex*, in early 1938 he felt the likelihood of war was no greater than it had been three years earlier, though he did believe that Austria had been threatened. Like many others, he failed to anticipate the Nazi move into Czechoslovakia. Scepticism about Soviet Communism, expressed to Warman and others, seemed to him at the time borne out by the mysterious death of Maxim Gorky. On the other hand, the idea of avoiding war and all the political uncertainties of Europe by moving to the United States momentarily lost its appeal because of what he saw as the danger of 'class war' there (though it is not clear what form he thought such a conflict would take.) By late in the year the threat of war was in the forefront of European consciousness. Aldington planned to return to France at the end of summer, and by then felt there would be no war, as the German people did not want it and the Italians and Japanese were too weak. When the 1938 war scare had subsided, he told Warman he entirely favoured Chamberlain's campaign of appeasement. 'The English Left seem to me quite crazy', he wrote to Warman on 9 November. 'For nearly twenty years they did everything possible to discourage the military spirit in England and to make the fighting forces inefficient, and then they want to commit us to a policy which must mean war with a formidable military coalition and the certainty of no support from U.S.A.'

Back at the Villa Koeclin, he continued work on *Rejected Guest*. His first approach was to write in autobiographical form, but after six months (70 000 words) of work he felt his tactics were mistaken and began again, writing the same story from the outside. By early November he had accomplished 15 000 words of revision and felt that his new opening chapter was the best thing he had done since the Prologue to *Death of a Hero*. When, however, he wrote with some embarrassment to Leonard Bacon in mid-November his mood had changed. Referring to *Rejected Guest* as his 'swan song', he remarked, 'I need hardly say that this is not exactly the crowning glory of twenty-five years hard work at literature I had hoped for'. In view of world conditions and (a new note, this) his own seeming loss of public appeal, he felt it would be senseless for him to continue writing:

> ... conditions are becoming almost impossible for the author without a private income. In England and the U.S.A., royalties to an author not domiciled in the country are treated as unearned income (!), so that in England I have to pay six shillings on every pound, plus 10% to my agent. The U.S. income tax is lower, but unluckily my earnings in America have declined. Other countries don't tax, but then they just don't pay! For example, I have an alleged credit of about 2000 dollars in Russia. When I made repeated applications for payment, I was sent 75 bucks! And so on. The Albatross Continental editions (printed in Germany) now pay only a meagre advance and just owe all accrued royalties.

In addition to this, I went through the English divorce court last year, and was mightly [sic] socked for costs and damages. I married again and we have a baby girl, and that was expensive too.

Further my sales have declined, not I think because my work is really falling off but simply because people are tired of what I have to say (however well it may be said) and because there is so much skilled competition.

Quae cum ita sint, I have been feeling for some time that the only thing to do is to retire temporarily or permanently from writing, and try to find some other means of subsistence. The good old days of political corruption and sinecure are unfortunately over, otherwise I might apply to His Majesty for the job of Pipe-Lighter to the Queen Mother or something equally lucrative and distinguished. There is nothing for it but a job in these degenerate days.

His embarrassment was due to the fact that he had not written to Bacon for two years but was now asking a favour, broaching the possibility that he might seek a university post in the United States, to teach English literature, and expressing a particular interest in California.[26]

Bacon replied almost at once to say that, through Professor Chauncy B. Tinker, there was some chance of an appointment at Yale University. Aldington seemed to retreat before the immediacy of this prospect and told Bacon that he had the means of subsistence until he had completed *Rejected Guest*, and even then he could draw on an advance from his new American publisher, the Viking Press. Yet he continued to toy with the idea of an academic job and the Yale position remained in his mind right up until Christmas. While the possibility was a real one, he hedged; when Bacon wrote in late December to say that Yale after all had no money for hiring, Aldington responded that he was anxious to get to America as soon as possible. In mid-November he had confided in Orioli that he was 'longing to get away from Europe altogether'.

Aldington and Netta were, in fact, very close to leaving Europe and, in retrospect, one action by him at this time takes on almost the symbolic quality of a farewell gesture. On receiving a cable from Orioli that Reggie Turner had at last died of cancer on 7 December, he arranged that a wreath be sent although he regarded such things as absurd superstition, a profanation of beautiful flowers. In *Pinorman* he explains that Turner, when poor, had denied himself to send a wreath to Oscar Wilde's funeral. Aldington and Orioli had agreed that, when Turner died, each would send a wreath.[27]

One last activity of Aldington's in 1938 is a very early engagement of C. P. Snow's in the question of 'Two Cultures'. The December number of *Discovery*, a periodical published by Cambridge University Press and edited by Snow, ran a letter from Aldington as editorial leader under the title 'Science and Conscience', the point of which is that working scientists should be bound by some equivalent to the Hippocratic Oath. What he had in mind is that scientists should hesitate to contribute their expertise towards war preparation. His view, as Snow says in a reply twice as long as the letter, is that of a defender of humanism. Snow responded that scientific preparations in Germany must be met by scientific preparations at home, and that there are worse things than war!

15 Farewell to Europe, 1939–40

Although he had complained to Orioli about his slender means in November 1938, Aldington's financial situation was not as precarious as he made out. Netta had just inherited a legacy of $2500 and he reported to Leonard Bacon on 2 January 1939 that the Viking Press, to whom he had switched from Doubleday, had recently advanced him $1500. He had also unexpectedly received $300 in Continental royalties. As to the future, C. P. Snow spent a couple of days at the Villa Koeclin early in January and the question came up of Aldington's taking a 'chair' at Cambridge, an idea said to be supported by J. B. Trend and F. L. Lucas. He therefore was entertaining thoughts of abandoning total financial reliance on writing and of entering academic life, and not merely as a means of moving to the United States. Nothing came of the Cambridge idea, but he had the foresight to apply for quota numbers for himself and family, necessary for entering the United States as landed immigrants.

They left the Villa Koeclin for good in January to return to London, and sailed on *S S Acquitania* on 11 February, arriving in New York 17 February. Two days later, Aldington wrote from the Hyde Park Hotel, East 77th Street, to Harold Rugg, the Dartmouth College librarian, who had enquired about purchase of manuscripts. He told Rugg he intended to remain indefinitely in the United States, on the quota, and that some manuscripts were following him from Marseille, though he could not tell what would happen to the great bulk which remained in Florence.

Throughout March he was in New York and had use of library facilities at Columbia University. He continued to entertain some idea of taking an academic post and late in March went to Princeton to meet Professor Abraham Flexner. Paul Willert, a friend, and head of Oxford University Press's New York branch, took him for a trip of several days to Cambridge, Massachusetts, and Aldington mulled over settling in some area of New England, though all would depend on establishing a steady source of income.

In April he took Netta and Catherine to Rhode Island, to stay with the Leonard Bacon family at the Acorns, Peace Dale. The Bacons gave them use of an upper floor and Leonard had a largish library in a separate building, where he and Aldington worked, at opposite ends. After a month at the Acorns, Bacon made available another, smaller Peace Dale house until the middle of June, and then yet another house, at Crowfield, Saunderstown, Rhode Island. During these months Aldington was again working at *Rejected Guest*, which was published by Viking and then Heinemann in Autumn 1939. He wrote articles, including one for *Atlantic Monthly* on Norman Douglas, for which he was disappointed to receive only $100 (and, later, an appreciative letter from Douglas). A *Saturday Review* piece which took two days work paid only a paltry $6.50. He liked his present situation, however. Although he came to consider them 'too Henry Jamesy', he first thought the old New England families among the finest people he had met. Like Emerson before him, he admired the pure speech of the ordinary working-people and rejoiced that, even more than the old families, they were free of 'Yankee facetiousness'. Among the old families he found admirable both the level of cultivation and standard of morality ('high without being puritanical or snuffling'), and regretted that the 'old money' would not outlast another generation. These Americans seemed all the better for being free of absurd inherited titles, but he does not admire them as democrats, rather as an elite, for, he asserted to Slonimsky, 'absolute democracy simply means the triumph of the mob and mob instincts'.[1]

If he was charmed with the people, he was delighted with the territory, especially at Saunderstown, where they had a house on a small private road about 500 yards off the Boston Post Road, with stands of sumac and half-wild country juniper, oaks, maples and apple trees. They looked out over a slope to Narragansett Bay and Conanicut Island, with Aquidneck Island (the original Rhode Island) beyond. In the garden they had chipmunks, woodchucks and jack rabbits and nearby was practically impenetrable tangled woodland. Aldington felt more tranquil than he had for a long time. His only serious problem was that of earning an income. He worked hard at writing magazine articles during this whole summer, but they were a precarious source in a new environment and the pieces he sent back to England took a long time to yield anything.

The playwright, Basil Dean,[2] spent the first week-end in June with the Aldingtons at Saunderstown. Dean wished to create a stage version of *Seven Against Reeves* and had in mind the highly successful Edmund Gwenn for the leading role. Re-plotting the novel for a scenario interested Aldington and although the project came to nothing the collaborators may have got quite far along with it as in 1942 he spoke of the script to his Hollywood agent, Al Manuel, under the working title 'My Wife Won't Let Me'. As, at the moment, Aldington hoped for little from *Rejected Guest*, he felt that a stage success would make a great deal of financial difference to his family.

Indeed, despite substantial income the Aldingtons' financial position was anything but secure. Crossing the Atlantic had complicated matters and in addition Aldington's London literary agent, Ralph Pinker, was in process of being prosecuted for misappropriation of a clients' funds and general malpractice. Aldington several times requested transfer of funds on the grounds that he would not be returning to England. A few months later he wrote in *Life for Life's Sake*: 'In September 1929, when I sat in the Paris café reading letters and telegrams about *Death of a Hero*, it seemed reasonable to think that I had achieved such ambitions as I possessed. By September 1939 nothing was left'. 'There isn't much to be said, is there?', he wrote to Warman on 5 September, after Britain had entered the war. Yet, though he feared half his income (British and Continental royalties) would be cut off, a great deal was 'left'. He had just lived a most satisfying New England summer; he was father of an infant daughter, a circumstance of extreme importance to him; his freelance writing life was still intact.

Later in September he saw his old friend Henry Slonimsky in New York City and wrote afterwards, 'Things base and petty wither away when you are near. The strange thing is that you are quite unaware of your own grandeur'. He had always felt a sort of admiration for Slonimsky's idealism. Slonimsky now advised him to continue seeking an academic post, and Aldington even discussed with Oxford University Press the possibility of writing an academic book, but he was encouraged otherwise by the first reviews of *Rejected Guest*, which led to a burst of enquiries from editors about his fiction. However, he had agreed to lecture at Harvard and Yale and was willing to accept other spot assignments, such as the informal reading he gave at Wellesley College in late September. Slonimsky learned of another possible new direction for 'the free life of the free-lance writer', the chance that Aldington 'might get 3 months (whoring) at Hollywood at a large salary'. Such 'prostitution' was acceptable, for two reasons: it would provide means for writing another book and would allow leisure to wait for the best academic post on offer.

The Hollywood opportunity was being negotiated through the New York literary agent Leland Hayward, whose representative also arranged meetings for Aldington with the editors of such publications as the *New Yorker, Harper's Bazaar* and *Cosmopolitan*, and with the representative of Paramount Pictures, who invited him for drinks, to 'renew acquaintance with Sinclair Lewis', on the evening of 26 September. Several such contacts proved to be old acquaintances, but Aldington soon began to discover the hazards of New York journalism. The *New Yorker* rejected two articles they had commissioned and then, after apparently commissioning an article on Portugal, returned it saying they had actually sent a man to Portugal. Aldington was told that if he wished to leave his article with them for two weeks they would eventually let him know. If their man in Portugal sent nothing back, they might well reconsider the matter! He was so upset by the implications of this episode, that his hard-earned reputation counted for so little, that he could not write for a week.

Although the reviewers were generally favourable, he had mixed feelings about the subscription for the Viking Press *Rejected Guest* (4000 plus 1200 for a bookclub of 'pre-reviewers'), but was pleased to tell Pinker, 'the Viking are advertising it handsomely, along with the *Grapes of Wrath*'.[3] Reviewers noted the book's momentum (one called it 'sprightly') and Mary Colum declared it 'a very intelligently written novel'.[4] It tells the story of David Norris, a boy of good background who must, because of poverty, struggle for a good education in the England before the Second World War. He has experiences, both in London and on the Continent, similar to those of the protagonists of *Women Must Work* and *Very Heaven*. While it is not exceptional, the book has competence and verve and the note of stridency is absent.

By early October Aldington had negotiated for a series of articles in the *Atlantic Monthly*,[5] with the coat-trailing title 'Farewell to Europe', and for *American Mercury* a trial piece with the possibility of his being engaged to write the magazines's monthly literary article; but he complained to Warman that intellectual and artistic work were underpaid in the United States and that topicality dominated. He felt it was now his ambition never to write another book, and may have been prompted to this because in a short period he was invited to six academic institutions to read or to lecture. Opportunity to give these lectures was his financial salvation, though the fees were sometimes moderate.

At the end of the year he had $2000 in hand with the prospect of earning $1000 in 1940 from lectures, but what was to be his long-term source of income? With *Rejected Guest*, he appears to have felt written out as a novelist. He told Slonimsky that through fiction he could make several thousand dollars a book, but alas he had nothing to say. An alternative suggestion came from two quarters. Bacon had just completed his memoir, *Semi-Centennial*, and urged Aldington to try something similar. Quite independently Howard Lowrie, of Oxford University Press, suggested that he write a book along the lines of Irwin Edman's *Philosopher's Holiday*,[6] published by Viking a year or so earlier. Aldington took to the idea and set about it at once. Despite a seasonal bout of bronchitis, by 20 December he had written between six and eight thousand words of *Life for Life's Sake*, which developed from 'Farewell to Europe'.

He always felt his own limits as a novelist, which he expressed to H.D. as early as publication of *Death of a Hero*. Herbert Read appears to have believed Aldington made a double mistake: first desiring to outvie Eliot as a poet and second aspiring to be a novelist—the latter ambition being his 'ultimate misfortune'. While it cannot be denied that Eliot's success bothered Aldington, there is no evidence that he wished to rival him as a poet. On the contrary, there is substantial evidence that he was modest about his attainments in the genre. Read believed Aldington's true *métier* was in criticism and biography, whereas in the 1920s Eliot had offered Read the opinion that Aldington's critical work was pedantic and diminished his true bent, for creative work. Read underestimated Aldington as a novelist, if only because *Death of a Hero*, written under pressure of the need to make a statement about the First World War, remains an impressive and important creative work. Eliot, on the other hand, undervalued Aldington's critical and biographical skills, which have afforded us *Voltaire, Portrait of a Genius, But . . .*, the fine, though problematical, *Lawrence of Arabia: A Biographical Enquiry*, and several valuable anthologies.

Aldington's chief aim as a novelist was to satirise English society as one in which the individual found self-fulfilment very difficult. He tends to see this society from a bourgeois perspective, or rather one which is highly critical of bourgeois characteristics such as the desire to maintain an image of respectability even at the cost of outright hypocrisy, and the propensity of most bourgeois-conditioned people towards materialism (concentration on making money), conformity, the cult of 'manliness', sexual prudishness and lack of imagination.

Through George Winterbourne in *Death of a Hero* Aldington put forward the artistic temperament as an ideal, but he also portrays the fashionable 'art-world' as shallow and self-serving. Both in this novel and elsewhere he introduces personal friends or acquaintances such as Pound, Eliot, Ford or Lawrence, in order to lampoon them as representatives of the art world he is attacking. A typical example is the portrayal of D. H. Lawrence as 'Comrade-Editor Bobbe', quoted above. Such a passage as this makes it more difficult to maintain that his later booklength treatment of Lawrence, in *Portrait of a Genius, But* . . . is balanced and objective, which, valuable as that book is, one would wish to do. The fact that the portrait of 'Comrade-Editor Bobbe' was published within the last year or so of Lawrence's life makes it easy for those who accuse Aldington of 'venom' to sustain such an accusation. Yet this and the other portraits are part of his all-out attack on English society. However, like the two women in George Winterbourne's life, the representative artists are marginal in effect compared with the elders. 'It was the regime of Cant *before* the War which made the Cant *during* the War so damnably possible and easy.'[7]

Aldington, in this novel and later, is always aware of the savagely ironic contrast between the profiteers who stay at home and the young men massacred in the trenches, between the happiness of young bourgeois lovers and the huddles of 'miserable, ragged human beings' on the Embankment benches.[8] But in *Death of a Hero* the part most often admired, the high point, is Part III where he offers a graphic portrayal of the horrors of active service in or near the front line trenches. Here he shows remarkable aptitude for realistic reportage, which carries a more subtle charge of satire:

> They were in the German trenches, with many dead bodies in field grey. Winterbourne and Evans went into a German dug-out. Nobody was there, but it was littered with straw, torn paper, portable cookers, oddments of forgotten equipment, and cigars. There were French tables and chairs with human excrement on them.
>
> They went on. A little knot of Germans came towards them holding up their shaking hands. The took no notice of them but let them pass through.
>
> The barrage continued. Their first casualty was caused by their own shells dropping short.[9]

For his second novel, *The Colonel's Daughter*, he took off from the realism of Part III of *Death of a Hero* and abandoned formal experiment. In the Smitherses, he portrays a bourgeois family still fixed in Victorian values, and consequently ineffectual. The book's title-heroine, Georgina, is the daughter of Colonel Fred Smithers, who embodies the cult of 'manliness', and has hypocritical double standards about women. A womaniser who keeps up an outward image of moral probity, he insists on Georgina's being brought up in a narrow fashion aimed to make her a model of respectability, but providing her with little education and no polish. As with many of Aldington's leading characters, Georgina is severely handicapped by lack of money. She conforms to the bourgeois model which means that the only role for which she is in any way suitable is that of average bourgeois housewife, but here she comes up against an insuperable obstacle, the extreme shortage of eligible young men, for most of them have been killed or badly disabled in the war.

The haranguing and invective of *Death of a Hero* are missing from *The Colonel's Daughter*. Aldington makes his social commentary through the characters and their interaction and he does not buttonhole or browbeat the reader. By implication, he continues to criticise the life-denying effects of bourgeois society, but finds a specific villain in the person of the local 'squire', Sir Horace Stimms, representative of big capital. Here as elsewhere, Aldington does not allow his hatred of capitalism to lead him towards any form of socialist solution, though he is extremely wary of tendencies towards Fascism or any set of social conditions which could lead to autocracy or concentration of wealth and power in the hands of a few men such as Stimms, who care nothing for the well-being of others.[10]

By the standards of the novel form in the early 20th century, *The Colonel's Daughter* is more fully achieved than *Death of a Hero* because the action carries or implies the commentary, and there is little direct moralising or author-intrusion. What limits *The Colonel's Daughter* is its very reason for being. The heroine, Georgina Smithers, is a sociological case history, interesting as such, but too passively the victim of circumstances to be a satisfactory central character.

Aldington's third novel, *All Men Are Enemies*, takes as its theme 'love vs. marriage' or authentic individual relations against those socially-conditioned and socially maintained. His sentiments, made the central theme of this novel, are close to the famous lines in Arnold's 'Dover Beach':

> Ah, love. Let us be true
> To one another! for the world, which seems
> To lie before us like a land of dreams,
> So various, so beautiful, so new,
> Hath really neither joy, nor love nor light,
> Nor certitude, nor peace, nor help for pain.

Aldington's individualism, for all that he rejected the cult of 'manliness' (or *machismo*), was male-focused and included the need for an empathetic heterosexual partner, so that they should 'be true to one another', such a bond being the most they could expect from life. Antony Clarendon, the protagonist of *All Men Are Enemies* believes in living life to the full and that all forms of government are inimical to the healthy and free growth of the individual. This novel manifests what may be called the opposite face to Aldington's 'venomous' social satire. With his long poems *A Dream in the Luxembourg* and *The Crystal World*, *All Men Are Enemies* represents his vein of lyrical romanticism. Although he is not always entirely free of triteness or mawkishness, Aldington has a gift for evoking the feelings of heterosexual love.

In *Women Must Work* (1934) he presents another female protagonist. Unlike the colonel's daughter, Georgie Smithers, who is both poor and plain, Etta Morrison is poor but attractive. *Women Must Work* deals with Etta's chances of leading a full individual life. She attempts this by adapting to the patriarchal world, by becoming wealthy through business success and by purchasing a simulacrum of love. Having achieved power and possessions, she has lost contact with her own natural being. She has simply adopted the patriarchal role without effecting any deeper change.

What Aldington does in all of these novels is to portray a world whose collective values have gone badly wrong, a world dominated by materialism on the one hand and the deadening pressure towards conformist respectability on the other. Into this nexus of 'suspense, decay and the loss of hope',[11] he places an individual who is striving for self-fulfillment against the odds posed by distorted values. Chris Heylin, hero of *Very Heaven* (1937), is driven to the verge of suicide by his circumstances as a cozened scion of the bourgeoisie who is suddenly deprived of the wealth which supports what we would now call his 'lifestyle'. He is saved at the very cliff-edge by his own reaction to the destruction of a butterfly caught in a downdraught of wind. This event triggers off in him a long meditation in which he rehearses (for the reader) another version of what is, in fact, Aldington's stoicism, an account of human experience which entails fealty to the 'life-process' (somewhat related to Darwinian evolutionism). Heylin ponders his own apparent failure in life:

> At this thought his almost ecstatic confidence in positive goodness of life hesitated. He lost the grandiose vision of a continuous and developing life process, stretching back into an almost inconceivably remote past and moving triumphantly through an illimitable future, lost too the sense of himself as a sharer, however humble and insignificant, in this extraordinary and exceptional destiny. It came to him that however true this vision might be, it was only true in a huge general sense and over a vast time-scale. Did it necessarily hold good in his particular case or over a very brief period like a century? The great energies which create also destroy, eliminate as well as foster. Whole races of living things as well as countless individuals have been rejected. How if he were one of the rejects, an end after all and not a beginning, one of those who must be content to be scrapped to make way for more adaptable organisms?[12]

Heylin at the last, accepting his own comparative littleness as part of 'this astonishing adventure' (it is not clear whether he means of the universe or of human consciousness), declares: 'I disown all formal codes, creeds and temporary fanaticisms, and trust myself to the living impulse'.[13]

After *Very Heaven*, Aldington wrote three more novels, two of these in the 1930s and the third, *The Romance of Casanova*, in 1946. *Seven Against Reeves* (1938) is a digression away from his main themes and characteristic satirical manner. Subtitled 'A Comedy Farce', the book concerns the adventures of a retired businessman in the art-world and the world of week-end house-parties. The situation affords Aldington opportunities to poke fun at intellectual chit-chat and the trivia of social life, both British and Continental. Reeves, the protagonist, is obliged, happily for himself, to return to work to pay off the debts for these trifling adventures.

Rejected Guest (1939) again deals with the effects of poverty and impending world disaster on the life of a young man, David Norris. Norris suddenly and temporarily becomes wealthy and sets out to 'lead the good life' (yachting in the Mediterranean, and so on), but in the end he must face the everyday world, symbolised by his being given, in the closing sentence of the novel, 'a third-class ticket to London', along with advice for dealing with the obduracies of the 'real' world: 'Be artful, mistrustful, selfish, and unscrupulous—as I am—and get to know the law and the stock market. *Much* more use than biology [that is, sexual love] and poetry'.[14]

Aldington's first two novels, *Death of a Hero* and *The Colonel's Daughter* are generally held to be his strongest, although *Women Must Work* has also received firm praise. As we have seen, the thematic range is limited by his focus on individualism, which does not, however, enable him to create a strongly memorable or deeply realised protagonist. There is little to distinguish one hero from another, from George Winterbourne through to David Norris. Oddly, perhaps, his two most distinctively realised characters are his leading women, Georgie Smithers and Etta Morrison, but apart from these his women tend to be types.

Repeated characters are matched by repeated plots, and the plots themselves very often seem little more than convenient vehicles for Aldington's ideas about life. These ideas centre on the distinctive effects of war-producing capitalism on human lives. Although he vaunts individualism, he is not especially concerned with the extraordinary or highly-gifted individual. Rather, he is interested in people of sensitivity who are otherwise quite ordinary, people he classifies in *Rejected Guest* as 'the silver change of humanity'.[15] A disadvantage of such people, from a novelist's viewpoint, is that they are unlikely to dominate life, but will more probably be its passive subjects. Despite the fact that Aldington often has his characters *thinking* panegyrics to inner freedom, they are not free though they may feel the need to escape. But there is no strong sense that they know where to escape to.

His ambivalence about this is shown by the apparent reversal of *Seven Against Reeves*, where the comic protagonist escapes from the world of 'higher values' (the art world) *back into* business. As an alternative to the bourgeois world, Aldington examines the art-world (in *Death of a Hero* and elsewhere) only to find it equally false and shallow in its own way.

Throughout his novels, he carries the message of self-fulfilment of the individual and of living life with 'gusto', but all of his characters are weighed down by social and universal circumstance. As a novelist, his main achievements are the great realistic third section of *Death of a Hero*, the evocations of the Mediterranean in *All*

Men Are Enemies and *Rejected Guest*, and the flawed but savagely effective indictment, in several novels, of the lingering and life-denying effects of Victorian cant.

After 1939 he published only one more novel, *The Romance of Casanova* (1946), and that different in kind from the work of his fiction-writing decade. In retrospect, it appears as if his careers as poet and novelist both terminated with the 1930s, and some feeling that his writing career had 'come to nothing' is understandable at this stage, with the onset of the Second World War as an overwhelming cut-off line. Despite this, a certain magnanimity is discernable in his Doubleday booklet *W. Somerset Maugham: An Appreciation*. Aldington's somewhat obsessive preoccupation with Eliot, and the latter's 'different voices' as T. S. Pym, Rev. Thomas Stearn, and so on, in his fiction are there for all to see, but charges of general rancour and envy fail to account for his detached appraisal of Maugham's work. He admires Maugham's cultivation, acuteness, range, and storytelling ability. His attitude to Maugham is clear and without overtones at a time when he must have felt the contrast with his own perceived lack of success.

Beyond his writing, he was undoubtedly depressed by the war and, more surprisingly, by Britain's involvement, though he rejoiced 'at the signs of British energy and courage at sea'[16]; but he had dire forebodings—of mutual distrust among European countries, economic disorder, even revolution in which low and violent elements in society gain power. In his personal life, he felt used up, though he had Netta and Catherine. Of his apparent literary success, he told the Slonimskys it was salutary to learn and accept that it amounted to nothing. In fact, some of the best of his writing career was still ahead. He was regrouping, finding new directions for his talents.

Yet for the time being he continued to consider becoming an academic, partly because teaching opportunities came up regularly. He prepared a series of 'show' lectures, to be given at Columbia in 1940. Topics were: Housman; Yeats, 'the patron of superstition'; D. H. Lawrence and H.D., 'passionate pilgrims' and 'martyrs of aesthetic righteousness'; Osbert and Sacheverell Sitwell, 'the dilettanti'; Eliot and Pound, 'les professeurs manqués'. He was also invited to read at Kenyon College, where John Crowe Ransom had recently become Professor of Poetry.

At the Poetry Society of America annual dinner in January 1940 he again met Wyndham Lewis, who was the featured speaker.

Despite years of animadverting against the British, especially the British middle-classes, Aldington had strong patriotic feelings about the war and now felt distaste at the idea of meeting Lewis, because of Lewis's Fascist sympathies. As it turned out, he enjoyed Lewis's wit, although he regretted that Lewis read in an unintelligible mumble from a prepared script. He had, however, 'piped down considerably on Fascism'. Lewis was not doing well financially and soon had to retreat to Toronto. The Aldingtons themselves were none too cheerful because they were constantly anxious about funds. He felt he could not find the 'formula' to write regularly for the paying magazines and that academic lectures meant a good deal of work for moderate recompense. But soon he had begun another large project alongside his memoirs.

In discussing the memoirs, *Life for Life's Sake*, with Harold Guinzburg, president of Viking Press on 31 January, the idea was mooted of a general anthology of poetry, which became *The Viking Book of Poetry of the English-Speaking World*. This undertaking was perceived as rival to standard works such as the *Oxford Book of English Verse*, but with 'a much larger selection of American poets'.[18] Such a project, along with lectures and completing the memoirs plus writing another novel would, Aldington estimated, take two to three years. Work on the anthology would be best done at the Library of Congress in Washington.

Guinzburg was at first enthusiastic, but the Viking editors began to have reservations. They felt that perhaps Aldington's name was not well enough known in the US for him to be sole editor. He asked for freedom to test the idea with other publishers, but Viking eventually decided to go ahead and his immediate worries about making a living were somewhat relieved.

A diversion from literary work occurred early in April when he was a guest of Colonel Roosevelt, a director of Doubledays, at the Dutch Treat Club. Another guest asked pointedly what was his particular assignment for British intelligence. 'What made you ask that?'. 'Oh just the general suspicion that all the English here are working for the Intelligence?' 'Evidently you don't feel that way about the Germans and Russians', Aldington snapped, and at once left the Club. Walter Winchell in his *New York Post* column then accused him of being a 'British spy'. On Aldington's behalf, the lawyer Morris Ernst wrote to Winchell and on 14 April Winchell's column carried the offhand apology: 'Richard Aldington is no more a British Intelligence agent than you and I. Mistake arose from a gag of someone kidding him. Appears he is a nice guy'. Bacon considered this worse than the original insult, but Aldington ironically objected only to being called 'nice', though he was shaken enough to suspend writing for a few days.

Prompted by Leonard Bacon, the Hollywood agent Alvin Manuel contacted Aldington in mid-April to express interest in representing him. Manuel, agent for well-known stars such as Robert Taylor and Alice Faye, also had some writers on his books, though none of major reputation. Familiar with most of Aldington's work, he formed a favourable impression on meeting the man. Bacon assured Manuel that Aldington would be co-operative and understanding on technical matters to do with writing for film. Manuel aimed at obtaining for him a guaranteed $1000 per week and soon was negotiating with the British-based producer Alexander Korda, first for a single fee for one short story and then on the possibility of writing a screenplay on Cyrano de Bergerac, on whom Aldington claimed he 'used to be the world's expert'. But Manuel's first efforts came to nothing.

Aldington, in any case, quite suddenly more secure and busy, was not keen to move to Hollywood. Discussions with Guinzburg had yielded a three-year agreement with Viking Press for two non-fiction works and a novel. Viking tied up $40 000 in the anthology and advanced $7500 on the novel and the memoir. Excerpts from the latter were to be serialised in the *Atlantic Monthly* at $1000 for each of three or four instalments. Fees for the Columbia University lectures arranged through Professor William York Tindall must have seemed small compared with these figures. Aldington felt that Viking drove a hard bargain and indeed these arrangements put him on a treadmill, but he was a compulsive worker and responded with typical industry. In the first week of May, for example, he wrote a full-length lecture on Housman, added 3000 words to his memoirs and made anthology selections from the work of Housman, Poe and Yeats.

This work was done from his apartment at West 115th Street but in mid-June he took Netta and Catherine up to Old Lyme, intending to spend a working summer in Connecticut, though distracted by being thoroughly depressed at news of the fall of France. Some of the time he worked in the Sterling Library at Yale and by the end of June was steadily labouring to meet deadlines: lectures for Columbia by late July, memoirs by the end of October. Mornings and afternoons were given to these, evenings to the anthology. When he delivered the Columbia lectures, starting in an August heatwave, he was pleased that the size of the audience increased for each lecture. He felt afterwards they may have been scandalised by his frank analysis of the pretentions of Pound and Eliot. As Tindall was in the chair for his Lawrence lecture he took perverse delight in expressing a position opposed to the professor's.

The Aldingtons remained at Old Lyme until October, a month of Indian summer, by then having arranged to winter in Washington, DC. The Library of Congress offered Aldington a private study for work on the anthology, a task he decided to finish before taking any holiday. At Old Lyme he had completed the basic selection up to the Romantics. Still to be chosen was 19th- and 20th-century English and American poetry. 'I wrote to Ezra at Rapallo for permission to use some of his poems, and received a letter I will show you', he told Slonimsky on 15 October. 'He asks an exorbitant price for his not very valuable verse, and is so Fascist that he expresses a hope Churchill will be hanged. He has even managed to persuade himself that the attack on England is a modern version of the American Revolution!' Throughout the early war years Aldington was anxious about the fate of Britain and afterwards he often referred to Pound's response, that Churchill ought to be hanged in front of the (non-existent) Gold Exchange in London. The remark brought an 11-year gap in their correspondence.

After ten days in New York City, the Aldingtons moved to Washington, DC, early in November 1940, the moment when, as Richard put it to Violet Schiff a decade later, 'our best time began'. He was happy, though the news from Britain stirred and depressed him—both his father's former law offices and his old school had been damaged in the blitz. The 'best time' also began with political anxieties and with Aldington spending his first Washington days bedridden with a severe cold. The year had been hard on him, salved by friendships with the Slonimskys and the Bacons. With Bacon his relationship was intensely practical, the two were similarly hardheaded and cynical towards human affairs. In contrast, his relationship with Harry Slonimsky touches a gentler side. He felt for Slonimsky's vulnerabilities as he had years earlier felt for Flint's, and appreciated a vein of tenderness in the man, whose sensitivity helped him at a moment of complex and difficult adjustment.

In Washington he met Edward Dahlberg, whose first novel

Bottom Dogs had been championed by no less than D. H. Lawrence. The meeting was opportune because Dahlberg, an original of independent mind, was deeply versed in the American writers. Aldington read aloud his proposed American choices for his anthology. Dahlberg especially approved his discovery of Melville's poetry and his intention to include a large selection.[19] Dahlberg, in retrospect, saw Aldington as 'lonely and thwarted' and told Kittredge that Netta had sought him out and asked him to befriend her husband, who had nobody to talk to (an ordinary enough circumstance for anyone on first arrival in a large modern city). By Dahlberg's account, the two men became 'warm friends', and certainly the American was just the kind of acerbic spirit Aldington would admire and like, though he told Bacon he found Dahlberg 'as over-sensitive as a racehorse'.

In December 1940 he heard from Frieda Lawrence, who had read 'Farewell to Europe' in the *Atlantic Monthly*. She invited the Aldingtons to visit her in New Mexico. He had months of work to do on the anthology, and at first was cautious about driving so far in the harshest of winter, but the idea struck him as adventurous and that escape from 'this mechanical East' might lead to something creative. Restless, he was tempted to start out at once and quickly entertained the possibility of settling in New Mexico, at least for a time. But common sense prevailed and reunion with Frieda Lawrence was delayed.

16   1941–42

Viking Press published *Life for Life's Sake* in January 1941 and Aldington by then had completed work on the anthology, which on 7 January he trumpeted to Pat Covici as 'the nicest thing we've done together'. He was confident he had done better than all predecessors, including wiping out 'Mr Q [Sir Arthur Quiller-Couch] and his Oxford Book'. Beyond editing, he was careful of other details, from the book's physical weight (he tested books for their wieldiness in the hand) to the question of whether to include his own poems—an idea rejected as giving critics a potential weapon, that he had chosen himself while omitting this, that or the other worthy poet. While tactfully accepting many in-house editorial suggestions, he endeavoured to keep the book nicely proportioned, and especially not overweighted with moderns.

The introduction to the anthology, which he was determined to keep brief and simple, nonetheless gave him considerable trouble and in late January he was still working at it, having scrapped one whole version. His problem, as he told Covici, was to hit the right tone, which depended on the range of potential readers, from the neophyte to those steeped in the poetry. Kittredge has an excellent paragraph on how Aldington's approach derives from his whole sense of prose style, which,

> while remaining essentially French in qualities of simplicity and lucidity, aimed at a manner softened by fluidity and personal candor, and invigorated by the deliberate interjection of the author's personality. Having seen developments in poetry narrow its focus to an audience of the erudite and having witnessed the drift of the novel into mazes of obscurity and preciosity, Aldington was concerned with preserving the main body of English poetic tradition as an open terrain for the unspecialized, average cultivated reader—that is, for those bred in the vanishing tradition of the 'good European' or his natural offspring, the 'good American'. Like the contents of the anthology itself, the introduction must, he felt, address itself to such an audience.[1]

Winter's discontents, chiefly in the form of 'flu and colds, kept before Aldington the enticements of a change of scene, to Florida perhaps or New Mexico. He began discussing with Frieda Lawrence and her husband, Angelo Ravagli, the possibility of renting a small house in New Mexico, perhaps from April to October, and he thought of purchasing a trailer for the journey. What held him in Washington through February was the anthology introduction, which he ultimately used to describe his selection principles. What the Aldingtons needed was a base where he could read anthology proofs in April or May. Contract commitments meant he must begin work at once on another book, and therefore needed a workroom.

Eventually he decided to make first for Florida. In fact, work pressure was mostly in his own mind, because he was months ahead of schedule for the Viking contract. They enjoyed the 1100-mile drive, via West Virginia and 'through all the Gone With the Wind country' and their Florida quarters were at Jamay Beach, Nokomis, about 35 miles south of Tampa. The natural setting greatly appealed to Aldington. Their cottage was on a long narrow island joined to the mainland by two bridges over a narrow creek, which opened into a large lagoon. Behind the cottage, built no more than 30 yards from the Gulf of Mexico, was a sandy stretch of land, with southern pine and mangrove. It fascinated him that the mangrove roots were covered with oysters, which therefore literally grew on trees. The beach after a storm, scattered with conches, sponges, bits of coral, sea cucumbers and king crabs resembled a Dali painting.

Though the water was cooler than the Mediterranean, by late March they were able to indulge in a little sea bathing. The anthology proofs began to arrive and Aldington tackled them in a rested and relaxed frame of mind. Probably because they planned to move on to New Mexico in April, he was also rereading much of Lawrence's work. Weeks of peace were disturbed only by a measles scare for Catherine. Apart from proofs, little came to him from the outside world, although a letter reached him from Robin Douglas to say that Norman Douglas was in northern Portugal. In January Aldington had reported to the *New York Times* that Douglas had managed to pass from Italy into Switzerland and from there to Portugal. Robin Douglas was anxious for his father to cross to the United States, but Aldington felt, as he suggested to Frieda Lawrence, that Douglas would not like it 'though I'd give a great deal to see him again'.[2] Evasive with Robin, to his other son, Archie,

Douglas said bluntly: 'The only way to get me to America would be to handcuff and chloroform me, and to keep me in an iron cage all the way across'.[3] Around the same time, he told Nancy Cunard he would have taken the trip but felt too old and frail. Orioli, too, was in Lisbon, until his death the following January, and it was only then that Douglas left Portugal.

The tedium of galley proofing continued, but when he could escape his desk Aldington resorted to a childhood pastime. He sent to New York for an entomologist's outfit to investigate the local lepidoptera. The abundant tropical seashells on Jamay Beach also interested him and he had collected and named over 50 species, and a dozen more for which he had the genus. He was confident enough to ask if Slonimsky knew of a biologist or entomologist who might be contacted in case there was any minor investigation which could be undertaken in the district.

Another old associate of Aldington's, from the First World War, now came into his life again as a consequence of the Second. The French poet André Spire had barely managed to escape from France and was virtually destitute, with a young and pregnant wife. Aldington asked Slonimsky if he could help find employment for Spire in New York, saying that he would contribute financially, if necessary.

All through May the Aldingtons remained at Nokomis, Richard enjoying the country life despite a plethora of nagging details over the anthology—unexpectedly having to do the bibliography himself, dealing with poets' demands for more space, making changes to the actual contents. The months at Jamay Beach were among the happiest of his life. His health improved and be boasted to the Slonimskys that for a time at least he was getting the better of a chronic weight problem and had lost 12 pounds. He found the local people congenial and the terrain of the Gulf region constantly interesting, so he was not surprised that the great American naturalist Audubon had made many trips there.

They set out for New Mexico, regretfully enough, in late May and as Aldington later told Dahlberg, 'Of course we stopped in motels, and Catha thought I created them in some mysterious way at the appropriate moment'.[4] From his letters one senses that the journey was just as phantasmagoric for him as for his daughter, and equally so their arrival. When they reached San Cristobal, their destination, the weather was rainy and cold and the place itself remote, though they had a superb plateau view with glimpses of the canyon of the

Rio Grande. He and Catha were both unwell and by early June Netta was complaining of lung pains. Aldington's first reaction was a desire to return to Florida, and the feeling that life at 9000 feet would be too strenuous for the lungs.

By the end of June the weather had cleared and they had settled in. He sent Slonimsky a detailed sketch of their quarters:

> We live in the little adobe cottage Lawrence built, and I work in a shack which was used by Dorothy Brett in 1923. On a hill slope about 50 yards away is the Lawrence memorial chaple [sic], with a white phoenix on the roof-tree, and inside a plain slab inscribed D.H.L. ... The great pine tree Lawrence loved so much still stands, and Brett has put a phoenix on it. Beside the chimney in our cottage there is the stone seat he built and the rope mat he wove for it.[5]

Taos, the nearest town, was 20 miles off, Santa Fe 70. Four summers earlier Aldous Huxley had lived at San Cristobal and was impressed by the violent thunderstorms and dramatic cloudscapes, the sparsity of human settlement (Taos then had 2000 people). He told his brother Julian that he had never lived in a place which seemed so alien, even hostile, to man,[6] but for a time at least Aldington was content to be there, in an immediate environment partially created by Frieda and Ravagli, with a grove of pines, firs and junipers and a richness of wild flowers.

They remained until late July, Aldington continuing to deal with details of the anthology. At his suggestion, Viking circulated a pre-publication questionnaire, though he was chagrined to realise that copies had gone to poets whose work was not presented. Most replies contained comments on the book's modern section, and inclusion of work by nearly a hundred extra poets (mostly American) was suggested. From the moment he arrived in San Cristobal on, he was writing to Ralph Guinzburg and Marshall Best at Viking Press long letters commenting on and rebutting replies to the questionnaire, though it was a fruitless pursuit, attempting to placate numbers of minor poets who bitterly resented their exclusion. The fracas continued into the reviews.

Partly because of Netta's health (she had a vulnerable lung and tubercular tendency) they curtailed their stay in New Mexico and in late July set out to return to Florida, Aldington driving 450 miles a day to get there. At once he wrote to Warman that he could well understand why Lawrence had returned to Europe, for apart from the extreme climate the region around Taos was rife with a variety of diseases and the so-called society of the area (apart from the Pueblo Indians and the Mexicans) was too predominantly made up of artists, 'a weary remnant of the Montparnasse champagne bohemia'. But he had enjoyed the butterflies, making a collection which he transported safely back to Florida. In response to hospitality, he promised Frieda Lawrence a set, together with a collection of Jamay Beach shells and various translations of his novels.

The Viking Book of Poetry of the English-Speaking World was published in September 1941 and reviews began to appear at once. Some commentators felt the anthology was a genuine renewal or new look at the tradition of poetry in English, but more expressed dissatisfaction at omissions of one kind or another, most of them ignoring the fact that such omissions were in line with the prescription stated in the introduction. Perhaps inevitably, many of the reviewers' requirements were mutually contradictory. Among others, Malcolm Cowley (*New Republic*, 22 September) felt that American poetry had not been well-served. Aldington considered the 20th-century selection the least important part of the book. His main task had been to re-examine the whole tradition and to do a better job of it than 'Q' had done in the *Oxford Book of English Verse*. As to the contemporary poets: 'Who can tell? The whole damn lot may be forgotten in twenty years'.[7] As if in direct contradiction of American avant-gardism, he declared: 'This myopic concentration on the newest things in poetry is very characteristic of great cities, a kind of metropolitan provincialism'.

Out of touch as he was with Pound, discussion of the anthology with Slonimsky brought their old friend to the forefront and Aldington dilated on the topic at some length:

> The itch to be encyclopaedic is indeed strange in a man who is so neurotic that he is almost incapable of reading a book. I have often watched him with books. He pecks at them, like an intelligent cockerel, and having discovered a grain of wheat, crows over it as the pith and essence of the book. I am quite unable to give you any account of the Cantos, for I don't know what they are about or what plan if any they are formed on or what they aim to express. . . . Yet if you have the patience to plodge through those swampy Cantos (I don't know why you

should) you will find occasional phrases, lines, even brief passages of real poetic beauty. But no man can write without betraying himself, and those Cantos are a faithful picture of Ezra's strangely chaotic mind and nature.

He had occasion to speak again of Pound to Slonimsky a week or two later, to express shock at a report in the *Nation* that in one of his Rome broadcasts Pound had exhorted the blacks to revolt against 'the white Jew' Roosevelt. Writing to Slonimsky on 19 October, Aldington sadly recalled the charm, generosity and vitality of the gifted Pound of the early days in England and wondered if such present degradation could derive from 'mere rancour, the disappointment of comparative failure'. A sad foreshadowing, this, of comments on himself 15 years in the future.

He himself was nagged by feelings of failure. The anthology had lifted him out of the depression into which the war had driven him, but its reception was far less reassuring than he needed. Many of the reviews seemed to be written by poets whose work had been omitted, with the obvious consequences. Even the book's brief appearance in the lower reaches of the *New York Herald Tribune Book Review* list of best-sellers did little to offset Aldington's feeling of discouragement and for the time being he found it difficult to work.

Furore about the anthology far exceeded responses to his memoirs, *Life for Life's Sake*, published at the beginning of 1941. Intended as a dispassionate look by a 'good European' at the 'good Europe' which was at its vanishing point, the book is also personal and highly selective. (There are merely fleeting allusions to Dorothy Yorke and Brigit Patmore). In writing of such figures as Pound, Eliot and Lawrence, Aldington gives direct and candid impressions, making each portrayal concrete through personal anecdote. Other friends, less famous, such as Henry Slonimsky or Thomas MacGreevy, are treated on the same scale, the criterion being his interest in them. Otherwise, the book offers a reckoning of his literary opportunities and preoccupations and a clear and straightforward account of travels and the aesthetics of travel comparable, say, with the travel passages in Hemingway's *The Sun Also Rises*. As a memoir, *Life for Life's Sake* may be placed alongside such books as Gerald Murphy's *Living Well is the Best Revenge* or John Glassco's *Memoirs of Montparnasse*.

But by the last weeks of 1941 Aldington was struggling with a more exacting kind of task. He had begun reading around the subject of the Duke of Wellington and forming the idea of writing a biography. Dealing with the figure of a 'plain man' fighting through against long odds, such a biography might, he felt, even have propaganda value and influence Americans' view of the war. Exhausted from labouring over the anthology and, as usual, from the aftermath of letdown, Aldington had been drawn into grappling with the Wellington materials and was in the midst of finding his way to a new commitment.

Much as he liked Florida, he felt isolated there and fearful of what war was doing to England and Europe, but United States involvement charged him with optimism, and he was surprised to find himself proud of Churchill's warm reception in Congress and of Americans' positive response to the Battle of Britain. Even what he regarded as peculiarly American forms of vulgarity (broadcasts of the Pearl Harbour emergency interlarded with Coca Cola advertising) for the moment appealed to him, as did alliterative references to 'sneaking sycophants of the snivelling Son of Heaven' and Westbrook Pegler's allusions to 'Benny the Bum'. Such titbits were passed on for the amusement of Eric Warman.

That winter and spring he read Wellington materials as intensively as possible; his letters to Leonard Bacon, with whom he was regularly corresponding at this time have the peculiar interest of displaying side by side his anxious attention to current war events and his notes on political and military developments during Wellington's career.

He relished the solitude afforded by miles of uninhabited Florida sea coast, finding special beauty in the barren shoreline. For news of Europe he relied chiefly on the *New York Times* and Eric Warman's letters, which gave a clear picture of the austerity of life on the English 'home front'. For himself he had 'a small part-time unpaid war job' as a Deputy Sheriff of Sarasota County, with credentials labelled 'Defense Only', which meant he had no authority for normal policing responsibilities. He had night patrol coastal duties, to guard against the possibility of enemy agents infiltrating from Cuba or the Antilles. Saboteurs did, in fact, land in June 1942 and Aldington may have participated in the incident (at least, writing to Bacon about it, he avoids saying that he did not!).

After a 21-month silence, Alvin Manuel, the agent, contacted him in mid-April. Manuel had temporarily gone out of the agency business but was now back and represented, among others, Erskine Caldwell, for whom he had just negotiated a $70 000 fee (for a novel) with Metro-Goldwyn-Mayer. This approach from the direction of Hollywood made Aldington restless and by mid-year he was seriously considering abandoning his Wellington manuscript. He felt that the 100 000 words produced by eight months of work had not brought the subject to life and that 'no literary power on earth' could make 100–150 pages on the Peninsular War interesting reading. Instead of giving up, he decided to regroup, to start again.

Late July and early August saw an interruption of his regular routine. Travelling to Boulder, Colorado, he took part in the 13th annual Writers Conference in the Rocky Mountains. Conference Director was the poet Edward Davison. Aldington's assignment was 'General Adviser' and in addition there were as 'Group Leaders' Katherine Anne Porter, Carl Carmer, Witter Bynner and Harry Shaw. Although the local papers dubbed him 'Poet Richard Aldington', Bynner was the chief 'resource person' for poetry. Aldington joined Carmer, Bynner, Davison and two other poets, Thomas Hornsby Ferril and Charles Edward Eaton, in a joint poetry reading and also gave a paper on 'The Poet and Its Habitat'. He enjoyed the trip to the Rockies more than the conference, which he saw as something of 'a mild racket', its formalities quite absurd. Predictably enough, he found the students' manuscripts semi-literate and the students themselves semi-educated. He got on well with Bynner, who had figured in D. H. Lawrence's New Mexico life, but the contact seems to have led to nothing.

By now the Aldingtons had become unsettled in their Florida haven. Netta came increasingly to feel the isolation of Jamay Beach and the school to which they had intended to send Catherine closed down. Just as important, Aldington needed to put himself in the way of opportunities to earn an income. By the end of 1941 75 000 copies of the Viking anthology had sold, including 60 000 through the Literary Guild, and this meant quite solid earnings for him, but he had also received, and spent, a solid advance and now needed to make more money. The likely place to do that appeared to be California, where Manuel was making moves on his behalf.

Writing to the producer Doré Schary on 21 August 1942 Manuel pointed out that Aldous Huxley had recently called Aldington 'one of England's greatest living novelists'. Huxley and Aldington had links going back to the early 1920s when both were on the editorial board of the short-lived periodical *Coterie*, and both were involved in the life and work of D. H. Lawrence. Huxley was well-established in Hollywood and remained so during the period the Aldingtons were in the United States, but throughout Aldington's Hollywood sojourn the two writers kept their distance. Such considerations would be no concern of Manuel's. His pitch about Huxley was part of the game and by mid-September he had circulated to the Hollywood studios a hyperbolic account of what he called Aldington's 'writing credits'. Events moved swiftly and by mid-October the Aldingtons were in Hollywood, having driven westward 'slowly because of the tires'.

Aldington made the move westward almost on impulse and at some risk. On 21 October 1942 he signed an open-ended contract with Paramount Studios for $500 a week, with $1000 for the final week. Quite quickly, on 19 November, this first contract terminated, not without some difficulty about the final payment. There was a certain arbitrariness to the whole process. Aldington had been given a book to read and then had an interview with the producer (Manuel had sent him various scripts and scenarios while he was still in Florida, to familiarise him with Hollywood writing techniques). He and the producer had about an hour's discussion, with Manuel in silent attendance. The producer suddenly stood up to leave and told him to report to the studio at nine next morning. Afterwards Manuel explained that this meant he had been hired to write a 'treatment' of the book in question. Later, Aldington described a 'treatment' to Slonimsky and Warman as a sketch of narrative in the present tense arranged in scenes and sequences, with indications of 'shots' and bits of dialogue. But before he had completed it a meeting of the Paramount board decided not to proceed with the film. The work in question was probably Maugham's *The Hour Before the Dawn*, for which Aldington did produce a treatment at this time. By the end of the year, however, he had emphatically decided that he liked Hollywood. They had found living quarters on Sunset Boulevard, strategically distanced from all the major studios. The geographical location of Los Angeles appealed to him, the physical openness of the town and even the encounters with movie stars, such as Veronica Lake and Don Ameche. 'I wish I had come here twenty years ago', he told Eric Warman. 'Whatever happens I shall never return to Europe.'[8]

17   1943–46

But Aldington's feelings were more complicated than this. He always felt he had to work hard, pressured by a need to earn, and this increasingly affected his health. Now at the turn of the year came a long bout of indigestion and he told Bacon he was unwell, depressed and discontented. Thanking the Slonimskys for a money gift to Catherine he contrived to suggest backhandedly that she had more than enough already. Having earned well in 1942, he was for the moment in comparatively easy economic circumstances, but seemed restless, even confused. 'We like the "city of dreadful joy" very much indeed. To me, at any rate, it is the most civilised town in America, with more genuine interest in art than any other. . . . If I were not worried to death and on the verge of a nervous breakdown, I should be very happy here,'[1] he wrote to the Slonimskys. He was not on the verge of a breakdown but, despite liking Hollywood, neither was he at ease.

At this moment he was approached by the FBI about Pound. One of Pound's biographers, C. David Heymann, asserts that 'Richard Aldington, like Williams, inundated the FBI with letters from the chief imagist' and also identified Pound's recorded voice.[2] No evidence is provided by Heymann. Moreover, Aldington can have received few such letters ('full of political and economic babble', is Heymann's phrase). Why then does Heymann find it necessary to imply that these men eagerly betrayed a friend? To choose between friendship and patriotic duty in a time of national emergency can be no easy matter. Both Williams and Aldington, though the latter more obliquely, had shown strong if personal patriotic feelings. Williams once said, 'Disgust is my most moving emotion', and the same point might appropriately be made about Aldington. Clearly, in those overwrought times both men were disgusted with Pound's behaviour. Quite understandably so, given the indictment for treason that was issued against Pound on 26 July 1943 by the US District Court of the District of Columbia. By making a series of pro-fascist broadcasts the indictment stated Pound 'knowingly, intentionally, wilfully, unlawfully, feloniously, traitorously, and treasonably did adhere to the enemies of the United States'.[3] Whatever action they took (and Aldington later assured H.D. he had only one meeting with the FBI) did not prevent Williams later from befriending Pound, and Aldington from carrying on friendly correspondence in the early 1950s and again (after a gap due to crises in his own life) from the late 1950s until his death. Pound saw himself in his old age as a friend of both men. A year after the war, Aldington wrote to H.D., who was carefully protected from any disturbing tidings, his version of Pound's wartime fate and his own involvement in it:

> The story of Ezra is very painful, but I think it is absurd for you not to be told. During the war (as you probably know) he broadcast for the Mussolini government in the most violent terms, screaming like Hitler (so I'm told), telling England it would be wiped out, cursing the Jew Roosevelt and all the rest of the nonsense. (He wrote me in 1940 that 'Churchill will be hanged on the London Gold Exchange'!) After the boys landed in Sicily Ezra saw he had pulled a terrific boner and tried to get away to Switzerland, but was arrested by the Italians on the frontier and sent back. When the yanks got into Rapallo, a man came up to some G.I.s and announced he was an American stranded in Italy. They were very friendly until they heard his name, whereupon the[y] put him under arrest. General Clarke kept him from summary execution and eventually sent him home, and he was put on trial in Washington as a traitor to the U.S. Just before the trial he broke down, and the doctors humanely announced that he was suffering from paranoia and must be confined as not in a fit state to plead. When I last heard he was in St. Catherine's [sic] Hospital, Washington, D.C. Several attempts were made to get me to declare myself [on] one side or the other and to contribute to his defence funds. I eluded them all, as I think most were from F.B.I. agents provocateurs or Communists. I was denounced to the F.B.I. as 'a friend of Pound's' in 1942, but was not molested beyond a long interview with a couple of cops, awful-looking thugs who took voluminous notes.[4]

Just before the FBI contact, Aldington completed the typescript of his biography of the Duke of Wellington. Neither magazine assignments nor studio work came in, so he made an attempt at writing a children's story. Still he continued in a confused psychological state. Despite persistent depression, he enjoyed Hollywood links and the professional trappings of film work, such as the opportunity to book a small private viewing room and run through old movies or, for that matter, any movie to make technical notes. Existence in the film colony generally he found a curious mixture, though, for town life, as near an 'earthly paradise' as could be. Some aspects of it appealed to the epicurean in him. Certainly his view of it was a long way from Faulkner's often-repeated Beckett-like summation; 'Nothin' ever happens an' after a while a couple of leaves fall off a tree and then it'll be another year'.[5]

William Faulkner worked with Howard Hawks on Hemingway's *To Have and Have Not*, released that year, and was a colleague of Aldington's at Warner Brothers. He did not drive and for a time Aldington drove him to the studio. Fascinated by Faulkner's distinctive southernness, he quoted him to Bacon, 'Of our colleagues he remarked: "Suh, Ah have neveh known a set of writehs less acquainted with their profession—suh, I doubt whetheh any of them eveh read a book!" '.[6]

Proofs of *The Duke* arrived at Sunset Boulevard in the first week of August 1943. Aldington was obviously now satisfied with it as he already pondered working on another biography, of Whistler, a project for which he made notes as late as October, though he told Bacon he would prefer George III as a subject. With October came at least material improvement in the Aldingtons' life. When *The Duke* was published, within three weeks 9000 copies sold, netting what was for him huge royalties of $4600. By mid-November a third printing was in press and the book's financial success was assured, so he spoke of the 'sudden change in our fortunes'.

In late November he began a six week Metro-Goldwyn-Mayer assignment at $1000 a week, working on a screenplay of Robert Nathan's *A Portrait of Jenny*. But he found a screenwriter's life as uncertain and unsatisfying as did Faulkner, with whom he lunched occasionally. Aldington's agreement with M-G-M had apparently been purely verbal and quickly lapsed. To make matters worse, on 30 November his old car was stolen—'as if in compensation', he remarked ironically. It was found after a few days at Long Beach with a flat battery. Meanwhile, he maintained interest in the idea of writing a 'genial' protrait of Whistler; but once more Hollywood intervened. Early in December Warner Brothers asked him to work on *The Miracle*, a movie to be directed by Wolfgang Reinhardt. The salary was lower than he had been offered by M-G-M, but higher than anything Faulkner was paid or would be paid until he was awarded the Nobel Prize for Literature nearly a decade later.

For Aldington this assignment meant another chance to establish himself as a writer in the Hollywood industry. Produced by Henry Blanke, *The Miracle* was to be a technicolor musical, and Aldington began work on 10 December, looking over old texts and scripts, conferring with Wolfgang Reinhardt (son of famous European director Max Reinhardt who had a generation earlier produced *The Miracle* with Lady Diana Cooper in a starring role[7]). The work was exciting, but Aldington had no illusions about his capacities or likely success as a screenwriter. Where Faulkner despised such work, he appreciated it as a difficult and highly technical business. Faulkner was indifferent to the idea of success in it whereas Aldington would have liked to succeed but felt chances were minimised by the political intrigues of insiders. If we go by screen credits, Faulkner certainly achieved more.

Details of the work fascinated Aldington, involving as it did something akin to scholarly research. *The Miracle* was based on a mediaeval legend, but Reinhardt shifted period to the 17th century and Aldington enlisted Slonimsky's advice in finding accurate accounts of how nuns lived in southern Europe, consulting such sources as C.G. Coulton's *Five Centuries of Religion* and Lina Eckenstein's *Women Under Monasticism*. Reading of this sort appealed to him and he enjoyed preparing the treatment despite the hazards of dealing with religious material under the vigilant eyes of the Catholic Church and the Hays Office, the Hollywood self-censoring organisation. Everything, of course, depended on Warner Brothers. His future was in their hands. If they liked the treatment he could very likely stay on, but if not he might never be given another assignment. He decidedly wanted to remain in California, because the only other part of the United States he cared for was Florida.

His other mainstay was the success of *The Duke*. The book was not intended to be a definitive biography, for the author himself described it to Viking editor Marshall Best as 'a compact handbook',[8] not 'a professor's book' but 'a popular and superficial work with no claim to original scholarship.'[9] Whatever may be its claims to authority, *The Duke* is done with great skill in choice of detail and general balance. Interestingly, too, it is a cooler look at the values Aldington explored in the best of his novels. Wellington obviously appealed to him as a great professional, a man who did his job as a soldier with outstanding competence and commitment and remained uncorrupted by public status. Predictably, Aldington admired his subject's capacity for holding himself above the praise or blame of the mob, his aristocratic aloofness, and yet he rejoiced enough in Wellington's position to include all his titles and honours, which occupy 21 lines of the American edition's title-page. Despite admiration for this 'decent landlord and humane general' he does not gloss over faults, but gives a rounded portrait.

His choice of Wellington as his first biographical subject since the rather more 'professorial' treatment of Voltaire nearly 20 years earlier, was partly dictated by his inner response to the times in which he was writing and his desire to celebrate a British hero. But Wellington was a hero to him for reasons beyond a brilliantly successful soldiering career. Modesty, openness and professionalism, these were the qualities in Arthur Wellesley which appealed to him, plus an opportunity in another medium to pursue the main theme of his fiction, 'to discover and expose the *idées fixes* of prejudice that cripple a free and genuine response to literature, to knowledge and to life'.[10]

After *The Duke* Aldington was deflected from literary writing by the demands of Hollywood. He had come to feel that the Whistler biography would be better handled by an American. Work on *The Miracle* continued into 1944 and he submitted a completed treatment on 11 February. He felt that the nine weeks working on it had been a sort of invisible tug-of-war with Wolfgang Reinhardt, though both were quite pleased with the result. The relation between producer, director and writer fascinated Aldington, who felt the last should be more respected because he tended to pull the script his way and thus had a pervasive influence on the film. In practice, even those of considerable literary reputation were not much respected in this milieu. Few of Scott Fitzgerald's treatments had remained untouched, for example, even though Fitzgerald took the job very seriously.

As Aldington saw, the life of someone such as himself, who was not on long-term contract was most precarious. The industry could employ only about two hundred writers and perhaps ten times that number were seeking jobs. The British writers generally (Isherwood was an example) did not succeed because, like Faulkner, they despised Hollywood and showed it, but they tended to underestimate the problems of the medium whereas Faulkner never presumed himself an expert in it and never particularly wished to be.

Other than his screenwriting Aldington was able to do little at this period even though he was employed by the studios not more than a quarter of the time. His studio income, therefore, was crucial. His treatment of *The Miracle* apparently pleased Jack Warner, to whom it had been fed piecemeal, putting Aldington's job repeatedly on the line. Warner invited him to his office, paid him compliments, made suggestions and ordered him to write the screenplay. This degree of success occasioned surprise in the studio generally and the news made an item in the Hollywood papers. Aldington, delighted, told Slonimsky he had no reason to complain about his treatment by Hollywood, which had been civil and patient, affording him every chance to show what he could do and making no bones about payment. His next concern was to succeed with the screenplay to the extent of getting a screen credit, an achievement which would make future studio employment much more certain.

Several years later he told H.D. he had made $25 000 at Warners, though most of it had gone in taxes, and certainly *The Miracle* was financially vital to him and in that respect made life a great deal easier. His 72-page treatment and the resulting appointment to write the screenplay led to a quarrel with Reinhardt, who had wanted another writer, but by early April Aldington had completed more than a hundred pages. It was his 18th week at Warners and he anticipated a further eight weeks work, but when at the end of the month he handed in the screenplay it was passed on to be worked over by someone else. Such hard realities of the screen writer's trade disturbed and depressed him.

Meanwhile he was assigned to collaborate on a different project with a regular screenwriter, Tom Job ('author of *Uncle Harry*'). The subject for treatment was a murder story, with the possibility that some major movie stars—Ida Lupino, Charles Boyer and Sydney Greenstreet—would be in the cast for the film. Aldington hoped to learn a great deal from Job, but the assigment fizzled out after a few weeks. At that point he left Warners to work for an independent producer, Lester Cowan, but this too proved an abortive move as did a return to Metro-Goldwyn-Mayer where he worked for five weeks on a treatment of a subject titled *Diamond Rock*, based on the novel *No Truce With Time* by his old friend Alec Waugh. Waugh says in his memoirs that the war ended just as M-G-M were to go into production with the film, so the project was permanently shelved.[11]

In August 1944 life took a difficult turn for the Aldingtons. First, Netta suffered from a bone splinter caused by the removal of a tooth and then Aldington sustained serious financial losses from the peccadilloes of his former agent Ralph Pinker. Pinker had never paid income tax on $12 500 received for the film rights of *All Men Are Enemies* and, although Aldington lived in Provence at the time of non-payment and knew nothing about it, he was now obliged to pay the tax plus a delinquency fine.

In contrast, after a long absence from print, H.D. had published a new book in England, *The Walls Do Not Fall*, part of a long poem sequence.[12] Osbert Sitwell reviewed it favourably in May in the *Observer*, and in consequence had its successor, *Tribute to the Angels*, dedicated to him. Aldington saw a copy, but he was unimpressed. 'The war certainly hasn't inspired her', he told Henry Slonimsky. In a somewhat Olympian tone, he professed himself also as uninspired:

> We have been two years in L.A. now, and sometimes yearn for a little simplicity and peace and silence—but where are these expensive luxuries to be had? You will see by the letter heading [Metro-Goldwyn-Mayer notepaper] that I still keep my restive Pegasus hitched to the extraordinary and improbable movie waggon; but as I cannot write seriously in these distressing times, it seemed sensible to try to earn and save a little money.[13]

Yet, despite these observations and the need to pay the film rights taxes, he told Al Manuel in September that he intended to rest for the remainder of the year, probably because further earnings would themselves be heavily taxed. Escape from the film studios meant that he could help in planning an exhibition at the Clark Library, UCLA, of his own works and career. Arranged through a new friend, the librarian Lawrence Clark Powell, this was held in November. He could also indulge his habit of voracious reading, harking back to the 19th century, ranging from the once popular novel *The Green Carnation* to William Morris's *The Earthly Paradise*. Briefly, he considered working towards a biography of John Addington Symonds. The Pre-Raphaelite period now seemed to him a golden age and he advised Warman to purchase whatever drawings and water colours from that era he could lay his hands on. Warman still had ambition for a writer's career, but Aldington suggested this had become much harder than it was before the First World War and strongly advised Warman to take the government job he had been offered. His own eye was still on studio work, although it was at this period he began to think of writing a novel about Casanova. On 15 December Manuel's partner Jules Goldstone cabled Mervyn Le Roy that the 'world famous novelist' Richard Aldington would be ideal for working on *The Robe*.

Nonetheless, 'free of hack work' until February, he followed his dip into the 19th century with substantial rereading in the classics (Homer, Virgil, Ariosto, Tasso). He saved enough petrol for a trip to the Mojave Desert, the first time his family had moved outside Los Angeles city limits in more than two years, and within an hour, at a place where they stopped for lunch, he took four species of desert butterflies, three of them rare. For several months he managed to work at fiction and in late March Manuel submitted to the Viking Press a portion of *The Romance of Casanova*.

The 'rest' period, however, brought on a crisis of confidence. Aldington's sense of his position in the movie colony wrung from him a lengthy *cri de coeur* to Slonimsky in mid-April:

> I am trying to make some money out of these fantastic movie people. If only I could pick up enough to have a very little income and move around the western states and sometimes to Florida. . . . As to my literary work . . . I receive too many cold shoulders not to realise that what I have said is not wanted, nor anything I might say. Weeks, even months pass without my exchanging a word with anybody outside my family but shop-keepers who still condescend to take what little money I have. Days pass without my even receiving a letter. . . . People no longer like me either as a writer or as a person. I don't blame anybody—even myself—it is just a fact. If only I had a little income this wouldn't trouble me in the least, I believe I should welcome it. Epicurus was right when he said—hide your life. Only in obscurity can one escape (perhaps) the curious moral cannibalism of democracy. But a writer's living depends on reputation, and mine has vanished. That is my fault—I never bothered about it, never cultivated or flattered anyone. That was a mistake—I was too indolent and conceited.[14]

This letter continues with an attack on 'Tom Eliot', and is a moment of instructive contrast. Of the two, Aldington was the more convivial, but he was socially, as he put it, 'indolent'. Awkward, even odd as he was at times, Eliot worked at cultivating people socially. He was diplomatic, whereas Aldington commonly felt free to make acidulous remarks to one friend about another. Yet, socially careless though he was, there is plenty of evidence that he could be the soul of affection and generosity. Of course, his nomadic life was not conducive to a network of friends or social contacts, except of the most superficial kind.

Even the end of the war in Europe found him in a morose mood. Recommending to Slonimsky escape from politics into the music of Beethoven and Mozart, he nonetheless pondered whether or not the unaccountable Germans ought to be eliminated:

> But why do we worry about these things? Among the many detestable illusions of this age is the notion—fostered by all kinds of self-seeking publicists who make money out of it—that every one of us is 'responsible' for this complexity and muddle, that we ought to 'discuss problems' and in fact worry ourselves sick about problems we can't possibly know expertly and certainly can't solve. *L'homme constitutionnel est triste.* By God he is, and a dull dog too. Write in your tablets—there is no responsibility without power, and the power of a single vote seldom entitles one to more than a choice between two undesirable rascals.

Beetles, of which he noted 18 000 species north of the Rio Grande, he felt were a preferable species, and after all 'what is best in the universe is non-human'. From various directions the human world still came to him and he could not ignore it. Charles Madge, of the Pilot Press in London, approached him to write introductions for a group of four French novels to be issued as one volume. *Great French Romances* was published by them the following year jointly with the New York firm of Duell, Sloan and Pearce, who had become Aldington's American publishers.

Manuel sold a movie option on Aldington's Casanova material to Columbia Pictures for $10 000 and by July Aldington was working on the project; but he was not very happy with the work. He had written nearly half the novel and forwarded it to Viking with an outline of the rest, but was not confident they would want it. His hunch was accurate and the book ('this fetid novel I am writing') was quickly rejected by Marshall Best. Within a month, Columbia Pictures, stipulating only that *The Romance of Casanova* must be published by a reputable New York firm, contracted to pay $30 000 for film rights if they proceeded with it and a further $15 000 for the screenplay. 'I cannot believe they will be so foolish', Aldington told

Bacon. Nor were they; but placing the book itself was by no means as difficult as might have been expected. After a fruitless approach to Doubleday a contract was signed with Charles Duell, and this secured an initial $10 000 from Columbia.

Aldington was, in fact, coming to detest the movie industry. His involvement in it had the effect of commercialising his whole career. Even the possiblity of the huge film rights payment from Columbia did not excite him because the funds would have to be deferred until the next year for income tax purposes. However, he was entertaining the possibility of another mega-project, a poetry anthology for the Encyclopaedia Britannica organisation, and despite Viking Press's rejection of the Casanova typescript, he signed an agreement with them to edit an Oscar Wilde volume in their 'Portable' series of readers.

Working to the top of his bent, he put in ten hours a day—on the novel, the anthology, the Wilde selection and some projects with Netta. She had just received her first commission, for $100, to paint a portrait and had made drawings for a children's book for which Aldington wrote the text. This project came to nothing, but another joint venture succeeded. Duells published, under the title *A Wreath for San Gemignano* and with illustrations by Netta, the translation of Folgore da San Gemignano's 'A Garland of Months', first issued by Charles Bubb in 1917. This little book was intended for the Christmas market, but striking printers delayed its appearance until the new year.

After the German surrender, requests for Aldington's work began to come in regularly. He convinced himself that his relatively slight literary production during the war occurred because he was among those who chose to keep silence, and thus he was now being sought out. 'I am simply worked off my seat here', he told Warman in August: 'Literally I am working ten hours a day to get these three books done. Since V.E. Day it has been one request after another. This happens—the few authors who have the restraint to keep silent throughout a war are the people who are wanted immediately after, when readers are looking for something else'.[15] He began to feel he was back in demand as an author and, at the same time, to find Hollywood and the studio people 'unspeakably vile'. Weary of the system which could switch him from one project to another virtually at a moment's notice, he in any case found working on Casanova in either medium (film or novel) a chore. He rationalised this by saying that Casanova's character was distasteful to him, but in July he had admitted to Warman that: 'I fear I am making a poor job of this Casanova for Columbia, which seemed such a good idea. ... this is a misfortune. If I could have pulled this job off successfully I stood to make 30 000 to 40 000 dollars. But I fear that too recedes into the land of might-have-been. It is a disappointment, as I could have done with a little rest. I grow old, Eric, and weary and discouraged'.[16]

By early September, though, he had finished the Wilde selection and introduction, a task which pleased him. Shortly afterwards he began negotiating with Heinemanns for an English edition of the Wellington biography, though he wanted to defer detailed discussions until he had finished with Casanova and Columbia Pictures. This suited the British publishers as their reader, the popular novelist Georgette Heyer, had raised doubts about Aldington's historical accuracy.

1945 was one of the few years when he published no book, though he was engaged in many schemes. His determination of a few years earlier, never to return to Europe, was now going into reverse. Apart from feeling the Casanova book was little more than a pot-boiler and the cinema version a very uncertain undertaking, he began to find reasons everywhere for deploring his circumstances. Studio strikes he professed to see as Communist-connected. As for American workers:

> I must try to get our passports in order. You will grasp the insane condition[s] here when I tell you that assistants at petrol stations are walking off their jobs because $300 a month (900 pounds a year!) is not good enough pay. Worse than that is the utter insolence and idleness of the 'workers', who in my opinion are far more controlled by Herr Stalin than most Americans dream of. He could have a general strike here any time he wanted.[17]

Catherine, now seven and in private school, meantime was ensnared in another side of American life, private enterprise or 'muscular Christianity'. Having become attached to the idea of regular church-going, she arrived home from church with 52 little envelopes for her weekly offering, indubitably a manifestation of 'practical' religion. Certainly Aldington was in sceptical and sardonic humour, enough to call Huxley's recently-published *The Perennial Philosophy* 'an anthology of godology', and to hide from the 'eminent saint' Aldous in the supermarket.[18]

Another part of his state of mind was a deliberately ostrich-like approach to the wider world. Along with virtually everyone else, intimidated by the 'sub-atomic' bomb, his response was to cut off outside contact, cancel newspapers, shut off the radio, and concentrate on work. Nowhere was safe any longer and a strain of fatalism in him seemed to be confirmed, to point to the only possible attitude. So he continued to wrestle with the unwelcome problems of the *Casanova*, to hope Columbia Pictures would decide to go ahead, and that his next task would be the screenplay. But on top of his glum sense of the world at large, a troublesome currency inflation now set in to devalue what funds he did earn and to reinforce his particular disillusionment with Hollywood.

By the year's end he completed the 'fetid' novel, finding it better than he had believed, an organic whole beyond most people's capacities, or so he told himself, passing the feeling on self-deprecatingly to Bacon. He had recovered his spirits. Hearing C.P. Snow would shortly be in California, he looked forward to their meeting. Herbert Read wrote from France, playing back Henry Miller's catchphrase about the 'airconditioned nightmare' of the United States. Aldington responded that Americans were pretty much like anyone else, and that he found Hollywood pleasant living and intellectually stimulating, though the movie world was preposterous. At Read's suggesting a return to Europe he said this would be like giving up a Pullman de luxe for a tiny rattletrap French car.

He was still waiting to hear about the *Casanova* movie project in mid-February 1946 when the unions started to monopolise the attention of film executives. He began seriously to consider leaving Hollywood and perhaps the United States, though he still waxed eloquent to Read (who was planning a trip to North America) about the New England autumns. He explained he could not travel East to meet Read because work in hand must be finished by April, when he planned to drive his family to Florida on the first leg of a year's holiday, then on to Jamaica to visit Netta's mother.

The strain of working in Hollywood and yet making efforts to continue producing books had begun to tell, and in particular he was finding the anthology arduous. Ten to 12 working hours a day reduced him to near nervous collapse and chronic 'influenza'. Escape was imperative. In mid-April he surprised himself by beginning to keep a diary. On 15 April he wrote: 'We have come to dislike America very much . . . and as the place has nothing to offer but money, we go'.[19] A week later he observed that, after nearly four years, Hollywood 'has been a crucial experience, salutary perhaps, damaging perhaps, certainly profitable, and certainly a place to leave!' Amid all this are notes of reading—Francis Bacon, Spenser, Dryden, *Troilus and Cressida*, Coulton's *Mediaeval Panorama*, all by contrast reinforcing his pessimism about the present. He saw parallels both with the declining years of the Roman Empire and with restrictions on personal freedom characteristic of the Middle Ages. 'How hateful it is to live in these betwixt and between periods', he wrote to himself.

Very early on the morning of 23 April they left Hollywood for the last time, travelling through Arizona, Oklahoma and Texas, headed for New Orleans. By the time they reached Yuma, Arizona, Aldington was suffering from nervous exhaustion, so they decided to go at a much slower pace. For the time being he continued the notebook, which is peppered with sour observations about Americans and their culture. Even New Orleans, he noted on 3 May, offers little other than evidence of the triumph of the Yahoo. Former heroes such as Emerson and Whitman are now diminished in his eyes, and reading Audubon yields a sense of despoiled nature and maltreated Indians.

By mid-May they were at Montego Bay, Jamaica. The journal was resumed, and provides a detailed account of these Caribbean months. The sojourn allowed Aldington a brief period to concentrate on different elements in himself, and he spent much time examining the seashore life and making beach excursions with a glass-bottomed box to observe the fish. He also reveals the first inklings of a later writing project in reading 'Fiona MacLeod' (William Sharp), the exponent of Gaelic mystical prose and verse, whose work he determined to include in an anthology of the aesthetes ('If it ever gets done'), which became *The Religion of Beauty* (1950).

Problems over having his 'old Buick' shipped to Jamaica show something of Aldington's state of mind. The Kingston shipping agent forgot to tell him the car had arrived and when he was forced to go to Kingston for it he felt himself involved in the tyranny of red tape. The incident worked him up into a state of almost paranoid self-commiseration:

If only I could find some place of repose in simple dignified surroundings. But I fear the only rest nowadays is in the grave. It is a bitter confession for one who has loved life so well. I am defeated, not by any fault or failure in myself, but by the quarrelsome and tyrannical stupidity of mankind. I have money but it is taken from me by cheating governments. I ask only to be left alone, but am continually plagued by officials with demands of one sort or another.[20]

The annoying trip to Kingston and, worse still, several days of hanging about there at the mercy of the bureaucrats, brought on dysentery. On return to Montego Bay, more wasted days were needed to recover from nervous fatigue and general discombobulation. Arrival from London of two copies of *Great French Romances* caused Aldington to reflect that his literary reputation had virtually disappeared, and so depressed him further. He felt that he had been obliged to accept hack work from a minor publisher, but the book contains four minor French classic novels including one by Balzac.[21]

He was more or less right about loss of reputation. The war had pushed much literary activity into the background, but there were other factors, too. First, Aldington's unrooted existence: he had, or seemed to have, repudiated England and there was no country to which his literary fortunes were particularly attached. The original direction of his work had been poetry and translation, and (like William Carlos Williams, but for quite opposite reasons) he appears to have felt circumvented as a poet perhaps largely because Eliot created a milieu alien to his sensibility and talents. When, unexpectedly, he succeeded as a novelist, it did not seem his natural genre, and his career in it progressively weakened, partly because he eventually exhausted his theme of the social and psychological effects of the First World War, but also because Hollywood deflected him into the specialised trade of screenwriting, which had nothing to do with literary reputations and in which he made little mark. At this moment in 1946, his biography *The Duke* was a solid commercial success in the United States, but had yet to make its impact in Britain.

Within three weeks of arrival in Jamaica, the Aldingtons decided there was no possibility of their making a long-term commitment to the place. His sense of isolation and decay was compounded by the mosquitoes, enervating climate and repeated thunderstorms. By the end of June they had decided the only course was to return to France.

Early in August they were back in New York City. The best thing about this sojourn was the Slonimskys' hospitality, though Aldington did come to an understanding with Charles Duell about various publishing projects, including anthologies of Pater and of the late 19th century aesthetes. But finally Aldington and Catha (Netta was to follow) flew by freight plane via Newfoundland to Shannon, destination Paris.

18   1946–50

Aldington confided in his journal on 17 August 1946 that first impressions of the 'dirty poor old town' of Paris were 'rather painful'. From a base at the Hotel Aiglon, Boulevard Raspail, he began to look for an apartment and to reorientate himself. Awaiting Netta's arrival, he saw much of the Glovers, something of Richard Church and Edward Gordon Craig. An early highlight was a visit to the Goncourt Exhibition on 25 August:

> Really most exciting, especially the beautiful series of Watteau drawings in red chalk and the many other items of 18th century art. There was a room of beautiful Japanese colour prints, and oriental furniture from the Goncourt home. The walls were hung with portraits of contemporary literary men, and in cases were the originals of the Journals, many Goncourt first editions, and books from their library illustrated especially for them with portraits of the authors. In the centre of the room was the voluptuous naked statue of a beautiful (but seemingly stupid) woman of about 1840. She was lying half twisted in a sensual attitude with her head lower than her bottom to tighten her breasts. But if the statue is anywhere near realistic she must have had an exquisite body.

Next day proofs arrived of Heinemann's edition of the Wilde anthology. Arnold Gyde, the editor, spoke of Aldington's 'comeback' in English letters and this together with promised Norwegian translations of *All Men Are Enemies* and *Seven Against Reeves* somewhat assuaged anxieties about his position, especially financial. The Paris of Nancy Cunard and Henry Crowder seemed, at first, part of an irrecoverable past and the city, now peopled by Glovers and Churches, an inescapably dourer version. But both couples shortly left for England and Nancy herself reappeared, having spent much of the war in South and Central America. She and Aldington exchanged brief notes, but he darkly informed Warman that he was not anxious to link up with 'fellow travellers'.[1]

When it came, he was morose about Heinemann's *Wellington*, which seemed a shoddy production (this was still the era of distinctive British war-economy paper-and-ink-saving). Complaining to Gyde about 'fatal errors' in the text, he feared the book's bad features gave ammunition to hostile reviewers; but anxieties diminished when the 10 000 first run sold out on publication.

Friends such as Warman, Prentice and Gribble began to visit. Aldington's journal, with its daily catalogue of meals, gallery browsing and shopping, tailed off as he clicked into the rhythms of a new life. Another old friend, Gustave Cohen, helped him re-establish contacts, and thus he gradually settled in. On 25 September he wrote to H.D., who had returned to Switzerland, that he had five books planned and needed only to rescue his library from Customs and find a large, quiet room in which to work. 'Our decision to return to Paris was taken when we found that Jamaica was quite impossible—a kind of darky republic full of mysterious political intrigues. . . . But Paris has proved quite delightful . . . shabby and weather-beaten, but still a relic of civilization. It makes one think of what Rome must have been after Alaric—with public buildings and libraries and statues and paintings still almost intact, but a nation on the way out.'

Despite high food prices, the nuisance of obtaining rations and extreme difficulty of discovering a suitable apartment, by late October he felt Paris had greatly improved his state of nerves, and that Europeans were friendlier than Americans. Late in the year the Aldingtons found an apartment at 162 Boulevard Montparnasse, with stocks of wood and coal, and near Catha's school. By the end of the year 10 000 copies of the Wilde anthology had sold, *Wellington* continued to move, and Heinemann's edition of *The Romance of Casanova* was due. Through the London publisher, Nicholson and Watson, Aldington signed a contract for French rights covering all his books since *All Men Are Enemies*, with an advance of £150 for each title. Rights to various titles were negotiated in a number of countries, including Holland, Spain, Italy, Switzerland and Czechoslovakia (where, the Czech publisher said, *A Dream in the Luxembourg* was held to be one of the great modern poems).

Flourishing though it may seem, all this was in a context of uncertain and anxious endeavours. Now that Aldington was making a European comeback, the energy seemed to drain out of his American publishing ventures. Viking Press refused advance royalties for a Portable French Reader, Duells took only a small run of the Pilot Press *Great French Romances* and Aldington had signed no new agreement with them for American rights. Manuel's moves to negotiated a $20 000 contract for a period as a screenwriter with

Warner Brothers came to nothing—but, unquestionably, Aldington was relieved to escape Hollywood. His accumulated publications yielded a living; but return to the Europe once abandoned 'forever' was a mixed experience, and he felt too 'disordered' for genuine creative work.

Ironically, what he called the 'fetid' *Romance of Casanova* had a huge pre-publication subscription of 18 000 at Heinemann and was contracted for publication in nine other European languages. Heinemann received orders for 30 000 of the Wilde and reprinted it in May 1947. Such figures were typical. Through Warman, a reprint of *All Men Are Enemies* was now issued by Arthur Barker. In the throes of 'the worst grippe I have ever had in my life', Aldington was not greatly encouraged by these signs of commercial success, but worked doggedly on.

Basil Dean contacted him in January 1947 to say that his new production company wished to dramatise *Seven Against Reeves*. Dean wanted to make the story-line topical—with allusions to rationing, queues, restrictions, and so on, but Aldington felt it should be presented as an appeal to nostalgia for the pre-war era. He was briefly excited by the project, even seeing it as a Hollywood vehicle, but nothing came of it.

Soon after his return to Europe, he resumed frequent correspondence with H.D. She wrote repeatedly expressing concern over the fate of Ezra Pound who had begun his long sojourn at St Elizabeth's Hospital in Washington. H.D.'s feelings towards Pound had remained more unequivocally compassionate than Aldington's and he several times felt the need to assure her that FBI agents had visited him about Pound only once. in Los Angeles. On a more positive note, he relayed to H.D. details of his current publishing successes. All his correspondents at this time were regaled with the sales figures of his books and information about contracts and royalties. His years in the United States had made him more money-conscious, but from *Death of a Hero* onwards he showed intense interest in the business side of being a professional writer. Making a living as a writer became the central focus of his anxieties, though not necessarily the real cause. This winter and spring his sales and reprints in Britain and on the Continent flourished. Since September 1946 he had earned £5000 in British royalties. He complained about the resulting high rate of income tax and pointed out that his economic situation was less comfortable than it might have been, because of damages he must pay as co-respondent in the divorce proceedings with Netta's first husband, Michael Patmore.

A potential source of revenue was the British edition of *Poetry of the English-Speaking World*, galleys of which he worked on in mid-year. His own career as a poet had almost lapsed, but a selection, *Bilder*,[2] appeared in Hamburg in 1947, and the summing-up would come in 1948 with Allen Wingate's edition of *The Complete Poems of Richard Aldington*. 'The latter aren't really as bad as I thought they were', he observed to H.D., 'though the only really successful one is *A Dream in the Luxembourg* which is now in its sixth impression'.[3] To H.D. at least, he underplayed receiving the James Tait Black Memorial Prize for *Wellington* in March. Not lucrative (the 1946 prize was worth £185), it was nonetheless prestigious. He sent Manuel a matter-of-fact note about it in mid-June, but took care to explain it as the British 'Equivalent to the Pulitzer'.[4]

A new friend now entered his life. Alister Kershaw, a young Australian with literary ambitions of his own, had come to Europe partly with the purpose of meeting writers whose work he admired, among them Roy Campbell and Aldington. Kershaw arrived in England penniless but Campbell arranged for him a BBC assignment, which financed a trip to Paris to meet Aldington. Earlier, while Aldington was in Jamaica, Kershaw had sent two slim volumes of his poetry. This Paris meeting was to have far-reaching consequences for both men. An immediate one was that Aldington sent Campbell a copy of his booklet *The Squire*, on the eccentric naturalist Charles Waterton. Aldington was just returning to the subject of this essay, published in 1934. A much larger portrait of Waterton appeared in 1948 in *Four English Portraits 1801-1851*, followed a year later by a book-length study, *The Strange Life of Charles Waterton*. Campbell responded to the booklet, and thus began one of the warmest friendships of Aldington's life.[5] Kershaw visited him in late May or early June and on 9 July Netta wrote to Eric Warman:

> I wonder if you would meet a young friend of ours and tell us what you think of him.
> His name Alister Kershaw, he is twenty-six writes poetry, comes from Australia, and has apparently brought himself up on Richard's books, all of which he knows almost literally (pause a moment for I mean this) off by heart . . .

She adds that Kershaw is shy and nervous and it had taken them four days to 'dig him out of his shyness', to find a vivid, charming and amusing companion. In effect, Warman was being asked to check on Kershaw, but also to look after him to the extent of seeking him out.

Neither Netta nor Catherine had been in the best of health and in May a vaccination left Netta nastily indisposed for several weeks. This, plus cramped studio space at Boulevard Montparnasse turned Aldington's thoughts once more to the Mediterranean. He found the Villa Aucassin at Le Lavandou, which was available from August to November. In Paris he had become irritated by endemic shortages of food, fuel and clothing. He hated the consequent bureaucracy and declared this 'eternal frustration of socialism' maddening. Once he sighted the Mediterranean he felt at home once more and enthused that this was 'the California of Europe', with its cypresses, palms, vineyards, and peach and almond trees. About a quarter of a mile from the sea, their villa was set in a valley green and gold with mimosa.

Glover and Church were at the Villa Aucassin together this summer and Church remarked on Glover's 'crushing' garrulity. Both men were convalescents, Glover both enfeebled and grieving the loss of his wife, so the villa had the air of a nursing-home. As for Aldington, he was benign, considerate and restrained, 'an aspect of his personality that, alas, rarely appeared in his books'.[6] One day he and the Churches took a picnic hamper into the hills and as they came to rising ground he actually carried Church across a series of stepping-stones. Noticing how Aldington was moved by the sound of the noon Angelus bells in the distance, Church in retrospect wished that such feeling might prove a key to Aldington's work. Church failed to see that the work's 'savagery' (his term) might be the obverse side of such feeling. In 1947 most of this 'savagery' was in the future, in the biographies which followed *Wellington*.

Manuel, still attempting to boost his client's career in the United States, wanted Aldington to produce another novel or a popular biography. He made suggestions, usually historical subjects with motion picture possibilities, such as the lives of the Apostles after the Last Supper, which seemed to recommend themselves, Aldington thought, because most had met violent ends. Meanwhile, Aldington worked for the London publisher Evans Brothers on *Four English Portraits*, a 'gallery' of mini-biographies: the young George IV, the young Disraeli, the young Dickens, and his 'old friend' Squire Waterton. He sent Manuel the Disraeli piece in

November, with suggestions for magazine placement. Larger tasks were in his mind, though possibly not suited to Manuel's aims, such as ' a really full biography of D. H. Lawrence.'

Both Aldington and Manuel had become restive about Duell's handling of Aldington's work in New York. He now set his hopes on returning to Viking Press, through his link with Covici. Should this occur, he thought of including a special contract provision for an emergency payment if he wished to move his family quickly to Switzerland, Spain or Italy. This odd proviso was in case of a sudden takeover of France by the Communists, which, he thought, had just narrowly been averted and which if it happened would mean a Communist world within ten years.

For the time being, however, he did quite well financially where he was. To add to his other sources of income, the London edition of *Poetry of the English-Speaking World* appeared in time for Christmas sale and, though under attack from reviewers, sold rapidly. On New Year's Eve he wrote to H.D. describing it as a 'body blow for the Eliot school', which re-established the main tradition of English poetry ('to which you and Ezra belong'). The book sold in an initial burst of 30 000 copies, and these heady figures momentarily prompted Wingate to consider risking a 10 000 run for *The Complete Poems*.

Despite the commercial success of *Poetry of the English-Speaking World*, Aldington, as usual, was not happy with the reviewers. One, in the *TLS* on 21 February 1948, pointed out a notable absentee from the book, Edith Sitwell, then at the height of her reputation. (Work is included by both Osbert and Sacheverell.) Gyde responded on 28 February that Miss Sitwell had refused permission. She, in turn, explained that she had done so because she had been asked for only one short 'undistinguished' poem first published in 1924. Implying that her later work had been ignored and unread by the editor, she said she saw no reason to allow herself to figure in the anthology 'disguised as a chaffinch' (6 March). She was not mollified by Aldington's explanation, two weeks later, that the modern section of the anthology was little better than token. All along he had held that his central interest was to take a fresh look at the main tradition. Offended and offensive, Sitwell observed that: 'Mr Aldington could be trusted to set innumerable booby-traps for himself and to blunder into them with no outside aid'. This was not the sort of controversy Aldington minded, but he cannily refrained from replying and thus prolonging the exchange, contenting himself with remarking privately to Gyde that it was Sitwell who had stumbled into the booby-trap of her own vanity. The tiny tempest did nothing to damage sales of the book, which continued high.

Difficulties with Duell, Sloan and Pearce continued, however. On 9 March John Browning of Evans Brothers wrote from London about *Four English Portraits* and the same day Duell wrote from New York. Browning spoke effusively of 'this very brilliant book'; Duell, saying his people were 'greatly impressed', nonetheless admitted hesitation about sales possibilities. Manuel proposed seeking a different New York publisher, this time E. P. Dutton, but the situation is symptomatic of the fact that Aldington never achieved a secure long-term publishing arrangement in the United States. The problem, as Manuel saw it, was a cultural gap. Such projects as the anthologies of Pater and the Aesthetes, or portrait sketches of distinctly English types were, Manuel felt, not suited to the United States market. Along with Duell and Covici, Manuel pined for the full-length novel or biography he felt Aldington should be producing. Browning had suggested the Waterton portrait might find a market as a full biography, and late in May Aldington wrote to Duell that he had nearly completed this book (having been temporarily deflected from his concern with D. H. Lawrence). By now he had come to feel that an overall contract was the best American publishing arrangement, but Duell could not agree and wrote, courteously enough, to say so.

In contrast, Aldington's literary affairs continued to flourish in the European marketplace. In May Kershaw, who had become a largely voluntary live-in assistant, despatched the typescript of *The Religion of Beauty* to Heinemann. The selection was rounded off with the work of a family friend from early in the century, Rachel Annand Taylor, and Aldington's bookseller William Dibben discovered that she was still alive. Characteristically, on hearing this Aldington wrote to John Gawsworth, editor of *Poetry Review*, suggesting he ask for her poems.

He now became heavily engaged with the subject of D. H. Lawrence. Besides the biography he contemplated, he linked in to a new scheme of Heinemann's. Jointly with Penguin Books, they planned to publish ten Lawrence titles, and Frere suggested that a Lawrence biography by Aldington might be part of the project. Accompanied by Allen Lane of Penguin, Frere travelled to Le Lavandou for discussions. The plan was for Aldington to write an introduction to each Lawrence reprint, with Penguin reissuing his

Lawrence booklet (first published by the University of Washington and then by Heinemann. Penguin never did print it). By mid-August Aldington had completed the Waterton biography and begun writing on Lawrence. In April he had told H.D. he intended to write 'the story of his days, and as much favourable comment on his work as possible . . . . ' Now, on 4 October, he remarked to Frere, 'it's a real challenge to a writer—to try to win sympathy for a guy with so many lousy aspects to his character'. But, for all that, he had written 25 000 words of what he termed 'a marvellous story', and felt he would complete the book by the end of February.

Though he complained to Warman about the long delays of publishing, which made it seem as it one's work were having no effect, Aldington advised Frere to delay publication of *The Religion of Beauty* for over a year, as he already had several books scheduled for 1949 and such matters always affected his tax status. Of the three titles published in 1948 *The Complete Poems of Richard Aldington* added nothing significant to the corpus of his poetry and, as he expected, caused no great stir in the world; *Walter Pater: Selected Works* is a competent and useful selection, comparable with the Wilde volume in scope and range. Competence also characterises *Four English Portraits*, a peculiarly native genre of essay-portrait, much dependent on anecdote, though the Dickens piece is actually commentary on a string of quotations from the master's work. Such professionalism seemed to be recognised, at least in London where the book was chosen for a Book Society Recommendation.

His London success was exploited by Manuel in the United States to win over publishers, but some of his efforts were offset by Aldington's abrasiveness. Convinced by now that Duell was too small, too conservative and too slow-moving for his purposes, he nonetheless put off E. P. Dutton because they stipulated only ten per cent author's royalty in ancillary radio, dramatic, television and motion picture rights. Interested as he was in such negotiations, they made him tense and suspicious. When Duell said they were prepared to match anything proposed by Dutton, this meant they would publish *Four English Portraits* and the Lawrence biography, but neither publisher wanted *The Complete Poems*. Aldington responded to Charley Duell's remark, 'we rather deserve a chance at the D. H. LAWRENCE book' with 'they want to pick out the juiciest plum and leave the others'.[7] He particularly blamed Duell's for poor American marketing of *The Romance of Casanova*. His London-induced mood of confidence, bolstered by the Book Society

Recommendation of *Four English Portraits*, was to conclude in disappointment. Despite its *succès d'estime*, pre-publication subscription was a mere 3000, far below expectations. Aldington, reacting hastily, instructed Manuel on 27 November, two days after the London publication date, to take the best available offer from either Dutton or Duell, for this book, the Lawrence and the Waterton, 'before they hear from London'. He had, however, by then alienated Dutton and his contract remained with Duell.

His business affairs became so extensive that dealing with them interfered with writing and Kershaw was asked to take them over wholesale, even while he was away in London, as he sometimes was. Even so, Aldington overworked and in late October was forced to rest, and questioned whether he should continue with the Lawrence book. He stopped work on it again briefly in November, because of anxiety about the way Heinemann were handling his affairs. Before the war he had made a contract through Frere which gave them all rights in his work published in the decade 1929-39. As far as he was concerned this was a device to minimise divorce payments to the Patmores, but he now felt this had been forgotten by Heinemann, who took the agreement at face value and did not advance some royalties due to him.

A different perspective on Aldington's life at the Villa Aucassin is given by his Australian friend, Denison Deasey, who was introduced by Kershaw. In late June and into July Deasey stayed at Le Lavandou, lodging at an inn, visiting the Villa Aucassin frequently in the afternoons and evenings. 'Lunch at the villa', Deasey wrote later[8] 'was a sort of quest, a gateway to finding out what was left in our worlds'. By now, apparently, Kershaw was fully at home and led the conversation, Aldington making quieter contributions. Deasey's account probably telescopes several occasions as he mentions the arrival of Henry Williamson, John Arlott and Richard Church plus a variety of London publishers and fellow-Australians, especially Geoffrey Dutton and his wife Nin. In contrast to a rambunctious Roy Campbell, Deasey portrays a sometimes withdrawn Aldington. He sets him off, tapping a long morning away on the typewriter in his upstairs workroom, against the flow of socialising visitors in the rest of the villa.

In January 1949 Aldington heard from the widows of two old friends. Violet Schiff sent Heinemann's reprint of Stephen Hudson's *A True Story*, which prompted an exchange of reminiscences. Aldington gave her news of Frieda Lawrence, who had moved to Port Isobel, Texas, close to the Mexican border. Memories of that area caught him once more in a regretful state at a missed alternative, though he was pleased that the ebullient Frieda found satisfaction in his Lawrence work. By now she had come to see Lawrence virtually in the guise of a saint, though she says tantalisingly at one point 'You remember yourself how jealous he was, at Port Cros, though he was fond of you, as you know!'[9] Continuing with his life of Lawrence, Aldington's attitude towards his subject shifted continually, but he told Kershaw about this time that he was 'liking him again'.

In London there was a sudden surge of interest in *Four English Portraits*. After a slow start, Evans Brothers expected a spring reprint to follow their first run of 10 000 copies. Yet the book remained a stumbling block in re-establishing Aldington's American publishing arrangements. Duell would publish the Waterton biography if they got an option on the Lawrence and were not obliged to take *Four English Portraits*. Moreover, they insisted *Portraits* not be offered to any other American publisher, as it would compete with the Waterton. Manuel was unhappy about this, but took heart from the British success of *Portraits* and Penguin's decision to issue *Seven Against Reeves* and *Soft Answers*. Perturbed at the downturn in his American publishing fortunes, Aldington yielded ground to the extent that he was willing to seek an American publisher for *Portraits* after Duell had published *The Strange Life of Squire Waterton*. Meantime, he attempted to manoeuvre Duell into paying the Lawrence permissions fees. But nothing came of efforts towards an American edition of *Four English Portraits*, and eventually he paid the Lawrence permissions fees himself. While all these negotiations were going forward between London, New York and Hollywood, at the Villa Aucassin he was completing the Lawrence manuscript.

The novelist Henry Williamson and his new bride stayed there this spring. Like Campbell and Aldington, Williamson was a Kershaw enthusiasm, and the visit was suggested by him. Aldington had found in the young Australian not merely a secretary, but someone who counteracted his tendency to ignore social life. Many visitors, some of whom became Aldington's devoted friends, first arrived at Kershaw's instigation. At Le Lavandou in April and into May, Williamson's account of his host confirms the impressions of many others. He noted Aldington's guardedness, observing that he had been hurt when young, as was discernible from much of his writing. Aldington delighted in childhood memories, but 'I was told that his mother had been a strong, self-willed woman who had dominated both a gentle husband and a gentle son. This, it seemed to me later on, was the key to his gradual dislike turning to contempt when he learned that T. E. Lawrence's mother had ruled her sons and their father with a self-will tautened at times to fury'.[10] T. E. Lawrence was a figure Aldington respected at this stage, regarding him as one of the few who had written sensibly about the other Lawrence.[11] In January 1949 Aldington had suggested Kershaw write a critical study of T. E. Lawrence.

1949 witnessed the summing up of Aldington's career as poet. The *Complete Poems* appeared in January, when he sent Kershaw a grim valedictory:

> I have not looked at them [he wrote on 27 January] just put them away, and am not sending any copies except those merely 'business' ones. Why? I think it is because the publication of them hitherto has never brought anything but jeers and disagreeables. Just as, after the reception of the Crystal World 12 years ago, I promised myself I would never write another line of poetry, & have kept my word; so I feel I never want to hear of them again. Were it possible to annihilate them, I would. Failing that I believe that the best way to kill them is to publish them now in this form and let the jackals devour them.

Most notable immediate response was a *TLS* review on 5 February. To this reviewer, the Imagist movement seemed like the naive beginnings of a return to naturalness. In measured tones, he characterised Aldington's poetry as lacking in rhyme and in compression of ideas, and the poet himself as making no attempt at organisation or formalisation of material. His work suffered from rhythmic sameness, monotony of pitch, lack of intensity, though some poems were 'almost Chinese' in their clarity and simplicity, and the poetry was undeniably readable, especially *A Dream in the Luxembourg* and *A Fool i' the Forest*, which were 'remarkably successful in an age unsuited to the long poem'. The best shorter pieces tended to be the war poems. These comments are prefaced with the observation that 'the refreshing honesty and passion, the tireless erotic preoccupations, the prettiness, the lack of intellectual and technical equipment, remains pronounced now as in the earliest poems'. A response was quickly forthcoming from Roy Campbell (that 'typhoon in a beer bottle', as Edith Sitwell once called him) whose letter appeared in the *TLS* on 26 February, declaring the reviewer an intellectual bureaucrat who perceived the art of poetry as a process of problem-solving.

That same month, John Gawsworth's new *Poetry Review* ran Aldington's version of 'The Vigil of Venus', translated in neatly managed metrical rhyming couplets, which won the approval of the venerable Gilbert Murray. *Poetry Review* followed in its next number with Campbell's 'Richard Aldington, Happy Pagan'.[12] Continuing from his *TLS* letter, Campbell claims that Aldington's clarity and explicitness accompany 'great profundities of thought and feeling' and that his work does not need the conventions of rhyme and meter. As to the supposed 'tireless erotic preoccupations', these are the source of 'some of the finest love poetry of our time'. Campbell's review reveals his strong affinities with Aldington—both were individualists, anti-socialist and anti-modernist, and each markedly displays an acerbic mental and verbal temperament. From his perspective, Aldington more than once declared Campbell the greatest living poet. Modest about his own poetry, he was glad enough to be championed by Campbell. Rejoicing in the energy fo the South African's verbal sallies, for himself he said little.

He overworked again this spring and summer, and meanwhile continued to appear before the public–the Albatross paperback edition of *Rejected Guest* in April, Evans' edition of *The Strange Life of Charles Waterton* in May, and Kershaw's bibliography. In April he received another of Frieda Lawrence's jaunty letters. She wrote as if he had been very close to Lawrence and may well have felt him so; yet Aldington remarked to Gyde: 'I was never one of his "closest friends", never even conscripted for Rananim'[13] (which H.D. had been). How close the two were has not been fully established, but it would say much for Aldington's disinterestedness if he felt this about the relationship, found much to criticise in Lawrence's personality and conduct, yet continued as an outspoken champion of his genius. In any event, he worked hard at the Lawrence biography until completion of the first draft on 20 May. By mid-July copies of the revised typescript had been sent to London and New York.

He also wrote a publicity brief for Carol Reed's film version of 'The Rocking-Horse Winner'; the first Penguin Lawrence had gone to press and Heinemann were to start work shortly on their Lawrence project, a proposed hardback reissue of 14 titles. In early August Kershaw informed Manuel that Heinemann were 'one hundred per cent' enthusiastic about the biography and that the Waterton was having a 'magnificent press' in England. A month or so later Charles Duell was equally positive about both books. Once again Aldington seemed to have reason for optimism about his literary fortunes, and once again he was in a financial pinch and looking for an advance from Heinemann.

But his sense of financial pressure may have been due to depression on finishing the book. 'Never before have I had the feeling of complete blankness and sterility', he wrote to Kershaw on 13 September, but it was something he had experienced many times, due to overwork and relative idleness after sustained effort. He was in this state when he heard from Bacon about Pound's receiving the Bollingen Prize for *The Pisan Cantos*, and the negative reactions to the award. The Harvard poet Robert Hillyer led the attack on Pound in two June 1949 issues of the *Saturday Review of Literature*, 'Treason's Strange Fruit' (11 June) and 'Poetry's New Priesthood' (18 June). Despite his own harsh views of the 'new priesthood', Aldington felt Hillyer was brash, but the award nonetheless wrong; for 'after all, damn it, even if Ezra was cracked, he wasn't cracked on our side, but on the side of Musso and Hitler. Don't persecute him, but don't reward him . . . .'[14]

Aldington set to work on the Lawrence introductions. From being modest about writing the life-story, he now used the phrase 'the standard Lawrence biography', but was steeling himself for virulent attacks. This other side showed in an exchange with Alec Waugh, whose anthology *These I would Choose*[15] included his poems, praised him in its introduction and, equally pleasing, ignored Eliot. Waugh's book, he said, was like a glass of fresh spring water after nauseating cocktails.

Another friend of this time was John Arlott. As Arlott's whole public presence affirmed his Englishness, and he was a personage in that despised organisation the BBC, not to mention a socialist and a sports commentator, the relationship may seem odd, but Aldington confided in him in tones of genuine affection. Twice in November he wrote giving Arlott details of current writing and publishing activities. He spoke of his feeling of nostalgia for the old lost English country life and, indeed, asked Arlott to send a book on English village life for Catha. Continuing to sense a conspiracy against himself among the British intelligentsia, he spoke to Arlott of 'British efforts to discredit me'. That he felt the British attitude to Lawrence was similar, may partially explain his admiration for 'the only real genius . . . who has come right out of the English industrial working class'. (A remark which reveals limited knowledge, but no matter). He considered the Heinemann-Penguin project of publishing 21 Lawrence titles a real monument to 'the last great English writer'. Fourteen titles eventually had Aldington's introductions (one which did not was *Lady Chatterley's Lover*, because the text had been mutilated by prudery). In writing of all this to Arlott,[16] Aldington makes no mention of the Penguin reprint of his *Soft Answers*; he fought hard with publishers and literati for his own interests, but characteristically knew the moment to be modest.

In a letter of 6 November 1949 he also gives Arlott something of the flavour of life at Le Lavandou, although the environmental developments he describes are, in fact, a cover for a serious impending change in his personal life, which was obviously taking shape as he wrote:

We had a really lovely October on the whole—just enough rain to moisten the earth and bring out the early winter flowers. The sweet alyssum is wonderful this year; and scents the air with honey all along the abandoned railway. Today we have our first mistral, but as there is a blue sky and we now can keep the central heating on permanently[,] it is rather nice.

We had rather *too* many people calling in this year, and I don't mind telling you that Netta and I would gladly have swopped [sic] many of them for you and Dawn. But visitors along this coast should have a car—the local transport is so bad it's a penance. But if it were not we should be swarmed over. As it is there is too much new building going on for my taste. Serge's annexe at the end of the bay nearest Lavandou is complete, and very luxurious. A new milk bar has been built near the Bastide, and three new houses between us and the Tabac. On the hill some genial collaborator is building a large mansion. And two places are going up on the Aiguebelle side of the valley. They began the rebuilding of Toulon on the first of this month; which incidentally had to wait until the harbour was cleared of ships sunk by various friends of humanity.

By the end of 1949 he was working on proofs of *Portrait of a*

Genius, But... For the first half of December he was laid up with a bronchial condition, but despite the obviously damaging effects of overwork was already contemplating, at Kershaw's suggestion, his next task. On 2 December he wrote hoping that Kershaw's discussion of the new project with John Browning of Evans had been useful, and that he had written of it confidentially to Duell. He was contemplating something that a year earlier he had proposed as a good project for Kershaw—a biography of Lawrence of Arabia.

To please Catherine, the Aldingtons spent Christmas at Monte Carlo, partly because it had the best aquarium in Europe and had just been restored to pre-war standards. The trip, and especially the tropical fish, reminded Aldington of warmer climes, and the glass-bottomed boxes in the Caribbean. Netta had a plan to visit her mother in Jamaica in the new year, but Aldington had no desire to see that particular paradise again.

19   1950-54

The 1950s were ushered in for Aldington in a paper nightmare, English and American proofs of the Lawrence biography, and 'interminable Lorenzo Penguins' all error-ridden. Endeavours of this sort were not helped by his learning that *The Strange Life of Charles Waterton*, despite relative British success, sold poorly in New York. He blamed this in part on paraphrasing and summarising review articles which, no matter how commendatory, obviated the reader's need to purchase the book. Other reasons may be adduced—chiefly that American readers have not the British taste for whimsical eccentrics. His Waterton portrayal is sympathetic, sometimes lighthearted and amusing but sometimes ponderous or locquacious. Perhaps reviewers resorted to summary because not much can be made of such a book in the way of judgements.

A distraction came when Peter Russell, editor of *Nine*, asked for a contribution to a Pound *festschrift*. Aldington could quite genuinely plead overwork, but he offered to be what use he could for 'your book on Ezra, though in fact I haven't seen him since about 1930. I thought even then that he was a bit nuts. As a human being he was at his nicest before 1913, when London made him self-conscious and artificial'.[1] Apart from being weak and exhausted, Aldington had plenty of worries. His solicitor-brother, Tony, who had become his business agent after the end of the war had not kept up payments to the Patmores so Aldington was now compelled to disgorge a large sum, money he had intended to set aside for Catha's future. Because he was proofing the D. H. Lawrence biography he began to feel anxious about reviewers, suggesting to Gyde that they 'forget' to send a review copy to the *TLS* and beware of the *Spectator*, the *New Statesman*, the *Listener*, the *Tablet* 'and all the Beaverbrook crowd'.[2]

After the Second World War Aldington was in continuous communication with his brother Tony, perhaps more in a business sense than a personal one, though Tony also acted as mediator between him and their mother. A few months before he left Hollywood in 1946, for example, Aldington had written:

> Talking of hideous [earlier in the letter he had said his Casanova novel was 'hideous']—I have had a hideous grouse from Mother

on the usual trouble. Netta, who is probably sound, says she is just trying to get some dibs out of me to go pub-crawling behind your back. Well, old boy, I leave it to you. Take any money of mine you need to make the old girl comfortable, but of course protect yourself from the horrid results of her convivial habits. It is an awful task. I understand I am due for a screed from Molly telling me I am neglecting my pore old mother, etc. Dear me![3]

Now, when he informed Tony that he had finished writing the Lawrence biography, he felt obliged to explain:

Well, the magnum opus—benedicite opera omnia—is completed and copies despatched to London, New York and Paris. We must now wait for them to be lost or mutilated or made the occasion of a strike of what are jokingly referred to as 'working' printers. What I am talking about is my life of D.H. Lawrence, which runs to 125,000 words; and will I hope hit the jackpot.[4]

Later in this letter he apologises: 'I have been so completely absorbed by that Lawrence book, which I began exactly a year ago, that I seem to have neglected everybody, and now I have leisure again I have no news. How are you? And Daphne? And when do I acquire a new nephew or niece?'

Family demands for money, particularly on behalf of his mother, continued over the years. Aldington's wariness of reviewers had increased with time, but the anxious tone of many of his letters at this period was most immediately due to another worry, the deterioration of his relations with his wife, Netta. From time to time he had complained to Kershaw about her lack of organisation, in keeping household accounts, for example, and recently of her unwillingness to help with his work, by filing, typing, and so on. She was now in London, having gone there from visiting her mother in the West Indies. By late January Aldington realised she intended to remain in England and look for a job. Upset for Catha's sake, he affected a sardonic attitude. 'I realise I am a cow', he told Kershaw '—even the "Literary" Supplement of the London Times says so—but this alacrity of ships leaving the sinking rat shocks my naivete'.[5] Netta soon wrote to say she proposed to set up in London as a painter. She suggested that his prospects for making a reasonable income were very dim. Little was put on paper about this crisis between them, but it appears that Netta had become disenchanted with the isolation and the drudgery of having little to do except act as an unpaid office secretary.

Matters seemed to go from bad to worse. As he waited uneasily for March publication of *Portrait of a Genius, But* . . . , the Penguin reissue of *Soft Answers* was a flop. Heinemanns were unenthusiastic about his proposed Lawrence of Arabia project, and the Patmore solicitors were adamant that back taxes on the divorce settlement be paid in full from royalties. Various Continental sources of income (such as Czechoslovakia) dried up. 'In fact', Aldington moaned to Kershaw, 'it is ruin. . . . ':

> You see EVERYTHING has gone wrong. Loss of [royalties from] Czechoslovakia, loss of Albatross, failure of my books in France, Scandinavia, etc.; refusal of Alberto to transfer even the paltry sums I earn in Italy and to issue fresh books; failure of Four Portraits and Waterton; cabal of Times, Listener, B.B.C., Eliot and Sitwell gangs etc.; loss of Viking; idiocy of Al Manuel and Duells. Final touch is that since Duells sent Frieda [Lawrence] proofs of Portrait she has ceased to write, which means she dislikes the book. If she publicly repudiates it that will kill it as surely as those T.L.S. people killed the Squire.
>
> Netta is quite right—my career as an earning writer is finished, owing partly to my own imprudence, partly to political events, partly to the malice of enemies. . . .
>
> I don't know quite what to do, for, as Netta so sweetly says, even if I could 'squeeze out another book' it would 'probably not be worth while economically'.[6]

To pursue the Lawrence of Arabia proposal became imperative because of the need for a publisher's advance and therefore precisely to 'squeeze out another book', so Kershaw was instructed to make whatever bargain he could with Evans Brothers. When Aldington's advance copy of *Portrait of a Genius, But* . . . arrived he howled treachery. Disgust overwhelmed him at the cheap production and the number of undetected printing errors, especially as Frere had said this was 'the biography of the century'.

Worries about reviewers were less well-founded than Aldington had feared. He could only complain about the *TLS* and *Daily Telegraph* (both reviews apparently by Malcolm Muggeridge) for praising *him* more than Lawrence. Thanking Frere for one batch of reviews, he remarked, 'I could not expect better'. The only sour notes from this first wave came from Peter Quennell and Christopher Sykes, whom Aldington dismissed as 'an Eliot bootlicker' and 'a Sitwell ditto'.[7] Yet large numbers of positive notices did not soothe him and he complained to Violet Schiff that the reviewers were either ill-educated barbarians or over-educated highbrows out to show their talent superior to Lawrence's.

Late in April 1950 Frieda Lawrence wrote to say how much she liked the book, though she felt a curious detachment in reading about herself. She wrote again on 2 May, 'an avalanche of reviews—It surely is what's called success . . . '; she also upbraided Aldington gently for not mentioning the help *he* had been to *them* during the First World War; 4 May: 'Do you remember in Port Cros you did so much for L and you say not a word in your book. I at the time was so grateful for your friendship and the life you gave me, with L so ill—when you yourself were in one of those difficult moments of your life'; 22 May: 'It is really exciting this Lawrence revival—I get a swelled head—aren't you really pleased at the *effect* you have had?' Finally, on 27 May: 'You seem to have unleashed a whirlwind with your very human book!'

Twice Frieda mentions H.D., once to observe with typical airiness, 'what a strange marriage of yours that must have been'. Aldington explained to H.D. herself that, except for a passing reference, he had kept her name out of the Lawrence book because he felt she would prefer it so, though H.D.'s biographer Janice Robinson has asserted that the omission was due to Aldington's jealousy.

Frieda's approval by no means anticipated the mixed criticism the book was to receive in the future. Claims have been made that it is the culmination of Aldington's long championship of Lawrence (Frieda's view), or that he merely jumped on the Lawrence bandwagon. Even Lawrence's biographer Harry T. Moore, who became a friendly contact of Aldington's and at one stage intended to write his biography, suggests ambiguously that he 'managed to keep in the public eye with a variety of books, some of them about Lawrence'.[8] Aldington's book, which just preceded Moore's *Life and Works of D. H. Lawrence* (1951), was a full-scale portrait unlike any Lawrence memoirs which had appeared from the early 1930s onward. He had no intention of being eulogist or destroyer, but wished to put Lawrence's life and career into perspective. In his own mind he succeeded well enough to consider this the best biography he had so far done. Moore, who had some technical criticisms and like other reviewers regretted that no new material was offered, felt the book was 'as fair as it is believable'.[9] Aldington took issue with both Lawrence's detractors and adulators.

Lawrence, by precept and example, had rooted him out of his Berkshire cottage into a life of travel and wider cultural contact. If Pound had led the way in despising London intellectual life, Lawrence had shown how to stand apart from it. Above all, Lawrence was the great instance of intuitive engagement with life and commitment to sense experience. As an epicurean, Aldington too desired to pursue life with spontaneity and gusto, without being dominated by the staleness of second thought. But another part of his nature sought detachment, objectivity, the scholar's distance, and in any event was wary and sceptical.

All these elements of his character come into play in his important study of Lawrence. A great admirer of his heightened sensitivity to life, his gift for contact, he was unmoved by Lawrence's 'blood' mystique and all the trappings of his view of psychology. Especially in the opening section of *Portrait of a Genius, But . . .* , Aldington's writing is temperate, distinguished and empathetic, with admirable variation of mood, style and pace to suit the immediate context, and a narrative momentum founded on masterly syntax. In this biography, in a genuine attempt to comprehend and record the baffling complexity of Lawrence's nature and his struggles, he applies some of the skills of a fine novelist, without in any way diminishing the portrait's value by introducing obvious fictionalisation. Harsh things are said about Lawrence, but also friendly and appreciative things, the sum amounting to this, that though he was 'wayward', domineering and self-righteous, Lawrence was 'the most vividly alive man of his time'.[10] Certainly Lawrence is excoriated, but his genius is fully acknowledged. *Portrait of a Genius, But . . .* , while it breaks no new ground, is forceful, determinedly non-idolatrous, and in final effect is a balanced study of a complex and extraordinary temperament.

As to that, biographer and subject, though of markedly different natures, have some notable similarities. Aldington speaks of Lawrence's 'fierce dogmatism and even hectoring style' (which he links back to Ruskin and Carlyle);[11] both qualities characterise his own early novels and some of his criticism, though he lacks Lawrence's fieriness. Aldington is contemptuous of Lawrence's utopianism, his 'philosophy' (in quotation marks), his obtuseness about Frieda's relationship to her children, and other matters, but he is quick to pounce on Henry James's condescending remark, which pictures Lawrence hanging in 'the dusty rear' of the procession of contemporary English novelists, scoffing that James mixes his metaphors and locates the procession in a rowing boat.[12] Yet despite all the cutting-down-to-size of Lawrence as a human being plenty of evidence is provided to balance the picture and one comes away from it feeling that, warts and all, Lawrence's greatness has been demonstrated.

Aldington's satirical powers sharpened as his prose style became more polished and flexible. The portrait of Lawrence, while it contains a personal element, is not a sudden lashing out at him, but its character is a foreseeable development from the head-on satire of Aldington's fiction, ranging from *Death of a Hero* to 'Stepping Heavenward'. Undeniably, he was contentious, but there is no record that he resented being lampooned in Lawrence's fiction and letters. He seems to have accepted such internecine exchanges as a matter of course.

His publishing affairs in the United States were much tamer than the London success of *Portrait of a Genius, But. . . .* By 1950 *The Romance of Casanova* had stopped selling, leaving an unearned balance of $350. Two months after New York publication, *The Strange Life of Charles Waterton* had earned its author only $600. Now Duell's edition of *D. H. Lawrence* (the American title of *Portrait of a Genius, But . . .*) had a poor subscription. Even the London sales of *Portrait of a Genius, But . . .* could not cover all the difficulties of Aldington's financial situation nor mitigate the fact that he must continue to work hard at what writing tasks came to hand. He felt stripped by the demands of the divorce settlement and payment of back taxes, and complained to Kershaw in April that he felt near nervous breakdown.

At this stage Roy Campbell, a friend by correspondence, entered his life in person. Campbell at first treated Aldington very carefully and wrote of him to Peter Russell: 'He seems a bit like W.L. [Wyndham Lewis] in the way that most of his reactions are hostile. He is a recluse and seems anti-everything. For him everybody is a "jew"—including Eliot, Lewis and Pound. He is unlike Lewis however in that he is goodnaturedly "anti"—there is no real rancour in what he says. . . . '[13] Campbell was mistaken about the anti-semitism. According to Kershaw the 'Jew' by-play was a parody of Campbell himself. Once the two had got each other's measure, Campbell came to the Villa Aucassin almost daily. He was the sort of man Aldington could take to, big, convivial, an outdoors adventurer whose physical activity had been curtailed by his being lamed, and a man with an impressive war record (active service in both World Wars and—on Franco's side—in the Spanish Civil War). Aldington had already made friendly gestures to the Campbells—advising Roy on his famous contretemps with Stephen Spender, expressing admiration for his poetry—and this visit filled out and confirmed their friendship.

Aldington had been corresponding with David Garnett, chiefly on the question of how much Lawrence had actually contributed to *The Boy in the Bush*, a novel written in collaboration with Molly Skinner. He believed Lawrence had recreated the book using Skinner's plot ideas, but Garnett was able to show that the work was much closer to genuine collaboration. Late in June Aldington told Garnett he had begun making notes for a biography of Lawrence of Arabia. Asking for general assistance, he particularly mentioned newspaper cuttings, which he felt he ought to read because 'much of the poor devil's misfortunes were clearly due to newspaper persecution'.[14] During the writing of *Portrait of a Genius, But . . .* , there is evidence that Aldington's feelings towards his subject veered a great deal between disgust and admiration, which may reveal a certain instability of temperament in himself, but may equally show that he was genuinely 'living with' Lawrence. In the T. E. Lawrence case the matter seems rather different. Aldington and Kershaw began with unquestioning acceptance of him as a national hero-figure. Even now, Aldington's mind was open on the matter, though to Kershaw he expressed serious reservations.

> I am not AT ALL encouraged by Frere's zeal for my writing on T.E.L. On the contrary. Like all these war-demented Brits, Frere's one idea is to try to bully or cajole or starve me into accepting and praising the WAR in which he [Lawrence] was a hero.[15]

In the early stages of dealing with Lawrence, he was angry with the hero simply as a 'warmonger'.

Unwell with bronchial trouble and incapable of doing much else, by mid-July he had stockpiled notes on Lawrence and pursued a helpful correspondence with Professor A. W. Lawrence, T.E.'s brother. Throughout the summer Aldington could do little. He had few visitors, and depended on Kershaw to deal with his professional correspondence. In a state of nervous exhaustion, he paid daily visits to the doctor. On 23 September he told Bacon he was ill from overwork, adding: 'probably you know that Netta unable to stand the strain has left me and gone to London'. For a time he had wished to hide Netta's defection, but realised gradually he could not avoid telling friends. When Edward Dahlberg, who had not been in touch for nearly a decade, sent his novel *The Flea of Sodom*, seeking a review article, Aldington found the writing 'lavish and prodigal', professed admiration for its 'apocalyptic reality', but begged off because he had suffered 'a sort of crack-up'.[16]

Notwithstanding large sales in the recent past, his professional life now seemed to him in no healthier a state than his marriage or his own body. The British edition of the D. H. Lawrence biography had done well enough, with 10 000 sales, but only one-third that number had sold in the United States. Richard Aldington, professional author, with many books in print was advised by a tax expert that outstanding debts because of an unpaid instalment of the Patmore divorce settlement might well make his best course a declaration of bankruptcy.

Dreary, rainy weather plagued them throughout January 1951, making the villa grounds a quagmire. To add to his 'everlasting toilsome climb over barren hills of frustration' Aldington learned the Harmsworths had a use for the Villa Aucassin, so he must move house in April. Worry made him vituperative, but he channelled these feelings largely into the discoveries he was making about Lawrence. 'I have had to slow down and almost stop work on TEL', he told Kershaw on 27 February. 'The strain with all the other worries is too great, and it makes me unfair to him through irritation. I have done nearly 30 000 words, but it will all have to be re-written and a lot of it cut'. Even so, he continued painstakingly seeking material, asserting in the same letter, 'I MUST have all FIRST HAND evidence about TEL or take the rap from Graves, Garnett et al'. Through March, as letters to Alan Bird, Kershaw and others show, he was heavily engaged in seeking details. His aim was to prepare the biography for autumn publication, so presumably legal and other complications had not yet been foreseen. In gathering a prodigious quantity of information, he made use of the talents of both Bird and Deasey, as well as Kershaw, and with this help it may have seemed at first no more than another routine task. Several years were to elapse, however, before the book could appear. During those years the project took heavy a toll of him psychologically and physically.

On 25 April he and Catha vacated the Villa Aucassin after a tenancy of nearly four years. They spent a few days in Aix, then moved on to Avignon for two days. From Avignon to Arles and Nîmes they followed the tourist's path of museums, churches and Roman ruins. Aldington drove quite far west and then in heavy spring rains headed north to visit the Gribbles at Sancerre. Such assiduous touring is surprising given that he really was run-down, but for the moment he felt very much like postponing house-hunting, school-searching and the heavy task of dealing with Lawrence. Motoring raised his spirits, especially through territory which was one of his cherished pre-war wandering places, so he arrived in Montpellier refreshed. Once settled in, however, he began to feel his 'solitude'.

A renewed link was now established with Ezra Pound, still at St Elizabeth's Hospital. Aldington had cut off from him in 1940, but began writing again as if nothing had happened, though he complained to Bird that Pound's cryptic and allusive letters were in the style of the Katzenjammer Kids, a feature of those same Hearst newspapers which had shaped some of Pound's political views. Pound urged him to write a life of Ford, but the most Aldington would do was offer to help Pound revive Ford's reputation.

When, a couple of years later, Pound's son, Omar, wrote asking support for a petition to the United States' President for Pound's release, although then corresponding regularly with Pound and giving him bulletins on H.D., Aldington in effect refused Omar Pound's request. He said that the President had no power to order the release of someone certified insane, or to show clemency to a citizen who has not been tried and convicted. He was among those who realised that if Pound was declared sane he would have to stand trial.

No satisfactory publishing arrangements had been concluded for the book on which he was labouring so prodigiously. Now, through August and September, secret contract negotiations were carried on with the firm of William Collins, which had the means, not available to Evans Brothers, to provide funds to ease his financial troubles. The premier agent in these negotiations, John Holroyd Reece, obtained a huge advance of £4 500 (£1 750 to go to Evans in repayment of advances). Kershaw then turned his attention to the American scene, extricating Aldington from a less than satisfactory arrangement with Duells, so he could seek a more profitable arrangement with another American publisher.

In mid-September 1951 Aldington told Kershaw he had found the right tone for the book. 'I want it to be cool, impersonal, without bias, but interesting', he said[17] though he continued to fear censorship by the Lawrence family even if most of his information were verifiable from published and widely available reference books. If Collins could get the necessary clearances, however, he felt the book could be a great success, 'And nothing mean in it'.

By necessity, his preoccupation with Lawrence had become almost total. Netta's departure had put a much greater domestic burden on him, hence his decision to set up quarters in a *pension*. Les Rosiers served well enough, but it was cramped. He and Catha lived in communicating rooms, with about half his library available and a large influx of Lawrence materials. Yet by mid-December he had completed one-third of the final draft of what he described to Minnie Slonimsky as 'the most difficult and dangerous job I ever undertook'.[18] Thus the struggle with the Lawrence matter continued, Aldington sitting daily at Les Rosiers writing, Kershaw in London and Paris, gathering materials and negotiating with publishers; but Kershaw was now persistently ill and proved to have a spot on the lung. Aldington worried, and was embarrassed to feel he should have done more in return for Kershaw's friendship and service; but his own problems monopolised his attention, though he urged Kershaw against spending winters in the north and in March expressed pleasure that he might soon come to Montpellier, at least for a brief spell. A month or so later, on 20 April, he reported to Alan Bird that he had completed work on Lawrence, apart from a couple of footnotes.

On 1 May he asked Kershaw's opinion of a plan to write a short book about Norman Douglas, perhaps a mixture of critique and reminiscence and 'a panegyric of his way of living'. On 7 February 1952 Norman Douglas had died on Capri and this news Aldington took with equanimity though at one time Douglas had meant much to him. In *Pinorman* (a project yet to come) he makes no mention of Douglas's death, though he hits a sour note or two about Douglas's old age. Now he suggested to H.D. 'The inevitable epitaph—we could have better spared a better man', adding that Douglas had experienced the ghastly misfortune of outliving himself. But he adds an anecdote of the 1930s in good-natured valediction:

I give you one memory which I think will recall the real Norman. He was staying with me at Le Canadel (Var) and I suggested a run in the car to the little hill town (then unspoiled) of Bormes. We descended at the one cafe. I explained that it was only a village place so we'd better have a vermouth. 'I'll go and see'. Off he went and in about ten minutes returned with the patron, a plate of English ham sandwiches (where did they get the loaf?) and *two* bottles of vintage champagne—for which needless to say I paid. Dear Norman.[19]

A month later Aldington began work on *Pinorman*. By late August he had completed the first draft, having decided to focus the book on the triumvirate of Douglas, Orioli and Prentice.

The writing of these recollections cannot wholly be separated from the long debilitating engagement with T. E. Lawrence. Aldington had both tasks very fresh in mind when he wrote to Bird in mid-August 1952 defending Bertrand Russell's right to attack D. H. Lawrence in the public media.[20] False reticence, he felt, destroyed honest criticism and honest biography. 'Why must we be so mealy-mouthed?' It was a question he had raised before, a propos of similar matters. This letter shows once more that Aldington can write about the same person at the same time acerbically and even-handedly. When he remarks that Russell 'met Lawrence at a time when much of L.'s finer self was eclipsed by his passionate worryings about the war', he shows his fluid sense of human nature. This conviction, that external circumstances could bring out a less attractive side of one's personality, must be considered in viewing the stresses and strains of his own life, most particularly in the 1950s, after his marriage had come apart and when he was persistently dogged by financial worries.

The question of tone came up in relation to another work in which he was intimately involved, a fictional account of his first marriage. During an enforced idleness, with a temperature of 101°, he read a typescript of H.D.'s 'Madrigal', in effect an earlier version of her *roman-à-clef*, *Bid Me to Live*. He agreed to read the work with some show of reluctance and admitted, 'towards the end I found myself rather exhausted, by the intensity of all these self-absorbed emotionalists'.[21] But he tried to interest Secker and other publishers in it.

Collins continued to delay with the T. E. Lawrence and Frere at Heinemanns suggested that *Pinorman* be published first, though he warned Aldington that Douglas's friends would not be happy with *this* book. When it did appear in April 1954 it was quickly followed by Nancy Cunard's indignant riposte in *Time and Tide*.[22] To this was added her letter of protest to Heinemanns about *Pinorman* and, shortly, publication of her eulogy of Douglas, *Grand Man*.[23] A contrast of temperament and attitude between Aldington and Cunard may be gauged from one small aspect of their treatments of Douglas. Several times in *Pinorman* Aldington expresses vehement disgust at what he perceives as Douglas's blatant pederasty, a characteristic which had been broadly hinted at a good many years earlier in *The Georgian Literary Scene* where Frank Swinnerton says of Douglas that he loved 'life, women, boys, food, drink and knowledge'.[24] Cunard's biographer, Anne Chisholm, notes that the descriptions of Douglas's books in *Grand Man* are uniformly eulogistic, though peppered with random asides. The most peculiar of these must be when, in discussing Douglas's attacks on formal education in his *How About Europe* . . . Nancy remarks: 'But oh what a contradiction is here! Why did *he* take such pains in educating a number of boys himself?'[25]

From Frieda Lawrence came a very different response to Aldington's book. 'Of course I swallowed your "Pinorman" like a raw oyster', she says. 'You treat Pino with special tenderness.'[26] Aldington contended Orioli had turned against Lawrence under the influence of Douglas. 'I don't think Lawrence ever knew how much Douglas hated him', Frieda wrote. She liked the vitality of *Pinorman* and the obvious care for Lawrence the book expresses. But in May came a communication from Graham Greene in a very different tone. Greene had been asked to review *Pinorman* by the *London Magazine*[27] and decided to send Aldington a carbon copy. Noting that his review was susceptible to a charge of libel, he moved to pre-empt action on Aldington's part by implying that for him to take action for libel would be an act of cowardice.

At his own suggestion, as a joke, Kershaw replied: 'Mr Richard Aldington asked me to acknowledge your letter and to inform you that it is not his custom to reply to unknown correspondents. (Signed) Alister Kershaw, secretary to Mr. Richard Aldington'. Greene's piece never appeared and indeed, the very next number of the *London Magazine*, for June 1954, ran a Heinemann advertisement for *Pinorman*, quoting a *Daily Telegraph* review which seems to discount most of the subsequent hostile criticism: 'Its sheer readability sets PINORMAN far above the commonplace . . . with its freedom from attitude, its frank acceptance—free at once from sloppy compassion or spiteful malice—it is at once a penetrating study of abnormality and an amusing interlude'. Obviously, Aldington too had friends at court. Greene himself appears to boast of Douglas's heterosexual abandon in his introduction to *Venus in the Kitchen; or Love's Cookery Book*, a collection of aphrodisiac recipes by one Pilaff Bey (in fact, two—Douglas and Orioli): 'He was no modest follower of Epicurus, practising frugality as pleasure. I should say he went far beyond Aristippus in praising purely sensual pleasure without the vestment of any moral law, the very existence of which Norman denied'.[28]

As to *Pinorman* itself, it feels like 'an amusing interlude' and was so intended—a book patched together from letters and anecdotes and even scribbles on menu cards. Yet no doubt Aldington meant it as a serious if minor contribution to literary history, and had thought as far back as 1940 of writing it. He characterises it as a source book for a future biographer of Douglas, which will provide the 'personal touches' some biographers value highly.

The book sets out to reminisce about three men, friends of each other and of Aldington. Perhaps regrettably, he writes least about the man for whom he felt the most, Charles Prentice. Of the three he had least liking for Douglas, but because part of his theme is that Orioli was dominated by Douglas, Douglas himself became the main focus of *Pinorman*. Others besides Cunard have written about Douglas in quite a different spirit from *Pinorman*, so it cannot be denied that the book is a particular response to the man. Is it, as Douglas's biographer Mark Holloway suggests, a 'malicious and spiteful attack'? If Holloway is right, is he also right in asserting (unless I have missed an irony) that the book contains 'passages of unadulterated truth'? Why did Aldington write of Douglas in this way?

He had admired Douglas's writing, its style and concerns, and many aspects of Douglas's hedonistic way of life. Both men were gastronomes, each thought himself pagan, and both were sexual libertarians, though this was one of Aldington's points of attack, as had been suggested. Considered in the light of peculiarly British social gradations, Douglas was from a higher social stratum. He also had enough of a private income to free himself from the kind of compulsive writing of which Aldington had become victim. Two of Aldington's ideals had long been the aristocratic and the model of a 'good European' and Douglas in his own bohemian way matched these. In short, Douglas was cultivated, stylish and erudite in a deliberately dilettante fashion. To discern what caused the gap between them is no easy matter, though one explanation begins with D. H. Lawrence and his quarrel with Douglas over the case of Maurice Magnus. In a glancing rebuttal in *Life for Life's Sake* (a passage which had first appeared in the *Atlantic Monthly*) Aldington complains about Douglas's attack in *D. H. Lawrence and Maurice Magnus: A Plea for Better Manners*.[29] He felt that Lawrence had endured as much of Magnus's sponging as he could afford and had written a superb introduction to Magnus's *Memoirs*,[30] where he explains with candid sensitivity his involvement with the man. Pointing out that Douglas had more money than Lawrence, Aldington asks: 'Why didn't he lend Magnus the money for lack of which the poor man killed himself?'[31] Douglas responded to the two questioning pages of *Life for Life's Sake* with several scalding paragraphs in his *Late Harvest*.[32] His tactic is to quote an Aldington statement then answer it directly, for example: ' "Norman had the crust to abuse Lawrence for not being a gentleman". Of course he was not a gentleman'. Lawrence, Douglas continues, was not to be entrusted with confidences. Moreover, he was one of a brood who vilify their benefactors. Whether Aldington took personally any of the comments aimed at Lawrence, is not known, but he was aware he had offended Douglas when his piece on the Lawrence-Magnus affair appeared in the *Atlantic Monthly*. Douglas had been compelled to fight off offensive charges about his behaviour towards Magnus for nearly a quarter of a century, starting with Lawrence's introduction to the American's *Memoirs*, though *A Plea for Better Manners* was prompted by an unsigned article in the London *Outlook* for 1 November 1924, in which Douglas is identified as the person criticised in Lawrence's Magnus introduction. To return to *Late Harvest*, the unkindest cut, as far as Aldington is concerned, may have been that Douglas's scathing rebuttal of his comments does not deign to mention their author by name. So much is background to *Pinorman*.

Long ago, then, in that *Plea for Better Manners*, Douglas had castigated Lawrence for his 'idiosyncrasies in the matter of portraiture; what he contrives to see and what he fails to see; or rather, what he makes a point of seeing, and what he makes a point of not seeing'. Such charges were to be laid against Aldington over *Pinorman* and there is no denying an edge of personal animosity, but this did not prevent him, here as elsewhere, from admiring the economy, vigour and lucid elegance of Douglas's writing: 'What he lacked, as his novels show, was not style but invention. His prose had that natural dignity which he retained in spite of his scallywag behaviour. ...'[33] If the man had wounded him and provoked retaliation, it was not the the extent of destroying his powers of critical objectivity.

He claimed that he could not understand the fuss about *Pinorman*. Douglas's sexual predilections had been freely referred to at the time of his death by obituaries in the American papers and other Aldington points are supported in Douglas's printed confessions: 'Haven't his bloody friends read Alone, Looking Back and so on?' he wondered aloud in a July letter to Netta. Perhaps because it did not fit snugly into any specific genre, the book did not sell especially well, subscriptions and two months' sales adding up to 5000 copies, a low figure for Aldington in his heyday.

Roy Campbell now conceived the idea of producing a booklet (or plaquette) to rebut Cunard and others who had attacked Aldington's portrayal of Douglas. Campbell enlisted the help of his son-in-law Rob Lyle, heir to the sugar family. Lyle offered to finance the plaquette, to be titled 'What Next? or, Black Douglas and White Ladyship, Being an Herpetology of Literary London', a somewhat laboured literary joke.[34] The question, 'What next?' had become a favourite of Aldington's but was mimicry of Douglas. Contents were to include Lyle's introduction, an essay by Campbell, and letters of Frieda Lawrence which had been turned down for the correspondence sections of several journals, juxtaposed with reviews of *Pinorman* by pro-Douglasites such as Nancy Cunard, Graham Greene and the cartoonist D. M. Low. It was the method of Douglas's own *Late Harvest*, turned against him and his friends. Besides actively promoting the project, Aldington was to provide a postscript.

While this affair of the plaquette was brewing, he was at work already on his *Introduction to Mistral*. Writing to H.D. in mid-July 1954, perhaps mindful of her fragile health, he gives a misleading sense of the tenor of his midsummer days. After a night's rain and a good deal of mistral, not unwelcome at this season, he reports, 'But now the sun blazes, the cicadas chirr, and it is just like a summer noon in Theocritus'.[35] He was not so mindful of H.D.'s sensitivities that he failed to include his customary grumble about Pound's anti-semitism and Fascism, and this time he sent a pull of the title page of the Peacocks Press *Ezra Pound and T. S. Eliot*.

Some relief came late in August, when he received additional and perhaps unexpected support in the *Pinorman* affair. Writing to say he would be passing through Montpellier en route to Spain, Somerset Maugham asked Aldington to dine with him on the evening of 7 September. Of *Pinorman*, Maugham asserted, 'All you say is true. How stupid the reviews have been! Sickening and perverse'.[36] Encouraging as this was, subsequent attempts by Aldington's friends failed to get Maugham's participation in the plaquette. To Aldington this seemed a serious blow, for the *Pinorman* fuss was in his eyes far more than a mere literary squabble, particularly against the concurrent background activity concerning the Lawrence biography. Financially crucial as the Collins venture was, Aldington pointed out to Bird, 'still more my reputation is at stake, particularly since the Pinorman affair'.[37]

Four or five times a week throughout September 1954 he wrote to Rob Lyle concerning the contents and production of the plaquette in support of *Pinorman*. As with the T. E. Lawrence book, copyright difficulties arose. It became impossible to follow Aldington's design of quoting Douglas's friends against Douglas and against themselves. Discussions about it continued until the end of the year, but the plaquette never appeared.

20 The T. E. Lawrence Affair, 1950–55

Long before he thought of writing *Pinorman*, on 22 June 1950 Aldington told David Garnett that he was making notes towards a biography of T. E. Lawrence. Very quickly, these notes became a stockpile, and just as quickly he realised that a study of Lawrence's life raised questions which he had not foreseen, and that Lawrence was a highly problematical character. His intention to write a straightforward life story changed as he proceeded, into a quest for evidence. As he accumulated it, the evidence called for checking by both military and scholarly experts and for the eventual publishers, Collins, to have lawyers go through the typescript in minute detail. Publication was delayed for years and Aldington was prevented from quoting copyright materials under the control of the Lawrence family. Instead, he was obliged to paraphrase, which made it considerably more difficult to substantiate his claim that the whole work was carefully documented. He told Kershaw, 'it is a colossal subject to treat with competence, and most difficult to treat frankly, without being or seeming hostile'.[1]

By the spring of 1952 he had forwarded the typescript to Collins, then had followed a delay of 17 months due in large part to legal questions, with the lawyers insisting on alterations amounting to some 10 000 words. Aldington observed sardonically that the title page should acknowledge the joint authorship of lawyers, publisher, himself, Kershaw and the New York attorney (United States publication was still being negotiated.) Collins's publicity man assured him that despite the cuts there was more than enough left to stir the biggest literary controversy in years. Indeed, he felt that this was the most controversial book Collins had ever published.

For some time the projected publication date of *T. E. Lawrence: A Biographical Enquiry* was 1 February 1954. The fuss began, but the book did not emerge. Articles appeared in sources as wide-ranging as the *New Statesman* and *Newsweek*. On 19 January the *Evening Standard* expatiated at some length, helping to make the book notorious even in advance of publication. The writer observed that the 'reputation and integrity of Lawrence of Arabia are about to come under the most devastating attack ever launched upon them' and added that the publishers claimed the book would 'erase Lawrence from the pages of history'. Nothing could have been better calculated to mobilise animosity against Aldington and his book.

When *Pinorman* appeared in April 1954, he was heavily preoccupied elsewhere. Two members of what he called the 'T. E. Lawrence Bureau', Basil Liddell Hart and Eric Kennington, were actively attempting to prevent publication of the Lawrence biography. On behalf of the Lawrence trustees, Liddell Hart requested a set of proofs and it was agreed he should have them. Almost immediately he was asked to return them, but apparently kept some.[2] At this moment Robert Graves threatened to start an affray with physical aggression against Aldington, who should also be sued for breach of copyright or for personal libel, after publication.[3] Another Lawrence supporter, Pat Knowles, Lawrence's onetime neighbour at Cloud's Hill, Oxford, pathetically and ridiculously forwarded to Winston Churchill a petition addressed to the Queen in an effort to stop publication. Others, including Lady Astor and the historian Lewis Namier, began to campaign against the book's appearing. Meanwhile Liddell Hart attacked the publisher, questioning his patriotism. Kennington asserted, more reasonably, that the public airing of Lawrence's illegitimacy would kill old Mrs Lawrence, who was then in her 90s. Collins repeatedly delayed publication.

Aldington, who was being persecuted, began to show signs of it and felt that one Collins editor deliberately raised difficulties, sabotaging publication by questioning details which he did not fully comprehend. To Netta, Aldington offered quite a different explanation for delay, which, he said, 'had nothing to do with Churchill and Hart. It was over a very complicated set of agreements turning the property into a Trust for the little one, tax-free—a lawyer's masterpiece'.[4] Collins apparently valued this trust property at £13 000 and documents show that negotiations towards it were indeed complex, But it was a genuine effort on Aldington's part to provide for his daughter's future. He at one point began to feel he had disentangled all legal problems regarding the Lawrence book and even that he had an American publisher, Putnam, ready to hand, but trust arrangements continued to cause delay.

In late August 1954 Kershaw succeeded in having Collins sign the last of various documents relating to the Lawrence biography, the trust arrangement, so that Aldington on 25 August was able to whoop at Kershaw an exultant, 'Victory, my dear Lord! And it is all yours. ... ' The plan was to have the book out in October, though that gave a very short production time. A few days later Aldington wrote again: 'How good and patient you are with me, and how infinitely I am in your debt'. Without Kershaw, he could never have negotiated his way through all the difficulties attendant on this publication.

Collins again delayed, but through them in October was signed an agreement for Spanish-American publication rights, and similar signings were due in Germany, Italy and the United States. Efforts in London to suppress publication were therefore thwarted. The French edition of the book was the first to appear. By mid-November it had created its own tensions. Aldington found the title, *Lawrence L'imposteur*,[5] which had not been cleared with him, deplorable and the translators 'illiterate'. A radio review in Paris resorted to the old trick of highlighting its programme by quoting some of the book's strongest anecdotes. At least one pro-Lawrence Bureau review appeared in Paris prior to publication and English editors were seeking review copies from the publisher, Amiot-Dumont, who sent these against Aldington's express wishes.

He felt that the French edition needed at least five pages of *errata*, some for errors which distorted or misrepresented evidence. Georges Roditi, Amiot-Dumont's literary director or editor, had sent him the translation typescript. After reading two chapters he returned it as unacceptable, requesting that it be entirely rewritten. Roditi had corrections made and then rushed the book into print, so Aldington claimed, without sending proofs. He and Kershaw each thought the other had received them. Consequently, Aldington felt himself vulnerable in England and by late November Kershaw was negotiating in Paris for some appropriate procedure to correct the errors, threatening that otherwise the book would be disavowed.

Collins' edition was in the press mid-November, scheduled for January 1955 publication. With his highly-developed awareness of publishing economics and strategies, Aldington wanted Collins to steal a march on the reviewers by bringing the book out unexpectedly in December. He felt that if Collins got 10 000 copies into the hands of the public before the appearance of a single review, then 'the battle would be won' and whatever was said afterwards would count for little.

Behind the scenes, the question of his personal attitude to T. E.

Lawrence had progressively become more of an issue and, indeed, proved in the long run to be the central issue of this period of his life. Collins' Canadian manager felt Aldington's 'unfairness' to Lawrence would damage prospective sales there. In New York his former publishers, the Viking Press, judged that he wrote the book in the spirit of a prosecuting attorney, and he had reported to Bird that another American publisher, Harcourt Brace, accused him of 'extreme bias and obvious prejudice'.[6] That he reports these accusations and does not trouble to deny them suggests his confidence in his way of handling the book. On the other hand, speaking of Lawrence's aged mother, he admits, 'I can't help thinking that she has a good case for damages, however right I might be'. Factual correctness was extremely important to him, as the continuous discussion of details, repeated checking and rechecking, willingness to emend where necessary and to provide extra footnotes, all demonstrate.

Direct news came from England in mid-December 1954, when Richard Church wrote from Kent:

> Of course, the fore-shadow of your Lawrence has been looming ominously over the literary (and indeed social and political) skies for the past two years, and everybody has been whispering in corners about it, some with glee, other with shocked horror. Now that the book is at last to appear, I am certain that it will have enormous sales, and you will have to seek a refuge in the South Seas as the fanatics come after your blood. What about all the deeply entrenched vested interests in the great Legend? How are you going to cope with them? However, you are not lacking in courage and punch. ... [7]

For the time being, Aldington had no thought of the South Seas. He and Catha spent an unexpectedly cheerful Christmas with Geoffrey and Nin Dutton in Florence. Yet he felt Italian life had deteriorated and the country had become a soulless American satellite. Everywhere the pretence of democracy had fostered a brutal materialism. British journalists phoned for copy about what the *Sunday Chronicle* headlined on 9 January 1955 as the 'Lawrence Sensation'. Still the book was not out, but the first impression of 25 000 had all but gone through pre-publication subscription. Manoeuvring was on for reviewers and Aldington was dismayed that the BBC review was to be done by the pro-Lawrence Sir Ronald

Storrs. Storrs was believed to be among those who had tried to prevent publication, according to Philip Knightley, and took the attitude that Aldington was destroying an 'inspiration to youth'. Aldington riposted: 'For anyone who has read the *Seven Pillars* it is a bit thick to hold Lawrence up as an example to boy scouts'.[8] Malcolm Muggeridge, interviewing Storrs on television on 26 January, defended Aldington 'splendidly', friends reported. In the British papers, articles on the not-yet-published book appeared by the day, in such sources as the *Daily Express*, *Evening News* and *Daily Mirror*. Aldington felt that on the whole the popular papers sided with him, the 'upper class' ones against him. On 19 February, the very eve of publication, he told Frieda Lawrence that Collins, on discovering that the Lawrence Bureau had cornered the reviewing in all the 'upper class' (the inverted commas are his) papers, had cleverly cancelled one thousand pounds' worth of advertising in them and instead had window advertising displays set up all over London. One, in Foyle's Bookshop in Charing-Cross Road, included a huge scroll which read: 'Is this the end of a Legend?'

In the 'Introductory Letter to Alister Kershaw', which prefaces *Lawrence of Arabia: A Biographical Enquiry*, Aldington explains that he began the book 'with the hope of investigating a hero and his deeds', as he had done ten years earlier in his biography of the Duke of Wellington. What diverted him into examining his subject's *bona fides* was the discovery of Lawrence's apparently false claim that in 1922 and 1925 he had been offered the post of British High Commissioner for Egypt. What reveals the importance of this is that Captain Liddell Hart, the military expert among those who attempted to prevent publication of Aldington's book, wrote to both Winston Churchill and Leo Amery (both of whom had been approached on Aldington's behalf on the same matter) asking them, as key members of the 1922–24 Conservative Cabinet, to support Lawrence's claim that such an offer had been made. Each replied equivocally, although Aldington quotes a categorical denial from Amery.

He uncovered numerous apparently contradictory statements of Lawrence's and formed a sense of his 'tortuous psychology'. Gradually he came to feel that Lawrence had 'been dealt a terrific blow by Fate' at some time in his early life. Through the Australian historian W. Denison Deasey, he found out that Lawrence was the illegitimate second son of Sir Thomas Chapman, an Anglo-Irishman, who had run away with the governess of the children of his first family. In the British Museum, Deasey came on a letter from Lawrence to Mrs George Bernard Shaw dated 14 April 1927 in which Lawrence speaks of his parents' 'living in sin' and of his mother having been 'brought up as a child of sin' (that is, that she, too, was illegitimate).[9] Aldington saw this as the clue he had been seeking, the clue to Lawrence's personality.

From this point, he proceeds to demonstrate that from earliest childhood Lawrence tended to exaggerate his own attainments, boasting that he could read and write by the age of four, began Latin when he was five, and so on. Comparable points are linked to Lawrence's career at Oxford and his work as a field archaeologist in the Middle East, for example, the claim (recorded in Robert Graves' *Lawrence and the Arabs*).[10] that in six years he read virtually every book in the Oxford Union Library, then approximately 50 000 volumes.

Such points are interpreted by Aldington as symptoms of a need to compensate for social inferiority. The same impetus might prompt one to desire 'some great achievement', for which the First World War provided notable opportunities. Lawrence, given the chance, proceeded to stage-manage his own role in the drama (and even part of the drama itself), turning his immediate accounts of military events into worked-up 'stories for his own glorification, stories which were untrue in precisely those parts which made them sound extraordinary and made him sound remarkable'[11]; in short, transforming the *Secret Despatches*[12] and other official accounts into the imaginative reconstructions of *The Seven Pillars of Wisdom*.[13] 'The difficulties of a biographer trying to discover the facts are baffling, discouraging and at times insuperable. If Lawrence's statements were all false the task would be comparatively easy; but they are not. Some are true; some, in fact many of them, are at least partly true; others are or seem to be quite unfounded.'[14] Many other commentators have encountered similar problems, but for some at least this does not ultimately invalidate Lawrence's reputation as a war hero.

Aldington's biographical method, generally speaking, is to compare Lawrence's claims, or those made on his behalf, with other accounts of events. Lawrence, for example, suggested that he 'arranged' the surrender of the fortress of Erzerum in Turkey to the Russian forces. Aldington cites evidence to show that this could not have been so, such as the contemporary report of the incident by the war correspondent of the *Manchester Guardian*[15] or the fact that

General A. P. Wavell's account in the *Encyclopaedia Britannica* makes no mention of Lawrence's role. Aldington finds this the more surprising because when Wavell wrote the account he was a friend of Lawrence's.

Edged with scepticism, but initially temperate in tone, Aldington's presentation does gather animus as it goes along. What he saw as Lawrence's custom of circulating exaggerated or 'wholly invented' stories 'while trying to preserve a reputation for shrinking modesty' obviously irritated Aldington, who grumbles that 'in almost every case they were stories which could only have originated with himself'.[16] For instance, he takes Lawrence's reputation as a 'Train-Wrecker' and provides proof that French officers organised attacks on the railway line almost every week and that several British officers besides Lawrence planned and led such attacks. In Lawrence's versions, and those of the American journalist Lowell Thomas, all these attacks are minimised while Lawrence's are highlighted.

Aldington raises questions about the capture of Akaba, a town strategically placed at the southern tip of Palestine. For his part in this action, Lawrence was promoted to Major, made a Companion of the Bath and awarded the Croix de Guerre:

> It was the capture of Akaba which first brought Lawrence out of the obscurity of the Arab Bureau, and in view of the extensive claims made by himself and his friends certain questions arise which are worth discussing, even if definite conclusions are hard to reach. Was Lawrence the originator of the 'strategy of occupying Akaba?' Was Lawrence the originator of the idea of taking it from inland, from the Howeitat? Was Lawrence the commander of the expedition which set out from Wejh with Nasir, and was he 'the general' who really planned and directed their operations? Finally, what was Lawrence doing in that blurred-out period between the 3rd and 19th June, and why did he refuse to give any but ambiguous information about that period?[17]

Aldington finds no answer for the first of these questions, and finally agrees with the conclusions of George Antonius's book *The Arab Awakening*[18] (Aldington notes in his own introduction that Antonius is 'not impartial', that is, is pro-Arab) that, 'His (Lawrence's) summing up is that "Akaba had been taken on my plan by my effort"—a claim that will perplex the historian'.[19] Antonius asserts that the plan to capture Akaba was devised and implemented by the Arabs. Aldington says it was first suggested independently by the French Colonel Brémond and Lawrence's British colleague, Colonel S. F. Newcombe. From General Allenby's taking over as Commander-in-Chief of the Egyptian Expeditionary Force in 1917, it seems to have become easier for Lawrence to build a public image. Perhaps sensing his propaganda value, Allenby championed Lawrence, athough he privately wondered if he was something of a charlatan[20] and once remarked that he 'loves posturing in the limelight'.[21]

As evidence of Lawrence's 'tortuous psychology', Aldington cites his reportage of violent incidents. He notes in *The Seven Pillars of Wisdom* Lawrence's praise of an associate because he 'took as blithe a pleasure in deceiving his enemy (or his friend) by some unscrupulous jest as in *spattering the brains of a cornered mob of Germans with his African knob-kerri*'.[22] One of the most sensational elements in Aldington's book relates to the question of whether or not Lawrence was sodomised by the pederastic Bey of Deraa. Lawrence relates that he was repeatedly flogged, then taken to the Bey, only to be rejected 'as a thing too torn and bloody for his bed'.[23] Aldington adds that Lawrence later wrote to Charlotte Shaw, 'that he had yielded to the Bey's pederasty, and so secured respite and ultimate escape'. Knightley and Simpson give the date of this letter as 26 March 1924, and quote from it: 'For fear of being hurt, or rather, to earn five minutes' respite from a pain which drove me mad, I gave away the only possession we are born into the world with—my bodily integrity'.[24] George Bernard Shaw and others have denied the story and Aldington himself questions it, as possibly merely another 'startling tale' of Lawrence's adventures. It is a tale in which Lawrence can be made to look bad either way.

However, variations between the *Secret Despatches* and 'the romantic version cooked up in *Seven Pillars*' are not limited to enhancing Lawrence's personal image. Lawrence championed Prince Feisal, afterwards King of Iraq, to lead 'the Arabs', and so had an interest in portraying him heroically, though he does not always do so, and the actual character of Feisal also continues to have its defenders and denigrators. The Lawrence scholar, Stephen E. Tabachnick suggests that powerful proof of Lawrence's being unafraid of the truth is that he permitted so much evidence to remain available in the Bodleian Library and British Government archives.[25] Of course, this circumstance could equally well support a demonstration of Lawrence's divided view of himself.

Similarly, when Jeffrey Meyers declares, seemingly with Aldington's criticisms directly in mind, that, 'Though Lawrence was often the only witness of the events he records, and for political and propagandistic reasons deliberately minimises the French military role and maximises the Arab [Aldington sees the reason as self-aggrandisement], his account of the Revolt is essentially accurate',[26] the reader may quite legitimately respond: 'Which account? The details in the *Arab Bulletin* or the *Secret Despatches*? Which version of the *Seven Pillars*?' Meyers lists 19 'direct participants' in the Arab Revolt and considers that, while three of these are critical of Lawrence, 'the accounts of both colleagues and enemies confirm his veracity'.[27] But this cannot be strictly true. Of the three critics, one is cited by Aldington as objecting to Lawrence's carelessness in command of his Arab troops. The other two, Colonel Edouard Brémond and Major-General Sir George Barrow, both questioned Lawrence's version of the facts. One example, from Barrow's standpoint, will suffice:

> Barrow asked Lawrence to get his Arabs out of Deraa—'this place is a hell of a mess'. Lawrence retorted that he couldn't, and that anyway the murders, robberies and tortures of Deraa were the Arabs' idea of war. 'It's not our idea of war', said Barrow, 'and if you can't remove them, I will'. Lawrence replied: 'If you attempt to do that, I shall take no responsibility for what happens' . . . . Barrow's men brushed the Arabs away without difficulty, and then posted sentries to guard the train of wounded. Naturally, not a word of all this occurs in Lawrence's accounts; on the contrary, he loses no opportunity of sneering at Barrow, and passed statements by Graves which General Barrow describes as 'not in accordance with the facts', or 'entirely suppositious'. It is only Barrow's word against Lawrence's. Good enough. But on their records, which do you believe? (Barrow's remarks are quoted from p. 211 and p. 209 of *The Fire of Life*).

Lawrence on various occasions took the view that the Arab Revolt was a decisive element in the First World War, or alternatively that it was 'the side show of a side show'. In this latter judgement Aldington agreed with him. Lawrence developed the techniques of guerrilla warfare, but himself admits that he was not uniformly successful in applying them. Aldington mocks the scale of these tactics and says that they alone would have been insufficient, even to win 'the sideshow'.

The Seven Pillars of Wisdom exists in several versions, but all are covered by Lawrence's remark to George Bernard Shaw that the book 'was an effort to make history an imaginative thing'.[28] Allowances can perhaps be made for the form of autobiography, as a subjective attempt to bring to resonant life the events the writer is presenting. But Aldington was also concerned about the 'Lawrence legend', specifically as the creation of the American journalist Lowell Thomas, first in heavily-attended public lectures, with accompanying motion pictures, and then in his book *With Lawrence in Arabia*:

> Lecture and book (which sold approximately 200,000 copies in the English edition) were the first means of introducing Lawrence to large audiences, and so strong was the original impression created that for the whole of his life Lawrence was seen through this golden mist of spurious glamour. I must repeat that Lowell Thomas saw few, if any, of the exploits he relates with such sensational emphasis; he had to rely on what he was told by Lawrence, by Lawrence's associates and by the Arab Bureau.[29]

Thomas gave his lecture hundreds of times and one effect was to justify British Government expenditures and military losses in the Middle East campaign. Aldington concludes that 'Lawrence's immense popular reputation was wholly due to [Thomas's] successful propaganda'[30] and that Lawrence himself checked through Thomas's material in detail.

> The passage of time and Lawrence's reiterated protestations that one of his reasons for enlisting in the ranks [of the Army and then the Royal Air Force] was to be 'ordinary' among ordinary men did not prevent him from telling ... extraordinary and unfounded stories designed to show how important he was. Perhaps the most striking of these was his reiterated claims that he had been offered and had refused the great office of High Commissioner for Egypt.[31]

Lawrence wrote to his mother on 15 February 1922 that, in talking to Winston Churchill, the Colonial Secretary: 'There was a question of me for Egypt if Allenby [General Allenby, High Commissioner since 1919] came away; but that of course I wouldn't accept. I don't think ever again to govern anything'.[32] Aldington points out that Egypt came under the Foreign Secretary and not the Colonial Secretary, that Lawrence was in a very junior official position to have received any such offer (or indeed for the post of Secretary to the Imperial Defence Committee, or reorganiser of 'Home Defence', which he also claimed later to have been offered.) Aldington cites responses from various figures in high places on the likelihood of Lawrence's having been 'offered Egypt'. Leo Amery's reply 'extremely unlikely', was consistent with what he had told Liddell Hart; Lord Lloyd, son of the first Lord Lloyd, who did become High Commissioner for Egypt in 1925, responded that such an offer could not have been made without his knowing about it; Churchill provided two responses, 'certainly unfounded' and (as Aldington's footnote has it) that: 'although he never offered the post of High Commissioner to Lawrence officially he *may* have talked over the possibility of his being offered it unofficially with Lawrence'.[33] On the offer of 'Home Defence', Sir Ronald Storrs replied, 'an emphatic NO . . . . grotesquely improbable'.[34]

Aldington virtually ends his book on this note, perhaps to demonstrate how far from the truth Lawrence's delusions of grandeur eventually took him.

This account of *Lawrence of Arabia: A Biographical Enquiry* indicates briefly what the fuss, before and after publication, was about. By the February 1955 publication date nearly 30 000 copies had sold and Collins had ordered a third impression. The French version, originally published in a run of 4 000, was also reprinting. By 3 March Aldington had collected nearly two hundred press cuttings concerning the biography. Three-quarters of these were hostile, and he began to feel many attacks were rooted in personal animus against him. Through February debate raged in the columns of the *Daily Telegraph*, with himself and Liddell Hart at the centre of it. In mid-March Aldington began to send Rob Lyle material supporting his general position.[35] Prompting Lyle for a rebuttal of Liddell Hart's article, 'T. E. Lawrence, Aldington and the Truth', which appeared in the April *London Magazine*,[36] he strongly advised sticking to the facts and ignoring Bureau invective. His tone in writing to Lyle throughout the early months of 1955 is confident, even magisterial. When charges arose of inaccuracy (or deliberate falsification) he reassured Lyle by checking and rechecking. By 2 May he had admitted to three errors of detail, but none of significance and certainly none that altered the tenor of his arguments. The controversy continued into the June and July numbers of the *London Magazine*.

Placing the Lawrence book in the United States proved extremely difficult, but now came an unforseen possibility in Roy Campbell's American publishers Henry Regnery of Chicago. While the Regnery contract was being negotiated, Aldington considered writing an epilogue for the American edition, to deal with events and problems which had arisen since the book's European publication. He did not do this, possibly because the American advance was far less than he had expected ($3 000 instead of an original possibility of $15 000). 'How weary I am of the Colonel!' he exclaimed, after one of several French radio debates, this time occasioned by a French pro-Lawrence book.[37]

The Regnery advance was much needed, funds from any source were, and Aldington again sought magazine writing. Matters became so grim that at one point in October he thought even Kershaw might be dropping him. By then he had lost confidence in his position. In mid-September he pleaded with Kershaw to try to find more money, feeling that Collins ought to be paying more royalties. He quite soon felt that he was failing to obtain magazine work, while his agent sought in vain for an American commission for a biography of Robert Louis Stevenson. The subscription to the Regnery Lawrence was a mere 3500 copies.

1955 proved a fateful year for Aldington's fortunes, both financially and in reputation. If his evidence about Lawrence is largely correct, why did this book damage Aldington so severely? Some observers considered that there was no chance of salvaging his reputation while Lawrence proponents such as Robert Graves could prevent it. Reviewing Aldington's book in the *New Republic*, Graves, (whose own book *Lawrence and the Arabs*[38] Aldington had called into question), fulminated: 'Instead of a carefully considered portrait of Lawrence I find the self-portrait of a bitter, bed-ridden, leering, asthmatic, elderly hangman of letters—the live dog who thinks himself better than the dead lion because he can at least scratch himself and snarl'.[39]

Once Aldington had begun to discover the 'facts' about Lawrence were not as they seemed, it was natural literary tactics to change his approach to 'biographical enquiry' to ascertain the true facts. The problem with such an 'enquiry' was that by the time he got the book's final version into shape he knew all the answers he was going to provide, and he allows this to affect the tone *from the start*. From the outset many small points are made, some gratuitous, with a touch of malice which runs counter to an otherwise objective perspective, and this undermines a genuine effort to present the real evidence in the case. For example, to establish a tendency in Lawrence to exaggerate statistics, of distances travelled by bicycle or on foot, or the number of books he read over a given period, Aldington presents this as self-aggrandising dishonesty without considering that it may be compensatory for some sense of personal deficiency or even, as he himself shows, that Lawrence was merely careless about figures.

The strategy of 'biographical enquiry' enables Aldington to maintain distance from his subject, with no need to empathise with him or attempt any kind of psychological identifying with him, but it has the disadvantage of producing a narrative tone without warmth, the tone of investigation. This in itself would be sufficient to repel some readers.

Aldington's *Portrait of a Genius, But . . .* is very well-written, and so is *Lawrence of Arabia: A Biographical Enquiry*, but there is a difference, in that the latter book is written entirely 'from the outside'. The very competence of its prose is a barrier to easy acceptance, and this is compounded because the reader is given no opportunity to make up his own mind about T. E. Lawrence's character. It is not merely a matter of what the reader may decide about the facts. The case seems firmly established, though details may continue to be disputed. But the reader is given little opportunity to evaluate the evidence for himself, nor is he freely allowed to decide *how he feels* about it. Aldington claimed a number of times that he began working on the T. E. Lawrence material from a neutral perspective and it seems a tactical error not to have attempted to recreate this neutral position as a starting-point in writing a book otherwise 'most sedulously laboured' (his phrase regarding one of T. E.Lawrence's works).

What should be borne in mind is the whole context of Aldington's writings, his long-standing hatred of British hypocrisy and his (in practice, ambivalent) contempt for the British class system. What may easily be overlooked is the link between the *saeva indignatio* of *Death of a Hero* and the ferocity of some of *Lawrence of Arabia: A Biographical Enquiry*, a juxtaposition eventually posed by Deasey's 1970 *Australian Book Review* article on the biography, 'Death of a Hero'.[40] Behind Aldington's writing the novel in the late 1920s and this mid-1950s biography was the conviction that the British people had been betrayed by a portion of its leadership. As Aldington wrote to Bird: 'I believe this Lawrence book is more than a mere biography—it is the showing up and repudiation of a whole phase of our national life . . . . Our life as a nation must not be based on lies and liars, on slick "policies"'.[41]

Lawrence continues to be admired today, but the admiration is less widespread and more muted, and Aldington's investigation of him has not gone unappreciated. To sum up from his point of view, it seems fair to cite a recent comment by the respected scholar and critic Graham Hough:

> This was the first systematic debunking of the T. E. Lawrence legend, and as at the same time (1955) T.E.L was an almost universally accepted public hero, Aldington attracted widespread opprobrium and some extremely venomous attacks. As it turns out, he seems to have been right; and the bitterness and resentment expressed in these letters [to Frieda Lawrence] was justified.[42]

21   1954–57

In May 1951 Aldington and Catha had moved from the Villa Aucassin in Le Lavandou to the Pension Les Rosiers in Montpellier. At this point he was almost totally preoccupied with the question of T. E. Lawrence. Netta's departure had put a much greater domestic and parental burden on him, hence the decision to live in a *pension* where he remained until he left for a cottage in Maison Salle, Sury en Vaux in 1957.

One great benefit of his removal to Montpellier was that Aldington, who lived a more or less solitary life, found a new friend in Frédéric-Jacques Temple. A D. H. Lawrence enthusiast, Temple had published at his own expense a French translation of Aldington's *D.H. Lawrence: An Indiscretion*. Born in the Villa Les Rosiers, in the very room where Aldington lived, Temple became close enough to the Englishman over the eight years of their friendship to assume co-editorship with Alister Kershaw of the memorial volume *Richard Aldington: An Intimate Portrait*. In his own contribution to the volume, Temple conveys something of the character of Aldington's way of life during the Montpellier years, his serviceable though accented French, his solitary amble each day to the post office for mail, his occasional Sundays away from the writing table, when he might be seen driving with Catha on the roads leading to the *camargue* or the Languedoc *garrigue*. Temple's Aldington is very English and the Frenchman saw him as a' disappointed lover' of his own country, 'who lived here like an outcast or, rather, like a retired Indian Army colonel in exile'.

At about the time Aldington first met Temple, in 1954, Heinemanns commissioned him to write a small book on the Provençal poet, Frédéric Mistral. Because of his limited knowledge of the Provençal dialect and of Mistral's work, he hesitated at first. But while he still lived at the Villa Aucassin he had one day visited Mistral's house at Maillane, which had delighted him by its dignity and simplicity and the sense that happy people had lived in it. He must have been particularly struck by Mistral's rootedness. He admired the poet's sound judgement, his common touch and distinguished if anavailing efforts to save and old way of life. He decided to do that book and, in the summer of 1955 as the worst nightmares of his involvement with T. E. Lawrence receded, he was working steadily on it. Contrasting with the value of Mistral's poetry, he assured Alan Bird that, 'Poetry today is worthless, because it is neither fashionable nor popular. It is a languid diversion of affected intellectuals. May it perish!'[2]

His work on another, and weaker, book at this time, *Frauds* (published in 1957) prompted no such dismal animadversions, but a eulogy of Dickens' eye for the grotesque. But both *Frauds* and *Introduction to Mistral* were an enormous effort and his cry of despair over them was to echo through his last years. He told Kershaw, 'they are very bad books, so all the toil is probably wasted'.[3] *Frauds* was undoubtedly a pot-boiler, a bread-and-margerine book. Perhaps the sense of Aldington's revulsion towards such a project is best conveyed through his remark to Bird that: 'the moronization of "literature" proceeds apace. The English publishers are rapidly following the Americans, and insisting that books must be "popular" and not "academic". By "popular" they mean journalism in book form.'[4]

By now he had become disenchanted with the efforts of his London agent, Rosica Colin, especially what he saw as failure to retrieve his situation in the US, where efforts had been made to find publishers for the Mistral book and *Frauds*. None of these efforts had succeeded, so he turned directly to Alvin Manuel, able to tell him that Heinemanns were enthusiastic, at least about *Frauds*. Manuel approached another New York agent, Ann Elmo, touting Adington as 'one of the world's most distinguished writers', but admitting his work had not been too 'commercial'. Manuel recognised that at least in the US the best days of Aldington's 'commercialism' were behind him. In pressing Elmo, Manuel obviously tried to do a favour for a man he regarded as an old friend.

In spite of his painful experience over the Lawrence affair, Aldington felt the best thing he could do professionally was to continue working at biography. He had begun reading for a Robert Louis Stevenson book, but with little enthusiasm. He felt that Stevenson's grandfather, the Robert Stevenson who built the Bell Rock Lighthouse was far more interesting. Of the novelist he noted, 'I don't really like him enough', and he developed a positive distaste for Stevenson's wife, Fanny Osbourne. It was all rather depressing, but he still had friends to encourage him. On 12 March Roy Campbell wrote from Portugal, of the Lawrence: 'It has sunk in despite everything. Nobody can read that book without being convinced'. After a ten-year silence, Herbert Read sent him the typescript of an article on Lawrence, to which Aldington responded as 'a most remarkable piece of insight and inferential reasoning'.[5]

Comforting as these contacts may have been, what he most desperately needed was income. A financial embarrassment in all senses was the continuing requirement to pay the Patmore divorce settlement, an obligation met reluctantly and with increasing difficulty. In 1955 he had been compelled to borrow from Warman to do it; now he was served a Queen's Bench Writ for 1956 dues. Far from finding it easy to keep up he was beginning to have problems even in paying for his *pension* at Les Rosiers:

> I am nearly six months in debt to the pension here, and enclose a letter from the solicitor who is trying to get something out of Collins (or rather the Inland Revenue) for me.
>
> My last six months royalty account from Heinemanns amounted to £10.0.0.
>
> Catha and I live a most simple life . . .
>
> You tell them to make me a bankrupt. I don't care.[6]

Renewed contact with Read led to a three-way link between Aldington, Read and Edward Dahlberg. Dahlberg, then in Denmark, annoyed Aldington with his self-pity, goading him to write in June: 'I am old, tired, ill, poor, and fighting for very existence against the combination of practically all the periodical writers of England and America. I will do anything I can for you, but it is I who need comfort and succour'.[7] But he invited Read and Dahlberg to Montpellier, and when Dahlberg agreed to come a room was reserved at Les Rosiers. Charles De Fanti, Dahlberg's biographer, says that to escape the cold of the Danish island of Bornholm, Dahlberg wrote to virtually everyone he knew, fishing for an invitation to visit warmer climes.[8] Dahlberg later told De Fanti that Aldington had 'begged' him to come, but Rlene Dahlberg said her husband interpreted as an invitation some remarks of Aldington's about his loneliness.

On 21 May Aldington wrote Dahlberg a typically brief note explaining that he was tired and was attempting to meet a deadline for the 'difficult and boring' Stevenson biography, but nonetheless he would be happy to see the Dahlbergs in Montpellier. Dahlberg arrived on his own and suggested that his publisher, James Laughlin of New Directions, might be interested in *Introduction to Mistral*. As Laughlin was then vacationing in Europe, Dahlberg made moves to set up a meeting, but Laughlin did not come and this angered Aldington. Dahlberg showed him *The Sorrows of Priapus*, which was to be the American's passport to a second chance at fame, but Aldington did not care for it, finding it formless and without a backbone of thought. The day after Rlene Dahlberg arrived in Montpellier the two men had a violent quarrel, Aldington calling Dahlberg a fraud and a failure. Next day he wrote Read that Dahlberg was neurasthenic from neglect and 'he lost his temper, abused me, was furious when I retaliated, and went off in a huff'.[9] Within two weeks the deficiencies in Dahlberg's learning and writing had enlarged in Aldington's mind to the point where he had become 'a phoney Burton and a phoney Hebrew prophet'.[10]

Despite this squabble, the Dahlbergs remained in Montpellier for two further months and Aldington complained to Read later that he had kept his word and driven Dahlberg around the historic sites only to find the American insensitive to both the history and beauty of the enviroment. From Montpellier in October, Dahlberg went to visit R. F .C. Hull, the Jung scholar and a friend of Read's, who summed up the visit in a 1972 interview with De Fanti: 'He's a very wearing person to be with. . . . There's no conversation, it is an argument. You must listen to how awful every writer is. All of them are *ad hominem* attacks. The only writers he admires are safely dead'.[11] A good while after Dahlberg's Montpellier visit and after a silence of several months, Read wrote to Aldington repudiating Edward's resentment which flowered into a serious [sic] of the most vituperative letters I have ever read'.[12] Without other evidence, the contretemps which terminated the relationship with Dahlberg might seem to cast Aldington in the role of ageing and embittered failure, but it was of Dahlberg that Read said, 'Peace to his bitter soul'.

In June Aldington received Mistral proofs from Heinemanns. Briefly he tempted fate by mulling over the possibility of writing a biography of Kitchener for Evans but, perhaps luckily after the Lawrence onslaught, the idea was soon dropped. He struggled away at Stevenson, even with the Dahlberg distractions, and was able to despatch the typescript to London in July. A second copy was ready, to forward to the United States as soon as the first safely reached Evans Brothers' London office. So far, however, Ann Elmo had met with no success in attempting to place Aldington's work.

Just after the Dahlberg fracas, he learned that Frieda Lawrence had died. He had always felt towards Frieda a mixture of scepticism and affection and in August he wrote to Lawrence's biographer, Edward Nehls, 'for me part of my youth and my reason for living has died with her',[13] but only three months earlier he had written to Alan Bird regarding *Lady Chatterley's lover:* 'I blame Frieda for it to a great extent. She urged him to write the book, and then to publish it, when I am almost sure he realized it was a mistake'.[14] Nehls later dedicated the second of his three volumes of composite biography to Aldington and said: 'It was through you as much as any single person that Lawrence's rights and reputation were guarded from the very outset, and now I think you may look back with pride on all you have done for him'.[15] Such compliments in this shrunken time were precious but, of course, he could not live on them and waited impatiently for Evans' response to Stevenson. This favourable verdict came in mid-August.

Another compliment came his way when Gustave Cohen called the Mistral book 'inspired and inspiring'. Aldington was pleased with the care with which Heinemann produced this book but concluded that the Americans would not touch it. He feared, too, the British reviewers but need not have worried as there was a little British reaction of any kind.[16] A hold-up caused by a long printers' strike now ended and proofs of *Frauds* arrived from Heinemann, who had stuck with Aldington despite the Lawrence outcry. He had doubts about *Frauds*, feeling that the educated would find it redundant and to others it would be incomprehensible. He now tended to have doubts about what he chose to write; either it was tiresome because of his undeniable weariness from overwork, or, as in the present case, it was an ill-considered topic for earning funds or finding a particular audience. Certainly he had lost confidence to a degree in his professional touch.

He felt that his star had fallen. In contrast, H.D.'s seemed on the rise and he was pleased about a *succès d'estime* she achieved just then. Yale University was presenting an exhibition of her books, manuscripts and photographs; her recently published *Tribute to Freud* was receiving favourable reviews, though largely for its style. It was what he chose to praise, too–her 'beautiful prose', 'pure English undefiled, neither British nor American but the essence of the language'.[17] As to her book's reception, he felt her work was too good 'for this kind of ballyhoo'. During their periods of contact after 1929 he had adopted an attitude tender, solicitous and helpful towards her. From the mid-1950s on he wrote to her almost every week. In a sense he rejoiced in public neglect of her work, able to tell himself that she was 'too good', so her new prominence perplexed him a little.

Doubly beset by poor health and penury, perhaps the chief irony of Aldington's last years was that he, the determined individualist, often had to subsist on handouts from friends, this summer from Alec Randall (who visited Montpellier while Dahlberg was still there) and Eric Warman. Agents and publishers who did owe him moderate sums all seemed to be 'eywey' (that is, 'away', he used the word so frequently in this context that he adopted this sarcastic spelling for it) at the crucial moment. New York, of which he had continued hopeful for publication, was proving completely sterile, a circumstance he attributed to the efficacy of the 'Lawrence Bureau' in its campaign there. Four of his books, *Pinorman, Introduction to Mistral, Frauds* and *Portrait of a Rebel* (the now-completed Stevenson biography) could find no market there.

When *Poetry of the English-Speaking World* was reissued in London in mid-October he complained that no review copies had been sent out, and even that he had been obliged to purchase his own copy, though he could ill afford the 30 shillings. *Introduction to Mistral*, a 200-page book scheduled for the end of October, was to be sold at the then substantial price of 25 shillings a copy, which seemed to betoken 'extreme pessimism' and a likely sale of around a thousand copies; in other words, nothing that would help him financially. Cohen's wholehearted praise was on the book's dust jacket, 'But how to raise money I know not', Aldington grumbled to Kershaw. 'Frere won't spare a copper. Browning has disappeared. N.Y. is hopeless. The German edition of TEL sold 300 copies–repeat 300'. A desolate panorama, indeed. In mid-November he was tided over, more or less, by a 2000 franc subvention from Kershaw, but was heavily in debt even for his accommodation. Several friends, including Manuel (who had been urging it for many years) suggested the way out was to write another novel, but it was impossible. As Aldington put it acidly to Kershaw, 'Why don't I get a job as a circus clown?'[18] No further writing assignment came to mind which would meet the situation and his only 'plan' was to 'sell up' at Les Rosiers. He was being boycotted by editors, publishers and reviewers and it was having its effect. This boycott was no paranoid figment and appeared to extend even to the United States, as he claimed to Al Manuel. Manuel at first 'depreciated' the claim, but then wrote that Elmo had encountered it in attempting to place in New York the several books Aldington had available for American publication.

An ally appeared from an unexpected quarter. Aldington was corresponding with the Russian scholar Mikhail Urnov, professor of literature at the Moscow Institute of Printing Arts and member of the Soviet Writers Union. Urnov published 'Richard Aldington and His Books' in the April 1956 number of *News: A Soviet Review of World Events*,[19] and this was followed in May by Aldington's response, featured as a 'box story'. Subsequently, the two men were in regular contact. Urnov wrote to ask biographical questions and to tell him that discussions in Moscow might lead to a reprinting of his early novels. Despite 'cold war' anxieties, he answered Urnov's questions frankly and Urnov later showed in his memoir in *An Intimate Portrait* that he was convinced Aldington had been subjected to 'lying propaganda' because of his book on Lawrence of Arabia. Urnov suggests that the governing idea of Aldington's creative work is 'to live here and now', humanistically, unburdened by restrictive ideas and institutions, and of course this is a way of restating Aldington's fundamental Epicureanism.

He was indeed in dire straits, but 1957 opened with one happy note. *The Times* for 3 January carried a friendly article, 'Richard Yea and Nay' by Oliver Edwards (pen-name for an old friend, Sir William Haley). Haley decided to devote this issue of his column 'Talking of Books' to Aldington because he felt denigration of him over the Lawrence affair had gone quite far enough. He liked neither *Pinorman* nor *Lawrence of Arabia*, but felt that *Portrait of a Genius, But . . .* was 'first class' and *Death of a Hero* a pioneering work. The appraisal was timely and generous, despite putting Aldington's high period well in the past, in the decade 1925-35, between *A Fool i' the Forest* and *Artifex*. Haley saw him as a generous, perceptive critic, less dynamic perhaps than D. H. Lawrence, but healthier, a champion of the universal art impulse against the deathliness of industrialism. Naming six works which he claimed 'will stand',[20] Haley regretted what seemed to him to be a falling off in Aldington's writing since the late 1930s.

Haley's review could do nothing to ease his lot. Because he was broke, he had agreed to undertake a life of Balzac for the London publisher Paul Elek. To Kershaw he complained that he was so run down he could barely walk to the post office. Once more he was anxious that he had run up arrears at Les Rosiers and he and Kershaw were looking for a cottage, which Kershaw would buy as a holiday retreat, though with Aldington in permanent residence.

The novelist Lawrence Durrell, armed with an introduction from John Arlott, wrote late this January seeking to visit Montpellier.

Durrell reiterated praise of Aldington's work which he had first ventured a quarter of a century earlier, when in 1933 he had written him a fan letter. Durrell had then only 'a few unsung private publications to his name',[21] but Aldington wrote a friendly response which included an invitation for Durrell to visit him. The invitation was not followed up. Now, in 1957, Aldington again replied promptly and thus began a friendship which was to continue through the remaining years of his life. Following his custom, he suggested inexpensive nearby accommodation. The Durrells actually took a 'primitive villa' at Sommières and in late February visited Montpellier for lunch. Durrell quickly arranged to review *Introduction to Mistral* for the *New Statesman*. Loans from Kershaw and Warman allowed Aldington to pay off *pension* arrears. Mondadori had brought out an Italian edition of *Death of a Hero* (having in 1955 sold 17 000 copies of *All Men Are Enemies*) but royalties were not expected immediately, because Aldington had received an advance. Warman arranged assignments for him to write introductions to a series of photographic books on European countries, and he had some articles in hand, though nothing which would bring in sizeable income.

Roy Campbell's review of *Introduction to Mistral* for the *TLS* appeared on March 8 and pleased Aldington, though he confided in Read: 'The book is not as good as the *TLS* says, but it struggles to express (a) my love of the earth, (b) my hatred of Machines and machine-worship (c) my feeling that there should be a 'reciprocity' between the poet and the people, the real people,'[22] by which he apparently meant that a poet should be the voice of his people and they should be aware of his presence among them and of its value. The Mistral book pleased him more than any other at this period, but was largely overlooked, while there were enquiries about *Frauds* because of its sensational title.

Meanwhile, through Urnov, Aldington received an invitation to visit Russia as a guest of the Soviet Writers Union, to honour his 65th birthday in July. A thorough medical check-up ruled out any possibility of the trip. Besides his near-chronic bronchial problems he was much overweight and obliged 'to waggonize and diet', plus taking an elaborate battery of pills for his Falstaffian 'whoreson lethargy'—a catalogue of ailments including obesity, muscular fatigue, bronchial irritability and depression. Trying as usual to work, he observed to Kershaw caustically that he had 'the greatest difficulty in putting sentences end to end. A pity I didn't have this malady at 18.'²³ Instead of travelling he must take six months rest, at a time when he could not afford six days. The regimen of drugs made writing difficult and in mid-April he was still unwell and deeply depressed, but had lost 17 pounds.

Some time early this year, through Elmo, the possibility arose of Aldington's writing a book about Pound. 'I can't do the book in co-operation with him' he told Randall, 'because he is so damned unreasonable he would want me to praise his politics, his race prejudices, his Major Douglas economics, his music and pseudo-Chinese stuff. I can't. Besides I have written a masterly little essay proving that he and Eliot are plagiarists. On the other hand Ezra was my friend, a man of most generous impulses in his youth, and extremely kind to me. So I can't write a book about him behind his back, saying what I really think.'²⁴ When on 2 February there appeared what he described as 'a mean and cowardly attack' on Pound in the *New York Herald-Tribune,* accusing him of supporting John Kasper and the Ku Klux Klan, Aldington had the impulse to protest, but his shattered condition made him incapable of doing even that, for fear of becoming embroiled in a situation beyond his energies.

Wyndham Lewis died in March, which left Aldington with mixed feelings and brought about an interesting exchange of letters with Herbert Read. On 10 March Read wrote:

> I hope you have not thought of my recent silence as due to anything but concentration on other things—in particular I hope you did not think that I was in the least infected by Edward [Dahlberg]'s resentment, which flowered into a serious [sic] of the most vituperative letters I have ever read. Peace to his bitter soul—I haven't heard from him since January 28, and he was then ill and about to leave Ascona. I don't know why he hit on Ascona, but I had a good friend there and with the usual misgivings I introduced Edward to him, with the usual results. But this friend [R.F.C.] Hull by name, took infinite pains to find the Dahlbergs cheap and confortable quarters, from which began to issue immediately the usual diatribes. But he complained of being very sick, and of wishing to make for Paris. I urgently advised him to remain where he was, but that is now six weeks ago.
>
> I think it is Lewis's death that causes me to write to you just now, for such an event makes one think of the early days. Lewis, as you know, had suddenly turned against me in the last few

years, but I bear him no grudge and he was already a man sick in mind and body, with the dreadful affliction of blindness coming on him. But Lewis never loved anybody—there was some poison in his soul from the very beginning, and by the beginning I mean that I suspect it had to do with the mystery of his birth and his obscure childhood. In all my associations with him—and they were pretty close in the days of *Tyro*, I cannot remember a moment of ease and relaxation. Every meeting was turned into a secret plot, against someone or some group. I used to search for one drop of the milk of human kindness in him, but if I found it it immediately turned sour. There was never any question of his mind—*Time and Western Man* is the most terrific intellectual counterblast I have experienced in my lifetime. But I ask myself why then did it not have more influence on me—or on us all—and I can only suppose that so much intellect was combined with a complete absence of emotion, of affection, of heart. He talked about 'the vice of mildness'—he was a Prussian at heart, and came very near to being a fascist. A fierce, ugly, unhappy man—one could not pity him because like Nietzsche he despised pity. The only man who loved him, so far as I know, was Tom [Eliot], and this I could never understand, and it led Tom into some of the most crazy of his utterances—such as that Lewis was the greatest prose stylist of our time (he must be almost the worst). However, the agony is over, and though I can't feel sorrow, I think a great deal about him, and finally *of* him. I wonder very much what your conclusions are.

I have been pleased to see good reviews of your Mistral and intend to get hold of it this week. I think only the barrier of language has prevented me from becoming an enthusiast, for all I know about him inspires sympathy and admiration. What a contrast such a poet is to a man like Lewis—really can they be the same species? I read a good deal of Chinese poetry these days—in translation, of course and I imagine that Mistral is very like the best of them.

Tom [Eliot] has got married since I last wrote to you, and successfully foxed everybody—not even John Hayward knew until the night before. Though I have often spoken to her on the 'phone, I don't know his Valerie, but she comes from these parts and is said to be a nice competent girl. I have had lunch with him twice since he got back from the honeymoon, but the subject is not discussed—only the difficulties of finding a place to live in, and the expense of furnishing it!

Aldington responded two days later:

> Your very kind, interesting and friendly letter . . .
> (1) Dahlberg. This, as our French friends don't say, was a jolie bouillotte de poissons. I did my best, but he stayed too long and tried to exact too much. I knocked off fairly urgent work to entertain him and drive him round to some of the places near here—which he failed to register with that peculiar insensitiveness to natural beauty of Americans and Jews. Then he reproached me for neglecting him when I merely retired to my room to read his script! I had barely read half of it, with growing misgivings, when he tried to pin me down to the promise of a eulogy. I make every allowance for his disappointment in life, but I doubt if a masterpiece of prose is to be made out of transpositions from Bohn translations of minor classics not always understood. Individual sentences and even two or three together are remarkable (mainly because 'lifted') but the work as a whole, so far as I read, seemed to me as lacking in structure as the Book of Proverbs. But I feel he is a sick man, rather on the Ezra line . . .
> (2) Did you see the vile and violent attacks on Ezra in the Herald-Tribune? I got into hot water (comme toujours!) with Frere (who is absurdly chauvin) by saying that if any public protest were made I should feel obliged to sign it. In fact I began one on my own, but dropped it, feeling that Tom was the person to decide. Perhaps he was right to opt for contemptuous silence. But the 'attack' seemed to me so skunky-yank my temperature approached 212° Faht.
> (3) Wyndham. Alas, poor Yorick! I thought highly of him—more than you, not so much as Tom. His negative attitude was probably due, as you hint, to his birth. But I think he was a paranoiac. He and Ezra were much alike in their mania of grandeur and mania of persecution. Both have told me most impressively of the persecution they suffered from 'them'. I never found out who 'they' were. Of course it was absurd to use his sledge-hammer to crush such tiny little nuts as Alec Waugh and Godfrey Wynn. But surely the Apes is a magnificent sortie against what W.L. so rightly called 'the champagne bohemia'? His books begin with magnificent energy, and gradually peter out. Poverty and the need to produce? Evidently you suffered far more from him personally than I did. But he was strangely oblivious of responsibilities. Not long after I was married to H.D.

he came one afternoon and asked me to lend him my shaving things. As he completed he remarked that he had been copulating for three days! (I hated his attitude to women.) Now mark. Some time later I ran into him in a little restaurant in Church St (W.8) and halfway through dinner he announced he had a clap! Nice for me with a young wife to think he had used my shaving brush a short time before! Nothing happened to us, thank goodness, but might not the origin of the blindness be there? I think the same infection caused that malady of the bladder which put him in a nursing home. He sent me an SOS, and I went to the place and gave him fifty pounds. His 'reaction' afterwards was to send me the opening chapter of a 'novel' satirising me as a literary pretender who knew how to make money! (This based on a trip from Paris to London on the same train when he was 3rd and I 2nd.) It was witty and I told him to go ahead and publish, which of course stopped him.

(4) Mistral. I don't think he comes up to the terrific standard of the best Chinese; but he has given expression to the life of the Midi as nobody else has. I mean the life of the peasants and fishermen and, in brief, everything that is missed by the people who rush down Route Nat 7 from Paris to dear old Monte.

A more upsetting death than Lewis's occurred on 23 April. Roy Campbell was killed in Portugal when the worn front tire of his car burst and the car swerved and hit a tree. On 27 April Aldington sent a terse note of the news to Durrell. He wrote again on 30 April to say how upset he felt: 'I loved the man, and he was a really great poet. Did you read his *Light on a Dark Horse?* It had a mixture of laughter, bull-dusting, violence and prose poetry which reminded me of Rabelais'. A few days later, bringing the two recent deaths together, Aldington told Durrell: 'There's going to be trouble in heaven though when he gets together with Lewis, not an angel spared'.[25]

Durrell, meanwhile, sent a series of well-intentioned suggestions for publishing projects. He proposed offering Kingsley Martin of the *New Statesman* a series of Aldington's notes on figures such as Pound and Campbell (so that, 'you might correct the prevailing impression that you've turned into a grumpy Diogenes')[26], or Aldington's editing a memorial volume by Campbell's friends and admirers. Aldington had no energy for such tasks.

Domestic responsibilities preoccupied him—Catha's renewed assault on the baccalaureate examinations, their forcible retreat from Les Rosiers where he had been given three months notice in February, and as usual the funds needed but not available. H.D. was helping with cheques. 'You must not worry about the future', she wrote on 8 June. Alister Kershaw had purchased a house in the hamlet of Maison Salle, Sury en Vaux, Cher, and was having it prepared for occupancy, or as Aldington put it to Randall: 'My French and Australian friends are putting up cash to get us out of here and offering a rent-free cottage dans le Cher with nearly an acre of land'.[27]

These days Aldington and H.D. were in quite frequent contact. Both were in poor health, H.D. over 70 and housebound from aftereffects of a broken hip. As usual, part of their exchange concerned Pound and his continuing confinement in St. Elizabeth's. As usual, Aldington's attitude to Pound is ambivalent. Unwavering in his affectionate memory of the young Pound of pre-1914 London, he never overcame disgust at Pound's virulent pro-Fascism and the writings produced from it. Perhaps influenced by his own increasingly circumscribed situation, he now sympathised intermittently with Pound's decade-long incarceration in a mental institution.

Another element in his late letters to H.D. is voyeuristic. Largely because he knew the richness of H.D.'s aesthetic life, he for some years sent her a stream of art postcards. Many of these are paintings or sculptures of young women, largely from classical art. That May, for example, came pictures of an 18th-century painting of a Naiad, two Poussins, and Picasso and Matisse postcards which he described as 'the most cleverly suggestive drawings I had ever seen'.[28] That he catered to this special interest of H.D.'s is interesting in the light of his vociferous fulminations against male homosexuality.

Besides Warman, H.D., and most of all Kershaw, he received financial help from the Duttons, towards moving to the Loire. At Maison Salle, he could make a garden on the acre and live inexpensively. Its one disadvantage, as it was much further north than Montpellier and in a valley, was the foreseeable adverse effect on his bronchial condition.

He was fortunate that his friends rallied around, but he had some reason for bitterness that a long lifetime of near total devotion to writing had led to such a pass. Some of the mess was his own doing, he felt, and in his present poverty was particularly upset about what happened to his translations in the United States, such as *Candide* and the *Decameron*. These had become virtually standard works and the Voltaire in particular was pirated more than once, or published without attribution to him. Long ago he had sold of rights to the *Decameron* and these eventually passed into the hands of Doubleday, though not the anthology rights, and Aldington was understandably angry when the publisher mistakenly attempted to appropriate half a permissions fee. Contrasting their wealth with his poverty, he protested. 'I drafted a letter for my agent to send them', he told Tony Aldington, 'and made them feel so ashamed of this Uncle Shylocking that I got my [$]60 . . .'[29]

Unsettled by Campbell's death and the need to move from Les Rosiers, he continued to have severe anxieties about money and to suffer his general debility, of which he observed to Winifred Bryher: 'This mysterious illness makes me so allergic to work, I think I must join a Trade Union'.[30] Though Kershaw and Temple had arranged transport of the Aldington chattels to Sury, the remaining costs were high enough. Nor were earnings anywhere near sufficient to meet them. In 1956, for example, Italian editions of Aldington's books sold 15 000 copies and netted him £80; a proposed Polish reprint of *Death of a Hero* in a run of 10 000 brought in half that amount as an advance with promise of a very low percentage royalty.

Ten months rent (800 000 old francs, or around £350) was owing at Les Rosiers. A promised £600 from the Duttons had not yet penetrated the bureacratic labyrinth and was causing panic. Even an offered guarantee from Gustave Cohen was fouled up in red tape. A chance for Aldington to transport his books free was threatened when M. Michaud, the Les Rosiers proprietor, became suspicious and had them seized. In response to Aldington's plaints, Bryher sent her own guarantee of 200 000 francs, but this too was subject to bureaucratic delays. Uncertainty continued into late July, when they at last set off for Sury. In a further act of kindness, Kershaw provided a small stipend for a young Australian and had him come to Maison Salle to repaint the interior of the house. Aldington desribed the place to the Durrells, in Australian argot, as 'a weird kip' and was amused by the imposing entrance hall and a lavatory flush which suggested 'a Shakespearean stage direction – "peal of ordnance shot off within" '. But he had every reason to be grateful for these four walls and a roof, home for the remainder of his life.

22   Maison Salle, 1957–59

With abatement of his worst financial crisis and the move to fresh quarters, Aldington seemed due for a spate of new publication. On 9 September 1957 Evans Brothers issued *Portrait of a Rebel: Robert Louis Stevenson*; the same month Elek Books reissued Aldington's *Decameron*, to launch a proposed new series of world masterpieces; a paperback house, Four Square Books, planned to include *Lawrence of Arabia: A Biographical Enquiry* in its first batch of four titles and was also negotiating reprints of *Death of a Hero* and *All Men Are Enemies*.

Apparently plans were going forward for a Viking reprint of *Poetry of the English-Speaking World*. The Viking Press in August sent Aldington a cheque equivalent to 425 000 old francs and showed interest in the Stevenson biography. Aldington also hoped Covici, the Viking editor, would wish to publish an American edition of the biography of Balzac projected for Elek. The large sum from Viking was part of a payment because he had sold them full rights to the anthology, to help Catha finish her education.

Life at Sury proved dull at first. He had no energy to sort through his confusion of books, but sent the Durrells copies of whatever of his own work he came across. He began to lead a more and more supine existence, spending most of his time in bed, seven in the evening to as late as ten in the morning. He had one or two meals a day and alternated futile efforts to write with daytime rest periods. Feeble attempts to work at the Balzac were stymied by wretched health and lassitude, though he found energy for writing letters. Otherwise he read a little, dipping into Pepys's diary. Catha had returned to study at Montpellier, so apart from an old peasant woman who 'did' for him, he was alone. Despite all this, he felt more hopeful. The Four Square edition of *Lawrence of Arabia* seemed to presage a better day where publication was concerned. Several of his translated works were being reprinted, acknowledged, and paying royalties; Gustave Cohen's French version of *A Dream in the Luxembourg* was about to be issued; an Italian contract had been signed for the Stevenson biography; the Moscow Foreign Languages Publishing House had actually paid an advance for a new edition of *Death of a Hero* and a volume of short stories. To these satisfactions may be added another writer's diverting publication, *The Sweeniad* by Myra Buttle,[1] a lampoon of T. S. Eliot. Even better perhaps, Buttle proved to be a Cambridge don, Victor Purcell, and thus supposedly a pillar of the establishment so much admired by Eliot.

The year 1957 ended with a flurry of unpleasantness, partially mitigated by a further kindness from William Haley who took the occasion of Cohen's translation to publish a positive piece on *A Dream in the Luxembourg* in *The Times* (December 5). Next day a court summons on behalf of the Patmores was issued to Aldington for arrears of settlement payments. Meanwhile he squabbled with Heinemann because the publisher claimed subsidiary rights on the Four Square Lawrence. So worries continued and, on top of them, he felt he could not drag on with the Balzac biography. He decided to postpone work on it for a year.

Through the first half of 1958 he was generally unwell, most seriously with severe neuralgia of the right arm, brought on by nervous exhaustion. Ordered to take complete rest for several weeks, he dabbled at translating from 16th-century Italian. A Pound letter provided some savage amusement by 'instructing' him to find a publisher for a translation of Gourmont's novel 'The Horses of Diomedes'[2] printed in the *Egoist* more than 40 years earlier. But Aldington was in no mood for such endeavours.

On 29 January he wrote to Warman, 'the complete quiet and peace of this place are most healing', with a simple routine of shopping, cooking, reading, walking a little, driving to the nearby town of Sancerre to post letters and enjoy the panoramic view from the hilltop. The letter continues:

> Of course I should be most grateful for any work you can give me or get for me. I can do short things fairly quickly. Recently I did a review (about 1200) for an Australian paper, and an article (3000) for the N.Y. Saturday Review. For these I received about 88,000 francs. Now they took about six days, and a full-length biog takes about a year of frightful work and brings about 550,000 frances less 42 and a half % British tax in full. I am willing to pay a fair amount, but not to be mulcted in that vindictive way, and nuts to the Hellfare State. I am very pleased that I now have a review of about 800 words to do for USA—book not yet arrived—but it should not take more than 2–3 days and will earn me about 16,000 francs at minimum. Surely, surely if I can get such work—articles, reviews, introductions—it is much better than killing myself

with books which are not wanted and which give the highbrows another opportunity to be insulting. The RLS book sold about 2500 to Xmas and another 500 were bound up in January. About half the advance earned! Pah.

This hints at the loneliness he often experienced in the Sury period, and sketches the situation of one who has been foolhardy enough to commit his economic survival to professional writing. Turning naturally enough to reminiscence, as he often did in these late years, he continues:

> Wonderful how literary history is written. You may have heard of a little pre-1914 paper called the Egoist which ran Joyce's Portrait as a serial, and of which I was literary editor until I went to the wars, and then TS Eliot got my job. Well, of course Pound and Eliot gave Patricia Hutchins the dope for her Joyce book,[3] and I find that what I did for the paper is entirely credited to them, mainly to Pound. Now I discovered and published the first poems of Marianne Moore; André Spire was a friend of Frank Flint's and mine, and through the Egoist Press I published some of Spire's war poems at my own expense; and I found and translated some of Lautréamont. All of this is credited to Pound . . . .
>
> The same female is now composing a work called Ezra Pound's Kensington,[4] to which of course I am expected to contribute glowing tributes to the Maitre . . . .[5]

Charges are sometimes made about Aldington's envy of Pound and Eliot. A passage like this draws attention to his perspective, largely justifiable. Many things he did in the Imagist days have been forgotten or herded into the corral of Pound's influence. How galling this must have been to one in Aldington's sorry circumstances! Pound, of course, was in an even more disadvantageous position, being in the last stages of his long confinement in St Elizabeth's Hospital in Washington, DC 'But I notice,' Aldington had remarked to Alan Bird on 2 January, 'that Ezra's name is constantly cited by "the critics" as one of the five greatest writers &c'.

Another letter, to his brother Tony, summarises contract difficulties which led later in the year to severance of his publishing links with Heinemann:

I don't know whether I should write to Frere or still leave it with you. The first thing is not to allow it to become a matter of business. Frere is my great friend; in 1939 to protect my property during the war (say nothing about the Ps but he'll know) I asked him to make a purely personal arrangement giving him control as I was in USA. I have never understood why this document went out of his possession and on to the Heinemann files. Incidentally when he drew that document (i.e. the 1939 one you have) he made no allowance for the fact that under the Income Agreement of 1936, valid for six years, Heinemann owed me about 2000 pounds, from which they were released by him gratis!

When the matter was sprung on me in 1948 F. was in New York, and after much delay produced a release (according to him) which must be the document of which you have a copy. But I have never had a copy so far as I can trace, though Fs personal letters at the time certainly indicate that he intended to make a full release. How it happens that this 1948 document is not on my file and was apparently not on Heinemann's I don't know. Perhaps F. was called away, and we both forgot.

BUT does Frere himself consider that this 1948 document is a full and friendly release from the 1939 agreement?[6]

An unsettled question was whether Heinemann or Aldington should pay for a much earlier release from a contract with Chatto & Windus. Now he sought a clear and full release from both agreements, 1939 and 1948, and asked the pertinent question: 'What consideration passed to me in 1939 that I should give H. the rights in my books?' He had made the 1939 agreement with Frere as a personal matter, partly because his literary agent of the time was under legal duress, but largely to protect his literary property while he was not living in Britain. His summary of the matter is an accurate one. Within months the affair was to be concluded to his satisfaction.

He was still pretty much obsessed with Lawrence of Arabia. When he heard the J. Arthur Rank Organisation was making efforts to finance a film on Lawrence he suggested to Alec Randall (not an especially sympathetic listener on the topic) that there would be hand-barrows outside every cinema peddling his biography as 'the book of the film'. Randall was disturbed at his continued absorption in the 'sterile controversy'. Unwell right through to the end of May, Aldington had not entirely lost his sense of humour.

Writing to Warman about the prospective Lawrence film, he asked: 'Why don't they do a technicolor of Horatio Bottomley?[7] And let us write the script?'[8] He regaled Randall, himself bored and in poor health, with copies of Durrell's lighter books, farces of British diplomatic service such as *Stiff Upper Lip* and *Esprit de Corps*.

Warman did find some welcome work for him. Aldington had reviewed the *Selected Letters* of D. H. Lawrence for the *Saturday Review*,[9] the effort of which had caused him two sleepless nights. He had in prospect writing the introduction for volume three of Nehl's *D. H. Lawrence: A Composite Biography*,[10] but suffered revulsion from such toil, 'a just punishment for having written too much'. Warman, however, proposed an assignment he was prepared to cope with, translating a large portion of the *Larousse Encyclopaedia of Mythology*, a job which paid relatively well and did not get on Aldington's nerves.

His health was, indeed, poor. Obesity and general unfitness imposed a regimen of abstention and a two-mile daily constitutional he considered it a feat to perform. One consolation was Durrell's writing, especially the serious fiction. *Justine*, first volume of *The Alexandria Quartet*,[11] moved Aldington deeply, its exoticism and strange style reminding him of his long-ago reading of Pierre Loti. Durrell, for his part determined to be optimistic about Aldington, repeatedly attempted to chivvy him out of his lethargy, suggesting his problems were largely psychological. Perhaps, too, Durrell thought, the isolation of Sury was not right for him. Aldington knew he could not hope to change his circumstances. Some good news came his way, however. By mid-May, Tony Aldington had come to the arrangement with Heinemann which freed all Aldington's pre-1939 titles (apart from *A Dream in the Luxembourg*). There was a further 10 000 printing of the paperback *Lawrence of Arabia* and 20 000 *Death of a Hero*, so he gloated that over 50 000 copies of his 'dead' books had sold in eight months.

In May and June he worked on the Larousse translation and the Nehls introduction. In early June Gustave Cohen died, but Aldington showed little reaction, perhaps because of his own dismal state. Later that month he suffered what he described as an attack of 'pseudo-angina pectoris',[12] but he kept working and got off the Lawrence introduction to Edward Nehls. His isolation was alleviated in July when the Kershaws came to Maison Salle. That summer Aldington also renewed a link with Harry T. Moore, who had contacted him around 1950 on questions connected with D. H.

Lawrence. Moore, Lawrence's biographer, was now editing Lawrence's letters and arranged to come to Sury for talks. Despite Aldington's poor health, Moore recalled later that his 'eyes were bright and fine, with the look of a man who relished life'.[13] Moore saw no frustration or bitterness in him, nor dogmatism, saying 'he showed no corroding grievance. His wit was sharp, his tone cheerful'. On their first meeting, Aldington displayed himself as a raconteur with a gift for mimicry and as an engaging host. This, his friends would say, was the real Aldington.

Probably the most cherished aspect of his life then was his daughter Catha, over whose attempts to achieve the baccalaureate he agonised a great deal. A group of friends contributed to a fund for him at this time. From Adelaide, the Duttons sent £750 and this magnanimity was handsomely matched by Kershaw in providing the cottage. Tom MacGreevy, remembering Aldington's generosity a quarter of a century earlier, wrote offering help and he accepted £25. Grateful as he was to Kershaw for the Maison Salle cottage he would have preferred to be near Catha (and the Durrells) in the Midi, observing to Durrell of the Loire valley that, 'the climate here is simply one mot de Cambronne after another'.[14] From this time on, he accepted financial gifts from Winifred Bryher, chiefly aimed at sustaining Catha's education. In November he told her, for example, 'I think now that with that and what Hilda sent I can go down and spend Xmas with my daughter in the Midi instead of staying in the Loire fogs'.[15] This late link with Bryher is extraordinary, given that she was the person who definitively took H.D. away from him in 1919 (thereby resolving his dilemma about H.D. and Arabella—'I love you but I desire *l'autre*'). As Alister Kershaw recollects, Bryher 'had reversed the usual process by *becoming* a friend, and an incredibly generous one, when Richard's circumstances were at their worst',[16] which means during the last five years of his life. At one point she became a financial guarantor for loans against his expected royalties. From this period on, in his letters to Bryher, there are frequent references to cheques for Catha. There are indications that her interest in Aldington's daughter went beyond the merely financial. In May 1959, for example, he expressed his anxieties about Catha to her and said 'if you can spare a day or two this summer to see Catherine and to advise me, I shall be deeply grateful. It is almost impossible for a man to be both parents'.[17] Catha paid a successful visit to Bryher and H.D. in Switzerland, and then Aldington himself was invited. A year after anticipating his escape from the 'Loire fogs' to celebrate Christmas 1958 in the Midi, he wrote to Bryher: 'Your kindness is quite overwhelming. Of course, I should much like to come—more indeed to try to thank you and Hilda for your kindness to Catha than for my health'. He then explains that he must finish work on the Encyclopaedia Britannica anthology of poems of the Western World (never published): 'As to my health—the chronic bronchitis (due to phosgene in 17-18) is incurable. Apart from that the July examination in Montpellier showed nothing organic, but a "nervous depressive" condition due to prolonged work and anxiety. You have lifted my real anxiety, by giving Catha her chance'.[18] A few days later, on 7 November 1959, he wrote of Bryher's 'taking off my intense anxiety about Catha's future'.

Besides joining the throng of friends who helped assuage his financial difficulties, H.D. sent him the typescript of her *End to Torment*, an account of her relationship with Pound. In responding, Aldington said of Imagism: 'How bitterly and deeply do I regret having had anything to do with it! Why did I have to be dragged in? An attendant lord, I suppose'. Eliot's shadow is there still; but this interesting letter reveals another facet of Aldington, in a memory of Katherine Mansfield:

> Do you remember that day we met Katherine Mansfield with the Lawrences in the Vale of Health, and how much we disliked her? In his latest and valedictory book, Points of View, Maugham has some interesting remarks on her talent. That portrait of Carco[19] in Je ne Parle pas Français is a slasher—a revenge. The Prelude—the children's wonderful phantasmagoria as they move from the old home to the new—if only I could just *once* write something so true and so unaffected and so vivid! Why did Lorenzo write her that appalling, that unforgivable letter—'I hate you, stewing in your consumption, I think the Italians were right to hate you etc. . . . ' How *could* he? And why?[20] How much it meant to her in all her miseries when she had an affectionate letter from her father. I must remember that.[21]

Old wounds, from the 'English phase' of his career, took long to heal. *End to Torment* touched him on the raw and he was angry at once again being treated 'in the "poor Richard" style'.[22] But he was objective enough about it to advise H.D. not to publish it for the present, as she would be publicly caught up in the whole question of Pound's culpability for his wartime activities in Italy.

Aldington wrote to Randall making enquiries about Rome ('surely', he suggested to Harry Moore, 'the most attractive and endlessly interesting of all human creations'), hoping he and Catha could spend Christmas there, at an establishment called the Hassler: 'I have a vivid memory of the place in the early 30s. I passed G. K. C[hesterton] who was sitting alone in the hall. It was just after a pack of puritanical idiots had stopped his drinking entirely, and the poor old fellow sat there looking as gloomy as if he had already got to Malebolge, melancholy as a gib cat'.[23]

Randall was interested in having him write about Pound, who had been released from St Elizabeth's and left the United States for Italy, but Aldington made it clear that for him Pound's work was suspect. He had written to Pound himself in late September urging contact with H.D., who was upset at not having heard from him on his release. On that occasion he spoke of Pound's 'long martyrdom', his 'superb courage and determination'. Towards Pound the individual and onetime close friend, there is little doubt this momentary sympathy is sincere enough, but in December, on receiving a copy of Canto XCVIII[24] he told Durrell it is 'pretentious and repetitive drivel' and asked with some sarcasm, 'why write for Occidentals in Chinese and Classical Greek?' 'You should not take Ezra seriously, even as a poet . . . ', he told Bryher on 13 December. Many of Pound's friends must have felt such ambivalence and its vehement expression is something Aldington had in common with an older and closer friend of Pound's, William Carlos Williams.

The plan to travel to Italy fell through, first because the Kershaws were able to be in Sury for Christmas and Aldington wanted to be there to welcome them. Catha had neglected to renew her passport and they were as usual short of money, so even the cheapest on MacGreevy's list of hotels was beyond their means. They did drive as far as Menton, visiting the Durrells at their *mazet* in Engances. Aldington enjoyed the brief excursion, but was utterly exhausted, so the journey back took several days, for rest and recuperation. They arrived in Sury on 8 January and next day he wrote H.D. a long and vivid letter about the trip, rejoicing in going over scenes of remembered pleasure but deploring the effects of industrialism and rebuilding, especially around Toulon.

His life now was virtually embedded in the French countryside, in whose seasons he felt the ancient continuities. 'I've just returned from one of those silent winter walks in Sancerre', he wrote to Harry Moore on 5 February. 'There was no snow and a thaw had ended a long frost, and with one or two old people shuffling about in wraps the illusion of being in the Moyen Age was complete.' In contrast, in mid-month he wrote of the prospect of a hideous week, eye-test, haircut, purchase of car seat covers and new covers for himself to replace shabby too-long-worn clothes. Such expense he considered wasted. 'The only objects worth spending on are, I think, my daughter, books, reproductions of art, flowers, wine, travel.' Spartan conditions did not rule out epicurean ironies and he suggested to Moore how right D'Annunzio was to limit himself to gold, champagne and caviar, commodities that even the 100 000 sold copies of several Aldington paperback titles would not afford, as each copy netted him twopence.

Now he had rare news of another old friend and associate, Frank Flint, whose translation of *The Private Life of the Marshal Duke of Richelieu*, with Aldington's introduction, had just been reissued. For this new run of 10 000 Flint, living quietly in a cottage near Didcot, would receive £25, Aldington half that sum. He had not been in touch with Flint for a long time; the other man's hypersensitivity had cut him off from the literary world in general. Aldington had always felt a protective affection for him and still believed Flint had allowed himself to be intimidated by reviews and literary hangers on, whereas he could have claimed a place as English expert on French Symboliste and post-Symboliste poetry. Aldington had always admired a certain tremulous integrity in Flint and now wondered, at least in passing, about renewing contact with him.

His own knowledge of French literature bore late fruit in the award of the Prix de Gratitude Mistralienne, for his *Introduction to Mistral*. The prize prompted Harry Moore to arrange an American edition, to be published by Southern Illinois University Press. The Heinemann edition had sold out and Aldington knew the satisfaction of having *The Times* reviewer (Cyril Upton) declare it the most intelligent book on Mistral, a favourable response matched later by Henri Peyre in the *New York Times*.

Durrell still felt optimistic about the revival or resumption of Aldington's literary career and repeatedly urged him to work on another book; but Aldington knew he was finished with writing books. His focus now was Catha, soon to be 21 and busily working in Montpellier for the baccalaureate. Her father joined her there on

30 June. Catha's oral examinations were on 4 and 5 July and from Montpellier she could not easily have made it back to Sury for her birthday on 6 July. The Temples had offered the use of their Montpellier flat for July. 'The flat is too luxurious for the likes of me', Aldington said wryly to H.D., 'but perhaps C. will enjoy it.'[25] Catha duly passed her examinations and got her wish, though belatedly, to meet Durrell's friend Henry Miller at her birthday time. Late in July Durrell and Miller came to Montpellier. Miller later left his impressions of Aldington:

> He was not the sort of man I had expected to meet. That was my first impression. He was bigger, bolder, kinder, more sympathetic—and far less British—than I had pictured him in my mind. *A good human being*, I thought to myself . . . . Something in his eyes which spelled sadness—not human sadness, but the sadness of an animal which knows not why it is sad. Or, as if at some time or other he had experienced a profound betrayal.
>
> I had this feeling, though I made no mention of it, that he was not long for this earth. Not that he looked ill—on the contrary, he seemed like a mighty oak of a man—but rather, that he gave the impression of weariness, weariness due to combatting human stupidity, meanness, and so on. As if he had given up the fight.
>
> And then later in the day, after we had all had dinner together—the Temples, the Durrells, my wife and I—to my surprise he waxed jovial. He laughed, drank, told stories—as a man might who had been deprived of human companionship for many moons.[26]

Aldington told H.D.: 'I met Miller with Durrell, and liked him very much. He is a good kind of American—they exist!'[27]

Possibilities arose, perhaps largely in Harry Moore's mind, of Aldington's travelling to the United States, to lecture either at Bread Loaf Writers Conference (where he had been years earlier) or at Southern Illinois University. Aldington decided such a trip could not be profitable financially, but he was in any case too unwell to go. He could hardly walk a mile, much less travel to North America.

Active on his behalf, Durrell arranged for him to write a monograph on D. H. Lawrence for the German publisher Rowohlt Verlag. Durrell also circulated to the *Paris Review* and elsewhere Aldington's essay on Rome, later published as introduction to *Rome: A Book of Photographs*. Most of Durrell's well-meant efforts came to nothing, though Curtis Brown in New York did purchase first serial rights in Aldington's *Two Cities* piece, 'A Note on Lawrence Durrell'. Aldington professed momentary fears that Catha might take up the thankless vocation of writer. Fanchette, the 'ridiculous Mauritian' who edited *Two Cities*, had even encouraged this, commissioning an article on Cocteau and offering her a job as part-time bilingual secretary. Such inducements must have seemed sadly ironical to Aldington.

Durrell, obliged to travel to London in late August, prompted him several times to make the trip, and wrote from London in September disturbed that Aldington was not a known name among the young. He urged that something be done about it, perhaps through adroit use of television, and claimed that a number of admirers felt the same, such as John Davenport, who said 'Tell Aldington to come back for a bit'. But, of course, it was impossible. At that very time, he was suffering one of his bouts of extreme lassitude.

In the last week of August, he received a deeply affecting letter from Pound:

> CHER R/
>   amid cumulative fatigue, and much that has gone to muddle, thinking of early friendship and late. This to say I have for you a lasting affection.
>
>   E.P./
> 25 Aug 59
> Came on some notes of first walking tour in France, amid the rubble a week ago or so. 'Quanti dolci pensier'.

Aldington at once wrote in warm reciprocation. A week later he elaborated to H.D. that Pound's letter had upset him as 'far too valedictory', that in spite of his current 'damnable semi-coma' he hoped he had replied with all the affection H.D. would have wished, but in this very letter to H.D. his ambivalent feelings towards Pound soon surface again.[28]

23   1959–61

From London, Durrell continued to urge that Aldington take steps to retrieve his British reputation, but by now he was more interested in his daughter's future than his own. Late in September Catha flew to Switzerland to visit H.D. and Bryher, perhaps with a view to furthering their interest in her education. Early in October Aldington was happy that both women were impressed by Catha and was soon able to inform Bryher that she had been accepted for the Sciences Politiques course at the Sorbonne. Bryher had helped to make her enrolment possible by guaranteeing her the equivalent of $200 a month for three years. Around this time Aldington received a subvention from a less expected source. Deirdre Bair records that Samuel Beckett sent him a gift of 27 000 old francs.[1]

Days of feeling well alternated with spells of profound lethargy, his existence, 'a frightful daily dollop of pills'. He spent much time in bed, and heard from H.D. that Pound, too, was worn out and largely bed-bound. But Aldington was still working. Responding to Bryher's invitation to visit he said he could come once he completed work on the commissioned Britannica anthology, 'the end of a life's work in poetry'. By early November he was writing the introduction. When he had finished it he could travel to Switzerland to see the 'witch-doctors', that is, a physician and a psychiatrist. He motored to Zurich in the last week of November, even in poor health preferring the freedom of travelling by car, feeling he could switch to a train if the going proved difficult. He confided in Bryher another reason for travelling by road: 'I should like to say farewell to Vezelay and Dijon, and perhaps, returning, to Bourg and Cluny'.[2] Expenses for the journey and medical attention were to be paid by Bryher, so he felt it was an offer he could not turn down, though he told Alan Bird: 'I have no particular hopes of this, for there is no known cure for the universal disease of Anno Domini'.[3] Nothing especially came of the medical tests and he did not react much to his other reason for the trip, seeing H.D., though she still had difficulty in walking as a consequence of a broken hip suffered in a fall in 1956. He did take steps to promote her work, sending poems to Temple for *La Licorne* and elsewhere.

At this time the editors of *Encounter* sent him a copy of an article by Katherine Anne Porter on D. H. Lawrence and *Lady Chatterley's*

Lover, inviting comment. Porter labels the novel 'a dreary, sad performance', 'a very laboriously bad book', and implies that Lawrence took advantage of the censorship regulations to create a *succès de scandale*. To her, to use this novel to undermine censorship was a 'fraudulent crusade'. As for Lawrence, 'he was about as wrong as can be on the whole subject of sex'. Porter herself goes on at inordinate length, but she has fun at the expense of a clutch of pro-Lawrence intellectuals, including Edmund Wilson, Jacques Barzun and Mark Schorer, and approves in contrast a remark by Yeats about the lovers, that 'the coarse language of the one accepted by both becomes a forlorn poetry, uniting their solitudes'. But her central objection is to Lawrence's sexual presumptuousness, his authoritative presentation of how Connie Chatterley felt. To which Porter responds: 'This shameless, incesssant, nosy kind of poaching on the woman's nature as if determined to leave her no place of her own is what I find peculiarly repellent'.[4]

Aldington answers, first, through several quotations from an American judge's decision as to the book's obscenity: 'There is no question about Lawrence's honesty and sincerity of purpose, artistic integrity, and lack of intention to appeal to prurient interest. . . .'.[5] Apart from this, he mentions (without giving a specific source) that the situation in a case-history of Dr Wilhelm Stekel's was close to that of Mellors and Lady Chatterley and, further, their relationship resembled that between Frieda and Lawrence. He quotes Frieda on Lawrence ('He fought for the liberty of my being and won') and Katherine Mansfield ('Oh, there is something about him and his eagerness, his passionate eagerness for life'). Porter and Aldington each had their points, but more fun was provided in *Encounter*'s correspondence columns, including a letter which featured a mock-review from New York of *Lady Chatterley's Lover*, supposedly in 'our *Field and Stream*', which praises the book for its 'many passages on pheasant-raising, the apprehending of poachers, ways to control vermin, and other duties of the professional gamekeeper'. The reviewer regrets, however, that the book's 'many pages of extraneous material' mean that it 'cannot take the place of J. R. Milner's *Practical Gamekeeper*'.[6] What seems remarkable about all this is the request from *Encounter* itself and then the cantankerous verve Aldington displayed in answering Porter, though he remarked to Durrell privately that he felt *Lady Chatterley's Lover* was 'almost the worst' among Lawrence's novels. He added yet another item to his long list of writings on Lawrence by providing an introduction for his friend F. J. Temple's *D. H. Lawrence: l'oeuvre et la vie*.[7] By the end of the year he had completed a chapter of the Lawrence book for Rowohlt and could manage to work for as long as three hours a day, though he told friends wistfully that Bryher had offered him a subsidy so he could 'shut up for a year', a suggestion by which he was 'sorely tempted'.

Complaining to Alan Bird that British newspapers deliberately ignored him, he was able to impart some good news. He had heard from Urnov in Moscow that there were plans for a 1960 Russian edition of *All Men Are Enemies*, a new translation of *Death of a Hero*—with Urnov's introduction, and a selection of short stories, *Farewell to Memories*.

Thoroughly irritated by having to bother with the 're-boiled cabbage' of the Rowohlt monograph, Aldington dropped his daily stint of work to two hours. He was teased by the possibility of an annuity from Bryher, which would free him to work as and when he pleased. Soon after New Year he was forced to quit work altogether, though he fretted to complete tasks in hand. In mid-January he accepted gratefully Bryher's offer of a six-month subsidy. Unable to write, he occupied his time in desultory reading of Ruskin and Pepys. Durrell's bid to have him travel to Nîmes and take part in a television programme was thwarted. Aldington was able to claim justly that his body had let him down, but added that he had nothing to say to the British, in any case. From his point of view, he was waiting for the apology he felt the British owed him. The immediate cause of this feeling was the reception of *Lawrence of Arabia* and its after effects on his reputation, but he had felt a general grudge against his fellow-countrymen for most of his life. Durrell who said that David Jones, the BBC team producer, would ignore the Lawrence of Arabia question and wanted to enlist Aldington's help towards a special programme on D. H. Lawrence, felt it was a missed opportunity.

Buoyed by his new financial circumstances, he had mixed feelings about the Rowohlt monograph. He longed to finish it so that he could purchase a car with the publisher's advance, but he hankered after discarding the chore altogether and claimed all his attempts to correspond with the publisher met with frustration. With Bryher's financial help and the fact that he was one of three British writers to receive royalties from Russia (the others were Maugham and Priestley) he began once again to feel the possibility of more economic freedom, although he did go on to complete the Rowohlt book.

Signs of hope must have been boosted by news from Urnov early in February. 'Your novel All Men Are Enemies has just been published in Russian translation and is very warmly received here. As I passed the bookshops on Pushkin's Street the other day I saw it myself—copies of your book being unpacked and disappear at once among an eager throng of booklovers.'[8] What more could any writer expect? What indeed, except to be able to write to one's former publisher (in this case, Covici in New York) just three weeks later with the claim that 225 000 copies of the book had sold.[9] The prospect of such sales had prompted Aldington to boast to Durrell that he could live without the British. By his own calculation he could have garnered £11 500 in royalties, but Russian ways of dealing with such matters meant a far less spectacular monetary success. What he actually received was 'an annual pourboire' of £250. Nonetheless, for the Russians he was an important British author, so he could shrug off the absence of any of his books from a British Council exhibition of 3000 titles currently on show in Moscow. An added irony was that the Russians themselves had printed an English-language edition of *Death of a Hero* in a run of 20 000.

At the beginning of March Aldington heard from Haley that his old Imagist associate and friend Frank Flint had died at Oxford. This, as he noted, left only the 'original' three, Pound, H.D. and himself. He wrote at once to Pound with the news, and reported to Durrell: 'A letter from Ez, who is in Rome (It'ly). He writes about Flint, but some bastard has evidently showed him my lecture on Ezra Pound and T. S. Eliot, and he is Patriarchally reproachful. Don't like that—would rather he had cussed some'.[10] This was just when Faber & Faber brought out the English edition of *Thrones*, Pound's last completed book of *Cantos*, and Pound was still close to Eliot, so the Peacocks Press book had come to his hand unpropitiously.

Geoffrey and Nin Dutton visited Aldington in mid-March 1960 and took him motoring. They looked in on the Durrells, and went on to visit H.D. and Bryher in Switzerland (Aldington reported to Moore, of H.D., 'it was 10 minutes before she could be anything but hysterical').[11] About this time he received a pull of the dust jacket for H.D.'s *Bid Me to Live*, and news that she was to be presented a Brandeis Gold Medal for poetry. He thought the novel was bound to succeed in the United States and was delighted about the medal, though he felt she deserved a Pulitzer Prize. H.D. planned to travel to her home country for the presentation, and friends saw to it that she got plenty of publicity. She must have suggested Aldington accompany her. 'Can't you see the headlines: "Aged Poets Reconciled—Living Incog in 5th Av. Hotel"?', he asked Harry Moore.[12] He was inclined to advise against the trip, though he told friends H.D. certainly deserved the success and should have had it earlier. Anxiously, he suggested she make use of a wheelchair while travelling, to avoid the embarrassment of sticks. She should be sure to prepare an address of at least 5000 words! (In the event, she was asked to speak for ten minutes). His advice, that she employ an abigail (a lady's maid) was apparently followed. He showed *Bid Me to Live* to Kershaw, the Duttons and others, prompting friends to write H.D. kindly notes. He and H.D. had been in regular communication almost continually since his return to France in 1946. As Barbara Guest says, 'the two were closer each year. She was always legally known as Mrs. Hilda (or H.D.) Aldington'.[13]

By the second week of May he was going over the completed typescript of the Rowohlt book. In mid-May he declared to Bird, 'I shall write no more if I can avoid it':

> It is quite a mistake to suppose there is any interest in my books in England or even USA except for the translations (i.e. Boccaccio, Candide, Laclos, which I suspect are sold as pornography, not as literature) and the 'paperbacks' of Hero and TEL. My sales are nearly all in foreign translations, and even the English copies are mainly sold abroad. Most of my books are out of print, and those still in print are simply the fag-end of editions which will never be reissued. Some belated accounts from Heinemann received yesterday will give you the 'picture'. From June 1957 to June 1959 Religion of Beauty sold 28 copies, of which 19 were export; Pater sold 57, of which 35 were export: Portrait of a Genius, But . . . sold 322, of which 226 were export. All my novels, stories, biographies, essays, poems are out of print—except of course in foreign translations, on which I live. If the Anglo-American public really wanted to read me their enquiries for the books would soon stimulate reprinting.[14]

Rowohlt now offered a contract for a paperback edition of *Death of a Hero*, with an option on *The Romance of Casanova*, but Aldington disliked it and refused it, claiming the publisher asked for '50% of all rights in all languages', a provision which, if true, would effectively have deprived him of half whatever income his books did afford, at least in regard to titles Rowohlt might publish. *Death of a Hero* was at this time being reprinted in Russia, Poland and Czechoslovakia. The American edition of *Introduction to Mistral* received a boost from a favourable three-column article in the *New York Times* by Professor Henri Peyre on 24 July. Aldington was quickly asked to write on Mistral for Collier's Encyclopaedia and, at the same time, nervously toyed with the prospect of writing on T. E. Lawrence for an Odhams Press periodical, *Today*. As he wrote to Durrell, a trifle desperately, on 16 August:

> I . . . find I have just published or shall publish books (new, reprints, foreign translations) in Chicago, Carbondale Illinois, New York, London, Paris, Hamburg (thanks to you), Moscow, Warsaw, Prague, Milan, Sofia, and Tokyo. Mostly lesser breeds outside the glorious victorious subtopian state, but I begin to think that after all they have not altogether succeeded in obliterating me.

By early September he was enduring a badly inflamed throat, he thought might be Vincent's Angina,[15] which he had suffered in 1931 after a period of overwork writing *Soft Answers*. Otherwise he was busy seeing Catha enrolled and settled in at the University of Aix. The plan was for her to find an apartment in Aix with an extra bedroom so he could stay there from time to time, and perhaps to locate an out of town cottage she could use as a retreat at weekends. The drive down to Aix forced him to memories of the lost past, lost through ribbon development of gas stations, billboards and industrial plants, along routes which had in the 1930s been among the most beautiful in Europe. 'The Provence of Mistral is dead indeed', he wrote to H.D. on 13 October. 'A land where there used to be time for everything, where it was "always afternoon" has become a land of gum-chewing hurriers'. He hoped that in Provence Catha would be fortunate enough to experience what remained of an old civilisation, but getting her there was not easy to bring about. Excusing himself for neglecting to write for months to Alan Bird, he explained:

> I have been occupied with the difficulties arising from the fact that my daughter could not endure Paris or the Institut de Sciences Politiques, and wanted to transfer to the Faculté des Lettres at Aix-en-Provence. I got recommendations to various

people . . . but in spite of many kind words, we are still entangled in the coils of all-conquering Bureaucracy.[16]

They could not recover the original of Catha's Baccalaureat Certificate from the Sorbonne, or get a replacement, or have her dossier transferred from Paris to Aix, but she attended lectures while waiting to become fully registered.

Early in November Aldington returned to Maison Salle for six weeks, having planned to go south again and take Catha to Rome for Christmas. Money worries were lessened because in 1960 the Russians paid £750 in royalties, three times the 1959 figure. They were, in fact, his main current source of literary royalties. The Britannica anthology had been a full 12 months at the publishers, but was apparently waiting in the production line as one of a series, and so produced no income. Rowohlt's *D. H. Lawrence in Selbstzungnissen und Bilddokumenten* still had not appeared. Aldington was back in Aix by 5 December. On 10 December they rendezvoued with the Durrells at Maussane, spent a few days in their company, and then took off in the Caravelle for Rome on December 17.

Aldington profoundly wished he was setting out for the Rome of 1912 or 1922 and was nervous of returning to a city made over to Vespa motor scooters and Coca Cola, but quickly adjusted to the changes and enjoyed escorting Catha through the whole long list of tourist spots, from the Piazza di Spagna to St Peter's. 'The journey has made the greatest difference to me', he wrote to Bryher (who had largely financed it) on New Year's Eve. He was able to replenish his stock of photographs and postcards, lost during the Second World War. By this time Spring Books had published *Rome: A Book of Photographs*, with a cut-down version of his introduction. Chagrined, he commissioned Potocki to issue it in full as a Melissa Press booklet, intending it as a 'Christmas card' for Bryher and H.D.; but the plan misfired. The 'King of Poland' bungled the job to the extent of leaving Aldington to sew the sheets. *A Tourist's Rome* is not, in any case, an inviting looking production; drab, riddled with misprints, it is a printer's mediocrity.

Aldington was happy in Rome, wallowing, as he put it, in Paterian aestheticism; he even thought some things about the city had improved, such as the performance of church music, which he believed had benefited from American influence. But Catha had arranged to spend a few days with friends on the Carmargue before starting classes again on 3 January 1961, so they returned to Aix on 30 December and he spent a solitary *Jour del'an* at the Hotel Sévigné. He remained in Aix until the end of January, but the good health he had experienced over the holiday soon dissipated and he complained to Bryher about feeling 'idiotically nervous' and 'almost suicidally depressed'.

Bryher sent a copy of the *Times Literary Supplement* for 13 January, containing a notice of the 90th birthday of Bruce Richmond, Aldington's editor of the 1920s. Written by Eliot, the piece irritated him by suggesting that not he but Richmond himself had instigated the meeting with Eliot, the one where he had arrived in a bowler hat and goatee beard. Aldington felt that not only Eliot but Herbert Read owed to him the swiftness of their acceptance by the *TLS*. It was perhaps nagging at a small point, but understandably so; the record had not treated him kindly, especially of late years, whereas the rival Eliot had become a noted pillar of the Establishment.

Finding life with Catha in Aix expensive, he planned to leave the Midi and return to Maison Salle at the end of January, when the worst of winter was over. En route north he lunched with Durrell and Claude, warning them jovially against their plan to marry, but nonetheless celebrating the prospect with champagne. Back in Sury he was greeted by a series of dim tidings. Both Alec Randall's health and his wife's had broken down; MacGreevy had recently suffered another in a series of heart attacks and Osbert Sitwell (never a close friend, but one remembered with affection) had cancer. Amid this gloomy news, Bryher offered to finance a further excursion to Italy. From Russia came the gift of a fur cap from A. Puzikov, head of Russian State Fiction Publications, and news of an article by Dilyara Zhantieva in *Literaturnia Gazeta* for 3 December 1960, supporting Aldington's position on T. E. Lawrence, a matter which continued to be of considerable consequence to him though friends advised him to forget it. As against this, the now-published Rowohlt pocketbook annoyed him because of poorly chosen photographs, dismal production and miscaptioning.

At this point he was asked to write an introduction to John Gawsworth's collected poems. Gawsworth was, in some ways, a less spectacular or perhaps more comical version of Potocki, Pretender to the throne of Poland, in being self-styled 'King of Redonda', a tiny Caribbean island inhabited only by ghosts and seabirds.[17] To enlist aid in claiming his 'kingdom' from the Crown, Gawsworth created many dukedoms, including those for Durrell,

Miller and Aldington. Aldington was at first cool to the idea of introducing Gawsworth's poems, which, privately, he did not much admire. Claiming he was 'Public Enemy Number One' of British letters, he tried to fob off the task on Durrell, but by June was actually looking through the typescript.

Before then he had taken advantage of Bryher's latest offer, and spent this April in Venice. Leaving Maison Salle on 13 March, he sent a postcard to Durrell with a picture of the Venice Museo Archeologieo and mentions having a room opposite the Isola di San Giorgio. An unlikely date of 16 March heads it. To motor from Sury to Venice in three days seems very rapid, especially as he visited Catha, who had the flu, at her out of town quarters in the Mas Dromar near Aix. Twice in late March Aldington wrote to Durrell, once from the Mas Dromar, and once from Saintes Maries de la Mer.

The plan had been for Catha to accompany him to Venice, but after being delayed by her flu he set out alone in the first week of April. Once he arrived, he remained in Venice or the region for six weeks or so, receiving supplementary funds from Bryher.[18] In Venice he visited St Marks almost daily, recalling that nearly 50 years earlier he had been in the city with Pound. Now he joked to Durrell that perhaps they might hire a palazzo between them. 'With Byron's apartment in the Palazzo Mocenigo, and a mere £5000 a year, two could job along very nicely here', he wrote on 7 May.

From Venice in mid-May he returned, via a stopover at the Mas Dromar, to Maison Salle where in early June he received proof copies of Harry Moore's two-volume edition of D. H. Lawrence's letters. Believing he discovered two criminal libels in them concerning H.D. and Dorothy Yorke, Aldington after consulting Kershaw persuaded Moore to omit two paragraphs. H.D., hypersensitive at her strongest, was under treatment at a Zurich clinic for cardiac trouble and a slight stroke, obliged to stay quiet at all costs.

By arrangement, Netta Aldington arrived in France in June. They met at Bourges and went on what Aldington described as 'a week's motoring jaunt', in fact some mild touring of the Loire region. Just as he was about to set out he received from Urnov the Russian edition of his selected short stories, *Farewell to Memories*,[19] 'with a woodcut of my fizzog as frontispiece'.[20] By Urnov's account, the Moscow bookstores were piled with copies and the first printing sold out in a few days.

In his dealings with the Russians over the years, while he never ceased to be suspicious of the Communist state, Aldington formed the impression that writers and publishers were more 'liberal' (the quotes are his) than portrayed in the Western media, and that the country was less politically monolithic. Of his own titles current in Moscow, *Farewell to Memories* and *All Men Are Enemies*, he wrote to Alan Bird on 6 July: 'Considering that our highbrows dismissed both books as negligible I feel some satisfaction in finding them accepted 30 years later by the countrymen of Tolstoy and Chekhov'.

The motor trip with Netta was revitalising, 'an odd mixture' of good French cooking, tropical heat and disaffected peasant farmers blocking the roads with tractors in some sort of anti-government protest:

> Someday [Aldington wrote to Harry Moore on 3 July] I must pilot you and Beatrice through 'my' routes between the Loire and the Mediterranean, and I'm sure you'll be as amazed as I am that such beauty still remains intact. At the Saintes Maries we ate langoustines (the British call them Dublin Bay Prawns, but I forget the American name) and soles with a good white wine of Provence. At Moulines we fed sumptuously on what they call 'white' ham—i.e. very mild local ham—followed by genuine brook trout, and a coq au vin for me and a real filet Charolais steak for my friend, with a white Hermitage and a red Moulin-a-Vent, both of 1959, the third greatest wine year of this century.

By the beginning of July he was back in his solitary life at Maison Salle. Signs were that some of his work at least was coming back into print; paperbacks of his *Decameron* and *A Book of Characters from Theophrastus &c* and a hardback reissue of his version of Cyrano de Bergerac's *Voyages to the Moon and Sun*. Paul Elek approached him with a proposal for a book on Venice and he collected an extensive preliminary bibliography before deciding that the outright fee offered was by no means commensurate with the amount of work involved. This same month Thames & Hudson approached him to do a D. H. Lawrence volume in their Pictorial Biography Series, a book eventually done by Harry T. Moore and Warren Roberts. In mid-July Aldington completed editing Gawsworth's poems, meantime attempting to get Gawsworth, as editor, interested in the *fin-de-siècle* poetry of Rachel Annand Taylor. Privately he was faintly contemptuous of Gawsworth, describing him to his sister Margery as 'the usual pub-crawling London bohemian', and was amused at being offered a dukedom of Redonda for a second time, the first being when he had financed Gawsworth's honeymoon some years earlier. Yet in dealing with Gawsworth about the poems he was both flattering and considerate, and even made 'a small offering' of cash to finance publication.

Late in July Kershaw visited Maison Salle, to work on a radio programme about wine-growing. Then Catha came, with her boy friend (and future husband) Jacques Guillaume. While he had these visitors to break his solitude, Aldington was faced with an embarrassment concerning T. S. Eliot. Seventy of Eliot's letters to him turned up in an exhibition at the University of Texas. Eighteen months earlier, at the end of 1959, Aldington had told Durrell that these letters had been put up for sale by someone (whom he does not name) at Sothebys. Now in consternation he wrote to Eliot on 25 July and again on 5 August explaining that the letters had been stolen from him long ago (the date was given variously to Harry Moore as 'in or about 1929' and 'in 1930') by a friend into whose safekeeping he had given them. Eliot's immediate responses were rather distant, though he accepted the explanation, and added in him memorial comment published in 1965: 'I have no reason to doubt his word and have nothing left but feelings of friendliness and regard'.[21]

Now Aldington received bad news of H.D. He told friends in early August that she would probably not be able to write again or read Greek, or perhaps anything at all. Bryher had suggested that he and Catha might visit in September for H.D.'s 75th birthday. It would be a last meeting, after which H.D. was to be flown to the United States to be near her daughter, Perdita, and to receive the best available medical attention. Aldington and Catha did motor to Zurich in the second week of September, remaining only briefly. Catha was allowed in to see H.D., but the doctors advised against Aldington's doing so. He and Catha shortly left for Saintes Maries de la Mer. Two weeks later Bryher informed them by letter that H.D. was dead. When the news came Kershaw was with Aldington, who was utterly distraught.

Subsequently he felt that the obituaries, both in the United States and Britain, insufficiently emphasised H.D.'s genius, though he did appreciate some perceptive notes by Herbert Read published in *The Times* on September 29. These caused him to contact Read again, though there is no record of a response, possibly because the letter contains a mocking pen-portrait of Eliot among his 'pen-slaves' at Fabers, frail and rather nervous, holding his wife's hand for moral support. It was not the sort of jibe to Read's taste. Almost as much on Aldington's mind as the death of H.D. was the latest upsurge concerning 'the Prince of Mecca'. Anthony Nutting's book on Lawrence[22] was being serialised in the *Sunday Times* and Aldington felt that Nutting virtually accused him of concocting the letter to Charlotte Shaw in which Lawrence admitted to yielding to the homosexual advances of the Bey of Deraa.[23] Aldington wrote to the *Sunday Times* claiming that a copy of the letter was in his possession, but the newspaper did not publish his protest, nor apologise, nor acknowledge it. Stanley Weintraub, who was then working on his book *Private Shaw and Public Shaw* (published in 1963)[24] also contacted the paper to protest, and wrote to Aldington:

> Nutting's insinuation that you concocted the letter to Mrs. G.B.S. alleged to be in the British Museum (but which he couldn't locate) was so annoying that I wrote an indignant letter to the editor announcing that I had just reread the letter and was sure that Nutting's statement was typical of the quality of his research in the rest of his book. But the *STimes* didn't print mine (so they wrote me) because another letter actually quoted the 'missing' letter. . . . But at least your statement is now actually confirmed by the quotation, which has received the *STimes* wide circulation.[25]

Aldington, in any event, had a witness, for his copy of the letter had been taken in the British Museum by Deasey. Support for his position came in a review by Malcolm Muggeridge in the *New Statesman* on 27 October, but he had come to feel that nothing would do much to change British official hero-worship of the 'bogus prince'.

Throughout November he remained in Aix to be near Catha, though he was contrary enough to claim that his current bout of the 'bronchs', which had hampered him during a brief visit from Eric Warman, was due to the climate and might have been avoided in Sury, despite its 'repulsive' fogs. The Durrells invited him to Nîmes for Christmas, and he accepted gratefully, though insisting on paying for the room at the Hotel du Midi himself and offering to bring a jar of mincemeat and a Christmas pudding (Crosse & Blackwell's, tinned). Less than a week before Christmas he described himself to his sister Margery as 'crawling about Aix like an old slug'. She suggested that he and Catha return to England and live with her in Watchbell House, Rye, at which he remarked to his brother Tony 'Give me the 50 megatons' (of a nuclear bomb). Durrell had a more optimistic picture of Aldington. ' 'Twas splendid to see you in good heart and unworried, and a delight to hear that your fortunes are steadily mending', he wrote on 28 December. Aldington, in reply, confessed to weariness, once he had returned to Aix: 'I was glad to get back here and to recruit with sleep and what Pino delightfully called "abstemy"'.[26]

24   1962

Aldington remained in Aix throughout January and February 1962, working little, except to deal with mail which consisted mostly of enquiries about printing paperback editions of various translations. Fanchette, the *Two Cities* editor, irritated him by trying to garner royalties from Southern Illinois University Press for his introductory piece in *The World of Lawrence Durrell*.[1] In mid-January Durrell drove to Aix to consult Aldington about a piece of historical fiction he was engaged in and we glimpse Aldington's writing experience when he advises against Wardour Street dialogue, suggesting that conversations should be in standard English and period and setting should be conveyed by accurate rendering of local colour.

This overnight visit was an occasion for comedy. Durrell had forgotten his car papers, a minor but inconvenient offence, and attempted to phone home about them, but meanwhile his phone had been changed, causing confusion all round. In the evening Aldington and he went to a café and got into conversation with a British naval petty-officer, who, somewhat to Durrell's dismay, had never heard of either of them (chiefly because he read Westerns). 'Salutary', Aldington remarked to Harry Moore, 'for a writer to be reminded how small the literary "world" really is!'[2] However small he might think that world, he was at pains to see that a copy of *The World of Lawrence Durrell* was sent to Professor Norman Jeffares at Leeds University, hoping it might lead to inclusion of a Durrell volume in the Writers and Critics Series.

Aldington, at the Hotel Sévigné, had his customary winter onslaught of bronchitis. His D. H. Lawrence biography was being issued in the United States as a paperback, and there was the possibility of a similar edition of *Lawrence of Arabia*. He told Moore:

> February looks like being 'my month'. There is your Durrell book; Orion announce a new illustrated edition of my Cyrano de Bergerac; and in London Folio are doing a very handsome reprint of Laclos. There is an American enquiry for a paperback Laclos . . . and from London paperback enquiries for the DHL and Life for Life's Sake.[3]

On D. H. Lawrence he wrote again to Moore on 3 February, assuring him that there did seem to be a reaction against Lawrence then, because people were fed up with hearing 'the Lady C. blather' and the cashers-in had promoted Lawrence too much. 'Lane has made a packet, but he had distracted attention from the best of DHL's work to one of his least succesful—it is sex-propaganda, not art.' He hoped Moore's edition of the letters would redress the balance. He realised that the American reprint of his D. H. Lawrence book was a consequence of the pother over Lady Chatterley, so he was not especially encouraged or flattered. He felt his own manifest unpopularity in Britain was due in part to championing Lawrence, which contributed to Lawrence's 'posthumous victory'. 'You can see from "the check-list"' [that is, of writings on D. H. Lawrence] he told his brother Tony 'that the revival dated from 1950, i.e. the year [my] book appeared'.[4]

With the worst of winter over, both economics and access to his papers made it advisable for him to return to Maison Salle. In his last few days at Hotel Sévigné he received an advance copy of the new Russian *Death of a Hero* and was disappointed to discover it had been issued in a run of only 100 000 copies, considerably lower than the 225 000 of the recent *All Men Are Enemies*. He was especially disappointed as Urnov wrote to tell him that the edition had sold out and there was no news of a further run.

He was back in the Loire region by 1 March, a return to winter. Shortly after settling in he wrote to his sister Margery, making cryptic reference to future plans: 'In the first half of May I have to take an old friend on a drive round France of 10 days—the annual holiday. Then I have had to accept for Catha and myself a three-weeks invitation roughly fixed for end-June-middle-July. Otherwise I shall stay here . . . .'[5] He issued Margery a general welcome to come and stay, but otherwise his coyly uninformative 'information' disguises the fact that he was planning another trip with Netta plus the momentous news that he had been invited by the Soviet Writers Union to visit Russia. This invitation, dated 9 February and signed by the Union Secretary, Alexei Surkov, is directed to a figure one might suppose to be very different from Aldington's British image:

Dear Mr Aldington,
    You probably know that your books are widely read, published and loved in the Soviet Union.

We appreciate you as a distinguished writer humanist who has devoted all his life to the cause of peace and human happiness. That is why we would be honoured if you would accept our invitation to you and your daughter to visit the Soviet Union and spend here 3 weeks as guests of our Union (the Union of Writers of the USSR). Your numerous Russian readers would welcome your presence here in July, and you will spend your 70th birthday among us.

And of course all the expenses during your and your daughter's stay in the Soviet Union, as well as the flight from Paris to Moscow and back, will be covered by the Writers' Union.

We do hope that you will accept our invitation and will let us know as soon as possible about your decision.

With warm regards, Alexei Surkov
Secretary of the Writers' Union, USSR

Forwarding a copy of the letter 'in confidence' to the Durrells, Aldington noted that: 'After consultation with Bryher and my solicitor-brother [Tony] I have rather grudgingly accepted for us both. Catha can visit schools for feeble-minded children, and I shall at least have the pleasure of annoying some people in G[reat] B[ritain]. We shake hands with murder some time in the second half of June. ...'[6] The curmudgeonly tone here is characteristic Aldington, but later he was proud to boast to Eric Warman, that receiving this invitation was '"ALL my own work", as the pavement artists say'.[7]

Meantime an American publisher had offered him a contract to translate Flaubert's *L'éducation sentimentale*, with a promised advance of $2500. Though he only began it, throughout these months he was rereading Flaubert, including the letters and some commentary and criticism. He also kept track of British responses to Moore's edition of D. H. Lawrence's letters, and his own review of the book appeared in the *Saturday Review of Literature* on St Patrick's Day. Aldington considered the Collier (American) paperback edition of his D. H. Lawrence book a flop, because of a low initial subscription of 1500 copies, but he was quite well off financially because his 'pension' from 'the tiny millionairess',[8] Bryher, had been increased.

On 7 April he wrote to Netta to arrange their mid-May motoring holiday. Two points of major interest are revealed in this letter, his solicitude for Catha and his attitude to the Russian trip. First, he warns Netta:

> we can't and mustn't ask Catha to leave her Aix-Carmargue run to meet us, because she is really working very hard for her exams in early June. We must go to her, however much extra driving it means. She is really interested in this psychology course, and we must remember that her future career and living depend on her getting this Licence. If she gets that I think I can arrange for her to have an extra course at Yale, which would put her far ahead of most French competitors. But she must first catch her Licence.

Buoyed and honoured as he was by the prospect of the Russian trip, to her he was privately sardonic about it:

> I hope to see Tsarskoe Selo, St Petersburg, and perhaps even Samarcand. Catha is to come with me, and is already longing to hear how the comrades treat feeble-minded children and 'fools', i.e. fous. I am telling the Russ frankly that I don't care a damn for their silly factories and Lenin's corp (sic), and all the usual crap, but shall be interested to see any surviving relics of civilisation. . . . But do please keep this wholly to yourself. I don't want any premature leakage, and you can see that the birthday celebrations will be a nice wipe in the mug from me for the British. Of course it will all be paid with my own money—they have sold 225,000 copies of All Men, and 100,000 of the new Hero. They have sent me about 1000 pounds in the past three years, but of course they owe me far more than that.
>
> If I can get hold of some of the roubles they owe me we'll try to bring you some furs by way of the Russian Embassy pouch—but how get them to bloody England?

The trip with Netta, Aldington's last extensive excursion in France, took them through the Southwest—Orleans, Azay-le-Rideau, Brantôme (so much connected with Brigit and the long past), Les Eyzies, St Bertrand de Comminges, Saintes Maries, Nîmes and Monluçon. He took pleasure in the fact that the church of St Bertrand in the Pyrenees contains the only extant remains of a dragon (so he told Moore), in fact a mummified crocodile brought back from Egypt by a 12th-century crusader. This was the sort of detail Aldington delighted in; and he was happy to tour an area so far undamaged by industrial blight.

News came of the death of an old friend, Carl Fallas, who had enlisted with him in 1916. Aldington heard in mid-May from another old friend, William Haley, who complimented him on his brief essay in *The World of Lawrence Durrell* '... typical of you', Haley said, 'still to be looking forward, eager to apprise the newer writers'.[9]

He left Maison Salle on 16 June to stay with the Kershaws in Paris, to make final visa arrangements for Russia. Prior to leaving the Loire he had arranged with a Sancerre tailor to provide him with a 'pseudo-gent's' wardrobe—black jacket and small check trousers, dark blue jacket with greys, nylon shirts and silk tie. But, like Oblomov—as Aldington noted—the tailor made the clothes too small.

During the few days in Paris he met at dinner in Kershaw's flat Sir Oswald and Lady Mosley and was much taken with them—as they were with him. Kershaw thought it amusingly typical of Aldington's total independence that he should dine with these scandalous 'fascists' on the eve of a trip to the USSR. He also crossed paths with Tom MacGreevy, returning from the Venice Biennale. The two friends had not seen each other for more than 20 years. 'I had understood', MacGreevy wrote later,

> that Richard's health, like my own, was not as good as it used to be. But he looked very well. In fact he looked as young and at least as debonair as he had looked a quarter of a century earlier. And he was as sympathetic as ever. We spent about an hour-and-a-half over a bottle of Krug, Richard and I reminiscing light-heartedly, the others letting us talk and joining in our laughter. Then they drove me to the Faubourg Saint-Honoré where I had business to attend to. It had been a happy reunion and as we said au revoir and they drove away, waving and smiling, leaving me on the pavement outside my picture gallery, I think we all hoped we should be meeting soon again.[10]

Aldington and Catha remained in Paris for the best part of a week, leaving Le Bourget on 22 June. At Sheremetovo Airport three-and-a-half hours later they were greeted by a phalanx of journalists and photographers, an interpreter—Oxana Krugerskaya, and Mikhail Urnov and his son Dmitri. Both Urnovs were literary critics, interested in Aldington's work; Mikhail was a translator and specialist in English and American literatures. On arrival at the Peking Hotel, a long dinner with the Urnovs was followed by a late-night drive through Moscow, including a viewing of the nightlit city from a height above the Moskva River.

Next day at lunch at the Peking Aldington met Surkov and Dilyara Zhantieva, who had written several times about his work; reporters continued to seek him out and people on the streets recognised him and approached him. He discovered that his books were widely known and liked and he found popularity, 'Quite a change!'

On Sunday 24 June they were driven to Tolstoy's estate at Yasnaya Polyana and met his daughter. And so the tour continued: a visit to the Gallery of Western Art and the discovery that it contains an excellent collection of Impressionists and Post-Impressionists; an evening of classical ballet at a conference hall in the Kremlin; a visit with Urnov to a publishing house. One day they went shopping and Aldington bought some wooden peasant dolls for the children of his Maison Salle neighbours. Kershaw in *An Intimate Portrait* describes Aldington's characteristic generosity and the gifts he purchased on this trip: 'a superbly embroidered handbag for my wife, marvellous Kazakhstan caps for my small son, a magnificent *rubashka* for me'.[11]

Norman Gates tells of an incident on 27 June when several journalists attempted to cajole Aldington into commenting favourably on the World Congress for General Disarmament and Peace, held in Moscow from 9 to 14 July 1962. Despite his long-standing disgust with British intellectual life and frequent assertions in letters that the Americans were chiefly responsible for the threat of nuclear war, he did not use the opportunity to castigate either, but responded instead that he saw in Russia no signs of desire for peace. It was a difficult beginning to a rather uneasy day. Next was a call at the State Publishing House and discussion of possible publication of a Russian edition of *Women Must Work*, and then a lunch at the Writers' Union Club where a discussion of his work was led by Urnov and Zhantieva. On this occasion Aldington was nervous that he might say something which could be used as propaganda.

From Moscow the took the night train for a five-day visit to Leningrad, something he had anticipated as a highlight, particularly the opportunity to explore the Hermitage Museum. One who greeted him off the train, D. M. Moldavsky, fortunately recorded the visit,[12] providing details such as that Aldington got off the train in full fig, 'a rosy-cheeked, blue-eyed, tall old man . . . rather proud of his new slightly crumpled suit-coat', the Sancerre tailor's black jacket.

The opulence of his suite at the Hotel European, even including such details as a bronze statuette of Voltaire on the inkstand, was in ironic contrast to the peasant simplicity of his accustomed life at Maison Salle. He was moved by such attentions as the greeting on arrival of a young girl who presented him with a posy of pinks and a battered copy of *All Men Are Enemies* for autograph. The obvious Russian regard for his work contrasted in his mind with the British view.

In Leningrad (he insisted on thinking of it as 'St Petersburg') he savoured the Museum of Russian Art, where Moldavsky noticed his appreciation of the traditional realism of 19th-century Russian work and his fascination with Russian icons. He was presented with a book of Russian woodcuts edited by Moldavsky and V. I. Bakhtin. They visited the Peterhof (Petrodvorets), the Summer Palace on the Gulf of Finland, where Aldington was struck by the fact that many of the garden statues were gilded, he felt this was partly due to 'barbaric tastes for display, but also to compensate for lack of sunlight'. Much of the statuary was copied from classical works, though this seemed not to be generally known. Most of the gardeners were women. During several tours of Leningrad, he was frequently surprised by the fame of his own work and the number of times he was approached by admirers.

The chief purpose of his visit to Leningrad was realised on Saturday 30 June, when he toured the Hermitage. Here more than anywhere he relaxed, showing considerable knowledge of the paintings, especially in the Italian galleries. His evident predilection for traditional art, rather than modern, must have appealed to his Russian hosts. Later he was shown the Voltaire room in the Leningrad Library, chiefly a collection of Voltaire's books, sold after his death to Catherine the Great. Just as the trip to Russia was itself a huge ironic capstone to Aldington's whole career, so that afternoon in the Leningrad Library focused his lifelong engagement with Voltaire, as a translator and biographer, and in particular his respect for *Candide*, whose mordantly satiric rationalism had for long been one of his guides. Certainly Voltaire's biting discursiveness is an influence behind Aldington's particular sense of social satire. Next day at the Hermitage, Moldavsky photographed him at the foot of Goudon's statue of Voltaire, noting that this visual link would serve to explain 'something in the work of the outstanding

English writer'. So, equally, does Aldington's amusement at Voltaire's inscription in his copy of translated Shakespeare: *'Le barbare Shakespeare traduit par le charlatan Le Tourneur'*.[13]

On Sunday morning, 1 July, he appeared on television, noting with good-humoured satisfaction that he was even paid a fee of 50 roubles. He was asked once more for autographs in copies of his books and some drawings ('almost caricatures') were made of him during the recording session. Although he recorded 20 minutes to be edited for a five-minute spot, he was delighted when the material was used unedited.

Returning to Moscow, the Aldingtons were entertained to lunch at the Writers Union, hosted by Boris Polevoi, a Georgian veteran of the Battle of Stalingrad, and then a Moscow editor, who impressed Aldington by drinking a bottle of wine and the better part of a bottle of vodka while displaying prowess as a raconteur. This lunch was followed by a high point of the trip, a reception at the All Union State Library of Foreign Literatures, where Aldington signed many copies of his books ('scores of them', he wrote to Durrell) and received an outpouring of invitations, flowers and billets doux. That day he wrote to William Haley, telling of his extraordinary and unforgettable Russian welcome and explaining that he had discovered he was one of the best-known English authors, especially among young Russians.

On 5 July the Aldingtons met the Russian novelist Konstantin Fedin[14] at his *dacha*. Fedin, Aldington's contemporary, hosted a literary gathering in his honour, at which he met the translator Countess Moura Budberg[15] ('formerly mistress of H. G. Wells', he noted in his journal),[16] and the widow of Maxim Gorky. This latter meeting was particularly appropriate, not only because Madame Gorky was an admirer of *Death of a Hero*, but because Gorky himself is often cited by Soviet critics as having helped to launch Aldington's Russian career, through a letter to Fedin on 9 March 1932. Fedin was an excellent host, 'amusing and well bred', who 'talked well and drank lots of vodka and white wine, paying many compliments to Catha' (Journal) and who appealed greatly to Aldington's epicurean side by providing a splendid luncheon including Russian caviare and smoked sturgeon.

On Catha's birthday, July 6, two days in advance of the actual date, the official celebration for Aldington's 70th birthday was held at the Writers' Club. Among the several speakers were Alexei Surkov and Mikhail Urnov. Aldington felt his own speech was poor and cut short by emotion, but Urnov later remembered his saying: 'Here, in the Soviet Union, for the first time in my life I have met with extraordinary warmth and attention. This is the happiest day of my life. I shall never forget it'.[17] He was presented with gifts, including 'a superb book of Eikons from East Berlin'. Fedin, who received a copy on his 70th birthday, had noticed Aldington's admiration for it, and so with a great deal of trouble another was found. He also received a specially bound copy of the recent Russian edition of *Death of a Hero*, bound in blue Russian leather with 'LXX' embossed on a silver plaque. This was accompanied by a letter from Pavel Chuvikov, Director of the Publishing House of Foreign Literature:

> The breadth and youthfulness of your writings, their true humanity and anti-militaristic feelings, bring your books to the hearts of the whole of progressive mankind.
>
> Your novels, *Death of a Hero, The Colonel's Daughter, All Men Are Enemies*, have been popular indeed among Soviet readers. We, the staff of this Publishing House, are proud that last year we published a very large edition of your collected stories under the title *Farewell to Memories*—short stories which had not appeared before in Russian. These stories, written like your other books, vividly, with talent, and with great courage, have had an enormous and well-deserved success.

Signed by 17 writers present, this letter was received with much applause and followed by a eulogy from Grigori Vladikin, the publisher responsible for the current reprints of *Death of a Hero* and *All Men Are Enemies*, who announced he had commissioned a translation of *Women Must Work*.

On 8 July, his actual birthday, Aldington lunched with the novelist Valentin Katayev[18] and his family. Katayev was enthusiastic enough to invite him to spend the winter at his *dacha*. Later Aldington dined with the Urnovs and recorded an interview. That night, even after he had retired, there were more visitors and telephone calls. The London *Sunday Times* to mark the occasion ran a brief ('half-hearted') feature, 'Richard Aldington at Seventy'; in Moscow the *Literary Gazette* printed a short extract from *Women Must Work*, together with a laudatory article. Next day, his last full day in Russia, included the most touching incident of Aldington's trip. A woman called Ludmilla Pavchinskaya made a 12-hour rail journey simply to spend ten minutes in his company. Moved by her little gift of a toy dog for Catha, Aldington saw her as a 'tragic figure', a type-figure of the Russian people, gave her a signed photograph, and promised to write.

The Aldingtons flew back to Paris on Tuesday 10 July and by the following Friday he was back into Maison Salle life. That day he wrote to his sister, Margery, sending her a piece of jasmine he had picked at Yasnaya Polyana. 'A tremendous reception everywhere', he told her. 'I knew I am read there but I didn't know how widely nor that I am revered and loved . . . words can't express the warmth with which I was greeted and the handsome treatment we received.' Of the Russians generally he wrote to Durrell next day, 'I found them the most cheerful and warm-hearted people I've ever met. Such a pity they have to be communists'. For the next two weeks he was still writing to friends about his Russian triumph. On 18 July he told Kershaw he was busy inscribing copies of his works to 'these amiable commos'. 'What a pity they have to be socialists', was an often-repeated, half-jocular and half-defensive remark. 'I was almost smothered in flowers, telegrams and letters' he told John Gawsworth.[19] At the same time he was trying, with half-assumed grumpiness, to evade contributing to a birthday issue of *Poetry Review* for Gawsworth, and responded to the suggestion that the sculptor Hugh Oloff de Wet do heads of both Durrell and Aldington by saying that Durrell would soon be in Britain and could sit for them both![20]

Settling back into Maison Salle meant a return to listening a great deal to classical music and for bedside reading he had Bryher's recent autobiographical book *The Heart to Artemis*. Busy as he was catching up on the bits and pieces of life at Sury and responding to the Russian hosts' generosity, he took time to remember another old friend, Florence Fallas. He had his agent redirect to her £10 due to him in London (after Fallas's death in May his widow received only a small pension) and asked Bryher if she could spare £50 for the same cause.

He resumed work on translating Flaubert's *Sentimental Education* and had reached the scene in which it was necessary to find counterparts for a number of technical terms in connection with the pottery factory of Monsieur Arnoux. Sceptical about Flaubert's use of such language, he asked Bryher for help, when he wrote to her on 24 July, in making sure that he arrived at the exact equivalents in English.

As was his custom, on the morning of 27 July he drove into the village of Sury-en-Vaux to collect mail. Shortly after his return to Maison Salle, Madame Rezard, a neighbour, noticed him sitting in the garden, his head in his hands. She crossed over to see if he was all right.[21] Finding him unwell, she called Maxime and Suzanne Gueneau, neighbouring wine growers. They helped him into the cottage and telephoned the doctor. Aldington was in great pain, but appreciated the help he was given. He died towards noon and the Gueneaus, not wishing to leave the body alone, spent the night in the cottage. With his peasant neighbours present, in Kershaw's phrase, to salute his passing, Aldington was buried without fuss in the small walled graveyard at Sury-en-Vaux.

Kershaw, Temple and others feared that their friend's death would occasion further disparagements in the British press. Certainly the moment was not marked by the widespread recognition Eliot was to receive a few short years later, but Aldington would have been surprised at some of the comments, such as Anthony Curtis's reference to him as 'an English literary all-rounder of formidable genius, one of the truly independent, creative minds of the age',[22] or David Holloway's remark, in an otherwise generally disparaging obituary: 'But Aldington's brilliance in so many fields of literature has been rivalled by few of his generation and is indeed rare at any time'.[23] In Moscow the *Literary Gazette* noted that his work preserved 'the best tradition of British critical realism'.[24] The Soviet Writers Union sent to Britain an expression of grief at the death of the writer whose name transliterated through the Russian alphabet as 'Oldington'.

Perhaps it is most fitting to conclude with a British comment from a long and searching obituary in *The Times* on 30 July. Judiciously noting that small groups of readers would remember Aldington for introducing them to French literature ('he revealed his quality best as a critic'), others for his portrayal of D. H. Lawrence, and others still for the freshness of *A Dream in the Luxembourg*, it goes on to suggest that, contributor to many genres—as poet, novelist, critic, biographer and translator, Aldington was yet something more than a man of letters. He would have relished the remark that *Dream in the Luxembourg* 'was perhaps more evocative of the 1920s than much more pretentious poetry'; but, 'He always conveyed the impression of having a driving force greater than writing itself. He was an angry young man of the generation before they became fashionable; he remained something of an angry old man to the end'. From this obituarist's viewpoint, sometimes Aldington's anger betrayed him, but at best it was thoroughly justified and the tendency to 'write him off as a discomfited railer of no consequence was wrong. His anger was directed at the stupidity of mankind. His ideal of what human society might be had something fine about it'.

Looking back through the stages of Aldington's life and literary career is to look across a span of honourable effort and considerable achievement: his part in the Imagist movement was at first unsought for, but he is the best British Imagist and the movement owes much to his work as editor. He was realistic about his own poetic gifts but others have underestimated them; his gifts as an editor for the *Egoist* and the *Criterion* deserve greater recognition; similarly his work as translator, both in connection with the Broadway Translation Series and for a number of texts which have become standard—such as the *Decameron, Candide* and *Les Liaisons Dangereuses*—might well be more widely acknowledged. Few other imaginative works on the First World War can match *Death of a Hero*, as George Orwell saw. A whole range of books, from *Poetry of the English Speaking World* to *The Religion of Beauty* and *The Portable Oscar Wilde* are testimony to Aldington's fine judgement as an anthologist and some of his best and most substantial critical work appears in introductions to anthologies. Turning to the most controversial aspect of his work, biography, we have a time span of nearly 40 years and a variety of subjects, from Voltaire and Mistral to the Duke of Wellington and Squire Waterton, D. H. Lawrence, Norman Douglas and T. E. Lawrence. Two studies, the early *Voltaire* and *Portrait of a Genius, But . . .* continue to be widely and justly respected. The biography of Wellington won a major British literary prize and the 'notorious' T. E. Lawrence book is now recognised as being accurate in its essentials.

A year or so before his death, T. S. Eliot, in response to Selwyn Kittredge, wrote with perhaps belated generosity that 'something more permanent and extensive should be written about Richard Aldington, whose place in the literary world of my time in London is or ought to be secure'.[25] Aldington began, as a very young man in London, simply wanting to be a writer, and succeeded beyond most people's wildest expectations. By chance his 'Choricos' was the first poem published under the Imagist label, but there was some justice in this as he was a pioneer who genuinely understood the link between French writing and the new Anglo-American movement. When nearly two decades later he achieved overnight fame as a novelist, he was modest about his attainments in fiction. Yet his breaking away from the post-Jamesian quest for formal perfection, the rough-hewn directness with which he wrote under pressure of recollected intense experience was itself both individualist and innovative.

Whe he wrote *Death of a Hero*, he rooted out for himself what he believed had caused the horrifying slaughter of the First World War – jingoistic humbug and class exploitation. A quarter of a century later, when he had moved from fiction to biography and came more or less by chance on the subject of T. E. Lawrence, this was his nemesis as a writer of reputation; but it also forwarded his deepest concerns. As he gradually uncovered what he believed to be the true story of 'Lawrence of Arabia', Lawrence came to epitomise all the self-serving hypocrisy which had for so long permeated British society.

T. E. Lawrence, or what Lawrence purportedly was, had become a myth which sustained an entrenched privileged Establishment which Aldington abhorred. He was a conservative of another kind, one who believed that the individual was far more important than any institution, and especially that the enemy of the individual was government and bureaucracy. He was also against the run of fashion in being more interested in classic literature than in the modern movements, even though he was part of one.

What happened to him in Russia in his last days, the adulation he experienced, is therefore all the more ironic. In his youth he held the ideal of the 'good European' and in the breadth of his literary interests and achievement he became one. Yet what he suffered for most of all, and chiefly at the hands of his own countrymen, was an individualism which many would claim was very British.

Notes

INTRODUCTION

1. C. P. Snow, in Alister Kershaw and F.-J. Temple (eds) *Richard Aldington: An Intimate Portrait* (Carbondale, Illinois, 1965) p. 134 (hereafter noted as *Intimate Portrait*). Snow's note here is taken from his earlier *Richard Aldington: An Appreciation* (London, 1938).
2. T. S. Eliot, letter to Selwyn Kittredge, 3 April 1964. See Kittredge, *The Literary Career of Richard Aldington*. (Ann Arbor, Michigan, 1976), p. 560
3. *Intimate Portrait*, p. 25.
4. C. P. Snow, *Variety of Men* (Harmondsworth, Middlesex, 1969) p. 217.
5. Miriam J. Benkovitz (ed), *A Passionate Prodigality: Letters to Alan Bird from Richard Aldington* (New York, 1975) and Richard Aldington, *Lawrence of Arabia: A Biographical Enquiry* (London and New York: Collins, 1955).
6. Ian S. MacNiven and Harry T. Moore (eds), *Literary Lifelines: The Richard Aldington-Lawrence Durrell Correspondence*. (New York, 1981).
7. *Imagist Anthology* (London and New York, 1930). See Aldington's memoir *Life for Life's Sake* (New York, 1941), p. 143.
8. R.A. to A. Lowell, 18 January 1916 (Houghton Library, Harvard University) Aldington, 'Modern Poetry and the Imagists', *Egoist* I, 1 June 1914, p. 201.
9. Richard Aldington, 'Some Reflections on Ernest Dowson', *Egoist* II, 1 March 1915, p. 42.
10. Richard Aldington, 'Loose Leaves', *Egoist* II, 6, 1 June 1915, p. 98.
11. T. S. Eliot, 'Contemporanea', *Egoist*, V, 6, June-July 1918, p. 84; and Patricia Clements, *Baudelaire and the English Tradition* (Princeton, N. J., 1985) p. 281.
12. *Life for Life's Sake*, p. 215.
13. Richard Aldington, *Images of War* (London, 1919 and Boston, 1921).
14. Bernard Bergonzi, *Heroes' Twilight* (New York and London, 1966), pp. 83-4.
15. *Intimate Portrait*, p. 147.
16. *Intimate Portrait*, p. 161.
17. A. C. Ward, *The Nineteen-Twenties: Literature and Ideas in the Post-War Decade* (London, 1933) p. 89.
18. Alister Kershaw broadcast script, Australian Broadcasting Corporation, n.d., p. 18.
19. Richard Aldington, 'The Prose of Frederic Manning', *Egoist* I, October 1914, p. 375; and see Clements, *Baudelaire and the English Tradition* (Princeton, 1985) p. 269.
20. Details of Aldington's works will be found in the bibliography of primary sources.

Notes

21. Kittredge, p. 564.
22. *The Religion of Beauty: Selections from the Aesthetes* (London, 1950) p. 543.
23. *Artifex* (London, 1935) p. 6.
24. Richard Aldington, *Four English Portraits* (London, 1948) p. 102.
25. *The Complete Poems of Richard Aldington* (London, 1948) p. 13.

CHAPTER 1. CHRYSALIS, 1892-1911

1. *Life for Life's Sake*, p. 11.
2. Margery Lyon Gilbert, 'Early Memories of Richard Aldington'. Unpublished typescript (copy in possession of the present writer).
3. *Death of a Hero* (London: Hogarth Press, 1984) pp. 60–1.
4. R.A.—letter to F. S. Flint, undated, Humanities Research Center, Austin, Texas.
5. Kittredge, p. 5.
6. 'Early Memories of Richard Aldington', unpublished typescript supplied by author, pp. 1, 5.
7. *Death of a Hero*, p. 17.
8. Late in life, Aldington's father, Albert Edward, was converted to Roman Catholicism.
9. Transcript of interview between Dorothy (Arabella) Yorke and Walter and Lilian Lowenfels, Maya Landing, New Jersey, 25 October 1964. (Transcribed by the late Miriam J. Benkovitz. Copy given to the present writer by Dr. Fred D. Crawford.)
10. See George Orwell, 'The Art of Donald McGill', in *Decline of the English Murder*, (Harmondsworth, 1965) pp. 142–54.
11. R.A. letter to P. A. G. Aldington, 21 May 1959 (Carbondale).
12. 'Childhood', *Complete Poems of Richard Aldington*, pp. 55–9.
13. Norman T. Gates, *The Poetry of Richard Aldington*, (University Park, Pa., 1974) p. 29; Richard E. Smith, *Richard Aldington* (Boston, 1977) pp. 60–1.
14. *Rejected Guest*, p. 21.
15. *Life for Life's Sake*, p. 36.
16. *Death of a Hero*, pp. 86–7.
17. Alun R. Jones, in *The Life and Opinions of T. E. Hulme* (London, 1960), pp. 28–9, suggests that Aldington was part of Orage's circle as early as 1908 (when Aldington became 16). Gates searched the *New Age* files for 1908 and 1909, but found no Aldington poems. Gates, *The Poetry of Richard Aldington*, p. 22.
18. *Life for Life's Sake*, p. 50.
19. *Death of a Hero*, p. 97.
20. Kittredge, p. 15.
21. *Intimate Portrait*, p. 112.
22. A. E. Houseman (1859–1936), famous as the author of *A Shropshire Lad* (1896), was a noted classics scholar.
23. Gourmont (1858–1915), described T. S. Eliot as 'the critical consciousness of a generation', was translated by Aldington, Pound

and Aldous Huxley. Gourmont's influence on Pound is well known, but it is not clear how his influence first came over to English writing. Interesting to note, therefore, is Rebecca West's opinion, expressed in a letter to Selwyn Kittredge, 20 March, 1964: 'I would think it would be Aldington who brought Remy de Gourmont to the attention of Ezra Pound and not the other way around' (Kittredge, p. 20).
24. Hugh Kenner, *The Pound Era* (Berkeley, Ca., 1971), pp. 55–8.
25. Kittredge, p. 20.
26. Kittredge, p. 18.
27. Letter to Winifred Bryher, 5 October 1918. (Beinecke Library, Yale).
28. *Life for Life's Sake*, p. 77.

CHAPTER 2. POUND AND H.D., 1912–13

1. Patmore, Mrs Brigit (1882–1965), born Ethel Elizabeth Morrison-Scott. Married Deighton Patmore, grandson of the Victorian poet Coventry Patmore. A member of Ford Madox Ford's circle at South Lodge. In 1928 she became Aldington's companion and remained so for nine years. She wrote an account of this in *My Friends When Young* (London, 1968).
2. *Life for Life's Sake*, pp. 70–1.
3. Letter to Amy Lowell, 20 November 1917 (Houghton Library, Harvard). Hugh Kenner, *The Pound Era*, p. 277, reads Pound's remark as ironic, suggesting that he was hinting at Aldington's ignorance of verse technique. This view should be assessed in the light of Pound's and Aldington's whole relationship at the time.
4. Some commentators have distinguished between '*vers libre*' and 'free verse', but the Imagists tended to use these terms interchangeably. It may perhaps be said that *vers libre* is French, whereas the British and American use of 'free forms' and 'free verse' was also influenced by Chinese and Japanese poetry and, in Aldington's case, by a chorus in Euripides' *Hippolytus*. Kittredge, p. 42; R.A. letter to A. Lowell, 20 November 1917.
5. Generally accepted as the approximate date.
6. *Literary Essays of Ezra Pound* (London, 1954) p. 3; first published in *Pavannes and Divisions* (1918).
7. The literature on Imagism is by now copious. Useful starting-points are: *Imagist Poetry*, edited by Peter Jones (Harmondsworth, Middlesex, 1972); J. B. Harmer, *Victory in Limbo: Imagism 1908–1917* (London, 1975).
8. The moment is referred to in many accounts of the period. Note Pound's remark to Harriet Monroe, that 'the whole affair was started, not very seriously, chiefly to get H.D.'s five poems a hearing', Monroe *A Poet's Life* (New York, 1938), p. 267. Pound locates the meeting at Church Walk, Kensington. In *End to Torment* (New York, 1979) p. 40, H.D. places the event in the British Museum tea-room. The founding of the movement and the finding of her name were different occasions, though it is possible that both occurred in the

tea-room. Aldington suggests that Pound kept the name 'Imagistes' *in petto* for the right occasion', *Life for Life's Sake*, p. 135. According to H.D.'s unpublished summary diary at Yale, the first time Pound introduced her *nom de plume* it was 'H.D.Imagist', but H.D.'s spelling was notably unreliable. Peter Jones, possibly following William Carlos William's *Autobiography*, says that Doolittle was already calling herself H.D. when she arrived in London in 1911. Jones, *Imagist Poetry*, p. 16.

9. Hulme's poems, without the note, were first published in the *New Age*, 25 January 1912.
10. *Life for Life's Sake*, p. 115.
11. H.D., 'Asphodel', unpublished typescript (1922), (Beinecke Library, Yale). Bk. II, p. 179; Janice S. Robinson, *H.D. The Life of an American Poet* (Boston, 1982) p. 42.
12. *Life for Life's Sake*, p. 118. These were said to have been published by Augener, but no details have been found.
13. Slonimsky completed a Ph.D. at the University of Marburg on Heraclitus and Parmenides, and published a book on the subject in 1912. He was for a long period a professor at the Jewish Institute of Religion, New York. Charles Norman records Pound's possessing a black velvet jacket a year or two earlier and this was possibly the same garment.
14. Author of numerous books on economics and international politics, Sir Norman Angell (1874–1967) is best known for *The Great Illusion* (1909), on the futility of modern war.
15. These very brief comments are from Angell's autobiography, *After All* (London, 1951) pp. 165–6.
16. *Death of a Hero*, p. 162.
17. In 'A Retrospect', Pound mistakenly dates this publication a year earlier, in 1911. See Cyrena N. Pondrom, *The Road from Paris: French Influence on English Poetry 1900–1920* (London, 1974) ch. I; see Aldington, *Collected Poems 1915–1923* (London, 1923) p. xi.
18. *Life for Life's Sake*, pp. 111 and 136. On p. 128 Aldington mentions discussing Verlaine with Stefan Georg at that period.
19. All three poems are included in *Complete Poems*, pp. 21, 24 and 34 respectively, with the last retitled (possibly because of the solecism in the French title) 'In the Old Garden'.
20. T. E. Hulme, *Speculations* (London, 1960) p. 132. First edition, 1924.
21. A. R. Orage (Alfred Richard Orage, 1873–1934) was a cultural and social critic, and literary reviewer, and proponent of Nietzsche's ideas. With Holbrook Jackson he purchased the *New Age* in 1907, and edited it 1909–22.
22. This is the poem Kenner discusses in *The Pound Era*, pp. 55–8.
23. Noel Stock, *The Life of Ezra Pound* (London, 1974) p. 158.
24. *Poetry*, vol. I (November 1912) no. 2, p. 65.
25. This is the date given by Joy Grant, *Harold Monro and the Poetry Bookshop* (Berkeley, 1967) p. 62. The actual opening was on the first of the year. Robert Frost, who was at the opening party by chance, could not afterwards remember whether it was in January or December.
26. R. B. Cunninghame Graham (1852–1936), a descendent of Robert II of

Scotland, known (he had Spanish blood) as 'The Modern Don Quixote' was also a political activist and the first socialist elected to the British House of Commons.

27. *Life for Life's Sake*, p. 128.
28. *Collected Poems 1915–1923*, p. xi.
29. Gates, *The Poems of Richard Aldington*, pp. 206–7.
30. *Life for Life's Sake*, pp. 128, 129.
31. *End to Torment*, p. 5.
32. Janice S. Robinson [see footnote 43 below], pp. 41–4.
33. *Complete Poems*, p. 38.
34. Aldington makes passing reference, in *Life for Life's Sake*, to Rebecca West as 'a brilliant writer' (p. 139). As we have seen (see above ch. I, fn. 19) after his death she offered a number of opinions on him.
35. Jane Lidderdale and Mary Nicholson, *Dear Miss Weaver* (London, 1970) pp. 76–82, esp. p. 77; Dora Marsden to Harriet Weaver, 16 November 1913.
36. Marsden to Weaver, 19 November 1913.
37. A 'large proportion of the contributions, though new to English readers, were translations or reprints of work that had already been published elsewhere'. Lidderdale, p. 80.
38. Fletcher to Amy Lowell, 7 September 1913 (Harvard), quoted from Charles Norman, *Ezra Pound* (New York, 1969) pp. 110–11. [The date of the letter is possibly incorrect, as Fletcher mentions that R.A. and H.D. are just married.]
39. *Life for Life's Sake*, p. 127.
40. The poem was published in the *Irish Times* on 8 September 1913 and, according to *The Variorum Edition of the Poems of W. B. Yeats*, is dated 'Dublin, 7 September 1913'. Yeats was at Woburn Buildings in early August 1913 when, according to Joseph Howe, he left to stay with friends in Ashdown Forest. Quite likely he returned to Woburn Buildings before settling in with his new 'secretary' (Ezra Pound) at Stone Cottage, Coleman's Hatch, in October, leaving Sussex for London occasionally (Hone, p. 272). This probably explains why there was no source. Aldington seems to have been mistaken in believing that the poem had just been finished the day before it was read to him.
41. Pound's letter was written on an unspecified date in November and he casually dates the wedding 'last week, or the week before'. The date is sometimes given as 28 October, but in a letter to F. S. Flint dated 18 October 1913 (U. Texas), Aldington says that he and H.D. were married 'today'.
42. 'Paint it Today' (Beinecke Library, Yale) ch. IV, p. 18.
43. See: Susan Stanford Friedman, *Psyche Reborn: The Emergence of H.D.*(Stanford, 1981); Janice S. Robinson, *H.D.: The Life and Work of an American Poet* (Boston, 1982); Barbara Guest, *Herself Defined: The Poet H.D. and Her World* (New York, 1984).
44. H.D.' *HERmione* (New York, 1981).
45. H.D. has provided at least two accounts of her reactions to this news: in *End to Torment*, pp. 17–18, Walter Morse Rummel is the messenger; in 'Paint it Today' it is Aldington.

Notes

46. *End to Torment*, p. 8.
47. At some point H.D. jotted a 'summary' of the events of her life in diary form. The typed pages are in the Yale Collection of American Literature in the Beinecke Library. These are listed by Barbara Guest as 'Autobiographical Notes'.
48. H.D.' *Bid Me To Live* (New York, 1960). For the passages quoted see pp. 24 and 11.
49. William Carlos Williams, *Autobiography* (New York, 1951) p. 52.

CHAPTER 3. EGOISTS, 1914

1. *Egoist*, vol. I (2 February 1914) no. 3, Accounts of the occasion are included in Stock, *The Life of Ezra Pound*, Norman *Ezra Pound* and Eustace Mullins, *This Difficult Individual Ezra Pound* (New York, 1961), in Joseph Howe, *W. B. Yeats: 1865–1939* (London, 1943); in Edith Finch, *Wilfred Scawen Blunt* (London, 1938); Richard Cork, *Vorticism*, vol. I (Berkeley, 1976); Longford, *A Pilgrimage of Passion: The Life of Wilfred Scawen Blunt* (London, 1979). See also William T. Going, 'A Peacock Dinner: The Homage of Pound and Yeats to Wilfred Scawen Blunt', *Journal of Modern Literature*, vol. I (March 1971) no. 3, pp. 303–10, and *Life for Life's Sake*, pp. 167–8.

    When Pound and Aldington visited Newbuildings again, in March 1914, Blunt appeared at dinner in the full fig of an Arab sheikh, a pair of gold-mounted pistols in his sash, and toasted, 'Damnation to the British government'.
2. *Egoist*, vol. I (15 January 1914) no. 2, p. 36. In *Poetry* in June 1915, Pound rated these parodies 'very excellent'. See also Hugh Witemeyer, *The Poetry of Ezra Pound 1908–1920* (Berkeley and Los Angeles, [U. Cal. Press], 1969) p. 197, 'Appendix: Richard Aldington's Parodies of Lustra'.
3. *Egoist*, Vol. I (15 January 1914) no. 2, pp. 35–6.
4. Rémy de Gourmont, *Le Latin Mystique du Moyen Age* (Paris: Mercure de France, 1893); *Egoist*, vol. I (16 March 1914) no. 6, pp. 101–2.
5. 'Some Recent French Poems', vol. I (15 June 1914) no. 12, pp. 221–3. For all these items an important text is Cyrena N. Pondrom, *The Road from Paris* (Cambridge, 1974).
6. Rémy de Gourmont, 'Tradition and Other Things', *Egoist*, vol. I (15 July 1914) no. 14, pp. 261–2, also 'A French Poet on Tradition' *Poetry*, vol. 4 (July 1914) no. 4, pp. 154–60. The links between Gourmont's ideas and Eliot's are discussed succinctly and usefully in Bernard Bergonzi, *T. S. Eliot* (New York, 1972), especially ch. II.
7. *Egoist*, vol. I (15 August 1914) no. 16, pp. 513–6.
8. *Life for Life's Sake*, p. 175.
9. Ezra Pound, *Selected Prose 1909–1965* (London, 1973) pp. 383, 385. First published in the *Fortnightly Review*, vol. 104 (July-December 1915) pp. 1159–66.
10. Pound, pp. 385, 386.
11. *Life for Life's Sake*, p. 148.
12. Norman, p. 115.

13. D. D. Paige (ed.), *Letters of Ezra Pound*, (New York, 1950) p. 288.
14. 'Modern Poetry and the Imagists', *Egoist*, vol. I (1 June 1914) no. 11, pp. 202–3.
15. Timothy Materer, *Vortex: Pound, Eliot and Lewis* (Ithaca, N.Y., 1979).
16. 'Vorticism', first published in the *Fortnightly Review* in September 1914, is now ch. XI of Pound's *Gaudier-Brzeska* (New York, 1970).
17. *Life for Life's Sake*, p. 151.
18. Stanley K. Coffman, Jr. *Imagism: A Chapter for the History of Modern Poetry* (Norman, Oklahoma, 1951) p. 113. In June 1914 in the *Egoist*, Aldington returned the compliment by declaring Ford's 'On Heaven' one of the best poems of the century.
19. Norman, p. 149.
20. Richard Cork, *Vorticism and Abstract Art in the First Machine Age* (Berkeley, 1976) vol. I Origins and Development, p. 246.
21. Stock, pp. 205–6; Coffman, p. 21f.
22. Cork, p. 235.
23. John Gould Fletcher, *Life is My Song* (New York, 1937) p. 149. Aldington on several occasions at this time praised Hueffer's [Ford's] 'On Heaven'. When Ford gave an account of this dinner in an essay on Gaudier in the *English Review* (vol. XXIX, October 1919, pp. 297–304) it included a virulent attack on Amy Lowell.
24. *Life for Life's Sake*, p. 165.
25. John Cournos, *Autobiography* (New York, 1935), p. 269.
26. *End to Torment*, p. 5.
27. H.D. to Amy Lowell, 23 November 1914 (Harvard).
28. Robinson, pp. 43–5.
29. *End to Torment*, p. 5.
30. Harry T. Moore, *The Priest of Love* (Harmondsworth, 1981) p. 262.
31. S. Foster Damon, *Amy Lowell* (Boston, 1935) pp. 237–40; Jean Gould, *Amy* (New York, 1975) pp. 129–32; *Life for Life's Sake*, p. 140; Robert Lucas, *Frieda Lawrence* (New York, 1973) p. 114.
32. R.A. to Harriet Monroe, 7 August 1914 (Reizenstein Library, University of Chicago).
33. Frank MacShane, *The Life and Work of Ford Madox Ford* (London, 1965) p. 127.
34. R.A. to Amy Lowell, 14 November 1914 (Harvard).
35. *Life For Life's Sake*, p. 158.
36. Frederic Manning (1882–1935). His works include *Poems* (1910), *Eidola* (1917), *Scenes and Portraits* (1930) and *Her Privates We* (1930). Manning was a friend of T. E. Lawrence.
37. These three essays appeared in the *Egoist* on 15 September 1914, 1 October 1914 and 1 December 1914. The Peguy essay appeared on 15 October.
38. R.A. to Amy Lowell, 7 December 1914 (Harvard). Pound had suggested the title *Some Imagist Poets*, to indicate that not all were represented and to maintain his 'copyright' on the French term 'Imagiste'.
39. *Egoist*, 15 November 1914, pp. 422–3.
40. Lidderdale, p. 86; *Letters of Ezra Pound*, pp. 31–2.

41. Coffman, p. 33.
42. R.A. to Amy Lowell, 7 December 1914 (Harvard).
43. Fletcher, *Life is My Song*, p. 177.
44. *Life for Life's Sake*, p. 170.
45. MacShane, p. 124.
46. R.A. to Wyndham Lewis, 13 December 1914 (Cornell).
47. R.A. to Amy Lowell, 3 October 1914. Jacob Epstein (1880–1959). American-born British sculptor. In his *Epstein: An Autobiography* (London, 1955) there are two incidental references to Aldington. One of these has him among those at Charing Cross Station seeing the 'terribly pale and shaken' Gaudier off to France in 1914 (p. 46).

CHAPTER 4. IMAGES, LOST AND FOUND, 1915–16

1. R.A. to Amy Lowell, 8 January and 1 February 1915 (Harvard).
2. Amy Lowell to Herbert Croly, 15 February; qu. in Damon, p. 287.
3. James Whitall, *English Years* (London, 1936) p. 57.
4. R.A. to Plank, two undated letters in early (February?) 1915 (Beinecke Library, Yale University).
5. Harriet Monroe to R.A., 26 March 1915 (Chicago).
6. David Perkins, *A History of Modern Poetry* (Cambridge Mass., 1976) pp. 370–1, says of this work: 'But in her work the new themes and forms seem hardly less conventional than the old, and the poetry they led her to write was even more willed and external'.
7. *Little Review*, March 1915, pp. 22–5. These remarks anticipate, interestingly, Marianne Moore on William Carlos Williams in her 'Things Others Never Notice'—see *Predilections* (London, 1956) pp. 136–9. (First published in *Poetry*, March 1934).
8. *Bid Me to Live*, p. 8.
9. *Bid Me to Live*, p. 24.
10. R.A. to Amy Lowell, 21 and 26 May 1915 (Harvard).
11. H.D., *Tribute to Freud* (Boston, 1974) p. 116.
12. *Bid Me to Live*, p. 12.
13. Guest, p. 73.
14. Peter E, Firchow, 'Rico and Julia: The Hilda Doolittle—D. H. Lawrence Affair Reconsidered', *Journal of Modern Literature*, vol. 8 (1980) no. 1, pp. 51–76.
15. D. H. Lawrence, *Kangaroo* (London, 1923). Phoenix edition, p. 219.
16. *Bid Me to Live*, pp. 24–5.
17. Kittredge, p. 105; Herbert Read, *The Innocent Eye* (New York, 1947) p. 100.
18. Harold Monro, 'The Imagists Discussed', *Egoist*, 1 May 1915, pp. 77–80.
19. R.A. 'The Poetry of F. S. Flint', *Egoist*, 1 May 1915, pp. 80–1.
20. Not included in Lawrence's *Collected Poems*, this is an anti-war poem in which killer and killed are portrayed as a kind of marriage of the flesh, and the killer is full of suicidal self-hatred.

21. George Lane, 'Some Imagist Poets', *Little Review*, vol. 2 (May 1915) pp. 27–35.
22. F. M. Hueffer, 'A Jubilee' in *Outlook*, 10 July 1915; cited in Glenn Hughes, *Imagism and the Imagists* (Stanford, 1931) p. 46.
23. Ford Madox Ford. 'On Impressionism', *The Critical Writings of Ford Madox Ford*, edited by Frank MacShane (Lincoln, Neb., 1964), p. 34.
24. A most valuable treatment of the links between this 'egoism' and Imagism is contained in Michael H. Levenson, *A Genealogy of Modernism—A Study of English Literary Doctrine 1908–1922* (Cambridge, 1984) ch. 5.
25. R.A. to Amy Lowell, 11 June 1915 (Harvard).
26. R.A. to Amy Lowell, 12 November 1915 (Harvard).
27. R.A. to Harold Monro, 12 November 1915 (Clark Library, UCLA).
28. *Intimate Portrait*, p. 132.
29. Thomas McGreevy, *Richard Aldington, An Englishman* (London, 1931) p. 15.
30. Gates, *The Poetry of Richard Aldington*, p. 35.
31. Harriet Monroe, *A Poet's Life* (New York, 1938) p. 352.
32. Norman, p. 89.
33. *Literary Essays of Ezra Pound*, p. 4.
34. *Complete Poems of Richard Aldington*, p. 14.
35. *Complete Poems*, p. 27, 'Stele'.
36. *Bid Me to Live*, p. 51.
37. R.A. to Amy Lowell, 29 October 1915 (Harvard).
38. Aldington, *Portrait of a Genius, But . . .* , p. 175.
39. Fletcher, *Life is My Song*, p. 223.
40. *Letters of Ezra Pound*, p. 69.
41. Lidderdale, p. 112.
42. *Letters of Ezra Pound*, p. 111.
43. Lidderdale, p. 118, fn. 9.
44. *Letters of Ezra Pound*, 5 March 1916, p. 71.
45. Cournos, *Autobiography*, p. 286.
46. John Cournos, *The Mask* (New York: Doubleday, Doran, 1919).
47. *Life for Life's Sake*, p. 175.
48. H.D. to Cournos, undated (Harvard).
49. H.D. *The Collected Poems 1912–1944*, p. 314, 'Amaranth'.
50. *Bid Me to Live*, p. 16.
51. Guest, p. 78; Fred. D. Crawford, 'Richard Aldington and H.D.', paper presented at the 'Aldington Symposium', University of Reading, 8–9 July 1986.
52. John Cournos, *Miranda Masters* (New York, 1926) pp. 100–1.
53. John Gould Fletcher, 'Mr Aldington's Images', *Poetry*, vol. VIII (April 1916) no. 1. pp. 49–51; Fletcher also dealt with R.A. fulsomely in the *Little Review*, vol. 3 (May 1916) 'Three Imagist Poets', pp. 32–41.
54. Kittredge, p. 143.
55. Kittredge, p. 154.

CHAPTER 5. WAR, 1916–18

1. Alfred Satterthwaite, 'John Cournos and H.D.', *Twentieth-Century Literature*, vol. 22 (December 1976) no. 4, pp. 394–410, esp. p. 401.
2. This reaction might well have interested Storm Jameson, a young writer who had the previous November in the pages of the *Egoist* attacked the complacency of contemporary writers, flabby-minded through lack of real hardship. 'One may wonder', she wrote, 'what would be the effect on the work of the finest poet among the Imagists if Mr. Aldington were partially flayed'—'England's Nest of Singing Birds', *Egoist*, 1 November 1915, pp.175–6.
3. D. H. Lawrence to Amy Lowell, 23 August 1916 (Harvard); quoted by Damon, p. 369.
4. Guest, p. 84.
5. Pondrom,. p. 583.
6. *Complete Poems*, p. 105.
7. *Complete Poems, p. 87.*
8. *Life for Life's Sake*, p. 186.
9. R.A. to Cournos, 8 March 1917 (Harvard).
10. *The Letters of D. H. Lawrence* (Boulton) vol. 3, p. 105.
11. How big a part may depend on whether one makes as much of the Lawrence-H.D. relationship as her biographer, Janice S. Robinson does, or rather less, as do Guest and Firchow.
12. *Intimate Portrait*, p. 123.
13. *Little Review*, III, 10, April 1917, pp. 12–13; Gates, *The Poetry of Richard Aldington*, pp. 261–2.
14. T. S. Eliot, 'The Borderline of Prose', *New Statesman*, 19 May 1917, p. 158.
15. T. S. Eliot, 'Ezra Pound; His Metric and Poetry', *To Criticize the Critic*, (London and New York, 1965) p. 173. First published as a separate title by A. A. Knopf in New York, in January 1918.
16. *Life for Life's Sake*, p. 209; Norman T. Gates, 'Richard Aldington and the Clerk's Press', *Ohio Review*, vol. VIII (Autumn 1971) no. 1, pp. 21–7.
17. *Intimate Portrait*, pp. 162–3; Harriet Monroe praised 'the small book's clear and rich lyricism' in Refuge from War', *Poetry*, vol. XII (April 1918) no. 1, p. 44.
18. Richard Aldington, *Roads to Glory*, (London, 1930) pp. 80–1.
19. *Death of a Hero*, p. 204.
20. Guest, p. 86.
21. R.A. to Amy Lowell, 4 January 1917 (Harvard).
22. *Bid Me to Live*, p. 16.
23. *Bid Me to Live*, pp. 131–2.
24. Cournos, *Autobiography*, p. 297.
25. Lawrence, *Aaron's Rod*, (London, 1954) pp. 23, 24.
26. *Letters of D. H. Lawrence*, (Boulton) vol. 3, p. 190.
27. *Bid Me to Live*, p. 46.
28. *Bid Me to Live*, pp. 58–9.

29. Harriet Monroe, 'Refuge from War', *Poetry*, vol. 12 (April 1918) no. 1, pp. 44–6.
30. *The Letters of D. H. Lawrence*, Boulton (Cambridge, 1984) p. 233, D.H.L. to C. Gray, 18 April 1918.
31. R.A. to Cournos, 6 April 1918 (Harvard).
32. H.D. to Cournos, ? July 1918 (Harvard).
33. R.A. to F. S. Flint, 7 July 1918 (Texas).
34. Kittredge, p. 154.
35. R.A. to H.D., undated (Yale).
36. R.A. to F. S. Flint, 27 October 1918 (Texas).
37. *Complete Poems*, p. 95.
38. *The Letters of D. H. Lawrence* (Boulton) vol. III (28 December 1918) pp. 313–4, Lawrence to Amy Lowell.
39. *Letters of D. H. Lawrence*, (Boulton) (Cambridge) vol. III (16 December 1918) p. 308, Lawrence to Selina Yorke.
40. *Bid Me to Live*, p. 81.
41. H.D., *Collected Poems 1912–1944* (New York, 1983). Introduction, p. xix.
42. Forrest Reid (ed.), *Pound/Joyce: The Letters of Ezra Pound to James Joyce* (New York, 1970) pp. 145–6.

CHAPTER 6. AFTERMATHS, 1919–20

1. *Life for Life's Sake*, p. 225.
2. H.D. to Conrad Aiken, 26 August 1933 (Yale).
3. *Life for Life's Sake*, p. 195.
4. Gates, *The Poetry of Richard Aldington*, p. 50.
5. R.A. to Lawrence Clark Powell, 12 January 1949 (UCLA).
6. *Intimate Portrait*, p. 163.
7. R.A. to Amy Lowell, 31 March 1919 (Harvard).
8. *All Men Are Enemies*, pp. 127–34.
9. The year 1919 is given by Valerie Eliot in *The Waste Land: A Facsimile* (New York, 1971) p. xvii. This date is accepted by Fred. D. Crawford in his useful chapter on Aldington in *Mixing Memory and Desire: The Wasteland and British Novels* (University Park, 1982).
10. *Life for Life's Sake*, p. 269.
11. 'Books of the Fortnight', *Dial*, vol. 66 (31 May 1919) no. 791, p. 576.
12. Marjorie Allen Seiffert, 'Soldier and Lover', *Poetry*, vol. XIV (September 1919) no. 6, pp. 338–41.
13. *American Review of Reviews*, vol. 60 (October 1919) no. 4, p. 446.
14. William Carlos Williams, 'Four Foreigners', *Little Review*, vol. VI (September 1919) no. 5, pp. 36–9.
15. R.A. to Harriet Monroe, 14 October 1919 (Chicago).
16. R.A. to Harriet Monroe, 1 April 1920 (Chicago).
17. Aldington, 'The Disciples of Gertrude Stein', *Poetry*, vol. XVII (October 1920) no. 1, pp. 35–40.
18. Aldington, 'English and American', *Poetry*, vol. XVI (April 1920) no. 2, pp. 94–8.

19. R.A. to Amy Lowell, 17 June 1920 (Harvard) *TLS*, 6 May 1920, pp. 277–8.
20. R.A. to Amy Lowell, 17 June 1920 (Harvard).
21. R.A. to Harold Monro, 7 July 1920 (UCLA). The lines are quoted from Eliot's poem, 'Mr. Eliot's Sunday Morning Service'.
22. Norman T. Gates, 'Richard Aldington's "Personal Notes on Poetry"', *Texas Quarterly*, vol. XVII (Spring 1970) pp. 107–13.
23. Aldington, 'The Walk', first published in Norman T. Gates, 'Richard Aldington and F. S. Flint: Poets' Dialogue,' *Papers on Language and Literature*, vol. 8 (Winter 1972) no. 1, pp. 64–5.
24. H.D. to F. S. Flint, 21 May 1920. Quoted from Pondrom, pp. 585–6.
25. Aldington, review of F. S. Flint, *Otherworld*, *Poetry*, vol. XVII (October 1920) no. 1, pp. 44–7.
26. R.A. to Edouard Dujardin, 21 June 1920 (SUNY, Buffalo).
27. R.A. to Harold Monro, 11 June 1921 (UCLA). *The Chapbook: A Monthly Miscellany* was published from Monro's Poetry Bookshop.
28. R.A. to Harold Monro, ? before 20 August 1921 (UCLA).

CHAPTER 7. MALTHOUSE COTTAGE: WORKING AT THE WRITER'S TRADE, 1921–25

1. *Letters of D. H. Lawrence* (Boulton) vol. 3 (1916–21) p. 183.
2. Lawrence, *Aaron's Rod* (New York, 1922) pp. 33–4.
3. Cyril Beaumont, *Bookseller at the Ballet* (London, 1975) p. 184.
4. R.A. to Amy Lowell, 26 August 1921 (Harvard).
5. *Life for Life's Sake*, pp. 262–3.
6. 'Sir Pious', *CP*, p. 180; 'A Garden Homily', *CP*, p. 181; 'Go Tell the Shepherd's Star', *CP*, p. 182. The first of these, part of 'Songs for Puritans', was among the poems rejected by *Poetry* in October 1922.
7. R.A. to Untermeyer, 19 February 1923 (Indiana).
8. *Complete Poems*, p. 156.
9. Aldington, 'The Art of Poetry', *Fortnightly Review*, vol. CXIII (January 1923) pp. 116–27.
10. *Literary Studies and Reviews* (London, 1924) p. 191.
11. *Literary Studies and Reviews*, pp. 146–7.
12. F. S. Flint, review, *Criterion*, vol. III (October 1924) no. 9, p. 140.
13. Richard Aldington, *Voltaire* (London, 1925) p. 237.
14. *Nation and Atheneum*, 6 March 1926, p. 780.
15. Alyse Gregory, *Dial*, vol. LXXXI (1926) pp. 438–9.
16. *New Statesman*, vol. 26 (6 February 1926) no. 667, pp. 520, 522.
17. R.A. to Herbert Read, 3 September 1924 (Victoria).
18. R.A. to Herbert Read, 23 December 1924 (Victoria).
19. Richard Aldington, *A Fool i' the Forest* (London, 1924) Preface.
20. Hughes, *Imagism and the Imagists*, pp. 100–6; Smith, pp. 79–86.
21. Robin Ancrum, 'A Fool i' the Forest: A Critical Edition' (M.A. Dissertation, University of Victoria, 1973). The passage derives from a chorus in Aristophanes' 'The Knights'.
22. R.A. to Herbert Read, 'King Charles the Martyr's Day', 1927.

338 Notes

23. Ancrum, p. 188.
24. *Life for Life's Sake*, pp. 293–4.
25. R.A. to Amy Lowell, 2 March 1925 (Harvard).
26. *New York Times*, 10 May 1925, p. 7.
27. Paul Rosenfeld, *By Way of Art* (New York, 1928) pp. 245–8.
28. 'A Letter from Richard Aldington', *This Quarter*, vol. I (1925) no. 2, pp. 311–15.
29. R.A. to Harold Monro, 14 July 1925 (UCLA).

CHAPTER 8. MALTHOUSE COTTAGE; ELIOT, 1919–27

1. T. S. Eliot, 'Reflections on Vers Libre', *New Statesman*, 3 March 1917, pp. 518–19.
2. T. S. Eliot, 'Ezra Pound His Metric and Poetry', see fn. V. 12.
3. R.A. to T. S. Eliot, 18 July 1919 (Harvard) (This is one of a group of nine letters in the Houghton Library.) In giving permission to Selwyn Kittredge to make use of these letters in his Ph.D. thesis, Eliot wrote: 'I would be very glad if these letters were made use of, as they show Aldington at his best, as when I knew him'. Kittredge, p. 218 (no date cited. 1964?).
4. Norman T. Gates, 'A Chronology of Aldington's Addresses', in *A Checklist of the Letters of Richard Aldington*, does not include this address for 1919, or the fact that in March 1919 Aldington wrote letters as from 52 Doughty Street.
5. R.A. to T. S. Eliot, 'Tues., 23rd' [September 1919?] (Harvard).
6. R.A. to T. S. Eliot, 11 June 1920 (Harvard).
7. Glenn Hughes, *Imagism and the Imagists*, p. 72.
8. Eliot, 'Reflections on Vers Libre', p. 518.
9. T. S. Eliot, 'The Borderline of Prose', *New Statesman*, 19 May 1917, p. 158.
10. 'Poetry in Prose' *Chapbook: A Monthly Miscellany*, no. 22 (April 1921) p. 17.
11. R.A. to Amy Lowell, 7 April 1921 (Harvard).
12. R.A. to T. S. Eliot, 11 November 1920 (Harvard).
13. Richard Aldington, 'The Sacred Wood', *Today*, vol. VIII (September 1921) no. 47, pp. 191–3.
14. Valerie Eliot (ed.) T. S. Eliot, *The Waste Land: A Facsimile and Transcripts of the Original Drafts Including the Annotations of Ezra Pound* (London, 1971) p. xx.
15. T. S. Eliot to R.A. , 16 September 1921 (Texas).
16. T. S. Eliot to R.A. c. 4 October 1921 (*Facsimile*, p. xxi).
17. T. S. Eliot to R.A. c. 11 October 1921 (*Facsimile*, p. xxi).
18. R.A. to Holbrook Jackson, 7 September 1921 (SUNYAB).
19. R.A. to Holbrook Jackson, 5 October 1921 (SUNYAB).
20. R.A. to Amy Lowell, 27 September 1921 (Harvard).
21. T. S. Eliot to R.A., possibly 21 October 1921 (Texas).
22. T. S. Eliot, 'Ulysses, Order and Myth', *Dial* (November 1923); no. 75,

	Aldington, 'The Influence of Mr. James Joyce', *English Review*, vol. XXXII (April 1921), pp. 333–41.
23.	Margaret Anderson, *My Thirty Years War* (New York, 1970) p. 170.
24.	Richard Ellman, *James Joyce* (London, New York and Toronto, 1965) p. 523.
25.	James Joyce to Harriet Shaw Weaver, *Letters*, vol. III (London and New York, 1966) p. 69.
26.	R.A. to H.D., 4 July 1918 (Yale).
27.	Selwyn Kittredge, 'Richard Aldington's Challenge to T. S. Eliot: The Background of their James Joyce controversy', *James Joyce Quarterly*, vol. 10 (Spring 1973) no. 3, pp. 339–41.
28.	Richard Aldington 'The Poet and Modern Life', *Poetry*, vol. XVIII (May 1921) no. 2, pp. 99–100.
29.	Richard Aldington, 'The Poetry of T. S. Eliot', *Outlook*, (London), vol. 49 (January 1922) no. 7, pp. 12–13.
30.	R.A. to T. Sturge Moore, 11 January 1922 (Indiana).
31.	Ezra Pound to R.A., undated (Texas).
32.	T. S. Eliot to R.A., 17 May 1922 (Texas).
33.	See, for example, *Literary Lifelines*, p. 187.
34.	Anne Olivier Bell (ed.), *The Diary of Virginia Woolf: Vol. II: 1920–1924*, (London, 1978) pp. 325–6.
35.	Dorothy Yorke to Selwyn Kittredge, 16 August 1963. Quoted in Kittredge, p. 222.
36.	*Chapbook*, no. 29 (September 1922) pp. 5–12.
37.	Herbert Read, 'The Nature of Metaphysical Poetry', *Criterion*, vol. I (April 1923) no. 3, pp. 246–66.
38.	*Life for Life's Sake*, p. 266.
39.	Fred. D. Crawford, *Mixing Memory and Desire: The Waste Land and British Novels* (University Park, Pa., 1982) ch. I.
40.	Richard Aldington, 'François Villon', *Criterion*, vol. IV (April 1925) no. 2, pp. 376–8; Humbert Wolfe's review is on pp. 459–63.
41.	R.A. to Herbert Read, 23 June 1925 (MacPherson Library, University of Victoria).
42.	'Richard Aldington's Letters to Herbert Read', edited and introduced by David S. Thatcher, *Malahat Review*, vol. 15 (1970) pp. 5–44. See pp. 6–7.
43.	Thatcher, p. 7.
44.	R.A. to Glenn Hughes, 26 November 1925.
45.	Herbert Read to R.A., 22 December 1925.
46.	R.A. to Herbert Read, 28 January 1926.
47.	See issues of the *Criterion* for 1926–27.
48.	Possibly Aldington may have circulated among these people, in any case. On 27 July 1927 Mary Campbell wrote to William Plomer that she had recently met Aldington, along with the Woolfs, at Long Barn, the home of Vita Sackville-West and Harold Nicholson. (See Peter Alexander, *Roy Campbell: A Critical Biography* (London, 1982) p. 80. On the other hand, Virginia Woolf wrote to T. S. Eliot just a month later, on 24 August 1927: 'Aldington I know nothing about, so must let that thrust of yours remain unmet; but I think he belongs to the

Murry world, where dog eats dog'. *A Change of Perspective: The Letters of Virginia Woolf 1923–1928* (London, 1977) p. 413.
49. Dated simply 'Wednesday' and 'Friday', the letters in question were written in the second half of August 1927 (see above note).
50. T. S. Eliot to R.A., 24 October 1927 (Texas).
51. Richard Aldington, 'Mr. Eliot on Seneca', *Nation*, vol. XLII, 29 October 1927, no. 4, p. 159.
52. T. S. Eliot, 'Seneca in Elizabethan Translation', *Selected Essays* (London, 3rd ed., 1951) pp. 65–105.

CHAPTER 9. MALTHOUSE COTTAGE: THE LATE 1920s, 1926–28

1. R.A. to Crosby Gaige, 18 May 1926 (Yale).
2. *Life for Life's Sake*, p. 300.
3. *All Men Are Enemies*, p. 323.
4. *All Men Are Enemies*, p. 325.
5. *All Men Are Enemies*, p. 326.
6. *All Men Are Enemies*. p. 338.
7. *All Men Are Enemies*, p. 340.
8. *Life for Life's Sake*, pp. 300–1.
9. *Life for Life's Sake*, p. 302.
10. Harry T. Moore (ed.), *The Collected Letters of D. H. Lawrence* (London, 1962) vol. 2, p. 901.
11. D. H. Lawrence, *Etruscan Places* (London, 1932).
12. Richard Aldington, *D. H. Lawrence: An Indiscretion* (Seattle, 1927).
13. *Life for Life's Sake*, pp. 306–7.
14. Richard Aldington, *Portrait of a Genius, But . . .* (London, 1951), pp. 319–20; Leo Hamalian, *D. H. Lawrence in Italy* (New York, 1982) pp. 153–4.
15. *Death of a Hero* (1984), pp. 124–5.
16. R.A. to Herbert Read, 29 November 1926 (Victoria).
17. R.A. to Herbert Read, 13 December 1926 (Victoria).
18. *The Exile* (Paris) (Spring 1927) no. 1.
19. *The Collected Letters of D. H. Lawrence* (Moore), vol. 2 (24 May 1927) pp. 978–9.
20. T. S. Eliot to R.A., [?] March 1928 (Texas).
21. Ezra Pound to R.A., 14 January 1928 (Yale).
22. Ezra Pound to R.A., 12 August 1928 (Yale).
23. Nehls, vol. III, p. 235.
24. *Intimate Portrait*, p. 119.
25. R.A. to Glenn Hughes, 31 August 1928 (Texas).
26. Kittredge, p. 317.
27. *Life for Life's Sake*, p. 312.
28. *Life for Life's Sake*, p. 319.
29. Richard Church, *The Voyage Home* (London, 1964) pp. 72–6; *Intimate Portrait*, pp. 12–16.
30. Church, p. 72.
31. Kittredge, pp. 313–4.

CHAPTER 10. PORT-CROS AND AFTER, 1928–29

1. See R.A. to H.D., 14 April 1929 (Yale), where he says: 'Brigit wrote me in 1926 to ask for assistance after the Deighton collapse'. Eliot, in an undated letter early in 1926, expressed doubts that Brigit was capable of contributing a volume to the Routledge Translation Series.
2. R.A. to Ezra Pound, 30 September 1928 (Yale).
3. Nancy Cunard, *These Were the Hours*, p. 52.
4. R.A. to Alec Randall, 13 October 1928 (British Library).
5. *Life for Life's Sake*, pp. 329–30.
6. *Life for Life's Sake*, p. 332; 'Nancy Cunard tells me that George Moore complained that he could not read my novel, because it begins at the end and is all mixed up in time. I said: Ask him if he has ever analysed a Greek tragedy. It is remarkable that only one reviewer, and then an American in some unheard of town, spotted the fact that the form of the Hero is shamelessly cribbed from Euripides'. R.A. to Charles Prentice, 26 March 1930 (Reading).
7. *Life for Life's Sake*, p. 333.
8. *My Friends When Young*, p. 137.
9. *My Friends When Young*, pp. 101–2.
10. *Pass. Prod.*, p. 193, fn. 18.
11. Kittredge, p. 317.
12. R.A. to H.D., 20 March 1929 (Yale-Pearson).
13. D. H. Lawrence to Aldous Huxley, 28 October 1928, *The Collected Letters of D. H. Lawrence* (Moore), vol. 2, p. 1096.
14. Moore, *A Priest of Love*, p. 576.
15. *The Collected Letters of D. H. Lawrence* (Moore) vol. 2, p. 1117.
16. R.A. to Glenn Hughes, 30 November 1928 (Texas).
17. Chisholm, *Nancy Cunard*, p. 127.
18. *My Friends When Young*, p. 117.
19. *Pinorman*, (London, 1954) p. 87.
20. Kittredge, pp. 259–62. (The H.D.-Cournos correspondence is in the Houghton Library, Harvard).
21. This photograph is included in Janice Robinson's book as *circa* 1920, but is probably later.
22. R.A. to Brigit Patmore, 16 May 1929 (Texas).
23. R.A. to Crosby Gaige, 9 June 1929 (Yale).
24. R.A. to H.D., 11 June 1929 (Yale-Pearson).
25. H. G. Wells to R.A., 29 September 1929 (Carbondale). Bennett's review is mentioned in *Life for Life's Sake* (p. 344) and a copy was sent to H.D. on 12 September 1929.
26. George Orwell, *Collected Essays, Journals and Letters* (Harmondsworth, 1970) vol. 3, p. 261. The review was in the *New English Weekly*, 20 September 1936.
27. R.A. to H.D., 29 March 1929 and 3 April 1929 (Yale-Pearson).
28. *Death of a Hero* (London, 1984 edition) p.x.
29. Kittredge, p. 339.
30. W. C. Frierson, *The English Novel in Transition 1885–1940* (London, 1940) p. 290.

31. *Heroes' Twilight*, p. 183.
32. Kittredge, p. 325.
33. *Death of a Hero*, p. 46.
34. *Death of a Hero*, p. 119.
35. R.A. to H.D., 14 May 1929 (Yale-Pearson).
36. *Death of a Hero*, p. 127.
37. *Death of a Hero*, p. 243.
38. *Death of a Hero*, p. 274.
39. *Death of a Hero*, p. 296.
40. *Death of a Hero*, p. 329.
41. *Death of a Hero*, p. 436.
42. Jon Silkin, *Out of Battle: The Poetry of the Great War* (London, 1972) p. 187.
43. Robert Wohl, *The Generation of 1914* (Harvard, 1979) p. 107.
44. Andrew Rutherford, *The Literature of War* (London, 1978) pp. 88–91; A. C. Ward, in a near-contemporary critique in *The Nineteen-Twenties: Literature and Ideas in the Post-War Decade* (London, 1933) sees as the central theme of *Death of a Hero*, 'that the war had been fatal to a whole generation of youth by inflicting death either morally or spiritually, or both, even when it had spared the fighters' bodies'. (p. 89).
45. R.A. to Herbert Read, 25 July 1929 (Victoria).
46. *Intimate Portrait*, p. 129.
47. *Mixing Memory and Desire*, pp. 10–13.

CHAPTER 11. A CAREER AS A NOVELIST, 1929–31

1. R.A. to John Cournos.
2. Henri Davray (1873–1944), translator of Oscar Wilde, editor and critic.
3. Aldington, *All Men Are Enemies* (London, 1933) p.375.
4. *All Men Are Enemies*, p. 378.
5. Harold Monro, review of Aldington *Collected Poems*, *Criterion*, vol. IX (1929–30) pp. 518–22.
6. James Hanley (b.1901). Novelist and poet, whose chief work is *The Furys* (1935). Aldington wrote introductions for two of Hanley's publications, *The Last Voyage* (London 1931) and *The German Prisoner* (London 1933).
7. Deirdre Bair, *Samuel Beckett: A Biography* (New York, 1978) p. 96.
8. *Intimate Portrait*, p. 3.
9. Reprinted in Gates, *Poems of Richard Aldington*, pp. 275–6.
10. R.A. to Brigit Patmore, dated '[Hotel] Select. Tuesday' (early 1930).
11. Miriam J. Benkovitz, 'Nine for Reeves: Letters from Richard Aldington', *BNYPL*, vol. 69 (1965) pp. 349–74, esp. pp. 351–3.
12. Two reviewers who make this point are Richard Church in the *Spectator* (3 May 1930, p. 746) and the *TLS* reviewer (23 May 1930, p. 428).
13. *Sunday Referee*, 15 and 22 June 1930; included in *Selected Writings of Richard Aldington 1928–1960*, edited by Alister Kershaw (Carbondale, 1970) pp. 24–31.

14. Wyndham Lewis, *Satire and Fiction* (London, 1930).
15. Huxley invited Aldington to visit him at Sanary and also expressed admiration for his Lawrence booklet.
16. Louise Morgan, 'Writing a Best-Seller in Seven Weeks', *Everyman*, vol. IV (1930–31) pp. 101–2.
17. Sidney Schiff (1868–1944) wrote fiction under the pen-name Stephen Hudson. Works collected under the title *A True Story* (London, 1965).
18. R.A. to Sidney Schiff, 16 October 1930 (British Library).
19. Kittredge, pp. 364–5, cites contemporary reviews from the *Spectator*, *Nation* and *New Republic*.
20. *Pinorman*, pp. 14–18.
21. Guiseppe Orioli, *Adventures of a Bookseller* (Florence, 1937).
22. Mark Holloway, *Norman Douglas* (London, 1976) p. 386. Charles Prentice of Chattos wrote to R.A. on 31 January 1931: 'Frieda certainly owes you a lot, for without your help Frere would not have been able to put this through'. (Carbondale).
23. Norman Douglas, *Paneros: Some Words on Aphrodisiacs and the Like* (London, 1931).
24. *Pinorman*, p. 24.
25. Reviewing the 1968 reprint of *Life for Life's Sake*, Cyril Connolly draws attention to two versions of an incident in which Douglas called for a small press edition of Athaneus. In *Life for Life's Sake* Douglas is recorded as calling for 'an edition of Athaneus "with plenty of notes"' (first edition, pp. 367–8). Aldington mentions that a scholarly edition is being prepared by a Harvard professor and observes that Douglas writes this in a black notebook. In *Pinorman*, Douglas is charged with, astonishingly and ridiculously, suggesting that the small press publish 'a complete Athaneus with a translation and plenty of notes . . . ' (p. 74), whereas the Loeb edition of Athaneus, in print in 1954, consists of seven 400-page volumes.
26. *Soft Answers* (London, 1932) p. 245.
27. *Intimate Portrait*, pp. 24–5.
28. *Soft Answwwers*, p. 189.
29. *Soft Answers*, p. 206.
30. 'Nine for Reeves', p. 365.
31. Michael B. Thompson, 'Richard Aldington and T. S. Eliot', *Yeats Eliot Review*, vol. 6 (1979) no. 1, pp. 3–9.
32. *Ezra Pound and T. S. Eliot*, p. 13.
33. Ibid., p. 16.
34. Ibid., pp. 17–18.
35. Ibid., p. 19.
36. Quoted from *Richard Aldington: Selected Critical Writings 1928–1960*, pp. 19–20.
37. 'Nine for Reeves', p. 365.

CHAPTER 12. 1931–33

1. Note, with covering letter to 'Dear Miss Leonard', dated 20 June 1931—Prentice Papers (Ms. 2444 Box 3190. University of Reading.)
2. R.A. to Schiff, 26 June 1931.

3. *This Quarter*, vol. iv (July-September 1931) no. 1.
4. *Published in Paris*, pp. 163–4.
5. D. H. Lawrence, *Apocalypse*, with introduction by R.A. (London, 1932).
6. R.A. to Slonimsky, 8 September 1931.
7. *Intimate Portrait*, p. 147.
8. 'Nine for Reeves', p. 368. 17 February 1932.
9. *Pinorman*, pp. 102–3; Guiseppe Orioli, *Moving Along* (London, 1934) p. 57.
10. *Pinorman*, p. 90.
11. *Life for Life's Sake*, p. 382.
12. Pierre de Bourdelle, Abbé de Brantôme (d. 1614) is author of *Vies des Dames Galantes*.
13. R.A. to Sidney Schiff, 6 August 1931. (British Library).
14. Jeffrey Meyers, *The Enemy: A Biography of Wyndham Lewis* (London, 1982) p. 159.
15. R.A. to Schiff, 19 January 1933. This remark about the 'poem of touch' is interesting for other reasons. Writing to Cournos that February, Aldington, in ebullient mood, said that Brigit, too, was active and 'has done a lovely little travel book which is now travelling on to publishers'. This is certainly the work referred to by Derek Patmore as 'a personal travel book called *A Diary of Touch*' of which Patmore said 'there is no doubt that Richard used many of [her] ideas in his new novel'.
16. R.A. to Herbert Read, 14 January 1933 (Victoria).
17. *All Men Are Enemies*, p. 55; American edn. p. 65. Norman Douglas apparently thought Henry Scrope was modelled on him. see *Pinorman*, p. 186.
18. *All Men Are Enemies*, pp. 279–80; American, pp. 325–6.
19. *All Men Are Enemies*, p. 248; American, p. 287.
20. *All Men Are Enemies*, p. 334; American, p. 388.
21. Unsigned *TLS* review, 2 March 1932.
22. Louise Morgan, *Everyman*, March 1933.

CHAPTER 13. 1933–36

1. W. K. Rose (ed.) *The Letters of Wyndham Lewis* (London, 1963) p. 217.
2. R. P. Blackmur, 'Richard Aldington', *Nation*, vol. 138 (30 May 1934) no. 3595, p. 625.
3. 'A Place of Young Pines', *Complete Poems*, p. 331.
4. John Wheelwright, 'A Poet of Three Persons', *Poetry*, vol. 45 (October 1934) no. 1, pp. 47–50; Gates, *The Poetry of Richard Aldington*, p. 100.
5. Guiseppe Orioli to R.A., 7 March 1934; *Pinorman*, p. 167.
6. *Life for Life's Sake*, p. 396.
7. Aldington, *Women Must Work* (London, 1934) p. 142.
8. *Women Must Work*, p. 382.
9. *Life Quest* (London and New York, 1935) 'Authors Note'.
10. The phrase is D. H. Lawrence's. See Aldington's introduction to

Notes 345

Apocalypse (London, 1932) p. xli; also *Portrait of a Genius, But* . . . , p. 354; Gates, *Poems of Richard Aldington,* p. 120 n.
11. Aldington, *Artifex: Sketches and Ideas* (London, 1935); *The Spirit of Place. An Anthology Compiled from the Prose of D. H. Lawrence* (London, 1935).
12. *Artifex,* pp. 56–7.
13. *Life for Life's Sake,* p. 407.
14. *My Friends When Young,* p. 41.
15. Ivan Anisimov (1899–1966). Corresponding Member of the Academy of Science of the USSR from 1960; member of the Communist Party of the Soviet Union from 1939; Director of the Gorky Institute of World Literature, 1952–1966.
16. *Intimate Portrait,* p. 151.
17. Douglas Goldring, *Odd Man Out* (London, 1935) pp. 224, 313–4.
18. "Beachcomber" was the pseudonym of J. B. Morton (1893–1979), journalist and author.
19. Alec Waugh, *My Brother Evelyn and Other Profiles* (London, 1967) pp. 60–72.
20. R.A. to Eric Warman, 22 April 1936.
21. *Life for Life's Sake,* p. 400.
22. *My Friends When Young,* p. 32.
23. William Soskin, review of *Very Heaven, New York Herald Tribune Book Review,* March 1937; R.A. to Eric Warman, 14 May 1937.

CHAPTER 14. 1937–38

1. H.D. *Tribute to Freud* (New York, 1956).
2. R.A. to H.D. 15 January 1937 (Yale); Guest, pp. 240–2.
3. H.D. to Frances Gregg, 10 February [1937] (Yale-Pearson).
4. *Pinorman,* p. 112.
5. Undated note to the present writer July 1983.
6. Carbondale, File 68/11/15, MS. p. 2.
7. *Very Heaven,* p. 368.
8. *Artifex,* pp. 162–3.
9. Ralph Bates (b. 1899) is best known as author of *The Olive Field* (1936), a novel of the Spanish Civil War.
10. *Published in Paris* (Yonkers, NY, 1975) pp. 376–7.
11. H.D. to Ezra Pound, 'Friday' [?1937] (Yale).
12. Guest, pp. 240–1.
13. 'Nine of his poems, translated by Mikhail Zenkevich, appeared in *An Anthology of New English Poetry*, published by the Leningrad branch of the Goslitizdat' [in 1937]. *Intimate Portrait*, p. 153.
14. *Intimate Portrait,* p. 153.
15. R.A. to Eric Warman, 19 September 1936.
16. Mikhail Urnov, *Intimate Portrait*, pp. 153–4 (D. G. Zhantieva, in *Soviet Literature* (1962) no. 12).
17. V. M. Moldavsky, 'Richard Aldington in Leningrad', *Neva* (1963) no. 5, pp. 164–7. English translation by Robert J. Winter.

18. Aldington, *Seven Against Reeves* (London, 1935) p. 305.
19. R.A. to Eric Warman, 19 March 1938.
20. Guest, p. 242.
21. C. P. Snow, *Richard Aldington: An Appreciation* (London, 1938) republished in *Intimate Portrait*.
22. Herbert Palmer, *Post-Victorian Poetry* (London, 1938) p. 328.
23. Kirker Quinn 'Aldington 1938', *Poetry*, vol. 52 (June 1938) no. 3, pp. 160–4.
24. Gates, *Poems of Richard Aldington*, pp. 111–12.
25. Richard E. Smith, pp. 98–101.
26. R.A. to Leonard Bacon, 16 November 1938.
27. *Pinorman*, p. 169.

CHAPTER 15. FAREWELL TO EUROPE, 1939–40

1. R.A. to Slonimsky, 12 May 1939.
2. Basil Dean (1888–1978). English actor, dramatist and theatre director; Second World War Director of ENSA (Entertainments National Service Association; author of *The Theatre at War* (1955).
3. R.A. to J. Ralph Pinker, 3 October 1939 (Carbondale).
4. Mary Colum, 'The Limits of a Skillful Talent', *Forum*, vol. CII (November 1939) p. 228.
5. Aldington, 'Farewell to Europe', *Atlantic Monthly*, vol. CLXVI, (July-December 1940): pp. 375–96 (September); pp. 509–30 (October); pp. 643–64 (November); pp. 773–96 (December).
6. Irwin Edman, *Philosopher's Holiday* (New York, 1938).
7. *Death of a Hero* (1984), p. 222.
8. *Death of a Hero* (1984), p. 186.
9. *Death of a Hero* (1984), p. 325.
10. Richard E. Smith, p. 125.
11. C. P. Snow, *Richard Aldington: An Appreciation*, p. 12.
12. *Very Heaven*, pp. 368–9.
13. *Very Heaven*, p. 375.
14. *Rejected Guest*, p. 378.
15. *Rejected Guest*, p. 288.
16. R.A. to Slonimsky, 22 December 1939.
17. *Ezra Pound and T. S. Eliot: A Lecture* (1954) and *A. E. Housman and W. B. Yeats: A Lecture*, both published by the Peacocks Press, Hurst, Berkshire.
18. R.A. to Ralph Guinzburg, 3 March 1940.
19. Dahlberg long afterwards complained to Selwyn Kittredge that Aldington 'cast away many' of Melville's poems. In fact, he printed 11 from an original selection of 17. Edward Dahlberg to Selwyn Kittredge, 22 May 1964 (Kittredge estate).

CHAPTER 16. 1941–42

1. Kittredge, p. 474.

2. R.A. to Robin Douglas, 7 April 1941 (UCLA).
3. Holloway, p. 450.
4. R.A. to E. Dahlberg, 16 June 1956 (Texas).
5. R.A. to Slonimsky, 30 June 1941 (Carbondale).
6. *Letters of Aldous Huxley* (London, 1969) pp. 421–2.
7. R.A. to Slonimsky, 21 September 1941.
8. R.A. to Warman, 30 December 1942 (Carbondale).

CHAPTER 17. 1943–46

1. R.A. to Slonimsky, 10 February 1943 (Carbondale).
2. C. David Heymann, *Ezra Pound: The Last Rower* (New York, 1976) p. 134.
3. Treason Statute (Section I, Title 18, United States Code, 1940 Edition). Quoted in Heymann, p. 135.
4. R.A. to H.D., 11 November 1946 (Yale).
5. Tom Dardis, *Some Time in the Sun* (New York, 1976) p. 119.
6. R.A. to Leonard Bacon, 9 April 1944 (Yale).
7. Philip Zeigler, *Diana Cooper* (Harmondsworth, 1983) pp. 152–8.
8. R.A. to Marshall Best, 28 April 1942 (Viking).
9. R.A. to Marshall Best, 3 July 1943 (Viking).
10. Kittredge, p. 528.
11. Alec Waugh, *The Best Wine Last: An Autobiography Through The Years 1932–1969* (London, 1978) p. 173.
12. H.D., *The Walls Do Not Fall* (London and New York, 1944).
13. R.A. to Slonimsky, 13 September 1944 (Carbondale).
14. R.A. to Slonimsky, 15 April 1945 (Carbondale).
15. R.A. to Eric Warman, 25 August 1945 (Carbondale).
16. R.A. to Eric Warman, 5 July 1945 (Carbondale).
17. R.A. to Eric Warman, 7 October 1945 (Carbondale).
18. R.A. to Eric Warman, 7 July 1945 (Carbondale).
19. Unpublished notebook CARB. 68/10/6, p. 1, 15 April 1946.
20. Unpublished notebook, p. 26. 26 May 1946.
21. *Great French Romances: The Princess of Cleves* by Madame de la Fayette; *Manon Lescaut*, by the Abbé Prévost; *Dangerous Acquaintances* by Choderlos de Laclos; *The Duchesse de Langeais* by Honoré de Balzac. (London,1946). Translated by Richard Aldington.

CHAPTER 18. 1946–50

1. R.A. to Eric Warman, 1 September 1946 (Carbondale).
2. Richard Aldington, *Bilder* (Hamburg, 1947), 103 pp.
3. R.A. to H.D., 2 May 1947 (Yale).
4. R.A. to Al Manuel, 12 June 1947 (UCLA).
5. Peter Alexander, *Roy Campbell: A Critical Biography* (London, 1982), p. 217.
6. Richard Church, *The Voyage Out*, pp. 75–76.
7. R.A. to Al Manuel, 7 November 1948 (UCLA).

8. W. Denison Deasey, "Lunch at the Villa", *Bulletin*, December 23–30, 1980, pp. 177–180. According to Peter Alexander, Campbell did not meet Aldington until 1950. Deasey seems to have telescoped several articles.
9. Frieda Lawrence to R.A., 21 January 1949 (Carbondale).
10. *Intimate Portrait*, p. 167. A great admirer of T. E. Lawrence, Williamson was author of *Genius of Friendship: 'T. E. Lawrence'* (London, 1941).
11. RA to Kershaw, 22 January 1949.
12. Roy Campbell, "Richard Aldington, Happy Pagan", *Poetry Review*, April-May 1949; reprinted in *Intimate Portrait*, pp. 4–11.
13. R.A. to Arnold Gyde, 4 May 1950 (Heinemann).
14. R.A. to Leonard Bacon, [? July—September] 1949 (Yale).
15. Alec Waugh, *These I Would Choose: A Personal Anthology* (London, 1948).
16. R.A. to John Arlott, 30 November 1949 (Recipient).

CHAPTER 19. 1950–54

1. R.A. to Peter Russell, 5 January 1950 (SUNYAB).
2. R.A. to Arnold Gyde, 12 February 1950 (Heinemann).
3. R.A. to P. A. G. Aldington, 19 March 1946 (Carbondale).
4. R.A. to P. A. G. Aldington, 16 July 1949 (Carbondale).
5. R.A. to Alister Kershaw, 27 January 1950 (Carbondale).
6. R.A. to Alister Kershaw, 24 February 1950 (Carbondale).
7. R.A. to A. S. Frere, 16 April 1950 (Carbondale).
8. Moore reviewed *Portrait of a Genius, But . . .* in the *Saturday Review of Literature*. Aldington told Bacon on 16 May 1950 that he had not seen the review, but he labelled it 'unfavourable'.
9. Harry T. Moore, 'Poet to Vagabond to Legend', *Saturday Review of Literature*, 29 April 1950, p. 20.
10. *Portrait of a Genius, But . . .*, p. 317.
11. *Portrait of a Genius, But . . .*, p. 105.
12. *Portrait of a Genius, But . . .*, p. 174.
13. Roy Campbell to Peter Russell, June 1950 (details in Alexander, p. 219).
14. R.A. to David Garnett, 22 June 1950.
15. R.A. to Alister Kershaw, 24 March 1950 (Carbondale).
16. R.A. to Edward Dahlberg, 12 September 1950 (Texas).
17. R.A. to Alister Kershaw, 19 September 1951 (Carbondale).
18. R.A. to Minnie Slonimsky, 12 December 1951 (Carbondale).
19. R.A. to H.D, 15 February 1952 (Yale).
20. Bertrand Russell had talked about Lawrence on the BBC Third Programme in July; *Listener*, 17 July 1952; R.A. to Alan Bird, 15 August 1952, *Pass. Prod.*, pp. 52, 53 n. 1.
21. R. A to H.D., 17 January 1953 (Yale).
22. Nancy Cunard, *Time and Tide*, 17 April 1954.
23. Nancy Cunard, *Grand Man: Memories of Norman Douglas* (London, 1954).

24. Frank Swinnerton, *The Georgian Literary Scene* (New York, 1934) p. 158.
25. Ann Chisholm, *Nancy Cunard* (New York, 1979) p. 296.
26. Frieda Lawrence to R.A., 29 March 1954; *Frieda Lawrence and Her Circle*, p. 103.
27. The review never appeared.
28. Norman Douglas (ed.), *Venus in the Kitchen, or Love's Cookery Book* by Pilaff Bey, introduction by Graham Greene (New York, 1953).
29. Norman Douglas, *D. H. Lawrence and Maurice Magnus: A Plea for Better Manners* (Florence, 1925).
30. *Memoirs of the Foreign Legion* by M[aurice] M[agnus]. With an introduction by D. H. Lawrence (New York, 1925).
31. *Life for Life's Sake*, p. 376.
32. Norman Douglas, *Late Harvest* (London, 1946) pp. 52–3.
33. *Pinorman*, p. 62.
34. Compare Nancy Cunard, *Black Man and White Ladyship* (Paris, 1931) and *On the Herpetology of the Grand Duchy of Baden* (London, 1894).
35. R.A. to H.D, 15 July 1954 (Yale).
36. W. Somerset Maugham to R.A., 7 September 1954 (Carbondale).
37. R.A. to Alan Bird, 9 September 1954; *Pass. Prod.*, pp. 136–7.

CHAPTER 20. THE T. E. LAWRENCE AFFAIR, 1950–55

1. R.A. to Alister Kershaw, 2 January 1951 (Carbondale).
2. Benkovitz notes that some galleys with Hart's autograph notations are at the Humanities Research Center, Texas. *Pass. Prod.*, p. 118, fn. 15.
3. In effect, the libel was perceived to be the suggestion that Graves and Liddell Hart had recorded as fact stories about Lawrence which they knew to be untrue. Philip Knightley says that the lawyers for the Lawrence trustees were prompted to libel Collins and Aldington and thus to precipitate an action. See Knightley, 'Aldington's Enquiry Concerning T. E. Lawrence', *Texas Quarterly*, vol. XVI (Winter 1973) no. 4, pp. 98–105.
4. R.A. to Netta Aldington, 12 May 1954 (British Library).
5. Richard Aldington, *Lawrence l'imposteur: T. E. Lawrence, The Legend and the Man* (Paris, 1954).
6. R.A. to Alan Bird, 13 November 1953, *Pass. Prod.*, pp. 98–9.
7. Richard Church to R.A., 12 December 1954.
8. Knightley, p. 104.
9. T. E. Shaw [Lawrence] to Charlotte Shaw, 14 April 1927. British Museum Addl. MS. 45903, 4.
10. Robert Graves, *Lawrence and the Arabs* (London, 1927) pp. 24, 25.
11. Richard Aldington, *Lawrence of Arabia: A Biographical Enquiry* (New York, 1955) p. 107. Hereafter cited as *L. Ab.*
12. *L. Ab.*, p. 109.
13. T. E. Lawrence, *The Seven Pillars of Wisdom* (London, privately printed, 1926; New York, 1926). Hereafter cited as *Seven Pillars*.
14. *L. Ab.*, p. 109.

15. *L. Ab.*, pp. 132–3.
16. *L. Ab.*, p. 160.
17. *L. Ab.*, p. 186.
18. George Antonius, *The Arab Awakening* (London, 1938).
19. Antonius, p. 322; *L. Ab.*, p. 192.
20. General Sir A. P. Wavell, *Allenby: A Study in Greatness* (London, 1940) p. 193.
21. General Sir George Barrow, *The Fire of Life* (London, 1942) p. 215.
22. *L. Ab.*, p. 201.
23. *L. Ab.*, p. 206; *Seven Pillars*, ch. 80.
24. Philip Knightley and Colin Simpson, *The Secret Lives of Lawrence of Arabia* (London, 1969) p. 214; British Museum Addl. MS: 45903, 4.
25. Stephen E. Tabachnick, *T. E. Lawrence* (Boston, 1978) p. 64.
26. Jeffrey Meyers, *The Wounded Spirit: A Study of the Seven Pillars of Wisdom* (London, 1973) pp. 25–6.
27. Meyers, p. 26.
28. Tabachnick, p. 67.
29. *L. Ab.*, p. 285.
30. *L. Ab.*, p. 290.
31. L. Ab., p. 381.
32. *Home Letters of T. E. Lawrence and His Brothers* (New York, 1954) p. 355.
33. *L. Ab.*, p. 385. According to Liddell Hart, Amery later said that his reply was 'irrelevant' and Churchill was much more positive regarding the possibility of his having offered Lawrence the post. B. H. Liddell Hart, 'T. E. Lawrence, Aldington and the Truth', *London Magazine*, vol. 2A (April 1955) p. 70.
34. Details are contained in a letter of 2 January 1951 from Colin Mann to Aldington. (Mann was then Public Relations Officer of the Conservative Party).
35. On file in the Berg Collection, New York Public Library: letter from Marshal of the Royal Air Force Sir Arthur Harris to General Barrow; letter from Squadron-Leader G. F. Breese concerning Lawrence's [T. E. Shaw's] service at R.A.F. Uxbridge; extracts from Sir Arnold Wilson's negative review of Lawrence's *Revolt in the Desert*, which appeared in the Journal of the Central Asian Society (1927); a letter from the Australian Major General Sir George Rankin, and more.
36. Liddell Hart, 'T. E. Lawrence, Aldington and the Truth', pp. 67–75.
37. Broadcast June 1955. The book was Jean Béraud-Villars, *Le Colonel Lawrence ou la recherche de l'absolu* (Paris, 1955); an English version, translated by Peter Dawnay was published in London in 1958.
38. See fn. 10 above.
39. Robert Graves, "Lawrence Vindicated", *New Republic*, 21 March 1955, p. 16.
40. W. Denison Deasey, "Death of a Hero" *Australian Book Review*, February 1970, pp. 84–6.
41. R.A. to Alan Bird, 11 February 1953; *Pass. Prod.*, pp. 80–1.
42. Graham Hough, review of *Frieda Lawrence and Her Circle: Letters from, to, and about Frieda Lawrence* Harry T. Moore and Dale B. Montague (eds.) (London, 1981) *TLS*, 6 November 1981, p. 1290.

CHAPTER 21. 1954–57

1. Frédéric-Jacques Temple, a poet and broadcaster. Author of *Lawrence: l'oeuvre et la vie* (Paris, 1960) and editor of *Hommage à Roy Campbell* (Montpellier, 1958). A book of his poems, *Foghorn*, was published by the Capricorn Press, Santa Barbara in 1971, with an introduction by Lawrence Durrell.
2. R.A. to Alan Bird, 7 July 1955; *Pass. Prod.*, p. 187.
3. R.A. to Kershaw, 23 July 1957 (Carbondale).
4. R.A. to Alan Bird, 7 July 1955; *Pass. Prod.*, pp. 187–8.
5. R.A. to Herbert Read, 29 March 1956. According to this letter, the article was to appear in *Bibliophile* but it has not been traced. See Thatcher, p. 35.
6. R.A. to P. A. G. Aldington, 8 February 1956 (Carbondale).
7. R.A. to Edward Dahlberg, 8 June 1965 (Texas).
8. Charles De Fanti, *The Wages of Expectation* (New York, 1978) p. 197.
9. R.A. to Herbert Read, 10 August 1956 (Victoria).
10. R.A. to Herbert Read, 26 August 1956 (Victoria).
11. De Fanti, p. 200.
12. Herbert Read to R.A., 10 March 1957 (Victoria).
13. R.A. to Edward Nehls, 16 August 1958 (Texas); *Pass. Prod.*, p. 328.
14. *Pass. Prod.*, p. 234. Aldington told Bird that Penguin Books were planning to issue a further ten Lawrence titles, six with Aldington introductions. *Lady Chatterley's Lover* appeared in 1960, without such an introduction.
15. R.A. to P. A. G. Aldington, 17 August 1956, quoting Nehls (Carbondale).
16. Reacting to one of the few reviews, that in the *Listener* of 15 November 1956, Aldington wrote Alan Bird a long, sound paragraph on the art and integrity of reviewing. R.A. to Bird, 26 November 1956. *Pass. Prod.*, p. 251.
17. R.A. to H.D., 22 October 1956 (Yale).
18. R.A. to Alister Kershaw, 13 November 1956 (Carbondale).
19. Urnov, *Intimate Portrait*, p. 155.
20. Voltaire, A Dream in the Luxembourg, Death of a Hero, All Men Are Enemies, Portrait of a Genius, But . . . , Life Quest.
21. Ian S. MacNiven and Harry T. Moore (eds.) *Literary Lifelines, The Richard Aldington-Lawrence Durrell Correspondence* (New York: 1981) p. vii.
22. R.A. to Herbert Read, 12 March 1957 (Victoria).
23. R.A. to Alister Kershaw, 18 March 1957 (Victoria).
24. R.A. to Alec Randall, 10 April 1957 (Victoria).
25. *Literary Lifelines*, p. 22.
26. Lawrence Durrell to R.A., 1 May 1957 (TPs from Moore).
27. R.A. to Alec Randall, 25 June 1957 (Huntingdon).
28. R.A. to H.D., 24 May 1957 (Yale).
29. R.A. to P. A. G. Aldington, 24 June 1957 (Carbondale).
30. R.A. to Winifred Bryher, 16 June 1957 (Yale-Pearson).

CHAPTER 22. Maison Salle, 1957–59

1. Myra Buttle [Victor Purcell], *The Sweeniad* (New York, 1957; Welwyn Garden City, 1957).
2. Remy de Gourmont, 'The Horses of Diomedes'. English translation by C. Sartoris published in parts in the *New Freewoman*, October to December 1913 and in the *Egoist*, January to March 1914.
3. Patricia Hutchins, *James Joyce's World* (London,1957).
4. Patricia Hutchins, *Ezra Pound's Kensington: An Exploration 1885–1913* (London, 1965).
5. R.A. to Eric Warman, 29 January 1958 (Carbondale).
6. R.A. to P. A. G. Aldington, 8 February 1958 (Carbondale).
7. Horatio Bottomley (1860–1933). Journalist, financier and Member of Parliament. He was expelled from the House of Commons in 1922 after being convicted of fraud.
8. R.A. to Eric Warman, 22 March 1958 (Carbondale).
9. Aldington, review of *Selected Letters of D. H. Lawrence*, in Diana Trilling (ed.) *Saturday Review of Literature* (1 March 1958) p. 17.
10. Edward Nehls, *D. H. Lawrence: A Composite Biography* (Madison, Wisconsin, 1957, 1958, 1959), three volumes. Aldington wrote the introduction to Volume Three (1959).
11. Lawrence Durrell, *The Alexandria Quartet* (London, 1962), a one-volume edition.
12. R.A. to Edward Nehls, 13 July 1958.
13. *Intimate Portrait*, p. 80.
14. R.A. to Lawrence Durrell, 15 November 1958. *Le mot de Cambronne* is a euphemism for *merde*.
15. R.A. to Winifred Bryher, 21 November 1958 (Yale).
16. *Intimate Portrait*, p. 48.
17. R.A. to Winifred Bryher, 11 May 1959 (Yale).
18. R.A. to Bryher, 2 November 1959 (Yale). Aldington's reference to 'phosgene' (gas) is more specific than his usual references to his wartime sufferings. In her interview with the Lowenfels in 1964, Dorothy Yorke said, 'he had been gassed a little, but it hadn't done anything to him'—Benkovitz typescript, p. 5.
19. Francis Carco (1886–1958). French Novelist, critic and memoirist.
20. Antony Alpers, *The Life of Katherine Mansfield* (New York, 1980).
21. R.A. to H.D., 21 November 1958 (Yale).
22. R.A. to Lawrence Durrell, November 1958; *Literary Lifelines*, p. 64.
23. R.A. to Alec Randall, 2 December 1958 (British Library).
24. In an Italian translation by Mary de Rachewiltz.
25. R.A. to H.D., 3 June 1959 (Yale).
26. *Intimate Portrait*, pp. 78–79.
27. R.A. to H.D., 30 July 1959 (Yale).
28. R.A. to H.D., 7 September 1959 (Yale).

CHAPTER 23. 1959–61

1. Bair, *Beckett*, p. 512.

2. R.A. to Bryher, 10 November 1959 (Yale).
3. R.A. to Alan Bird, 17 November 1959; *Pass. Prod.*, p. 272.
4. Katherine Anne Porter, 'A Wreath for the Gamekeeper', *Encounter*, vol. 14 (February 1960) pp. 69–76.
5. Richard Aldington, 'A Wreath for Lawrence', *Encounter*, vol. 14 (April 1960) pp. 51–4.
6. *Encounter*, vol. 14 (May 1960) Letters, p. 85.
7. Paris: Seghers, 1960.
8. Mikhail Urnov to R.A., 28 January 1960.
9. R.A. to Pascal Covici, 20 February 1960 (Viking).
10. R.A. to Lawrence Durell, 7 March 1960; *Literary Lifelines*, p. 135.
11. R.A. to Harry T. Moore, 22 April 1960 (Carbondale).
12. R.A. to Harry T. Moore, 9 April 1960 (Carbondale).
13. Guest, p. 316.
14. R.A. to Alan Bird, 14 May 1960; *Pass. Prod.*
15. Vincent's angina: an ulcerative inflammation of the throat, caused by bacilli and often foul-smelling.
16. R.A. to Alan Bird, 18 November 1960; *Pass. Prod.*, p. 282.
17. *Literary Lifelines*, p. 176.
18. While supplying Aldington and others with funds, Bryher lived quite simply.
19. *Farewell to Memories* (Moscow, 1961).
20. R.A. to P. A. G. Aldington, 23 June 1961 (Carbondale).
21. *Intimate Portrait*, p. 25.
22. Antony Nutting, *Lawrence of Arabia: The Man and the Motive* (London, 1961).
23. *L. Ab.*, pp. 205–7.
24. Stanley Weintraub, *Private Shaw and Public Shaw: A Dual Portrait of Lawrence of Arabia and G.B.S.* (London, 1963).
25. Quoted by R.A. in a letter to Lawrence Durrell, 10 October 1961; *Literary Lifelines*, p. 190.
26. R.A. to Lawrence Durrell, 29 December 1961.

CHAPTER 24. 1962

1. *The World of Lawrence Durrell* (London and Carbondale, 1961).
2. R.A. to Harry T. Moore, 22 January 1962 (Carbondale).
3. R.A. to Harry T. Moore, 21 December 1961 (Carbondale).
4. R.A. to P. A. G. Aldington, 26 February 1962 (Carbondale).
5. R.A. to Margery Lyon Gilbert, March 1962 (Temple).
6. *Literary Lifelines*, p. 208.
7. R.A. to Eric Warman, 30 May 1962 (Carbondale).
8. John Pearson, in *Façades: Edith, Osbert and Sacheverell Sitwell* (London, 1978), describes Bryher as 'this tiny millionairess in her old blue beret' and gives several examples of her generosity in subsidising writers.
9. R.A. to Harry T. Moore, 19 May 1962 (Carbondale).
10. *Intimate Portrait*, p. 62. My account of this last trip of Aldington's is

much indebted to Norman T. Gates's 'Richard Aldington in Russia',*Texas Quarterly* (Summer 1978) pp. 35–57.
11. *Intimate Portrait*, p. 50.
12. V. M. Moldavsky, 'Richard Aldington in Leningrad', *Neva* (1963) no. 5, pp. 164–7. Translated into English by Robert J. Winter.
13. R.A. to Lawrence Durrell, 14 July 1962; *Literary Lifelines*, p. 217.
14. Konstantin Fedin (1892–1977). Novelist and short story writer, Secretary of the Soviet Writers Union 1959 to 1971, when he became chairman of its Administrative Board. Author of *The Desert* (1923), *Cities and Years* (1924) and *The Rape of Europe* (1933–35).
15. Baroness Moura Budberg. Translator of Russian fairy tales and of the biography *Chekov, 1860–1904*, by Sophie Laffitte.
16. For a time in the 1920s Budberg was Gorky's secretary and mistress. In the 1930s she had an affair with H. G. Wells. Gates, *The Poems of Richard Aldington*, p. 57, fn. 4.
17. *Intimate Portrait*, pp. 158–9.
18. Valentin Katayev (b. 1897). Satirical writer, who achieved fame with *Lonely White Sail* (1936) and subsequently wrote on themes of revolutionary heroism, as in *I am the Son of the Working People* (1937).
19. R.A. to John Gawsworth, 26 July 1962 (Texas).
20. R.A. to Lawrence Durrell, 26 July 1962; *Literary Lifelines*, pp. 220–1.
21. *Intimate Portrait*, p. 50.
22. Antony Curtis, *Sunday Telegraph*, 29 July 1962.
23. David Holloway, *Daily Telegraph*, 30 July 1962.
24. *Literary Gazette* (Moscow), 31 July 1962, p. 4.
25. T. S. Eliot to Selwyn Kittredge, 3 April 1964. Kittredge, p. 560.

Bibliography

Two published bibliographies of Aldington's work are:
Alister Kershaw, *A Bibliography of the Works of Richard Aldington from 1915 to 1948* (London: Quadrant Press, 1950).
'A Chronological Check List of the Books by Richard Aldington' prepared by Paul Schlueter. *In Richard Aldington: An Intimate Portrait*, pp. 175–86.
There is a bibliography in Russian and a useful checklist of selected articles by Aldington is included in Selwyn Kittredge's *The Literary Career of Richard Aldington*, pp. 581–5.

(i) Works by Richard Aldington

Images (1910–1915) (London: The Poetry Bookshop, 1915) *Images Old and New* (Boston: Four Seas, 1916).
The Poems of Anyte of Tegea (London: Egoist Press, 1915 and Cleveland: Clerk's Press, 1917). [Poets' Translation Series, no. 1.]
Latin Poems of the Renaissance (London: Egoist Press, 1915). [Poets' Translation Series, no. 4.]
The Little Demon, by Feodor Sologub (pseud. of Feodor Teternikov). [Translated by Richard Aldington and John Cournos.] (New York: Alfred A. Knopf, 1916).
The Garland of Months, by Folgore Da San Gemignano. (Cleveland: Clerk's Press, 1917). [Poets' Translation series, no. 5]
Reverie. A Little Book of Poems for H.D. (Cleveland: Clerk's Press, 1917).
The Love of Myrrhine and Konallis, and Other Prose Poems (Cleveland: Clerk's Press, 1917 and Chicago: Pascal Covici, 1926).
Images of War. A Book of Poems (Westminster: C. W. Beaumont, 1919; London: Allen & Unwin, 1919 [expanded ed.]; and Boston: Four Seas, 1921).
Images of Desire (London: Elkin Mathews, 1919).
Images (London: Egoist, 1919).
War and Love (1915–18) (Boston: Four Seas, 1919).
Greek Songs in the Manner of Anacreon (London: Egoist, 1920). [Poets' Translation Series, Second Set, no. 1.]
The Poems of Meleager of Gadara (London: Egoist, 1920).
Medallions in Clay (New York: Alfred A. Knopf, 1921). *Medallions* (London: Chatto & Windus, 1931).
The Good-Humoured Ladies, A Comedy by Carlo Goldini . . . . To Which is Prefix'd an Essay on Carlo Goldini by Arthur Symons (Westminster: C. W. Beaumont, 1922). [Translator]
French Comedies of the XVIIIth Century. Regnard: *The Residuary Legatee*; Lesage: *Turcaret, or the Financier*; Marivaux: *The Game of Love and Chance*; Destouches: *The Conceited Count*. (London: Routledge & Sons, n.d. [1923]; (New York: E. P. Dutton & Co, n.d. [1923]. [Broadway Translations.]

Voyages to the Moon and Sun, by Cyrano de Bergerac (London: Routledge & Sons, n.d. [1923]); (New York: Dutton, n.d. [1923]). [Broadway Translations.]

The Berkshire Kennet (London: Curwen Press, 1923).

Collected Poems, 1915–1923 (London: Allen & Unwin, 1923).

Exile and Other Poems (London: Allen & Unwin, 1923).

A Fool i' the Forest. A Phantasmagoria (London: Allen & Unwin, 1924).

Literary Studies and Reviews (London: Allen & Unwin, 1924).

Dangerous Acquaintances (Les Liaisons Dangereuses), by Choderlos de Laclos (London: Routledge & Sons, n.d. [1924]); (New York: Dutton, n.d. [1924]). [Broadway Translations.]

Sturly by Pierre Custot (London: Jonathan Cape, 1924); (Boston: Houghton Mifflin, 1924). [Translator]

The Mystery of the Nativity, translated from the Liégeois of the XVth Century (London: Allen & Unwin, 1924).

A Book of Characters From Theophrastus; Joseph Hall, Sir Thomas Overbury, Nicholas Breton, John Earle, Thomas Fuller, and other English Authors; Jean De La Bruyère, Vauvenargues, and Other French Authors (London: Routledge & Sons, n.d. [1924]); (New York: Dutton, n.d. [1924]). [Broadway Translations]

Voltaire (London: Routledge & Sons, 1925); (New York: Dutton, 1925).

French Studies and Reviews (London: Allen & Unwin, 1926); (New York: Dial Press, 1926).

The Fifteen Joys of Marriage, Ascribed to Antoine De La Sale, c. 1388–c. 1462 (London: Routledge & Sons, n.d. [1926]); (New York: Dutton, n.d. [1926]). [Broadway Translations.]

Candide and Other Romances, by Voltaire. (London: Routledge, n.d. [1927]); (New York: Dutton, n.d. [1927]). [Broadway Translations.]

Letters of Madame De Sevigné to Her Daughter and Her Friends (London: Routledge, 1927). [Translator]

Letters of Voltaire and Frederick the Great (London: Routledge, 1927); (New York: Brentano's, 1927). [Broadway Library of XVIIIth Century French Literature.]

Letters of Voltaire and Madame du Deffand (London: Routledge, 1927); (New York: Brentano's, 1927). [Broadway Library of XVIIIth Century French Literature.]

D. H. Lawrence. An Indiscretion. (Seattle: University of Washington Book Store, 1927). [University of Washington Chapbooks, no. 6.] *D. H. Lawrence* (London: Chatto & Windus, 1930).

The Great Betrayal (La Trahison des Clercs) by Julien Benda (London: Routledge, 1928); *The Treason of the Intellectuals* (New York: Crosby Gaige, 1928); (London: Chatto & Windus, 1931).

Fifty Romance Lyric Poems (New York: Crosby Gaige, 1928); (London: Chatto & Windus, 1931).

Rémy de Gourmont. A Modern Man of Letters (Seattle: University of Washington Book Store, 1928). [University of Washington Chapbooks, no. 13.]

Hark the Herald (Paris: Hours Press, 1928).

The Eaten Heart (Chapelle-Réanville, Eure, France: Hours Press, 1929); (London: William Heinemann, 1931).

Collected Poems (London: Allen & Unwin, 1929); (New York: Covici Friede, 1929).

Rémy de Gourmont. *Selections from All His Works* (New York: Covici, Friede, 1929).

Death of a Hero. A Novel (New York: Covici, Friede, 1929); (London: Chatto & Windus, 1929). (Also published in German, Swedish, Danish, French, Russian, Czech, Romanian and Spanish. An unexpurgated English edition was published in Paris by Babou and Kahane [1930]. An English-language edition has also been published in Russia.)

Roads to Glory (London: Chatto & Windus, 1930); (Garden City, N.Y.: Doubleday, Doran & Co., 1930).

Two Stories (London: Elkin Mathews & Marrot, 1930).

At All Costs (London: Heinemann, 1930).

Balls and Another Book for Suppression (London: E. Lahr, 1930). [Blue Moon Booklet, no. 7]. *Balls*. Privately Printed, 1932.

Love and the Luxembourg (New York: Covici, Friede, 1930). *A Dream in the Luxemburg* (London: Chatto & Windus, 1930). (Also published in Czech and French.)

Alcestis, by Euripides (London: Chatto & Windus, 1930). [Translator]

The Decameron of Giovanni Boccaccio (New York: Covici, Friede, 1930). (London: G. P. Putnam's Sons, 1930). [Translator]

Letters to the Amazon, by Rémy de Gourmont (London: Chatto & Windus, 1931).

Last Straws (Paris: Hours Press, 1931).

The Colonel's Daughter. A Novel (London: Chatto & Windus, 1931); (Garden City, N.Y., Doubleday, Doran, 1931). (Also published in Danish, Swedish, French, Spanish, Italian, Polish and Russian.)

Stepping Heavenward. A Record (Florence: G. Orioli, 1931); (London: Chatto & Windus, 1931).

Soft Answers (London: Chatto & Windus, 1932); (Garden City, N.Y., Doubleday Doran, 1932).

Movietones. Invented and Set Down by Richard Aldington, 1928–1929 (Privately printed, 1932).

Last Poems, by D. H. Lawrence, edited by Richard Aldington and Guiseppe Orioli. (Florence: G. Orioli, 1932); (New York: Viking Press, 1933); (London: Martin Secker, 1933).

Aurelia, by Gérard de Nerval (London: Chatto & Windus, 1932), [Translator]

All Men Are Enemies. A Romance (London: Chatto & Windus, 1933); (Garden City, N.Y.: Doubleday, Doran, 1933). (Also published in Danish, Hungarian, Italian, Spanish, Russian, Czech and Norwegian.)

Women Must Work. A Novel (London: Chatto & Windus 1934) (Garden City, N.Y.: Doubleday Doran, 1934) (also published in Spanish, Swedish, Italian, Polish and Czech.).

The Poems of Richard Aldington (Garden City, N.Y.: Doubleday, Doran, 1934).

The Squire (London: Heinemann, 1934).

D. H. Lawrence. A Complete List of His Works, Together with a Critical Appreciation (London: Heinemann, n.d. [1935?]).

Artifex. Sketches and Ideas (London: Chatto & Windus, 1935). (Garden City, N.Y.: Doubleday, Doran, 1936).
Life Quest (London: Chatto & Windus, 1935); (Garden City, N.Y.: Doubleday, Doran, 1935).
Life of a Lady. A Play by Richard Aldington and Derek Patmore (Garden City, N.Y.: Doubleday, Doran, 1936); (London: G. P. Putnam's Sons, 1936).
Very Heaven (London: Heinemann, 1937). (Garden City, N.Y.: Doubleday, Doran, 1937). (Also published in Czech, Italian and German.)
The Crystal World (London: Heinemann, 1937).
Seven Against Reeves. A Comedy-Farce (London: Heinemann, 1938). (Garden City, N.Y.: Doubleday, Doran, 1938). (Also published in French, Spanish and Swedish.)
Rejected Guest. A Novel (New York: Viking, 1939). (London: Heinemann, [1940?].
W. Somerset Maugham. An Appreciation by Richard Aldington [with *Sixty-Five*, by W. Somerset Maugham, a Bibliography, an Index of Short Stories and Appreciations] (Garden City, N.Y.: Doubleday, Doran, 1939).
Life for Life's Sake. A Book of Reminiscences (New York: Viking Press, 1941); (London: Cassell, 1968).
The Viking Book of Poetry of the English-Speaking World (New York: Viking Press, 1941). *Poetry of the English-Speaking World* (London: Heinemann, 1947).
The Duke, Being an Account of the Life and Achievements of Arthur Wellesley, 1st Duke of Wellington (New York: Viking Press, 1943). *Wellington, Being an Account of the Life and Achievements of Arthur Wellesley, 1st Duke of Wellington* (London: Heinemann, 1946). (Also published in French, German, Spanish and Italian.)
A Wreath for San Gemignano (New York: Duell, Sloan and Pearce, 1945); (London: Heinemann, 1946).
Great French Romances: The Princess of Clèves, by Madame de Lafayette; *Manon Lescaut*, by the Abbé Prevost; *Dangerous Acquaintances*, by Choderlos de Laclos; *The Duchesse de Langeais*, by Honoré de Balzac (London: Pilot Press, 1946); (New York: Duell, Sloan and Pearce, 1946).
The Romance of Casanova. A Novel (New York: Duell, Sloan and Pearce, 1946); (London: Heinemann, 1947). (Also published in Czech, French, Swedish, Spanish, German and Finnish.)
The Portable Oscar Wilde (New York: Viking Press, 1946). *Oscar Wilde. Selected Works* (London: Heinemann, 1946).
Bilder [Selected Poems] (Hamburg: A. Keune, 1947).
Jane Austen (Pasadena: Ampersand Press, 1948).
Four English Portraits, 1801–1851 (London: Evans Brothers, 1948).
Walter Pater. Selected Works (London: Heinemann, 1948); (New York: Duell, Sloan and Pearce, 1948).
The Complete Poems of Richard Aldington (London: Allan Wingte, 1948).
The Strange Life of Charles Waterton, 1782–1865 (London: Evans Brothers, 1949); (New York: Duell, Sloan and Pearce, 1949).
D. H. Lawrence: An Appreciation (Harmondsworth, Middlesex: Penguin, 1950).
D. H. Lawrence: Portrait of a Genius, But . . . (London: Heinemann, 1950).

The Religion of Beauty. Selections from the Aesthetes (London: Heinemann, 1950).
Pinorman. Personal Recollections of Norman Douglas, Pino Orioli, and Charles Prentice (London: Heinemann, 1954).
Ezra Pound and T. S. Eliot. A Lecture (Hurst, Berkshire: Peacocks Press, 1954).
A. E. Housman and W. B. Yeats. Two Lectures (Hurst, Berkshire: Peacocks Press, 1955).
Lawrence L'Imposteur: T. E. Lawrence, The Legend and the Man (Paris: Amiot-Dumont, 1954). *Lawrence of Arabia. A Biographical Inquiry* (London: Collins, 1955); (Carbondale: Southern Illinois University Press, 1960).
Introduction to Mistral (London: Heinemann, 1956); (Carbondale: Southern Illinois University Press, 1960).
Frauds (London: Heinemann, 1957).
Portrait of a Rebel. The Life and Work of Robert Louis Stevenson. (London: Evans Brothers, 1957).
Larousse Encyclopedia of Mythology (New York: Prometheus Press, 1959). [Translated by Richard Aldington and Delano Ames; Felix Guirard (ed.), intro. Robert Graves.]
D. H. Lawrence in Selbstzeugnissen und Bilddokumenten (Reinbek bei Hamburg: Rowohlt Taschenbuch Verlag GmbH, 1961).
Farewell to Memories (Moscow: Foreign Languages Publishing House, 1963).
Richard Aldington: Selected Critical Writings 1928-1960 Alister Kershaw (ed.) (Carbondale and Edwardsville: Southern Illinois University Press, 1970).
A Passionate Prodigality: Letters to Alan Bird from Richard Aldington 1949-1962 Miriam J. Benkovitz (ed.) (New York: New York Public Library and Readers Books, 1975).
Literary Lifelines: The Richard Aldington-Lawrence Durrell Correspondence Ian S. McNiven and Harry T. Moore (Eds) (New York: Viking Press, 1981).

Aldington and D. H. Lawrence

Besides items 24, 56, 62, 84, 85, and 95 in the bibliography, Aldington edited: *D. H. Lawrence: Selected Poems* (London: Secker, 1934) and *The Spirit of Place. An Anthology Compiled from the Prose of D. H. Lawrence* (London: Heinemann, 1935). He also wrote introductions for the following: *Apocalypse* (London: Secker, 1932), *Mornings in Mexico* and *The White Peacock*, both published in London in 1950 by Heinemann; for the following Lawrence titles published by Penguin Books: *Aaron's Rod; Etruscan Places; Kangaroo; The Lost Girl; The Plumed Serpent; Selected Essays; St. Mawr, and the Virgin and the Gipsy; The Woman Who Rode Away, and Other Stories* (all published in 1950); *The Rainbow, Women in Love* and *Sea and Sardinia* (all published in 1953). He also compiled the Penguin edition of Lawrence's *Selected Letters* (1950, which has an introduction by Aldous Huxley. Aldington provided introductions to *D. H. Lawrence: A Composite Biography*, vol. III, Edward Nehls (ed.) (Madison: University of Winsconsin

Press, 1959) and *D. H. Lawrence: l'oeuvre et la vie* by F.-J. Temple (Paris: Seghers, 1960).

(ii) Articles

'Marinetti's Poems', *New Freewoman*, I (1 December 1913) p. 226
'Books, Drawings and Papers', *Egoist*, I, 4 (1 January 1914) p. 10.
'Modern Poetry and the Imagists', *Egoist*, I, 3 (1 June 1914) p. 7.
'Blast', *Egoist*, I, 4 (15 July 1914) p. 5.
'Free Verse in England', *Egoist*, I, 8 (15 September 1914) p. 2.
'Two Poets', *Egoist*, I, 11 (16 November 1914) pp. 3–4.
'Some Reflections on Ernest Dowson', *Egoist*, II, 1 March 1915.
'The Poetry of Ezra Pound', *Egoist* (Special Imagist Number), 1 May 1915, p. 4.
'Loose Leaves', *Egoist*, II, 6, 1 June 1915.
'The Poetry of F. S. Flint', *Egoist* (Special Imagist Number), 1 May 1915, p. 7.
'The Poetry of Amy Lowell', *Egoist*, II, 6 (1 July 1915), p. 2.
'Rémy de Gourmont', *Drama*, XXII (May 1916), pp. 167–83.
'Henri de Régnier', *Dial*, LXI (September 1916), p. 725.
'Poet and Painter: A Renaisssance Fancy', *Dial*, LXII (January 1917), pp. 7–9.
'Letters to an Unknown Woman', *Dial*, LXIV (March 1918) pp. 226–7: LXIV (May 1918) pp. 430–1: LXIV (June 1918) pp. 525–6.
'New Paths', *Dial* LXV (September 1918) pp. 149–50.
'Poetry of the Future', *Poetry*, XIV (August 1919) pp. 266–9.
'Rémy de Gourmont', *Anglo-French Review*, XXXI (15 September 1919), p. 27.
'Rémy de Gourmont', *Living Age*, CCCIII (13 December 1919) pp. 665–8.
'Campion's Observations', *Poetry*, XV (February 1920) pp. 267–71.
'English and American Poetry', *Poetry*, XVI (May 1920) pp. 94–8.
'Georges Duhamel', *Living Age*, CCCV (8 May 1920) pp. 362–7.
'Approach to Marcel Proust', *English Review*, XXX (June 1920) pp. 488–93.
'The Disciples of Gertrude Stein', *Poetry*, XVII (October 1920) no. 1, pp. 35–40.
'Review of F. S. Flint, *Otherworld*', *Poetry*, vol. XVII (October 1920) no. 1, pp. 44–7.
'The Art of Poetry', *Dial*, LXIX (November 1920) pp. 166–80.
'The Poetry of the Sitwells', *Poetry*, XVII (December 1920) pp. 161–7.
'Roman Letter', *Dial*, LXX (March 1921) pp. 309–12.
'The Influence of Mr. James Joyce', *English Review*, XXXII (April 1921) pp. 333–41.
'Poetry in Prose', *The Chapbook: A Monthly Miscellany*, XVI (April 1921) pp. 18–26.
'The Poet and Modern Life', *Poetry*, XVIII (May 1921) pp. 99–100.
'Rémy de Gourmont', *Times Literary Supplement*, 12 May 1921, p. 304.
'The Sacred Wood', *To-Day*, vol. VIII (September 1921) no. 47, pp. 191–3.
'Cowley and the French Epicureans', *New Statesman*, (5 November 1921) pp. 133–4.
'A Note on Waller's Poems', *To-Day*, IX (December 1921) pp. 20–2.
'The Poetry of T. S. Eliot', *Outlook* (London), vol. 49 (January 1922) no. 7, pp. 12–13.

'The Work of T. S. Eliot', *Literary Review*, III (14 January 1922), p. 350.
'Charles Dufresnay', *North American Review*, CCXV (August 1922), pp. 254–8.
'Marivaux and Marivaudage', *North American Review*, CCXVI (August 1922), pp. 361–5.
'The Poet and His Age', *Chapbook: A Monthly Miscellany*, XVII (September 1922) pp. 12–32.
'Roman Letter', *Dial*, LXXIII (October 1922) pp. 383–7.
'The Art of Poetry', *Fortnightly Review*, CXIII (January 1923) pp. 116–27.
'Voltaire's Advice to a Reviewer', *Literary Review*, IV (21 June 1924) p. 840.
'Conrad and Hardy', *Literary Review*, (6 September 1924) p. 8.
'Mark Rutherford in Old Age', *New Republic*, (24 December 1924) pp. 125–6.
'A Letter from Mr. Richard Aldington', *This Quarter*, vol. I (1925) no. 2, pp. 311–15.
'François Villon', *Criterion*, vol. IV (April 1925) no. 2, pp 376–8.
'A Note on Free Verse', *Chapbook*, 'Annual Issue', 1925.
'A Note on Contemporary English Poetry', *Nation*, (13 May 1925) p. 548.
'D. H. Lawrence as Poet', *Saturday Review of Literature* (1 May 1926) pp. 749–50.
'Voltaire and Frederick the Great', *Fortnightly Review*, CXXVI (17 October 1926) pp. 546–9.
'Light Novelists of the Eighteenth Century', *Vogue* (London), VII (June 1926) p. 74.
'How They Did It a 100 Years ago; The Hairy Jeaune-France of Romantic Paris Who Worshipped Byron', *Vogue* (London), VII (August 1926) p. 43.
'Napoleon', *London Mercury*, XVI (July 1927) pp. 257–65.
'William Blake', *Nation* (19 March 1927) p. 858.
'Mr. Eliot on Seneca', *Nation* (29 October 1927) p. 159.
'Mr Aldington Replies to Professor Bernbaum', *Modern Language Notes*, XLIII (February 1928) pp. 114–5.
'Science and Conscience', *Discovery*, n.s. I (December 1928) pp. 421–2.
'First Impressions of Portugal', *Spectator* (7 July 1933) pp. 10–11.
'The Squire', *Virginia Quarterly Review*, X (October 1934) pp. 576–86.
'Sea Verge', *Spectator* (23 July 1937) pp. 139–40.
'Archie's Dilemma', *Spectator* (8 October 1937) pp. 580–1.
'What Science Means to Us', *Living Age*, CCCLV (January 1939) pp. 406–9.
'Norman Douglas and Calabria', *Atlantic*, CLXIII (June 1939) pp. 757–60.
'D. H. Lawrence: Ten Years After', *Saturday Review of Literature* (24 June 1939) pp. 3–4.
'Des Imagistes', *Saturday Review of Literature* (16 March 1940) pp. 3–4.
'Percy B. Shelley', *Saturday Review of Literature* (7 December 1940) p. 7.
'Australian Revaluations: An Introduction to Frederic Manning', *Australian Letters*, II (June 1959) pp. 26–7.
'A Wreath for Lawrence', *Encounter*, vol. 14 (April 1960) pp. 51–4.

(iii) Secondary Sources

Alexander, Peter, *Roy Campbell: A Critical Biography* (London: Oxford University Press, 1982)

Alpers, Antony, *The Life of Katherine Mansfield* (New York: Viking Press, 1980).
Ancrum, Robin, *'A Fool i' the Forest*: A Critical Edition', M.A. thesis, University of Victoria, B.C., 1973.
Anderson, Margaret, *My Thirty Years War* (New York: Horizon Press, 1970).
Angell, Norman, *After All* (London: Hamish Hamilton, 1951).
Angell, Norman, *The Great Illusion* (London: Heinemann, 1910).
Antonius, George, *The Arab Awakening* (London: Hamish Hamilton, 1938).
Bair, Deirdre, *Samuel Beckett: A Biography* (New York: Harcourt Brace Jovanovich, 1978).
Barrow, General Sir George, *The Fire of Life* (London: Hutchinson, 1942).
Baum, Paul F., 'Mr Richard Aldington', *South Atlantic Quarterly*, vol. XXVIII (April 1929) pp. 201–8.
Beaumont, Cyril *A Bookseller at the Ballet* (London: Beaumont, 1975).
Benkovitz, Miriam J., 'Nine for Reeves: Letters from Richard Aldington', *Bulletin of the New York Public Library*, vol. 69 (June 1965) no. 6, pp. 349–74.
Benkovitz, Miriam J. (ed.) *A Passionate Prodigality: Letters to Alan Bird from Richard Aldington. 1949–1962* (New York: New York Public Library and Readex Books, 1975).
Béraud-Villars, Jean Marcel Eugène, *T. E. Lawrence; or, the Search for the Absolute*, translated from the French by Peter Dawnay (London: Sidgwick & Jackson, 1958).
Bergonzi, Bernard, *Heroes' Twilight* (London: Constable, 1965).
Bergonzi, Bernard, *T. S. Eliot* (New York: Collier, 1972).
Blackmur, R. P. 'Richard Aldington', *Nation*, vol. 138 (30 May 1934) no. 3595, p. 625.
Boll, Theophilius E. M., *Miss May Sinclair: Novelist* (Rutherford, N.J.: Fairleigh Dickinson University Press, 1973). British Museum Additional MS 45903, 4. Letters of Thomas Edward Shaw to Charlotte Shaw.
Burne, Glenn S., *Rémy de Gourmont. His Ideas and Influence in England and America* (Carbondale: Southern Illinois University Press, 1963).
Buttle, Myra (pseudonym for Victor Purcell), *The Sweeniad* (Welwyn Garden City: Broadwater Press, 1957; New York: Sagamore Press, 1957).
Campbell, Roy, 'Richard Aldington, Happy Pagan', *Poetry Review*, April-May 1949 (Reprinted in *Intimate Portrait*).
Chisolm, Anne, *Nancy Cunard* (New York: Alfred A. Knopf, 1979).
Church, Richard, *The Voyage Home* (London: Heinemann, 1964).
Clements, Patricia, *Baudelaire and the English Tradition* (New Jersey: Princeton University Press, 1985).
Cork, Richard, *Vorticism and Abstract Art in the First Machine Age* (2 vols.) (Berkeley: University of California Press, 1976).
Cournos, John, *Autobiography* (New York: G. P. Putnam Sons, 1935).
Cournos, John, *Miranda Masters* (New York: Alfred A. Knopf, 1926).
Crawford, Fred D., *Mixing Memory and Desire: The Waste Land and British Novels* (University Park, Pa.: Pennsylvania State University Press, 1982).
Crawford, Fred D., 'Richard Aldington and H.D.' Paper presented at the Aldington Symposium, University of Reading, 8 and 9 July 1986.
Cunard, Nancy, *Grand Man: Memories of Norman Douglas* (London: Secker, 1954).

Cunard, Nancy, *These were the Hours: Memories of My Hours Press, Réanville and Paris*, edited by Hugh Ford (Carbondale: Southern Illinois University Press, 1969).
Dardis, Tom, *Some Time in the Sun* (New York: Scribner, 1976).
Damon, S. Foster, *Amy Lowell: A Chronicle* (Boston: Houghton Mifflin, 1935).
Deasey, W. Denison, 'Death of a Hero', *Australian Book Review* (February 1970) pp. 84–6.
Deasey, W. Denison, 'Lunch at the Villa', *The Bulletin*, Sydney, (23–30 December 1980) pp. 177–80.
De Fanti, Charles, *The Wages of Expectation: A Biography of Edward Dahlberg* (New York University Press, 1978).
Delany, Paul, *D. H. Lawrence's Nightmare: The Writer and His Circle in the Years of the Great War* (New York: Basic Books, 1978). *Des Imagistes. An Anthology* (New York: Boni, 1914).
Doolittle, Hilda (H.D.),'Asphodel'. Beinecke Library, Yale University. Written 1921–22.
Doolittle, Hilda (H.D.), 'Autobiographical Notes'. Beinecke Library, Yale University.
Doolittle, Hilda (H.D.), *Bid Me to Live: A Madrigal* (New York: Grove Press, 1960).
Doolittle, Hilda (H.D.), *Collected Poems 1912–1944* With an Introduction by Louis L. Martz (New York: New Directions, 1983).
Doolittle, Hilda (H.D.), *End toTorment* Edited by Norman Holmes Pearson and Michael King (New York: New Directions, 1979).
Doolittle, Hilda (H.D.), *HERmione* (New York: New Directions, 1981).
Doolittle, Hilda (H.D.), 'Paint it Today', Beinecke Library, Yale University. Written 1921.
Doolittle, Hilda (H.D.), *Tribute to Freud* (New York: Pantheon, 1956).
Doolittle, Hilda (H.D), *The Walls Do Not Fall* (London and New York: Oxford University Press, 1944).
Douglas, Norman, *D. H. Lawrence and Maurice Magnus: A Plea for Better Manners* (Florence: privately printed, 1925).
Douglas, Norman, *Late Harvest* (London: Lindsay Drummond, 1946).
Douglas, Norman, *On the Herpetology of the Grand Duchy of Baden* (London: Adams Brothers, 1894).
Douglas, Norman, *Paneros: Some Words on Aphrodisiacs and the Like* (London: Chatto & Windus, 1931).
(Douglas, Norman), *Venus in the Kitchen, or Love's Cookery Book* Pilaff Bey, edited by Norman Douglas. Introduction by Graham Greene (New York: McGraw Hill, 1953).
Eliot, T. S., *Ezra Pound His Metric and Poetry* (New York: Alfred A. Knopf, 1917).
Eliot, T. S., 'Reflections on Vers Libre', *New Statesman* (3 March 1917) pp. 518–9.
Eliot, T. S., *Selected Essays* (London: Faber & Faber, 3rd ed., 1951).
Eliot, T. S., 'Ulysses, Order and Myth', *Dial* no. 75. (November 1923).
Eliot, T. S., *The Waste Land: A Facsimile Edition*, edited by Valerie Eliot (London: Faber & Faber, 1971).

Ellman, Richard, *James Joyce* (New York, London and Toronto: Oxford University Press, 1965).
Firchow, Peter E., 'Rico and Julia: The Hilda Doolittle—D. H. Lawrence Affair Reconsidered'. *Journal of Modern Literature* vol. 8 (1980) no. 1, pp. 51–76.
Fletcher, John Gould, *Life is My Song* (New York: Farrar & Rinehart, 1937).
Fletcher, John Gould, 'Mr. Aldington's Images', *Poetry* vol. VIII (April 1916) no. 1, pp. 49–51.
Fletcher, John Gould, 'Three Imagist Poets', *Little Review*, vol. III, (May 1916) pp. 32–41.
Ford, Ford Madox, *The Critical Writings of Ford Madox Ford*, edited by Frank MacShane (Lincoln, Nebraska: University of Nebraska, 1964).
Ford, Hugh (ed.), *Nancy Cunard: Brave Poet, Indomitable Rebel 1896–1965* (Philadelphia, New York and London: Chilton Book Co., 1968).
Ford, Hugh, *Published in Paris: American and British Writers, Printers and Publishers in Paris 1920–1939* (London: Garnstone Press, 1975; New York: Pushcart Press, 1980).
Friedman, Susan Stanford, *Psyche Reborn: The Emergence of H.D.* (Stanford University Press, 1981).
Frierson, W. C., *The English Novel in Transition 1885–1940* (Norman: University of Oklahoma Press, 1942).
Gates, Norman T., *A Checklist of the Letters of Richard Aldington* (Carbondale and Edwardsville: Southern Illinois University Press, 1977).
Gates, Norman T. *The Poetry of Richard Aldington: A Critical Evaluation and An Anthology of Uncollected Poems* (University Park, Pa.: Pennsylvania State University Press, 1974).
Gates, Norman T., 'Richard Aldington and F. S. Flint: Poets' Dialogue', *Papers on Language and Literature*, vol. 8 (Winter 1972) no. 1, pp. 64–5.
Gates, Norman T. 'Richard Aldington and Glenn Hughes: An Exchange of Letters', *Library Chronicle of the University of Texas at Austin*. N.S. no. 7, (Spring 1974) pp. 21–6.
Gates, Norman T.,'Richard Aldington and the Clerk's Press', *Ohio Review*, vol. VIII (Autumn 1971) no. 1, pp. 21–7.
Gates, Norman T., 'Richard Aldington in Russia', *Texas Quarterly* (Summer 1978) pp. 35–57.
Gates, Norman T. 'Richard Aldington's "Personal Notes on Poetry"', *Texas Quarterly*, vol. XVII (Spring 1970) pp. 107–13.
Going, William T., 'A Peacock Dinner: The Homage of Pound and Yeats to Wilfred Scawen Blunt', *Journal of Modern Literature*, vol. I (March 1971) no. 3, pp. 303–10.
Goldring, Douglas, *Odd Man Out* (London: Chapman & Hall, 1935).
Goldring, Douglas, *South Lodge* (London: Constable, 1943).
Gould, Jean, *Amy: The World of Amy Lowell and the Imagist Movement* (New York: Dodd, Mead, 1975).
Gourmont, Rémy de, 'A French Poet on Tradition', *Poetry*, vol. IV (July 1914) no. 4, pp. 154–60. Translated by Richard Aldington.
Gourmont, Rémy de, 'The Horses of Diomedes', Chapters translated by S. Sartoris were published in the *New Freewoman* in September to December 1913 and in the *Egoist* in January, February and March 1914.

Gourmont, Rémy de, *Le latin mystique du moyen âge* (Paris: Mercure de France, 1892).
Gourmont, Rémy de, 'Tradition and Other Things', *Egoist*, vol. I no. 14, pp. 261–2.
Grant, Joy, *Harold Monro and the Poetry Bookshop* (Berkeley: University of California Press, 1967).
Graves, Robert, *Lawrence and the Arabs* (London: Cape, 1927).
Graves, Robert, 'Lawrence Vindicated', *New Republic* (21 March 1955) p. 16.
Graves, Robert and Liddell Hart, T. E. *Lawrence to his Biographers* (London: Cassell, 1938).
Gray, Cecil, *Musical Chairs* (London: Home and Van Thal, 1948).
Guest, Barbara, *Herself Defined: The Poet H.D. and Her World* (New York: Doubleday, 1984).
Hamnett, Nina, *Laughing Torso* (London: Constable, 1938).
Harmer, J.B., *Victory in Limbo: Imagism 1908–1917* (London: Secker & Warburg, 1975).
Heymann, C. David, *Ezra Pound: The Last Rower* (New York: Viking, 1976).
Holloway, Mark, *Norman Douglas* (London: Secker & Warburg, 1976).
Hone, Joseph, *W. B. Yeats: 1865–1939* (London: MacMillan, 1943).
Hughes, Glenn, *Imagism and the Imagists* (Stanford University Press, 1931).
Hutchins, Patricia, *James Joyce's World* (London: Methuen, 1957).
Hutchins, Patricia, *Ezra Pound's Kensington: An Exploration 1885–1913*.
Huxley, Aldous, *Do What You Will* (London: Chatto & Windus, 1929). *The Letters of Aldous Huxley* edited by Grover Smith (London: Chatto & Windus, 1969). *Imagist Anthology* (London: Chatto & Windus, 1930; New York: Covici Friede, 1930).
Jones, Alun R., *The Life and Opinions of T. E. Hulme* (London: Gollancz, 1960).
Jones, Peter (ed.), *Imagist Poetry* (Harmondsworth: Penguin, 1972).
Joyce, James, *Letters* (London: Faber & Faber, 1966; New York: Viking, 1966 vol. III, edited by Richard Ellman.
Kenner, Hugh, *The Pound Era* (Berkeley: University of California Press, 1971).
Kershaw, Alister and F.-J. Temple, *Richard Aldington: An Intimate Portrait* (Carbondale: Southern Illinois University Press, 1965).
Kittredge, Selwyn B., *The Literary Career of Richard Aldington*. New York University Ph.D. Thesis, 1976. Reproduced by University Microfilms International, Ann Arbor, Michigan, USA.
Kittredge, Selwyn B., 'Richard Aldington's Challenge to T. S. Eliot: The Background of Their James Joyce Controversy', *James Joyce Quarterly*, vol. 10 (Spring 1973) no. 3, pp. 339–41.
Knightley, Philip, 'Aldington's Enquiry Concerning T. E. Lawrence', *Texas Quarterly*, vol. XVI (Winter 1973) no. 4, pp. 98–105.
Knightley, Philip and Colin Simpson, *The Secret Lives of Lawrence of Arabia* (London: Nelson, 1969).
Lawrence, D. H., *Aaron's Rod* (London: Heinemann, 1922).
Lawrence, D. H., *Apocalypse* (London: Secker, 1932).
Lawrence, D. H., *Etruscan Places* (London: Secker, 1932).
Lawrence, D. H., *Kangaroo* (London: Heinemann, 1923).

Lawrence, D. H., *Last Poems* (London: Secker, 1933; New York: Viking, 1933). edited by Richard Aldington and Guiseppe Orioli.
Lawrence, D. H., *The Collected Letters of D. H. Lawrence*, edited by Harry T. Moore (London: Heinemann, 1962). vol. 2.
Lawrence, D. H., *The Letters of D. H. Lawrence: Vol. III 1916–1921*, edited by James T. Boulton and Andrew Robertson (Cambridge University Press, 1984).
Lawrence, D. H., *Selected Letters*, edited by Diana Trilling (New York: Farrar, Straus & Cudahy, 1958).
Lawrence, Frieda, *Frieda Lawrence and Her Circle: Letters from, to and about Frieda Lawrence*, edited by Harry T. Moore and Dale B. Montague (London: MacMillan, 1951).
Lawrence, T. E., *Home Letters of T. E. Lawrence and His Brothers* (New York: MacMillan, 1954).
Lawrence, T. E., *The Seven Pillars of Wisdom* (London; private ed., 1926; New York: George H. Doran, 1926).
Levenson, Michael H. *A Genealogy of Modernism—A Study of English Literary Doctrine* (Cambridge University Press, 1984).
Lewis, P. Wyndham, *The Letters of Wyndham Lewis*, edited by W. K. Rose (London: Methuen, 1963).
Lewis, P. Wyndham, *Satire and Fiction* (London: Arthur Press, 1930).
Liddell Hart, Capt. B. H., *'T. E. Lawrence' in Arabia and After* (London: Cape, 1934).
Liddell Hart, Capt. B. H., *Colonel Lawrence: The Man Behind the Legend* (New York: Dodd, Mead, 1934).
Liddell Hart, Capt. B. H., 'T. E. Lawrence, Aldington and the Truth', *London Magazine*, vol. V (April 1955) no. 2, pp. 67–75.
Lidderdale, Jane and Mary Nicholson, *Dear Miss Weaver. Harriet Shaw Weaver 1876–1961* (London: Faber & Faber, 1970; New York: Viking, 1970).
Longford, Elizabeth, *A Pilgrimage of Passion: The Life of Wilfred Scawen Blunt* (London: Weidenfeld & Nicholson, 1979).
Lucas, Robert, *Frieda Lawrence* (New York: Viking, 1973).
Lyon Gilbert, Margery, 'Early Memories of Richard Aldington'. Typescript. Estate of Margery Lyon Gilbert.
MacShane, Frank, *The Life and Work of Ford Madox Ford* (London: Routledge, 1965).
Magnus, Maurice, *Memoirs of the Foreign Legion* by M. M. With an introduction by D. H. Lawrence (New York: Alfred A. Knopf, 1925).
Manning, Frederic, *Her Privates We* (London: P. Davies, 1930).
Manning, Frederic, *Scenes and Portraits* (London: Peter Davies, revised edn, 1930).
Materer, Timothy, *Vortex: Pound, Eliot and Lewis* (Ithaca, N.Y.: Cornell University Press, 1979).
McGreevy, Thomas, *Richard Aldington, An Englishman* (London: Chatto, 1931).
Meyers, Jeffrey, *The Wounded Spirit: A Study of the Seven Pillars of Wisdom* (London: Martin Brian & O'Keefe, 1973).
Moldavsky, V. M., 'Richard Aldington in Leningrad', *Neva* (1963) no. 5, pp. 164–7 (translated by Robert J. Winter).

Monro, Harold, 'The Imagists Discussed', *Egoist* (1 May 1915) pp. 77–80.
Monroe, Harriet, 'Refuge from War', *Poetry*, vol. XII (April 1918) no. 1, pp. 44–6.
Monroe, Harriet, *A Poet's Life* (New York: MacMillan, 1938).
Moore, Harry T. *The Priest of Love* (Harmondsworth: Penguin revised ed., 1981).
Moore, Harry T. 'Richard Aldington in His Last Years', *Texas Quarterly*, vol. VI (Autumn 1963) no. 3, pp. 60–74.
Moore, Marianne, *Predilictions* (London: Faber & Faber, 1956).
Morgan, Louise, 'Writing a Bestseller in Seven Weeks', *Everyman*, vol. IV (1930–31) pp. 101–2.
Mossop, D. J. R., 'Un disciple de Gourmont: Richard Aldington', *Revue de litterature comparée*, vol. XXV (October 1951) pp. 403–35.
Nehls, Edward, *D. H. Lawrence: A Composite Biography* (Madison: University of Wisconsin Press, 1957, 1958, 1959), 3 vols. Aldington wrote the introduction to vol. 3.
Norman, Charles, *Ezra Pound* (New York: MacMillan, 1960; New York: Minerva Press, revised ed., 1969).
Nutting, Antony, *Lawrence of Arabia: The Man and the Motive* (London: Hollis & Carter, 1961).
Orioli, Guiseppe, *Adventures of a Bookseller* (Florence: Lungarno Press, 1937. New York: R. M. McBride, 1938).
Orioli, Guiseppe, *Moving Along. Just a Diary* (London: Chatto & Windus, 1934).
Orwell, George, 'The Art of Donald McGill', *Decline of the English Murder* (Harmondsworth: Penguin, 1965).
Orwell, George, *The Collected Essays, Journals and Letters*, edited by Sonia Orwell. vol. 3. (Harmondsworth: Penguin, 1970).
Palmer, Herbert, *Post-Victorian Poetry* (London: Dent, 1938).
Patmore, Brigit, *My Friends When Young* (London: Heinemann, 1968).
Patmore, Derek, *Private History: An Autobiography* (London: Cape, 1960).
Pearson, John, *Façades: Edith, Osbert and Sacheverell Sitwell* (London: MacMillan, 1978).
Pearson, John, *The Sitwells; A Family's Biography* (New York: Harscourt Brace Jovanovich, 1978).
Perkins, David, *A History of Modern Poetry* (Cambridge, Mass.: Harvard University Press, 1976).
Pondrom, Cyrena N. *The Road from Paris: French Influence on English Poetry. 1900–1920* (Cambridge University Press, 1974).
Porter, Katherine Anne, 'A Wreath for the Gamekeeper', *Encounter*, vol. 14 (February 1960) pp. 69–76.
Pound Ezra, *Gaudier Brzeska* (New York: New Directions, 1970).
Pound, Ezra, *The Letters of Ezra Pound, 1907–1941*, edited by D. D. Paige (New York: Harcourt Brace, 1950).
Pound, Ezra, *The Literary Essays of Ezra Pound*. With an introduction by T. S. Eliot (London: Faber & Faber, 1954).
Pound, Ezra, *Pound/Joyce: The Letters of Ezra Pound to James Joyce*, edited by Forrest Read (New York: New Directions, 1967).
Pound, Ezra, *Selected Prose 1909–1965*, edited by William Cookson (London: Faber & Faber, 1973).

Read, Herbert, *The Innocent Eye* (London: Faber, 1933).
Robinson, Janice S., *H.D.: The Life of An American Poet* (Boston: Houghton Mifflin, 1982).
Rosenfeld, Paul, *By Way of Art* (New York: Coward-McCann, 1928).
Rutherford, Andrew, *The Literature of War* (London: MacMillan, 1978).
Satterthwaite, Alfred, 'John Cournos and "H.D."', *Twentieth-Century Literature*, vol. 22 (December 1976) no. 4, pp. 394–410.
Seiffert, Marjorie Allen, 'Soldier and Lover', *Poetry*, vol. XIV (September 1919) no. 6, pp. 338–41.
Silkin, Jon, *Out of Battle: The Poetry of the Great War* (London: Oxford University Press, 1972).
Sinclair, May, *Mary Olivier: A Life* (London: MacMillan, 1919).
Sinclair, May, 'Poems of Richard Aldington', *English Review*, vol. XXXII (May 1921) pp. 397–410.
Sinclair, May, *The Dark Night* (London: MacMillan, 1924).
Smith, Richard E., *Richard Aldington* (Boston: Twayne, 1977).
Snow, C. P., *Richard Aldington: An Appreciation* (London: Heinemann, 1938).
Snow, C. P., *Variety of Men* (Harmondsworth: Penguin, 1969).
Snow, C. P., *Some Imagist Poets* (Boston: Houghton Mifflin, 1915, 1916, and 1917).
Stock, Noel, *The Life of Ezra Pound* (New York: Pantheon, 1970; Harmondsworth: Penguin, 1974).
Swinnerton, Frank, *The Georgian Literary Scene* (New York: Farrar & Rinehart, 1934).
Tabachnick, Stephen E., *T. E. Lawrence* (Boston: Twayne, 1978).
Temple, F.-J. (ed.), *Hommage à Roy Campbell* (Montpellier: Editions de le Licorne, 1958).
Temple, F.-J., 'Richard Aldington', *Sud* (1973) no. 11, pp. 102–5.
Temple, F.-J. and Alister Kershaw, *Richard Aldington; An Intimate Portrait* (Carbondale: Southern Illinois University Press, 1965).
Thatcher, David S. (ed.), 'Richard Aldington's Letters to Herbert Read', *Malahat Review* (1970) no. 15, pp. 5–44.
Thompson, Michael B., 'Richard Aldington and T. S. Eliot', *Yeats Eliot Review*, vol. 6 (1979) no. 1, pp. 3–9.
Ward, A. C., *The Nineteen-Twenties: Literature and Ideas in the Post-War Decade* (London: Methuen, 1930).
Waugh, Alec, *The Best Wine Last: An Autobiography Through the Years 1932–1969* (London: W. H. Allen, 1978).
Waugh, Alec, *My Brother Evelyn and Other Profiles* (London: Cassell, 1967).
Waugh, Alec, *These Would I Choose: A Personal Anthology* (London: Sampson Low, 1948).
Wavell, A. P., *Allenby: A Study in Greatness* (London: George Harrap, 1940).
Whitall, James, *English Years* (London: Cape, 1936).
Williams, William Carlos, *Autobiography* (New York: Random House, 1951).
Williams, William Carlos, 'Four Foreigners', *Little Review*, vol. VI (September 1919) no. 5, pp. 36–9.
Williamson, Henry, *Genius of Friendship; 'T. E. Lawrence'* (London: Faber &

Faber, 1941).
Witemeyer, Hugh, *The Poetry of Ezra Pound 1908–1920* (Berkeley and Los Angeles: University of California Press, 1969).
Wohl, Robert, *The Generation of 1914* (Cambridge, Mass,: Harvard University Press, 1979).
Woolf, Virginia, *The Diary of Virginia Woolf. 1920–1924*, vol. II, edited by Anne Olivier Bell (London: Hogarth Press, 1978).
Woolf, Virginia, *A Change of Perspective: The Letters of Virginia Woolf 1923–1928* (London: Hogarth Press, 1977).
Yardley, Michael, *Backing into the Limelight: A Biography of T. E. Lawrence* (London: Harrap, 1985).
Yorke, Dorothy (Arabella), Interview with Walter and Lilian Lowenfels, Maya Landing, New Jersey, 25 October 1964. Transcribed by the late Dr Miriam J. Benkovitz.
Zeigler, Philip, *Diana Cooper* (Harmondsworth: Penguin, 1983).

Index

Aiken, Conrad 44, 68, 70
Aldington, Albert Edward 1, 2, 4, 15, 29, 53, 77–8, 239
Aldington, Catherine 185, 201, 203, 207–9, 213, 215, 225, 229, 242, 244–6, 253–4, 262, 264, 275, 277, 286, 289, 294, 296–300, 305, 306–7, 308, 310, 311–12, 314–17, 320, 322
Aldington, Jessie May 2–4, 7, 111, 239, 245–6
Aldington, Netta (formerly Patmore) 176–8, 180, 183–5, 189, 191, 201, 203, 205, 209, 220–1, 224, 226, 229, 233–4, 244, 246–7, 254, 259, 262, 275, 308, 309, 314–16
Aldington, P. A. G. (Tony) 3–4, 245, 288, 291–3, 312, 314–15
Aldington, Richard: aestheticism, xviii, 9, 306; Aldington Poetry Prize, 140, 154; anti-capitalism, 128–37, 156–63, 178–9, 197; Bel Esprit plan, 95–7, 101; Broadway Translations Series, 101–3; butterfly collecting, xvii, 5, 208, 210; divorce proceedings and aftermath, 180–2, 232–3, 238, 247, 250, 277, 290; Dover, 1, 4–5, 167; epicureanism, xvii, 84, 100, 126, 257–8, 281; Garton Peace Foundation, 15–16; General Strike, 106–7; ideal of the good European, xvii, 8, 28, 84, 107–8, 109, 172, 174, 211, 214, 258, 325; the Great War (First World War), 19, 33–7, 41, 54–67, 75, 128–37, 142–3, 196, 228, 248, 325; Hellenism, xvii, 10, 17–20, 27, 31, 46, 48; in Hollywood, 193–4, 213–24, 226, 228; Imagism, xiii–xiv, xx, 14–17, 22, 27–30, 33–5, 43–7, 49, 50, 91, 116, 119, 138, 324; Paris, 15, 21, 111, 114, 230–1; Poets Translation Series, 45, 51, 69; prose poetry, 91–2; Republic of Letters Series, 100–2; Russia, xx, 127, 138, 171–2, 182–3, 306, 308–9, 314–15, 317–22, 323, 325; Second World War, 201, 212, 223; *Sunday Referee*, xvi, 141, 144–5, 149, 151, 155–6, 158; University College, London, 9–12; *vers libre*, 10, 14, 16, 17, 27, 58, 82, 91, 165; sense of Victorian moral and social values, xv, 130–1, 196; Vorticism, 27, 29–31, 37
WORKS: Books and pamphlets: *All Men Are Enemies*, xvii, 70, 106–7, 119, 138–9, 156, 158–63, 164, 166 (film), 168, 177, 182, 185, 197–8, 201, 230–2, 282, 289, 302–3, 310, 314, 316, 319, 321; *Artifex: Essays and Ideas*, xvii–xix, 170, 180, 187, 281; *Candide* (Voltaire), 105, 113, 287, 304, 319, 324; *Collected Poems* (1929), 139, 143; *Collected Poems 1915–1923*, 18–19; *The Colonel's Daughter*, 142, 144, 146, 151–3, 156, 158, 168, 171, 185, 197, 200; *The Complete Poems of Richard Aldington*, xix–xx, 18, 47, 59, 80, 187, 233–4, 237, 240; *The Crystal World*, 180, 186–7, 198, 240; *Death of a Hero*, xiv, xv, xvii, 1–5, 16, 24, 56, 60, 62, 68, 110, 120–1, 124, 126–38, 141–3, 152, 154, 158–

Aldington, Richard – *continued*
9, 168, 171–2, 175–6, 180, 182, 185, 188, 193, 195, 196–7, 200, 232, 250, 274, 281, 288–9, 302–5, 314, 320–1, 325; *Decameron* (Boccaccio), 116, 288–9, 304, 309, 324; *D. H. Lawrence: An Indiscretion*, 109, 112, 275; *A Dream in the Luxembourg*, 114, 118, 141, 172–3, 198, 231, 233, 240, 289, 323; *The Duke*, 217–18, 228; English edition (titled *Wellington*), 230–4; *The Eaten Heart*, 119, 139, 173; *Exile and Other Poems*, 80–2, 86; *Ezra Pound and T. S. Eliot*, 260; *Farewell to Memories*, 302, 309–10; *Fifty Romance Lyric Poems*, 108, 110–11; *A Fool i' the Forest*, 69, 85–7, 99, 115, 129, 240, 281; *Four English Portraits*, 233–4, 236–9; *Frauds*, 276, 279–80, 282; *French Studies and Reviews*, 107–8; *Hark the Herald*, 119, 124, 139; *Great French Romances*, 223, 228, 231; *Images*, 46–9, 50, 69; *Images of Desire*, 69, 180; *Images of War*, xiv, 56, 59, 69, 180; *Introduction to Mistral*, 259, 276–8, 280, 282, 284, 297, 305; *Last Straws*, 144; *Lawrence of Arabia: A Biographical Enquiry*, 195, 254, 261–76, 280–1, 289–90, 302, 304, 313, 324; *Lawrence l'imposteur*, 263; *Les Liaisons Dangereuses* (Laclos), 82, 304, 324; *Life for Life's Sake*, xiv, xvii, 2, 7, 11, 13, 23, 56, 69, 90, 106, 117, 119, 121, 144, 146, 148, 174, 193, 206, 211, 258; *The Life of a Lady*, 164; *Life Quest*, 169; *Literary Studies and Reviews*, 83–4; *Love and the Luxembourg*, 127; *The Love of Myrrhine and Konallis*, 55, 58, 69, 111; *Medallions in Clay*, 45, 78; *Pinorman*, 126, 144–5, 189, 254–60, 262, 281; *The Poems of Richard Aldington*, 165; *The Portable Oscar Wilde*, xvi, 231–2, 237, 324; *Portrait of a Genius. But . . .* , xvi, 109–10, 195, 238, 243–4, 246–7, 249–52, 273, 281, 304, 324; *Portrait of a Rebel: The Life and Works of Robert Louis Stevenson*, 280, 289, 291; *Rejected Guest*, 4, 5, 188–9, 193–5, 199–230, 241; *The Religion of Beauty*, xvi, 227, 236–7; *Rémy de Gourmont: Selections from All His Works*, 115, 125, 155; *Rêverie*, 58–9, 63, 69; *Roads to Glory*, 56, 59, 142–3; *The Romance of Casanova*, 199, 201, 222–6, 231–2, 237, 250, 304; *Rome: A Book of Photographs*, 298, 306; *Seven Against Reeves*, 180, 183, 230, 232, 239; *Soft Answers*, 148, 155, 239, 243, 247, 305; *The Squire*, 233; *Stepping Heavenward*, 146–9, 250; *The Strange Life of Charles Waterton*, 233, 239, 241, 245; *A Tourist's Rome*, 306; *Very Heaven*, 4, 11, 167, 173, 175–6, 178–9, 183, 185, 194, 198–9; *Viking Book of Poetry of the English-Speaking World*, 202, 206, 209, 210–11, 213, 233, 235, 289, 324, later, British edition, 280; *Voltaire*, 84, 102, 108, 114, 195, 288; *Voyages to the Moon and Sun* (Cyrano de Bergerac), 79–80, 203, 309, 313; *Walter Pater: Selected Works*, 237; *War and Love*, 59, 69, 72; *Women Must Work*, 164–8, 194, 198, 200,

Aldington, Richard – *continued*
    318, 321; *A Wreath for San Gemignano*, 224; *W. Somerset Maugham: An Appreciation*, 201.
    ARTICLES, ESSAYS: 'Decadence and Dynamism', 39; 'The Disciples of Gertrude Stein', 73; 'Et in Arcadia Ego', 98; 'Farewell to Europe', 205; 'François Villon', 99; 'The Influence of Mr James Joyce', 93–4; 'Landor's Hellenics', 83–4; 'Mr Eliot on Seneca', 104; 'Notes from France', 56; 'Parochialism in Art', 35; 'Personal Notes on Poetry', 74; 'The Poet and His Age', 97; 'The Poet and Modern Life', 95; 'The Poetry of T. S. Eliot', 83, 95; 'Some Recent French Poets', 27; 'Theocritus on Capri', 18, 83; 'What is Wrong with English Poetry', 139; 'A Young American Poet', 40.
    INDIVIDUAL POEMS; 'After Two Years', 46; 'Amalfi', 18, 49; 'Au Vieux Jardin', 16–17; 'Childhood', 4–5, 49; 'Choricos', 16, 46–7, 63, 324; 'Cinema Exit', 49; 'Four Songs', 80; 'Inscriptions', 140; 'In the Tube', 49; 'In the Via Sistina', 18, 48; 'Lesbia', 48; 'On the March', 56; 'Pompeii', 19; 'To a Greek Marble', 16, 48.
Allenby, General Edmund (later Field Marshal, Lord) 268, 271
Amery, Leo (Rt Hon.) 265, 271
Anderson, Margaret 58, 93, 111
Angell, Norman 15–16
Anglo-French Review 69, 71
Anisimov, Ivan 171–2
Antonius, George 267–8
    The Arab Awakening 267–8
Apollinaire, Guillaume 27

Aragon, Louis 124, 127
Arlen, Michael (Dikran Kouyoumdjian) 142, 158
Arlott, John 238, 242–3, 281
Arnold, Matthew 197–8
Asquith, Cynthia 77
Atlantic Monthly 192, 194, 203, 205, 258
Austin, Francis (Rev.) 5, 7
Australian Book Review 273

Bacon, Leonard 146, 174, 188, 191–2, 195, 203–5, 212, 215, 217, 224, 226, 242
Bair, Deirdre 140, 300
Bakhtin, V. I. 319
Baldwin, Stanley (Rt Hon.) 106
Balzac, Honoré de 85, 182, 228, 281, 289
Barnes, Djuna 127
Barney, Natalie 95, 114
Barrow, George, Major-General Sir 269
Barzun, Jacques 301
Bates, Henry Walter 169
Bates, Ralph 180
Beach, Sylvia 124
'Beachcomber' (see under Morton, J. B.)
Beare, Mr (?) 11–12
Beaumont, Cyril W. 78–9
Beauduin, Nicholas 28, 40
Beckett, Samuel 127, 140, 300
Benda, Julien 114
Bennett, Arnold 128
Bergonzi, Bernard xiv, 130, 135
Benkovitz, Miriam 122, 150
Best, Marshall 209, 218, 223
Bird, Alan xiii, 252–4, 260, 274, 276, 279, 291, 300, 302, 304–5, 309
Blackmur, R. P. 165
Blast 29, 30–1, 37, 44
Blunt, Wilfred Scawen 26–7, 159
Bodenheim, Maxwell 58
Bosschere, Jean de 39
Brémond, Edouard, Colonel (later General) 268–9
Brett, Dorothy 209

Index

Brooke, Rupert 34, 72
Browning, John 236, 244, 280
Bryher (Winifred Ellerman) 11, 68–9, 71, 124, 182, 288, 294–6, 300, 302, 306–8, 310, 315, 322
Bubb, Charles C. (Rev.) 55, 59, 69, 224
Budberg, Countess Moura 320
Bunting, Basil 140
Buss, Kate 95
Bynner, Witter 213

Campbell, Roy xv, 233, 238–41, 250–1, 259, 272, 276, 282, 286, 288
Cannell, Skipwith 22
Cendrars, Blaise 73
Chapbook, The 58, 91, 97
Chapman, Arthur 9–10
Chapman, Sir Thomas 265–6
Chesterton, G. K. 296
Chisholm, Anne 256
Church, Richard 117–18, 230, 234, 238, 264
Churchill, Winston Spencer (Rt Hon.) 204, 212, 216, 262, 265, 270–1
Chuvikov, Pavel 321
Clerk's Press 55, 58, 69
Cocteau, Jean 99, 299
Cohen, Gustave 164, 231, 280, 288–9, 290, 293
Colin, Rosica 276
Colum, Mary 194
Colum, Padraic 44, 45
Cooper, Lady Diana 218
Cork, Richard 30
Coulton, C. G. 218
Cournos, John 2, 18, 31–3, 36, 41–2, 49, 51, 52–5, 57, 61, 63–4, 103, 117, 122, 138, 185
Covici, Pascal 111, 113, 120, 206, 289
Cowan, Lester 220
Cowley, Malcolm 210
Craig, Edward Gordon 230
Crane, Frank 133
Crawford, Fred D. 52, 136

Criterion, The xiv, xvi, 70, 73, 84, 92, 97–9, 103–4, 111, 117, 139, 324
Croly, Herbert 38
Crowder, Henry 124, 127, 230
Cummings, E. E. 154
Cunard, Nancy (Hon.) 119, 122, 124, 127, 139–40, 144, 164, 208, 230, 256, 257, 259
Cunningham-Graham, Robert Bontine 18
Curtis, Anthony 323
Custot, Pierre 82–3

Dahlberg, Edward 204–5, 208, 252, 277–8, 280, 283, 285
Dahlberg, Rlene 277, 278
Daily Telegraph 141, 247, 256, 271
Davison, Edward 213
Davray, Henri 69, 138
Dean, Basil 192–3, 232
Deasey, W. Denison 238, 252, 265, 273, 311
De Fanti, Charles 277–8
Des Imagistes, 28–9, 31
Dial, The xvi, 55, 58, 72–3, 84, 114, 125–6
Dibben, William 236
Discovery 189
Doolittle, Charles 23
Doolittle, Hilda (see under H.D.)
Doran, George 111–12
Doubleday, Nelson 151, 172–3
Douglas, Archie 207
Douglas, Major C. H. 283
Douglas, Norman xv, 126, 144–6, 155, 166, 170, 172, 178, 184, 192, 207–8, 254–5, 256–60, 324
Douglas, Robin 207
Duell, Charles 224
Dujardin, Edouard 74–5
Durrell, Lawrence xiii, 96, 180, 281–2, 286, 288–9, 293, 296–303, 306–7, 310–13, 315, 320, 322
Dutton, Geoffrey 238, 264, 287, 294, 303–4
Dutton, Nin 238, 264, 287, 294, 303–4

Edman, Irwin   195
Edwards, Oliver (see under William Haley)
Egoist, The   xiv, 26–7, 29, 30–1, 34–6, 39, 43–5, 49, 51, 56, 58, 291, 324
Elek, Paul   309
Eliot, T. S.   xiii, xiv, xvi, xvii, 28, 55, 58, 71, 74–7, 80, 82–3, 85–105, 107, 112–18, 132–3, 136–7, 141, 146–8, 154, 169, 195–6, 201, 204, 211, 222, 228, 235, 242, 247, 250, 260, 283–5, 290–1, 295, 303, 307, 310, 324; WORKS: 'Ezra Pound: His Metric and Poetry', 58, 90; *For Lancelot Andrewes*, 132; 'The Hollow Men', 149; *The Sacred Wood*, 28, 76, 92–3; 'Seneca in Elizabethan Translation', 104; 'Tradition and the Individual Talent', 92, 97; 'Ulysses, Order and Myth', 93; *The Waste Land*, 82, 86–7, 99, 131, 136–7, 148
Eliot, Valerie   284
Eliot, Vivien   92–3, 98, 147–8
Ellerman, Sir John   69
Ellerman, Winifred (see under Bryher)
Elliot Smith, Sir G.   169
Ellis, Havelock   19–30, 133
Elmo, Ann   276, 278, 280, 283
Encounter   300–1
English Review   34, 70–1, 93
Epstein, Jacob   37
Ernst, Morris   202
Evening Standard   158, 261–2
Everyman   139, 142, 162

Faber, Geoffrey   148
Fallas, Carl   51–4, 56–7, 64, 317, 322
Fallas, Florence   51–4, 322
Fanchette, Jean   299, 313
Falkner, William   217–18
Fedin, Konstantin   154, 320–1
Feisal Ibn Husein, Sharif   268
Firchow, Peter   41

Fitzgerald. F. Scott   219
Flanner, Janet   127
Flaubert, Gustave   14, 85, 115, 182, 315, 322
Fletcher, John Gould   22, 31–2, 36, 44–5, 50, 53
Flint, F. S.   xiv, 2, 26, 28, 31, 34, 44, 51–6, 59, 61–2, 71, 75, 78, 82, 84–5, 102, 115–17, 204, 291, 297, 303
Flint, Violet   75
Ford, Ford Madox   26, 29–37, 40, 45, 132, 172, 196, 253
Frere, A. S.   145, 164, 177, 236–7, 247, 280, 292
Friede, Donald   126, 128
Frierson, W. C.   130

Gaige, Crosby   106, 108, 110–12, 120, 123, 126, 164
Garnett, David   251–2, 261
Gaster, Vivian   9
Gates, Norman T.   46, 68, 159, 186, 318
Gaudier Brzeska, Henri   26, 31–2
Gawsworth, John   236, 241, 307–10, 322
Georg, Stefan   18
Glassco, John   211
Glover, Halcott   68, 79, 99, 129, 168, 173–5, 184, 230, 234
Goldring, Douglas   172–3
Goldstone, Jules   222
Gorky, Maxim   xiv, 154, 187, 320
Gourmont, Rémy de   10, 27–8, 35, 38, 100, 105, 110, 113–15, 155, 157, 290
Graves, Robert   60, 135, 252, 262, 266, 269, 272
Gray, Cecil   61, 63
Greene, Graham   256, 259
Gregg, Frances   23, 25, 177
Gregory, Alyse   84
Gregory, Lady Augusta   26
Grenfell, Julian   48
Grey, Dudley   8, 9, 10–11, 83, 131
Gribble, George   85, 184, 231, 253
Gueneau, Maxime and Suzanne   323

Index

Guest, Barbara 41, 52, 55, 60, 304
Guillaume, Jacques 310
Guinzburg, Harold 202, 203, 209
Gull, Cyril Arthur Edward Ranger (also known as Leonard Cresswell Ingleby or Guy Thorne) 7
Gyde, Arnold 230–1, 235–6, 241, 245

Haley, Sir William 281, 290, 317, 320
Hanley, James 139
Hamnett, Nina 46
Hardy, Thomas 154
Hart, B. H. Liddell, Colonel 262, 265, 271
H.D. (Hilda Doolittle) xiv, 13–25, 29, 31–3, 36–7, 40–2, 46, 50–9, 61–8, 70–1, 73, 75, 77, 96, 103, 116, 121–2, 124–9, 132, 177, 181–2, 184–5, 201, 215–16, 220–1, 231–3, 235, 237, 241, 248, 253–5, 259–60, 279–80, 285–7, 294–6, 298–300, 303–5, 308, 310, 311
  WORKS: 'Asphodel', 15, 19–20; 'Autobiographical Notes', 23; *Bid Me to Live*, 24, 40–2, 50, 52, 58, 61, 64, 66, 77, 255, 303–4; *Collected Poems 1912–44*, 66; *End to Torment*, 23–4, 295; 'Hermes of the Ways', 16; *HERmione*, 23; *Madrigal*, 255; 'Paint it Today', 23; *Tribute to Freud*, 177, 279
Hearn, Lafcadio 7
Hemingway, Ernest 124, 211
Henley, W. E. 19
Heseltine, Philip (Peter Warlock) 46, 50
Heyer, Georgette 225
Heymann, C. David 215–16
Hilbery, Malcolm 131
Hillyer, Robert 242
Holloway, Mark 145, 257, 323
Holroyd-Reece, John 253
Hough, Graham 274

Hours Press 119, 139–40
Housman, A. E. 10, 201, 203
Hughes, Glenn 29, 101, 108, 113–14, 116, 119, 123
Hull, R. F. C. 278, 283
Hulme, T. E. 14–15
Hunt, Violet 18, 31, 175
Hutchins, Patricia 291
Huxley, Aldous 50, 75, 91, 122, 142, 149, 156, 209, 213–14, 225
Huxley, Julian 93

Jackson, Holbrook 69, 92–3
James, Henry 165, 250
Jeffares, A. Norman 313
Jones, David 302
Joyce, James 70, 93–5, 111, 142, 291

Kasper, John 283
Kenner, Hugh 10
Kennington, Eric 262
Ker, W. P. 11, 13
Kershaw, Alister xv, xvii, 178, 233–4, 236–44, 246–7, 250–4, 256–7, 261–3, 265, 272, 275–6, 280, 282, 287–8, 293–4, 296, 308, 310, 317–18, 322–3
King, William 104–5
Kittredge, Selwyn xvi, 43, 48, 53, 64, 95, 97, 117, 122, 130, 205–6, 324
Knightley, Philip 265, 268
Knowles, Pat 262
Korda, Alexander 203
Koteliansky, S. S. 123
Krugerskaya, Oxana 317

Laforgue, Jules 83
Landor, Walter Savage 83–4
Lane, Allen 231
Lann, Evgeny xv, 154
Laughlin, James 277–8
Lawrence, A. W. 251
Lawrence, D. H. xvi, xvii, 33–4, 44, 49–50, 54, 57, 61–3, 65–6, 71, 74, 76–7, 82, 92, 108–10, 112–13, 116, 119–24, 132, 142, 149, 154–6, 158–9, 164, 170,

Lawrence, D. H. – *continued*
172, 185, 196, 201, 204–5, 207, 210, 211, 213, 235–9, 241–3, 245, 247–52, 255, 258–9, 275, 279, 281, 293–5, 298, 300–2, 307–9, 313–15, 323–4
Lawrence, Frieda 49, 61, 63, 108–9, 116, 119–20, 145, 205, 207, 209–10, 238–9, 241, 247–8, 256, 259, 274, 278–9, 301
Lawrence, Mrs Sarah 262, 264
Lawrence, T. E. xiii, xv–xvi, 82, 240, 247, 251–2, 254–5, 260–74, 275, 279, 292, 311, 324–5
Lewis, P. Wyndham 29–30, 32, 37, 96–7, 115, 128, 137, 141–2, 149, 157, 165–6, 170–1, 201–2, 250, 283–6
Lindsay, Vachel 86
Literary Gazette (*Literaturnia Gazeta*) 307, 321, 323
Little Review 40, 44, 55, 58, 72, 111
Liverpool Daily Post 97, 180
Lloyd, 2nd Lord 271
London Magazine 256–7, 271–2
Low, David 259
Lowell, Amy 7, 13–14, 22, 29, 30–40, 42–5, 50, 53, 54–5, 59, 62, 68, 70, 73–4, 78, 87, 96
Lowenfels, Walter 126, 140, 154
Lowrie, Howard 195
Lucas, F. L. 191
Lyle, Rob 259–60, 271
Lyon Gilbert, Margery (née Aldington) 1, 2, 309, 311–12, 314

Madge, Charles 223
Magnus, Maurice 258
Mallarmé, Stephane 17–18, 111
Manchester Guardian 266
Manning, Frederic 35, 76, 78, 91–2
Mansfield, Katherine 295, 301
Manuel, Alvin 193, 203, 212–14, 221–3, 231, 233–4, 236–9, 241, 247, 276, 280
Marinetti, Filippo 22, 30

Marsden, Dora 21, 44, 51
Marsh, Edward 33
Martin, Kingsley 84, 286
Martz, Louis L. 66
Materer, Timothy 29
Maugham, W. Somerset 172, 201, 214, 260, 302
McAlmon, Robert 124–5
MacGreevy, Thomas 46, 127, 136, 140, 146, 149–51, 211, 294, 296, 307, 317
Megata, Morikimi 7
Merriman, Sir Boyd 181
Meyers, Jeffrey 268–9
Meynell, Alice 18
Miller, Henry 180, 226, 298, 308
Mistral, Frédéric 275, 286, 305, 324
Moldavsky, D. M. 183, 318–19
Monro, Harold 16, 18, 28, 30, 33, 39, 43–6, 58, 70, 74–9, 88, 91–2, 97, 99
Monroe, Harriet 16–17, 22, 28, 34, 38, 39–40, 46–7, 51, 63, 72–3, 79, 96, 126
Moore, Harry T. 248–9, 293–4, 296–8, 303–4, 308–10, 313–16
Moore, Marianne 80, 82, 291
Moore, T. Sturge 95
Morgan, Louise 142, 162
Morrell, Lady Ottoline 93, 96, 103
Morton, J. B. (Beachcomber) 173
Mosley, Sir Oswald and Lady Diana 317
Muggeridge, Malcolm 247, 265, 311
Munson, Gorham 128–30
Murray, Gilbert 241
Murphy, Gerald 211
Murry, John Middleton 53, 69, 95, 100

Nahi, Bey of Deraa 268, 311
Namier, Lewis 262
Nash, John 46
Nathan, Robert 217
Nation and Atheneum 97
Nehls, Edward 279, 293

Index

Nerval, Gérard de   127, 155
New Age   7, 17
Newcombe, Colonel S. F.   268
New Freewoman   21–2, 26, 45
New Republic   38, 44–5, 210, 272
News: A Soviet Review of World Events   281
New Statesman   84, 154, 245, 261, 282, 286, 311
Newsweek   261
New Yorker   194
New York Herald Tribune   175, 211, 283, 285
New York Times   37, 207, 305
Nine   245
Norman, Charles   29, 47
Nouvelle Revue Française   116
Novy Mir   xv, 154
Noyes, Alfred   72
Nutting, Anthony   311

Observer   30
Opie, John   157
Orage, A. R.   17–18
Orioli, Giuseppe (Pino)   126, 138, 144–6, 149, 155, 166, 183–4, 189, 191, 256–60, 312
Orwell, George   128, 324
Osbourne, Fanny   276
Outlook (London)   45, 95, 258
Owen, Wilfred   xiv, 47

Palmer, Herbert   186
Patmore, Brigit   13, 41, 53–4, 103, 116–17, 119, 120–7, 136, 138, 142, 145–6, 149, 155–7, 159, 164, 166, 169–73, 175, 176–7, 211, 316; *My Friends When Young*, 122, 175
Patmore, Coventry   10, 18, 177
Patmore, Deighton   119
Patmore, Derek   164, 171, 175
Patmore, Michael   176–7
Paulhan, Jean   116, 119
Pavchinskaya, Ludmilla   321
Pegler, Westbrook   212
Péguy, Charles   35
Peyre, Henri   297, 305
Picasso, Pablo   127

Pinker, J. Ralph   141, 143, 163–4, 193, 221
Plank, George Wolfe   39
Poetry   xvi, 16–17, 22, 26–7, 48, 53, 72, 79, 92, 126, 186
Poetry and Drama   26, 33, 39
Poetry Bookshop, The   18, 29, 45, 50, 70, 76
Poetry Journal   51
Poetry Review   16, 236, 241, 322
Polevoi, Boris   320
Pondrom, Cyrena N.   55
Porter, Katherine Anne   213, 300–1
Poticki de Montalk, Geoffrey   306–7
Pound, Dorothy   33
Pound, Ezra   xiii, xiv, xvii, 10, 13–26, 28–37, 43–4, 47, 49, 51, 56, 58, 67, 70–2, 74–5, 82, 85, 87–90, 92–8, 100, 107, 114–16, 119, 125–7, 132–3, 137, 140, 142, 146–8, 157, 159, 181, 196, 201, 204, 210–11, 215–16, 232, 235, 242, 245, 249–50, 253, 259, 283, 285–7, 290–1, 296, 299–300, 303, 308
  WORKS: *The Cantos*, 33, 210–11; 'The Faun', 25; 'A Few Don'ts', 47; 'Hugh Selwyn Mauberly', 37; the Malatesta Cantos, 98; *Personae*, 89, 114; the Pisan Cantos, 242; 'A Retrospect', 14; *Ta Hio, or the Great Learning*, 114; 'Tempora', 33
Pound, Omar   253
Powell, Lawrence Clark   69, 221
Prentice, Charles   126–7, 146–8, 155–6, 164, 176, 231, 256–60
Preston, Hayter   155
Priestley, J. B.   158, 302
Proust, Marcel   83
Purcell, Victor (Myra Buttle)   290

Quennell, Peter   248
Quinn, John   51, 95
Quinn, Kirker   186–7

Randall, Alec 9–10, 34, 64, 101, 118, 138, 280, 283, 287, 292, 296, 307
Randall, Amy 116, 307
Rascoe, Burton 171
Ravagli, Angelo 207, 209
Ray, Man 127
Raymond, Harold 208
Read, Herbert 7, 43, 46, 57, 69–70, 84–6, 97, 99–104, 108, 110, 111, 117, 136, 152, 158, 164, 169, 173, 195, 226, 276–8, 283, 307, 310, 311
Reeves, James 141, 155
Reed, Carol 241
Reinhardt, Wolfgang 217–18, 220
Remarque, Erich Maria 135
Rezard, Madame 323
Richard Aldington: An Intimate Portrait 275, 281, 318
Richmond, Bruce 71, 90, 93, 99, 100–1, 146, 307
Roberts, Warren 309
Robinson, Janice S. 20–1, 25, 41
Roditi, Georges 263
Rodker, John 35, 95
Rogers, Bruce 111
Roosevelt, Colonel Elliot 202
Rose, W. K. 100–2, 141
Rosenberg, Isaac 72
Rosenfeld, Paul 87
Roth, Samuel 111
Rothermere, Lady 93, 97
Rudge, Olga 141
Rummel, Walter Morse 15
Russell, Ada 31
Russell, Betrand 88, 133, 255
Russell, Peter 245, 250
Rutherford, Andrew 136

Saturday Review of Literature 242, 315
Schaffner, Frances Perdita 68, 70, 310
Schary, Doré 213
Schiff, Sidney (Stephen Hudson) 142, 148, 151, 183, 238
Schiff, Violet 204, 238, 248

Schorer, Mark 301
Searle, Alan 173
Secret Despatches 266, 269
Shakespear, Olivia 32
Shaw, Charlotte 266, 268, 311
Shaw, George Bernard 7–8, 268, 270
Sherriff, R. C. 127
Silkin, Jon 135
Simpson, Colin 268
Sinclair, May 49, 68, 72, 86, 95; *The Dark Night*, 86; *Mary Olivier*, 72
Sitwell, Edith 85, 235–6, 241, 247
Sitwell, Osbert 201, 221, 307
Sitwell, Sacheverell 85
Skinner, M. L. 251
Slater, Montague 141–3
Slonimsky, Henry 15, 20, 114, 154, 177, 192–3, 195, 201, 204, 208–11, 214–15, 220–3, 229
Slonimsky, Minnie 254
Smith, Richard E. 186
Snow, C. P. xiii, 185–6, 189, 191, 226
Some Imagist Poets 41–2
Spire, André 208, 291
Squire, J. C. 102
Stekel, Dr Wilhelm 301
Stevens, Wallace 169
Stevenson, Robert Louis 272, 276–9
Stirner, Max 45
Storrs, Sir Ronald 264–5, 271
Strelets 154
Sunday Times, The 311, 321
Surkov, Alexei 314–15, 318, 320
Swinburne, Algernon Charles 9, 46, 48
Swinnerton, Frank 256
Sykes, Christopher 248
Symbolistes, The 16, 18, 111, 297

Tabachnick, Stephen E. 268–9
Taylor, Rachael Annand 236, 309
Temple, Frédéric-Jacques 275, 288, 298, 300, 301, 302, 323
Thayer, Scofield 93
This Quarter 87, 139–40, 154

Index

Thomas, Lowell 267, 270
Thorne, Guy (see under Gull)
Tietjens, Eunice 58
Times, The 26, 72–3, 105–6, 281, 290, 297, 310, 323
Times Literary Supplement, The xiv, xvi, 53, 69, 71, 73–5, 82–3, 85, 90, 100, 114, 151, 162, 235, 240–1, 245–7, 282, 307
Tindall, William York 203–4
Titus, Edward 139
To-day 69, 93, 173
Tolstoy, Leo 318
transition 115
Trend, J. B. 104, 117, 191
Turner, Reggie 166, 189–90
Two Cities 299, 313

Upton, Cyril 297
Upward, Allen 31–2
Urnov, Dmitri 317
Urnov, Mikhail xv, 182–3, 281–2, 302, 308, 314, 317–18, 320–1

Vladikin, Grigori 321
Voltaire, François Marie Arouet de xv, 319–20, 324

Waddell, Helen 104; *The Wandering Scholars*, 104
Walpole, Hugh 70
Ward, A. C. xv
Warman, Eric 158, 166, 174–5, 183, 187–8, 193–4, 209, 212, 214, 221, 224, 231–4, 237, 277, 280, 282, 287, 290, 293, 311, 315
Warner, Jack 220
Waterton, Charles xix, 245, 324
Watts Dunton, Theodore 9
Waugh, Alec 59, 70, 173, 220, 242, 285

Wavell, General Sir Archibald P. 267
Weaver, Harriet Shaw 21, 35, 51, 94, 111
Weintraub, Stanley 311
Wellesley, Arthur, Duke of Wellington 212, 218–19, 265, 324
Wells, H. G. 128, 175–6, 320
West, Rebecca 10, 11, 21
Wheelwright, John 166
Whibley, Charles 104
Whitall, James G. 38–9
Whitham, Jan Mills 51
Whitman, Walt 15, 65
Wilde, Oscar 5, 7, 54, 190, 224, 231
Willert, Paul 191
Williams, William Carlos 25, 43–4, 72, 82, 91, 116, 141, 215–16, 228, 296
Williamson, Henry 238–40
Wilson, Edmund 301
Winchell, Walter 202–3
Wohl, Robert 135
Wolfe, Humbert 99
Woolf, Leonard 103
Woolf, Virginia 96, 97, 103

Yeats, Georgiana 125–6
Yeats, W. B. 13, 19, 22, 26, 35, 48, 51, 83, 85, 125–6, 201, 203
Yorke, Dorothy (Arabella) 4, 59, 61–5, 73, 77, 79, 97–9, 103, 111, 113, 115, 117, 120, 122–3, 125–6, 128, 132, 136, 181, 211, 294, 308

Zenkevich, Mikhail 182
Zhantieva, Dilyara 183, 307, 318
Zukofsky, Louis 140